The West of
Billy the Kid

Billy the Kid.

Believed to have been taken at Fort Sumner toward the end of 1879 or the beginning of 1880, this image is a 2-inch by 3-inch carte-de-visite ferrotype—called a "tin-type"—one of the most common photographic formats used between 1860 and 1890. It was most probably produced by what was called a "multiplying camera" that used a number of lenses and/or a repeating back to make four nearly identical images which cost perhaps twenty-five cents. Battered, nail-pierced, faded by time and poor handling, it has nonetheless become a twentieth-century icon; it is the only authenticated picture of the boy they called Billy the Kid.

The West of
Billy the Kid

BY

Frederick Nolan

UNIVERSITY OF OKLAHOMA PRESS

Norman

Also by Frederick Nolan

The Life and Death of John Henry Tunstall (Albuquerque, 1965)
The Algonquin Project (New York, 1974)
The Mittenwald Syndicate (New York, 1977)
The Sound of Their Music: The Story of Rodgers and Hammerstein (New York, 1978)
White Nights, Red Dawn (New York, 1981)
Wolf Trap (New York, 1984)
A Promise of Glory (New York, 1984)
Blind Duty (New York, 1985)
Red Center (New York, 1987)
The Lincoln County War: A Documentary History (Norman, 1992)
Lorenz Hart: A Poet on Broadway (New York, 1994)
Bad Blood: The Life and Times of the Horrell Brothers (Stillwater, Okla., 1994)
Portraits of the Old West (London, 1997)

This book is published with the generous assistance of
Edith Gaylord Harper.

Library of Congress Cataloging-in-Publication Data
Nolan, Frederick W., 1931–
The West of Billy the Kid / by Frederick Nolan.
p. cm.
Includes bibliographical references and index.

ISBN 978-0-8061-3104-7

1. Billy, the Kid—Pictorial works.
2. Outlaws—Southwest, New—Biography—Pictorial works.
3. Frontier and pioneer life—Southwest, New—Pictorial works.
4. Southwest, New—History—1848—Pictorial works.
I. Title.
F786.N62 1998
364.1$'$552$'$092—dc21
98-17472
CIP

The paper in this book meets the guidelines for permanence and durability
of the Committee on Production Guidelines for Book Longevity
of the Council on Library Resources, Inc. ∞

Copyright © 1998 by the University of Oklahoma Press, Norman,
Publishing Division of the University.

Contents

Illustrations

Maps

Preface

You will observe, gentlemen, that I neither blame nor approve; I relate.
—*Talleyrand*

IN ALL THE YEARS THAT HAVE PASSED since I first came wide-eyed and eager from Walter Noble Burns to the subject of Billy the Kid, I have not anywhere found another account of his life that so kindled my enthusiasm and my desire to know more. And I wondered whether, knowing what we now know that Burns did not, it might be possible today to write another such book—but without compromising its historical accuracy. But even if it was possible, would it, could it contribute anything meaningful to a subject which has already inspired a thousand books and countless millions of words more in other media? Could there be anything new to discover? Could there be anything new to say?

Every book is a journey of discovery, and this one proved to be no exception. In retrospect I realize I set out to write it with considerable misgiving, far from confident I would be able to answer my own questions positively. Along the way I learned how little I actually knew about the real person whose life I was investigating and how much of the existing evidence describing that life has been overlooked or ignored by earlier writers. The real Billy, a boy growing up on a harsh frontier, had been lost beneath a mountain of stereotypes—the psychopathic killer, the gunfighter, the romantic outlaw—an infinitely malleable icon for each succeeding generation.

Once I laid these misconceptions aside, his true personality began to emerge. And as I continued to scrape off the layers of legend, false assumption, and downright lies which have accumulated on his story, a clear picture began to form, that of a bright, alert, intelligent boy with an impish sense of humor, thrown early and unprepared upon his own inner resources. A brave boy, too, forced to live on the sharp edge of frontier life, doing the best he could in a world that rarely extended a helping hand. Not by any means a perfect human being—there was a dark and vengeful streak in his nature, too—but understandable, entire, and real.

It is this real person I have tried to put into these pages: the young man as he (sometimes) saw himself and the young man his friends and enemies (sometimes) saw. To it are added more than two hundred and fifty pictures of his world—the places he lived, the scenes he visited, the people he knew—many of them published here for the first time and providing in sum as complete and rounded a picture of his life as it is possible to create. And perhaps with something new to say about him as well.

Let me here put my historical cards on the table. I do not here or elsewhere care to embrace the current (and I am confident, transient) fashion for what is called conceptual history in which the facts are massaged to fit and support a preconceived theory. I have no intention of trying to explain the Kid's life within a larger historical context or of dumbing-down his motivations to dimensions a child can comprehend. Nor do I desire to establish or even discuss whether he was a product of his environment or a supreme example of social Darwinism, a sociopath, a misfit, or merely another juvenile delinquent. I am going to present you with the facts. If you want them neatly packaged with nice, safe, politically correct conclusions that will spare you the necessity of thinking, this is not your book. My main, my only aim is to make this story as historically true as it is possible to make it, because I am still old-fashioned enough to believe that above all else, the truth matters.

Why does the truth matter? Politicians daily trample it to death, the media pervert it, government agencies strangle it with doublespeak—why should it be any different with the Kid's story? The answer is, of course, that if you need an answer the battle is already lost. Although we may be, today, as far away from the life of Billy the Kid as he was, in his day, from the life of George Washington, as distant from the night of his death as, on that night, he was from Patrick Henry's defiant speech about liberty or death, we are all part of the same unending panoply. Like the Kid, we, too, are history, already being drawn inexorably into the past. If it were our story, we would want it told truly, or at least as truly as it can be told.

History—the truth about the past from which we all emerged and to which we all belong—is too precious a commodity to be surrendered without a struggle to the fast-buck salesmen of fake photos and stolen documents, to the self-styled historians and even shabbier conmen who have over the last few decades infiltrated the historical forum. If we do not defend and protect the truth, they will cheapen and devalue it until only the sham remains—the replica cowtown, the concept museum, a shoddy theme-parked "experience" of the past packaged in the form of meretricious books, cheap movies, and second-rate TV programs masquerading as history under the catch-all title of "infotainment."

Billy the Kid—*even* Billy the Kid—deserves better treatment than this. For all his sins, and though we know so little about him, he was a real human being and deserves to have his story told with as much respect and accuracy as any other historical figure. This book, then, is an attempt to do just that, to reach back across the century and try to see the life and the West of Billy the Kid as it truly was almost 120 years ago, when what is now our history was his tomorrow.

FREDERICK NOLAN

Chalfont St. Giles, England

Acknowledgments

I WOULD LIKE TO BEGIN by acknowledging the pioneering research of two men: Robert N. Mullin, who located the Antrim-McCarty marriage record, and Waldo S. Koop, who first established that the family had lived in Wichita, Kansas. These two landmark finds were and remain among the most significant contributions made by anyone to the story of Billy the Kid.

I owe special thanks to Susan Berry of the Silver City Museum for her invaluable contribution to my chapter on the Kid's time in that city; Richard Rudisill, and Arthur Olivas of the Museum of New Mexico for their assistance in locating and identifying appropriate images; Colleen Salazar, Billy Charles Cummings, Donna Crandall, and Cindy Martinez all formerly of the Lincoln County Heritage Trust for valued research, assistance, and support; Jack Rigney and the staff of the Lincoln State Monument; Melba M. McCaskill, who acted as my most effective amanuensis in Midland; David L. King, who was my diligent sleuth in Wichita and other corners of Kansas; Bob Boze Bell of Cave Creek for his wonderful illustrations; Dick George of Tempe, Arizona, and T. Dudley Cramer of Oakland, California, for their excellent photographs; and to the descendants: Art Blazer, Mescalero, New Mexico; Joseph Brazil and Armene Brazil Green, Hot Springs, Arkansas; Mary Boulware Campbell, Redmond, Washington (Mary Richards); Alton R. Corbet, Dallas, Texas; Pauline Jaramillo, Los Lunas, New Mexico; Walter N. Jones, Jr., Pasco, Washington (Fritz and Whitlock families); George and Zella Linn, Turlock, California; Dorothy Mesenbrink, Denison, Iowa (John Kinney); Edward and Nancy Marxen-Phinney, Beavertown, Oregon (Juan Patrón); Herman Mills Miranda, Dallas, Texas; Joe Salazar, Lincoln, New Mexico; Hilary Tunstall-Behrens, London, England; Harvey H. Whitehill III, Albuquerque, New Mexico; Robert J. Widenmann, Brønshøj, Denmark; and David E. Winter, Beebe, Arkansas (Frank Clifford).

I am indebted also to Opal Baker, Crawford County Historical Society, Denison, Iowa; Allen and Ken Barker, Pine Grove, California; the late Robert L. Barron, El Paso, Texas; Alice Blakestad, Hondo, New Mexico; Susan Gardner Boyle, Little Rock, Arkansas; Maryln and the late Joe Bowlin, Ruidoso, New Mexico; James A. Browning, Charleston, South Carolina; Howard Bryan, Albuquerque, New Mexico; Sandra Burleson, Hackleburg, Alabama; Bonny Celine, Albuquerque, New Mexico; Joanne Classen, Denver, Colorado; Lee Cotten, Sacramento, California; Rob Cox, Organ, New Mexico; Wayne Daniel, El Paso Public Library, El Paso, Texas; James H. Earle, College Station, Texas; Conley L. Edwards, Library of Virginia, Richmond; Harold L. Edwards, Bakersfield, California; Ralph L. Elder, Eugene C. Barker

History Center, Austin, Texas; Chrystyn Elley, Missouri State Archives, Jefferson City; Patricia A. Etter, Arizona State University, Tempe; Deborah Ferrall, Office of Tourism/History, Lyons, New York; Robert Fisher, Tucson, Arizona; Elvis E. Fleming, Roswell, New Mexico; Alexandra Gressitt, Indiana Historical Society, Indianapolis; Dr. Geoffrey Gomes, Hayward, California; Andy Gregg, Albuquerque, New Mexico; Janean Grissom, Taiban, New Mexico; the late J. Evetts Haley, Midland, Texas; Robert and Linda Hart, Las Cruces, New Mexico; Walter and Nora Henn, Lincoln, New Mexico; Alice Henson, Jefferson City, Missouri; Q. Baird Hershey, Jr., York Springs, Pennsylvania; Dr. Austin Hoover, New Mexico State University, Las Cruces; Lynn Hunter, Artesia, New Mexico; Alan January, Indiana State Archive, Indianapolis; David Johnson, Zionsville, Indiana; Cleis and Jerry Jordan, Lincoln, New Mexico; Jens Kiecksee, Neuenkirchen, Germany; Michael J. Keleher, Albuquerque, New Mexico; Lewis A. Ketring, Jr., and his son, Lewis, Montebello, California; Terry Koenig, Roswell, New Mexico; Charles Lamb, University of Notre Dame, Indiana; the late Donald R. Lavash, Lubbock, Texas; Bernice Lear, Kerrville, Texas; Don McAlavy, Clovis, New Mexico; Patricia McCann, New Mexico State University, Las Cruces; Herb and Chula Marsh, El Paso, Texas; Katy Matthews, Topeka, Kansas; Leon and Cheryl Metz, El Paso, Texas; Joyce and Morgan Nelson, Roswell, New Mexico; Paul and Jayme Northrop, El Paso, Texas; Dorothy J. O'Brien, Mariposa, California; the late David Orr, Roswell, New Mexico; Chuck Parsons, Yorktown, Texas; Paxton P. Price, Las Vegas, New Mexico; the late Philip J. Rasch, Ojai, California; the late William D. Reynolds, Bakersfield, California; Nancy Robertson, Raton, New Mexico; Kenneth J. Ross, Department of History, Presbyterian Church, Philadelphia, Pennsylvania; Joseph G. Rosa, Ruislip, England; Nancy B. Samuelson, Eastford, Connecticut; Susan Seyl, Oregon Historical Society, Portland; Paul T. Shafer, Campbell, California; Judith Sibley, Archivist, U.S. Military Academy, West Point, New York; Beth L. Silbergleit, University of New Mexico Library, Albuquerque; Lee Silva, Sunset Beach, California; Gregory Scott Smith, Fort Sumner State Monument, Fort Sumner, New Mexico; Joe and Diana Stein, Las Vegas, New Mexico; Ellen L. Sulser, State Historical Society of Iowa, Des Moines; Eddie Taylor, Fort Walton Beach, Florida; Greg Thomas, Amarillo Public Library, Amarillo, Texas; Robert J. Torrez, State Records Center and Archive, Santa Fe, New Mexico; Stephen E. Towne, Indiana State Archive, Indianapolis; Jami Frazier Tracy, Wichita-Sedgwick County Historical Museum, Wichita, Kansas; Robert M. Utley, Georgetown, Texas; Herman Weisner, Organ, New Mexico; Robert R. White, Albuquerque, New Mexico; John P. Wilson, Las Cruces, New Mexico; Michael J. Winey, U.S. Army Military History Institute, Carlisle, Pennsylvania; Jim and Carla Wright, Albuquerque, New Mexico; Michael Wurtz, Sharlot Hall Museum, Prescott, Arizona.

And last and most especially, the fine and generous friend to whom I affectionately dedicate this book:

Robert G. McCubbin

The West of
Billy the Kid

Abbreviations

ACP file   Appointments, Commissions, and Promotions File,
            Adjutant General's Office, Letters Received 1871–80,
            Record Group 94, National Archives.
    HHC   History Center, Nita Stewart Haley Memorial Library,
            Midland, Texas.
MoNM   Museum of New Mexico, Santa Fe.
NMSU   New Mexico State University, Las Cruces.

CHAPTER ONE

The Kid from Nowhere

Few American lives have more successfully resisted research than that of Billy the Kid. It is almost as if he decided at birth to leave behind as little documentary trace as he could of his entry into, and passage through, the world. Thus, in spite of a century of effort by a legion of researchers to document his early life, little more is known about him now than was current at the time of his death at Fort Sumner in 1881.

Reduced to essentials, the sum of our certain knowledge about the origins of Billy the Kid is this: at the time of her second(?) marriage his mother's name (but not necessarily her maiden name) was Catherine McCarty. After spending something like a year as close friend and neighbor of William Henry Harrison Antrim in Wichita, Kansas, she married him at Santa Fe on March 1, 1873, and among the witnesses to that ceremony were her sons Henry and Joseph M. "Josie" McCarty. The family relocated in Silver City, where Catherine McCarty, said to have been Irish or of Irish descent (although, since she married Antrim in a Presbyterian church, she could as easily have been Scots-Irish), and believed to have been forty-five years old, died in 1874.

And that is all. We do not know where Catherine McCarty was born or whence she came. We do not know the name of the man who fathered her sons or even if the same man was father to both. We do not know for certain the year of birth of either son, the places of their birth, which of them was the older, or even their full names.

Out of the gazetteer of locations which have been advanced as Billy the Kid's birthplace in a thousand books about him, three main contenders have emerged: New York, Missouri, and Indiana, with New York, until comparatively recent times, the clear favorite. The reason is simple: his first biographer—Pat Garrett's ghostwriter Marshall Ashmun Upson—and a great many people who claimed to have known the Kid (but who in all likelihood assimilated their "knowledge" from the same newspapers and dime novels as did Upson) said he was born in New York.[1]

Adding minimal weight to this proposition is the fact that in his pension applications William H. Antrim stated that Catherine McCarty's first husband, and therefore theoretically the father of Henry McCarty, had died in New York City.[2] This evidence might carry more conviction were it not for the demonstrable fact that Antrim's memory of his wife and his stepsons was considerably short of perfect.

If the records are to be trusted, however, the Kid neither was born in nor ever lived in New York, city or state, nor did his father die there. Meticulous line-by-line examination of 1860 census records for the fifty-nine counties of New York state has produced no family configuration of a father, mother, and two sons named McCarty matching or even resembling the one sought. An 1860 Manhattan census showing a Patrick, thirty; Catherine, twenty-nine; Bridget, seven; and Henry McCarthy, the latter just one year old, has tempted many to accept it as the genuine article. Quite apart from the misspelled surname, however, it requires us to accept wishful thinking: because Henry is one year old, and therefore fits the entirely unproven proposition that he was born in 1859, everything else *must* be correct. But if it is, what happened to Bridget? Why is Catherine's age given incorrectly? And what happened to the father? Careful search of available New York records for an appropriate McCarty death—either a Bridget or a Patrick—between 1860 and 1867 has produced not a single possible candidate.

In the 1950s a self-styled "descendant," Lois Telfer proposed a different solution. She said the Kid's real name was Bonney, not McCarty, and that his father was one of the twin sons of Barnabas Bonney of Lyons, Wayne County, New York. Barnabas, born in Columbia County, New York, married Kezia Park, born at Lyons in 1794, and their twin sons Orris and William were born there, Telfer contended, on July 5, 1826. Since records at Lyons go back only as far as 1880, there is no way of establishing the validity of her proposition or confirming her claim that the Kid, William Bonney's son, was born in Brooklyn.

Could it then have been in Missouri that Henry McCarty was born? After all, we apparently have it on no less an authority than the Kid himself that this was so. Between June 17 and 19, 1880, Lorenzo Labadie, former Indian agent and former sheriff of San Miguel County, enumerated the census at Fort Sumner, New Mexico. In it he listed William Bonny, twenty-five, working in cattle, born in Missouri, as were both his parents.[3]

In a comprehensive search of the 1860 census for Missouri, applying the same criteria as those used in New York, a total of 148 McCarty households was checked, including two headed by a Catharine, one by a Catherine, twelve by a William (including two named William H.), and seven by a Patrick. Not one of them even remotely matched the desired configuration. Neither was any family with the correct sequence of names located in the city of St. Louis, which was separately enumerated. Ergo, on this evidence Billy the Kid was not born in Missouri.

Last came Indiana, in many ways a more logical birthplace for the Kid, since it appears to have been in Indianapolis or its environs that William H. Antrim, the Kid's stepfather-to-be, first met Catherine McCarty, and since it was probably from that state that she emigrated first to Wichita, Kansas, and from there to New Mexico.[4] Once the criteria previously applied are again employed, however, the proposition begins to evaporate. As with New York and Missouri, and despite the presence of a substantial number of McCarty entries, the Indiana state census for 1860 (about 40 percent of which is so badly faded that the entries are virtually illegible) appears to contain no family grouping with the appropriate details—a paterfamilias McCarty with a wife Catherine and sons Joseph and Henry or William Henry.

To be sure, there were McCartys in southeastern Indiana as far back as the 1830s, and in Warren, Owen, and Spencer Counties in the '60s. There was a Joseph McCarty in Cass County who had two sons, Joseph and Henry. There is a record of the marriage of a William H. McCarty to a Catherine Clark in Harrison County on November 18, 1858, which some Kid researchers believe might be the appropriate one. In the 1860 census there is a William H. McCarthy from Kentucky living with a group of McCartys we may presume to be his wife (Sophia, aged fifty-seven, from Pennsylvania) and their children. One of these is also a William H., aged twenty-four, born in Indiana, and about the right age to have been Billy the Kid's father, but he has no wife and does not appear in the 1870 census.[5]

He could of course have been married soon after the census was taken to a Catherine who would have been about twenty and who had two sons— one named for his father and born in 1861 and a second, Joseph, born two years later. (And as we shall see, 1863 may well have been Joe Antrim's year of birth, and on at least one occasion he appears to have given Indiana as his birthplace.) This husband then died and the widow moved on. But once again, the proposition is impossible to document. So in Indiana, as in New York and Missouri, the records thus far examined yield nothing but another series of negatives.

To sum up: despite exhaustive search, no McCarty family entry convincingly close enough to the parameters deemed appropriate exists in the 1860 state census records of New York, Missouri, or Indiana. Not a single one. Until and unless someone is determined enough—or insane enough—to undertake the Sisyphean task of individually following through on every single one of those entries to establish whether any of the hundreds of McCarty families enumerated—not to mention those named Bonney—expanded after 1860 to include sons named Henry and Joseph, the riddle will remain stubbornly unsolved.

To the findings so far adduced can be added a further, and probably equally unanswerable, conundrum concerning Henry and Joseph McCarty Antrim. At the time of the Kid's death, not just one but several newspapers referred to Joe as his *half*-brother. If this were true, it might explain all the anomalies and gaps in the timetable. We might then have Mrs. McCarty, widow of Michael, who had previously been married to a (shall we say) Mr. Bonney, who was Billy's father. Bonney, Sr., died (say, in New York, for want of better information), and his widow married a man named McCarty, with whom she went to Indiana or whom she met there; he was Joe's father, but not Billy's. McCarty died sometime before 1867 (let us say in Indianapolis, for want of better information), whereupon Mrs. McCarty, widow, starts to appear in Indiana directories. This theory (which of course is all it is) would accommodate Billy's being the older brother and explain why later on, looking for a new alias, the Kid reverted to the most natural one of all.

This is not a proposition to be summarily dismissed. Some of the earlier folklore about the Kid—propagated widely (but not solely) by the Upson-Garrett *Authentic Life*—suggested that the Bonney family, consisting of father William Bonney, Sr., his wife Katherine, and two sons William and Edward, left New York early in the summer of 1862 and headed west. After the father's death in Coffeyville, Kansas, the widow and her sons went in a wagon train to Pueblo, Colorado, and continued from there to Santa Fe and finally to Silver City. The possibility that William Bonney, Sr., died at Coffeyville was dismissed as fantasy because that town was not incorporated by its few white inhabitants until 1871.

Yet there was an earlier settlement on that spot called Possum Town, which at one time had its own cemetery, long since recycled. At Liberty, a few miles north, not only are there records of Bonneys but even a William (born 1859) and a Catherine McCarty, 1821–89; and in an item in the *Wichita Eagle*, August 25, 1935, old-time newspaperman and historian D. D. Leahy, writing about early Wichitans, noted, "They were not a paper collar crowd, but wore fine linen, laundered by such experts as Mrs. McCarty, the former Mrs. Bonney, mother of the subsequently notorious Billy the Kid, on North Market Street."

All this, of course, can as easily—and probably does—mean nothing.

Suffice it to say no more at this juncture than that, after having carefully and comprehensively examined the 1860 censuses for the states of New York, Missouri, and Indiana, one comes hesitantly to the conclusion that perhaps the simple, logical, obvious reason no one has ever been able to find legitimate documentation of the birth of Henry McCarty in these records is because he was not born when they were compiled.

The more the existing data—it is hardly evidence—is examined, the more everything about it suggests that Billy the Kid was probably younger than even Ash Upson made him. The recollections of more than a few Silver City residents who knew Henry McCarty Antrim when he lived there remembered him as being about twelve in 1874, while both Frank and George Coe said on different occasions that at the time of the Blazer's Mill fight the Kid was about seventeen, suggesting he might have been born anytime between 1861 and 1863.[6] That would suggest Joe was the younger brother but in turn poses another problem: the unlikely proposition that Catherine McCarty, characterized as "a jolly Irish lady, full of fun," bore no children until she was nearly thirty. In that era, and in her milieu, this seems at very best highly improbable—which brings us full circle.

It might be pertinent to ask why any of this matters. It might be relevant to propose that even if we knew now exactly where Billy the Kid was born and raised, or indeed, his complete genealogy, it would not add a scintilla to our understanding of him. Yet doubtless the search will go on, and perhaps one day someone will find the answers.

For the moment, however, the intensive four-year search for clues to the origins of Billy the Kid concludes more or less where it began, in the series of dead ends set forth above. It has established nothing and changed nothing; it never seemed remotely likely that it would. Instead, the story moves on to 1869, the first point in the life of Henry McCarty for which at least minimal documentation can be found: his brief sojourn in Wichita, Kansas.

CHAPTER TWO
Wichita

2.1. A purported photograph of Catherine McCarty Antrim.

Date and photographer unknown. Courtesy Leon C. Metz.

Familiar to every student of the Billy the Kid story, this is a genuine, large painted Civil War–era tintype. The original was owned by the George Griggs family, who exhibited it at their Billy the Kid Museum. It gained acceptance as a photo of the Kid's mother sometime in the late 1930s when Eugene Cunningham, author of the book *Triggernometry*, identified it as such to photographic collector Noah H. Rose in order to obtain from Rose an original photograph he wanted badly. The widespread propagation of this "fact" based on Cunningham's "authentication" became such a source of embarrassment to Cunningham that he finally confessed he had hoaxed Rose and did not have the slightest idea who the woman was. One thing seems certain: it is not Catherine McCarty.

Source: Eugene Cunningham correspondence with the author, 1953–57.

THE YEAR IS 1870. The population of the United States is 39,818,449, and the center of population is forty-eight miles east by north of Cincinnati, Ohio. During this year the states of Virginia, Texas, Georgia, and Mississippi will be readmitted to representation in Congress. John D. Rockefeller and his brother William will organize the Standard Oil Company. A cartoon donkey will become the symbol of the Democratic Party, roller skating the latest national craze. The boardwalk at Atlantic City will be completed. And America's best-loved soldier, General Robert E. Lee, will die.

As the year dawns, the strands that will intertwine to bind Catherine McCarty and her sons Henry and Joseph forever into the history of their era are still unconnected; in New Mexico the borders of the recently established Lincoln County have only just been laid out; the young English businessman John Tunstall has not yet left his London home; minister Alexander McSween has not yet abandoned his calling to enroll in law school at St. Louis; Fort Stanton post trader Lawrence G. Murphy has not yet collided irrevocably with the U.S. government; his clerk Jimmy Dolan is but a year out of the service.

Dick Brewer, a nineteen-year-old Wisconsin emigrant with an unhappy love affair behind him, is working for farmer John Schooler and his wife Mary in Mason Township, Jasper County, near Carthage, Missouri. Unassigned Major Nathan August Monroe Dudley, "North American" to his friends, is kicking his heels in Huntsville, Texas, where he has just been appointed military superintendent of prisons. Statesman Lew Wallace is in Mexico, Robert Widenmann in Michigan, attorney Montague Leverson in New York. Cadet Millard F. Goodwin is at West Point. Journalist Ash Upson is in Santa Fe. Jim Greathouse is peddling whiskey to Indians in Texas, Dr. Taylor Ealy is attending a Pennsylvania seminary, student Huston Chapman is attending the Portland Academy in Oregon, Warren Bristol is a Minnesota legislator, Frank Warner Angel is a Wall Street lawyer. And Henry McCarty is a schoolboy. But where?

As we have seen, there are reasonable grounds—although they are scarcely proof—for accepting that Catherine McCarty met William H. Antrim in Indianapolis sometime toward the end of the Civil War. How they met, what the affinity was between twenty-three-year-old Billy and thirty-five-year-old Catherine we shall never know. Antrim left no written account of how his association with her began or anything about her background before he knew her. Indeed, family members recalled in later years that whenever the subject of Catherine arose, he would become uncomfortable and change the

2.2. William Henry Harrison Antrim.

Photographer Furlong, Las Vegas, date not known.
Rasch Collection, Lincoln County Heritage Trust.

One of the eight children of Levi and Ida (Lawson) Antrim, William H. Antrim was born at Huntsville, near Anderson, Indiana, on December 1, 1842. In 1863, while working as a teamster in Philadelphia, he filed suit against the government for wrongful drafting and took his case successfully to the Supreme Court. By the time their verdict was handed down, Antrim had moved to Indianapolis, where in June 1863 he enlisted as a ninety-day volunteer; he was honorably discharged the following September. He lived at Indianapolis until 1869, moved to Kansas in 1870, and settled near Wichita adjacent to Catherine McCarty.

Following Catherine's death he became a wandering prospector and lived out the rest of his life without ever being asked, or himself choosing to set down on paper, the truth about his stepson's background or, for that matter, anything about him at all. After a trip to California to visit his family in 1907, he and his nephew Lon Irish homesteaded near Glenwood. He moved to California in 1920 to live with a niece and died at Adelaida "a pious and highly regarded old gentleman" on December 10, 1922.

Source: Philip J. Rasch, "A Man Named Antrim." *Los Angeles Westerners Brand Book* 6 (1956): 49–54.

subject as soon as possible.[1] Perhaps with reason: there are some strange anomalies about her life.

Be that as it may, by the summer of 1870, Mrs. McCarty had become well enough acquainted with William H. Antrim to accompany him—or have him follow her—to Kansas.

On April 10, 1869, less than a month after the inauguration of President Ulysses S. Grant, it was decided to make the Osage Indian Trust Land along the Kansas–Indian Territory borders available for settlement as of October 22, 1870. When news of this easily obtainable free land reached Indianapolis, William Antrim decided to make the seven-hundred-mile journey west to the Kansas frontier and try his hand at homesteading. He arrived in the early summer.

There are indications that he first spent some time in Allen County, so it may have been there he heard boomers for the new city that was to be built near the junction of the Little and Big Arkansas Rivers. Platted on March 25, 1870, by William Greiffenstein (town builders had anticipated the opening of the land for settlement and moved in early to file on and near the area), it was to be a substantial sixteen-block center set on an eighty-acre agglomeration, its main street ninety feet wide and all others seventy. It would be called Wichita.[2]

There had been settlements of one kind or another in the area since late 1863, when a band of Wichita Indians, loyal to the Union and fleeing for safety from Indian Territory, established an encampment in the densely timbered land where the Little Arkansas empties into the major river. Living with them was Jesse Chisholm, a veteran trader and guide. After the Civil War ended,

2.3. Earliest known photograph of Wichita.

Photographer unknown, June 1870. Wichita–Sedgwick County Historical Museum.

The "town" as it looked about the time Billy Antrim and Catherine McCarty and her sons arrived.

Chisholm built a trading post "between the two rivers" and began trading up and down the old Indian trail. Before long others were using the same trace, among them Greiffenstein and James R. Mead, later senator, who recalled that his and Chisholm's teams "were the first which ever passed over that route and marked out what afterward became known as the Chisholm Trail."[3]

The 1870 federal census for the State of Kansas, enumerated June 27, showed 607 people in the newly formed Sedgwick County. Bustling though it certainly was, the town was still primitive in appearance. J. P. Allen, who established a drugstore in Wichita that year, later recalled how seeing the little group of buildings that was Wichita sitting in the "sea of grass" created a vivid mental image of civilization amid wilderness. From the top of the Empire House Hotel on Main Street he could see over the treeless prairie for miles. A couple of years later it would be all the rage for folks to sit up there and watch the oncoming progress of the railroad construction train from Newton.

William Ross also arrived in Wichita in 1870. He especially liked the Episcopal Church, which was almost hidden by a huge crop of sunflowers. Prairie grass was everywhere, and a slough of water ran across the single main street, forcing citizens to enter some of the businesses on board planks. A few miles south of the town was "absolute wilderness."

James R. Royal was another local moved by Wichita's proximity to nature. He had come out on a dare by friends who had told him that Wichita was all sand, and he had made his first social appearance at the 1870 Fourth of July buffalo barbecue, held on the Little Arkansas River in what is now South Riverside Park. When he learned from "border ruffians" at the feast that there was wonderful hunting and fishing in the area, he had a twenty-yard fish seine made and that fall set himself up in the fishing business on the Little Arkansas. On a single haul he once caught 450 fish, ranging from small fry to a forty-pound catfish.

2.4. Wichita, North Main Street,
west side.

Date and photographer unknown.
Wichita–Sedgwick County Historical Museum.

The west side of North Main
Street, showing the Black & Nixon
Diamond Front Grocery Store
and the W. C. Woodman store,
which later offered a profitable
banking service. Catherine Mc-
Carty's City Laundry was near
here; the one-and-one-half-story
false-fronted buildings are very
similar to the one from which she
operated.

G. M. Weeks, from Knoxville, Illinois, also attended the Fourth of July buffalo barbecue, where he watched a dance given by a large number of Arapaho
and Sioux Indians. He reported that most of the buffalo meat at the barbecue was spoiled and had to be dumped in the river.

By the time Billy Antrim arrived that summer of 1870 with Catherine
McCarty and her sons—perhaps in time to have been at that same Fourth
of July barbecue—there was no longer any chance of obtaining homestead
land close to town, so William filed on a quarter section six miles northeast
of Wichita. There he built "a substantial frame house 14 x 14, one and ½ stories high, Pine Shingle roof, two doors and three windows," into which he
moved about the first of August. Over the next year he would plow and cul-
tivate five acres of land; build a pole stable roofed with boards and hay and
a two-acre corral with "good post and rail fence"; and have a hundred trees
planted and growing, a six-foot-deep well dug, and about one hundred fence
posts and two hundred rails on the ground for fencing.[4]

It would of course be absurd to attempt to reconstruct their life in Wichita
on the basis of the few documents in which their names occur, but that both
William Antrim and Catherine McCarty—and notably Catherine—took an
immediate, even leading interest in civic matters is indicated by an event
which took place on July 21, 1870. This was, remember, at a time when the
women in Wichita came in one of only two varieties: either the settlers' wives
and merchants' ladies who lived east of the river, or the buffalo girls who
danced by the light of the moon to the west of it. So it is the more remark-

able that on that July day, out of 124 Wichitans who presented to Probate Judge Reuben Riggs a petition for the incorporation of the town, only one was a woman, and that woman was Catherine McCarty. On this evidence it would seem safe to assume she also attended the first meeting of the board of trustees of Wichita, which took place in McAdams Hall the following day. She clearly intended to be something more than just another farmer's wife.[5]

Quite soon after their arrival Catherine set up a hand laundry service in a two-story building on North Main Street. Its success is attested to by the fact that commencing the following November, she also began buying and selling town lots; during her stay in Wichita she would be involved in a dozen such transactions. By March 15 of the following year, by which time the Atchison, Topeka & Santa Fe Railroad was completed as far as Cottonwood Falls, her laundry was sufficiently well established to be included in a roster of the town's mercantile establishments published in the very first issue of the *Wichita Tribune:*

2.5. The site of the Catherine McCarty hand laundry today.

Photograph by David King, 1996.

> CITY LAUNDRY
> The City Laundry is kept by Mrs. Mc-
> Carty, to whom we recommend those
> who wish to have their linen made clean.[6]

Just ten days later Catherine appeared before Andrew Akin, registrar of the land office at Augusta, in adjoining Butler County, to file on a Sedgwick County quarter section, adjacent to that of William Antrim (at what is now 21st and Oliver), for which she paid $1.25 an acre, or $200.00 dollars, clear proof that the City Laundry had become a thriving enterprise.

Appearing in person to support her application was Antrim, who attested to the many improvements already made: about seven acres enclosed or in cultivation, rose hedges about seven feet wide, fifty-one fruit trees set and growing, posts and rails on the ground for further fencing, a twelve-foot-deep well, and an outdoor cellar covered with earth and timber. These improvements were valued at between $250 and $300.

Interestingly, Antrim, who attested to having known Catherine for six years, said she was "a single woman over the age of twenty one years the head of a family consisting of two children." In the applicant's affidavit, signed by Catherine with her mark, she declares she is "a Widow & the Head of a family," and Wichita tradition has it that she was always known as "the Widow McCarty."[7]

The affidavits were witnessed by that of Fredrick Daily, who claimed to have known Catherine "for the three months last past." Who he was or what his connection to Catherine might have been is unclear. There is no Fredrick Daily in the 1870 census—only a Bernard Daily born in Ireland. In the 1875 census is an F. Daley, age thirty-seven, hotel keeper, born in Indiana, who arrived at Wichita from that place and was quite wealthy in comparison to his neighbors, with real estate valued at twelve thousand dollars and personal property at fifteen thousand dollars.[8]

Antrim's deposition dates Catherine's move into the twelve-by-fourteen-foot, one-story cabin, with its board roof and single window and door, at March 4, 1871. Since proper Wichitans would doubtless have frowned upon

William and Catherine's living together out of wedlock, we may deduce that at the beginning of their sojourn in Wichita, Mrs. McCarty and her boys probably lived in the North Main Street building.

Pauline Kimmerle, who arrived in Wichita in July 1870, wrote a memoir which caught the tenor of life there then. "Previous to our arrival," she recalled, "Mr. Kimmerle had engaged workmen to build a story and a half building, with living quarters on the second floor. Here we made our home, and when it blew, it rocked like a cradle. This building was the only structure in the second block on North Main Street."[9]

By November 1870, however, Wichita proper had 175 buildings and a population of eight hundred people, a considerable increase over the 16 buildings recorded shortly after the Camp Beecher soldiers left in the spring of 1869. There were three churches, a Masonic hall, two hardware stores, two drugstores, two saddlery and harness shops, two shoemakers, a jewelry store, two blacksmiths, two brickyards, three paint shops, six carpenter shops, a furniture store, three livery stables, a carriage and wagon shop, two restaurants, three hotels, two billiard saloons, two wholesale liquor outlets, four real estate offices, a tannery, "and too many law offices to count." There were two stage lines: Henry Tinsdale's Southern Kansas and Terry & Company's Kansas Stage Company. In addition, there was a clothing emporium (the New York Store) and even a district courtroom, although it consisted of only a chair for the judge and a lawyer's table made of goods boxes set end to end.[10]

The following spring—the day they chose, March 4, was a Saturday—the McCarty family moved into the cabin Antrim had built on Catherine's claim northeast of town. Life on the open prairie was considerably different from life in town, as attested to by Mary Weeks, whose family lived east of town and south of the McCarty claim. "The cowboys were bringing their herds of cattle through from Texas and we were constantly fearful lest they stampede. Mother often cautioned us children 'Be careful that you look out for the cattle.' The sunflowers and the blue grass were so high that we couldn't tell when the cattle were near. The wolves howled at our doors. We were not so very much afraid of them in the daytime, but we kept rather close inside after night."[11]

No doubt Henry and his brother Joe did, too. But there were other dangers, said Bertha Germen, who came to Wichita from London, England, with her husband and settled on a claim nine miles east of town in February 1871. "There were no doors or windows in our new house (or rather shell, as it seemed to me)," Mrs. Germen remembered. "The men . . . took the wagon sheet and made a shelter for the horses. Then they cut holes in the walls for windows. It began to snow. The men boarded up the windows, put up a cook stove. My, but it was cold. I, of course, got supper. The wind blew in the house, [and we] could scarcely keep a lamp alight, it was only a stable lamp."

As the storm raged on, she thought she heard someone calling outside, but the men told her it was her imagination. They made beds on the floor and "went to bed, very tired." Next morning, a Mr. Floxy from Dry Creek in Butler County rode up to the house and asked whether they had seen anything of two boys sent out by their stepmother to hunt cattle that had gotten away before the storm broke. A search party set out.

2.6. Wichita, Douglas Avenue.

Photographer unknown, 1873. Wichita–Sedgwick County Historical Museum.

Although Wichita was primarily a cattle town, it was also a market for sheep, here being driven along Douglas Avenue. If the picture had been taken a year or so earlier, one of the "street gamins" seen here might well have been Henry McCarty.

"The men found the boys in a hollow of the next quarter, East. The smaller boy was nearly dead. His older brother had covered him with his coat. His name was Joe Marshall. Joe said that after they saw our light he had shouted and shouted, but no one heard. The men took our wagon and team and took the boys home. The younger one died."[12]

It was not just the snow that could kill you. Amanda Ballard describes a prairie fire that happened on October 16, 1871:

> The corn crop had been good. My husband coming from the east thought he must cut the corn and shock it. . . . We also had about twelve acres of potatoes to dig. Thinking it too warm to bury them we put them in a pile and covered them with potato vines, then stood the cornstalks around them to keep off the rain. . . .
> My husband went down to the river [about a mile north of us] to cut some wood. About one half mile directly south of us was a camp of Texas herders with their cattle. My husband had not been gone an hour when I saw a fire start in their camp. . . . Imagine my feelings, my little girl and I out there on the prairie alone. The flames were leaping and creeping, coming straight toward us, there was no water, only a barrel sunk in the ground for a well. . . . In less time than it takes to tell we were surrounded by fire. Anyone who has ever seen a prairie fire knows how it will burn a strip through with the wind. Then what is called the backburn, doesn't burn rapidly. Our house and all were right in the strip with the wind. The only way we could live in all that heat was to stand at the north side of the house. Everything all around us was burning. The corn, being shocked, was burning, the potatoes being covered were roasted, the house, being made of logs and having a dirt roof saved that. . . . Everything was gone, everything that we had raised that summer.[13]

Drought, flood, fire, plagues of frogs, rattlesnakes—life on the prairie was a litany of dangers, but like all frontier kids, Henry and Joe grew up tough and self-reliant. There is no record of whether either or both of them attended the rudimentary school that had been built in 1869; it was anyway abandoned in 1871 when the sod roof collapsed. In all likelihood their life was a typical mixture of chores and pleasures, helping to put in the spring crops, going

2.7. Birds Eye View of Wichita, Kansas, 1873.

Drawn by E. S. Glover, published by Strobridge & Co., Cincinnati. Wichita–Sedgwick County Historical Museum.

The drawing shows the principal buildings in surprising detail. The Antrim and McCarty quarter-sections were off the lefthand side (north) of this panorama. The City Laundry is located on Lot 75 on the west side of Main about halfway between First and Second.

fishing, sawing firewood or swimming in the creek, going into town in the wagon or setting out hedge seedlings.

Food, at least, was plentiful. "We are having venison, buffalo, and ante-lope to our heart's content," said the *Vidette* in January 1871. Game was abundant and a three-day hunting trip would yield a three-month supply of tasty meat. If you were not yourself a hunter, William Mathewson bought and sold wild game in his feed store on Douglas well into the 1880s, and the walls and floors there were always covered with prairie chickens, quail, wild geese, and rabbits. Prairie chickens sold at two for twenty-five cents, quail were a dol-lar a dozen, buffalo rump was four cents a pound, and deer meat was fifteen cents a pound.[14]

By 1871 fifteen thousand to twenty thousand head of cattle a week were passing through Wichita on their way to the railroad towns, bringing with them the cowboys, "swearing, drinking and doing much as they please," as a traveler named George Anderson recorded. Most of the business houses kept whiskey to sell, he reported, and the tone of the town was not at all improved

2.8. Joseph Antrim.

Photographer not known, 1928.
R. N. Mullin Collection, HHC.

Joseph Antrim was probably born in Indiana in 1863 or 1864. He left Arizona about 1880 and spent some time in Trinidad, Colorado, as a professional gambler. The following year, an Albuquerque newspaper reported that Joe had claimed he was ready to shoot Pat Garrett on sight for killing his half-brother; Joe himself scotched the rumor by pointing out that he and Garrett had already met at that city's Armijo House, discussed the killing, and parted on a friendly footing. In 1883, Joe helped prevent the lynching at Silver City of W. H. "Doc" Kane (Cain), and a few months later he prevented a shooting at Las Vegas when he made gambler Joe Silks put up his gun. After a brief stint in Tombstone, where he was fined after an altercation with a black hotel porter, Joe drifted up to Denver, where he became a small-time gambler. In 1928 *Denver Post* reporter Edwin H. Hoover interviewed him, finding him so colorless that even when one of his colleagues pointed out that Joe was Billy the Kid's brother, Hoover replied, "So what?"— thereby missing out on one of the greatest scoops in frontier history. Joe Antrim died in poverty at Denver on November 25, 1930, at the (stated) age of seventy-six. His body was given to the Colorado Medical School for dissection.

Sources: Philip J. Rasch, "The Quest for Joseph Antrim," in *Trailing Billy the Kid*, 151–64; *Albuquerque Evening Review*, August 4, 1882; *Silver City Enterprise*, July 20, 1883; *Las Vegas Daily Optic*, October 3, 1883; *Denver Post*, April 1, 1928.

by the smell of fresh buffalo hides laid out in the streets, attracting clouds of bluebottle flies.

The morals of the town smelled little better. It might have been hard to get a drink on the Sabbath, but all the businesses were open and catered to "the hardest set of men," typically accoutered with "a huge bowie knife; a brace of Navy revolvers; large spurs with bells tingling from their heavy cavalry boots; rawhide breeches with the hair on."[15]

This, then, was Henry McCarty's boyhood world. No record exists of his sojourn in Wichita other than the later brief recollection of Marsh Murdock that Henry had been a "street gamin in the days of the longhorns."[16] Certain it is he would have been there, or thereabouts, on February 28, 1871, when Deputy U.S. Marshal Jack L. Bridges, accompanied by Lee Stewart, a scout, and a twenty-five-man detachment of the Fifth Cavalry commanded by Lieutenant Edward L. Randall, rode into town to arrest handsome Jack Ledford, who ran the Harris House (later the Tremont) just down the street from the City Laundry. It was said Jack had once been the leader of a gang of horse thieves and counterfeiters who roamed from Kansas to the Texas Panhandle, but he had turned over a new leaf, married a local girl (and named his hotel for her), and settled down in Wichita.

There was bad blood between Ledford and Bridges over an earlier collision in which Ledford "gave Bridges a sound thrashing," so when Ledford saw Bridges coming, he went to shooting. After emptying their revolvers at Ledford, Bridges, Stewart, and the young lieutenant turned and ran, Bridges collapsing in the street before he reached shelter. Ledford walked across to Dagner's store. Shot twice through the body and twice through the right arm, he was carried into a parlor where he died about half an hour later.[17]

Of more concern to Billy Antrim and her two sons was Catherine's deteriorating health. Whether she already had tuberculosis before she arrived in Wichita or whether, as seems likelier, she contracted it there, it can only have been exacerbated by the constant heat and damp of the laundry in which she spent her every working day. Her condition must have been serious enough for her doctor to recommend, as was the custom then, a higher, drier climate: Colorado, perhaps, or New Mexico. Catherine forthwith began to sell off her Wichita holdings. On June 16, 1871, she sold her quarter section and its improvements (it is now part of the Hebrew White Chapel Memorial Cemetery) to David Orr, and over the next couple of months she and Antrim completed a further flurry of real estate deals.[18]

On June 17, Antrim finalized the paperwork on his quarter section directly northeast of the one Catherine had sold.[19] Although he later experienced some difficulty in obtaining patent to this 160 acres because he had filed on the land from Humbolt in Allen County, he held on to the property until a few years before he died. Why he did so is uncertain; perhaps it was for income, or perhaps he hoped he might one day return to Wichita. Whatever his motives, eleven days later he deeded to Catherine the lots on Chisholm he had previously purchased plus "the building on lot 75, Court (now Main) Street." She in turn sold lots 48 and 50 on Chisholm Street for $445 to Massachusetts-born Henry J. Cook, sixty-two, a recent arrival from Illinois.[20]

When Cook later experienced difficulties with the title to this property, he executed a statement which has baffled everyone who has since tried to trace the dim trail of the McCarty family. After the appropriate six-month interval, he said, he sent payment in full to Catherine McCarty, who "then resided in the city of New Orleans, La.," and that "soon thereafter, the said Catherine McCarty died, to wit, about the year of 1873, [and] . . . at the time of her death said Catherine McCarty was a single woman."[21]

This "sworn statement" before a notary public was surely never intended as anything but a means to an end, enabling Cook, who died four years later, to prove his title to the property. A relative newcomer to Wichita when he made the purchase, he would not have known Catherine as "the widow McCarty" and in all likelihood attested to her marital status, her whereabouts, and her "death" confident that there was no one to contradict him. And he was right.

If nothing else, Cook's deposition pinpoints the last appearance in Wichita of Catherine McCarty; sometime after August 25, 1871—Antrim, famously unreliable, said it was in October 1872—the family left town, heading, if Joseph Antrim's equally vague later recollections are to be trusted, perhaps for Denver, but certainly west.[22]

CHAPTER THREE

Silver City

O<small>N</small> M<small>ARCH</small> 1, 1873, <small>THE SAME DAY</small> a young Englishman named John Tunstall was hunting duck "up the Arm" on Victoria Island with his friend Shears ("We had no luck they are so wild," he reported), William H. Antrim and Catherine McCarty were united in matrimony at the First Presbyterian Church of Santa Fe by its pastor, the Reverend David F. McFarland. Witnesses were Mrs. McCarty's two sons Henry and Joseph, pet-named Josie; Mrs. McFarland; her daughter Katie; and a man named Harvey Edmonds, who frequently acted as a standby witness on such occasions.[1]

Whence they had come and how long had they been in Santa Fe before this wedding no one can say; diligent research has failed to place the McCartys anywhere on the American map between the date of Catherine's last property sale, August 25, 1871, and this spring day in 1873. One possibility is that Catherine became too sick to maintain her own quarter-section and the other properties she owned in Wichita and moved in with Antrim, who had enlarged his own cabin substantially, and that they remained there until they were able to head west.

It might equally as convincingly be argued that Catherine, witnessing Wichita's transformation into a trail town with saloons and bordellos springing up on Water Street, two and one-half thousand cattle a day being driven up its main avenue, and rowdies and whores flocking to Delano, the red-light district across the river, decided it was no place to bring up two young boys and persuaded Antrim they ought to move.

Another theory, based on Joseph Antrim's late-life recollection, is that they went to Denver. This is to some extent reinforced by Frank Coe's recollection of the Kid's background: that "he was born in New York, got his schooling there, and must have been thirteen years old before he left. He came to Denver with his family and his father died there. His mother married a man named Antron. They went to Las Vegas, where they ran a restaurant; later they moved to Santa Fe and a year later to Silver City when the mining rage broke out."[2] Again, intensive search has failed to yield a single documentary clue to support these propositions. All we have is Antrim's unreliable recollection that he left Wichita in October 1872.

By what means and by which route the family arrived in Santa Fe, or how long they were there (or in Las Vegas) before the wedding took place, there is no way of knowing. Garrett's ghost writer Ash Upson suggested that Mrs. McCarty ran a boarding house in Santa Fe. Another possibility is that they stayed with Antrim's sister, Mary Ann Hollinger, believed to have been living in the Santa Fe area at that time, but there is no mention of their arrival in the chatty columns of Santa Fe's *Daily New Mexican* at any time between April 1871 and June 1873.

More surprisingly, there is not even a mention of the marriage in the newspaper, although two earlier marriages and another just two weeks later—those of Thomas McDonald, proprietor of the Exchange Hotel, to Laura Crothers, daughter of Moqui Pueblo Indian Agent Williamson Crothers on April 9, 1872; of Paul F. Herlow to Sophie Wollenwerber on New Year's morning; and of Katie McFarland herself to Mr. William Wallace of Fort Defiance on April 6, 1873—all officiated over by Reverend McFarland—were commented on at length in its columns.

Life in the "metropolis"—as owner-editors Manderfield and Tucker fondly referred to their home town—was a chronicle of small-town events, and the *New Mexican* tirelessly reported all of them: who had registered at the Exchange Hotel, the arrival of the "epizootic" (horse distemper), or the brilliant flourishes of Mr. J. M. Coon, the billiardist who played exhibition matches at the Exchange Hotel. An account of the funeral of Mrs. Stephen Elkins on October 20, news of the opening of Paul Herlow's new butcher shop on the southwest corner of the plaza a month later, and the establishment of Billy Bolander's new harness shop on San Francisco Street the following February received fulsome coverage. The weather, the depredations of the Apaches—Cochise's war with the military was raging in Arizona—and regular reports from correspondents in La Mesilla and on the mining activities at Silver City were interspersed with puffs for a forthcoming masquerade party or the appearance of the Fort Wingate Theatrical and Minstrel Troop at the Opera House on Lincoln Avenue, orchestra seats one dollar, dress circle fifty cents.

Lacking any kind of documentation, all that can be said with any certainty about Antrim and the McCartys is that they must have been in Santa Fe throughout the month preceding the wedding, because residence was a necessary qualification for the calling of the marriage banns over the three weeks preceding the ceremony—as the very proper Reverend McFarland would doubtless have insisted be done. Surprisingly, weddings did not always take place in the Presbyterian Church; McFarland seems to have been happy to conduct ceremonies in private homes, if required. However, in the absence of evidence to the contrary, we may assume that on Saturday morning, March 1, William Antrim, Catherine McCarty, and her sons proceeded together to the church, its square tower rising proudly above the one-story adobes surrounding it.

It was a cool, clear, fine day with a sharp nip in the air; the mean temperature, recorded by Observer J. P. Clum of the Signals Service of the U.S. Army, was 31° F. The handwritten record on pages 35–36 of Book of Marriages A of Santa Fe County reads as follows:

1873
March 1ˢᵗ Mr. William H. Antrim and Mrs. Catherine McCarty
Both of Santa Fe, New Mexico
by D. F. McFarland.
Witnesses
Harvey Edmonds Mrs. A.R. McFarland
Miss Katie McFarland, Henry McCarty, Josie McCarty.

The official record is confirmed by another in Dr. McFarland's own hand in the register of the Presbyterian Church, although he excludes the name

3.1. First Presbyterian Church, Santa Fe, ca. 1868–69.

Photograph by Nicolas Brown.
MoNM Negative No. 37895.

of his daughter as a witness. Taken together, these documents add one or two more interesting fragments of information to the sum of our knowledge. For example, Joseph Antrim is in both cases named second (and, in one instance, by his pet name, Josie), suggesting strongly that he was the junior of the two boys, a proposition that will be examined more fully later. The second item is that both parties to the marriage are stated to be "of Santa Fe," indicating, if entries above and below theirs are any guide, that they were residents of the town, making the absence of any mention of the marriage in the newspaper all the more puzzling.

Soon after the wedding, the Antrims left Santa Fe. They may have stayed briefly in Georgetown, a mining camp that had grown up around the first discovery of silver made in 1866 and which was experiencing something of a renaissance, then they may have moved on to busy, noisy, dirty, booming Silver City. Whether they had come to this locality because the excellence of its climate had already been remarked upon by a government commission seeking a location for a sanatorium for officers suffering from tuberculosis, or whether, as seems at least as likely, they came because Billy Antrim had the get-rich-quick bug, is unclear. Perhaps it was for both reasons.

Five years earlier, apart from the military establishment at Fort Bayard, the old copper mines at Santa Rita, the camps at Pinos Altos and Central City, and a few farms scattered along the Mimbres River, the whole area of which Silver City was now the undisputed center had been unexplored wilderness, homeland of the hostile Apache. The future site of the city itself was a pleasant grassy valley called La Ciénaga de San Vicente.

In the spring of 1870, news reached Pinos Altos of a big silver strike at a camp named Ralston (later Shakespeare), and a group of miners rode down to investigate. When they examined the ore, they realized there was plenty just as good back where they had come from—and no one knew about it.

3.2. Dr. David Fulton McFarland.

Date and photographer unknown.
Dept. of History & Records Management Service, Presbyterian Church (USA), Philadelphia, Pennsylvania.

David F. McFarland was born in Washington County, Pennsylvania, on March 12, 1820. A graduate of Washington and Jefferson College, Philadelphia, he was licensed by the Presbytery of Washington on October 8, 1851, and ordained at Peoria on July 8, 1852. In October 1857 he married Amanda A. Reed, born in 1832 in Brooke County, Virginia. During the Civil War he was a teacher and she his assistant at Mattoon Female Seminary in Illinois. He was assigned to set up Presbyterian missions in New Mexico and came to Santa Fe toward the end of 1866. Amanda crossed the plains several times by stagecoach between 1867 and 1873. The *Santa Fe Daily New Mexican* of August 9, 1871, noted the opening of Santa Fe University, proprietors W. F. Arny, Joab Houghton, and McFarland, one of his many efforts to educate his flock. Dr. McFarland retired in ill health to San Diego in 1873, but two years later he and his wife became missionaries to the Nez Percé tribe in Lapwai, Idaho. Dr. McFarland died on the reservation there May 13, 1876.

Source: *Biographical and Historical Catalogue of Washington & Jefferson College, 1802–1902*, 352.

They went back to the Ciénaga and staked out their claim—they called it the Legal Tender—which yielded silver ore that assayed as high as one hundred dollars a ton. News of the "Ciénaga Mines" spread fast, and the boom was on. Among the earliest of the mining camps in Grant County, Silver City outstripped all her competitors, a new place in every sense of the word.

John and James Bullard, H. M. Fuson, Elijah Weeks, J. T. Yankie, R. Yeamans, A. J. Hurlburt, and John Swisshelm, the men who located the Legal Tender claim, were considered "founding fathers," while among the town's earliest boomers were Lucien B. Maxwell, Harvey H. Whitehill, William Chamberlain, James Corbin, Richard Hudson, Singleton M. Ashenfelter, Colonel J. F. Bennett, Judge Hackney, and Brad Dailey.

Despite the constant presence and menace of the Apaches, Silver City flourished from its inception, and within a year about a hundred buildings had been erected. The first sawmill, installed five miles above town by M. W. Bremen, operated twenty-four hours a day to satisfy demand. The growth of the town was so fast and so spectacular that in 1871 the county seat was moved down from Pinos Altos. Later in the year rich deposits of chloride were found west of town, and Chloride Flats sprang up on the site. Even in those early days of rudimentary mining techniques, wealth was being torn from the earth in astonishing quantities: by 1875, Silver City mills would be producing sixteen thousand dollars' worth of bullion a week.

The town shed its mining-camp identity very rapidly; as early as late 1872 a brickyard was in production north of town, and solid business premises were being built. A sizeable community of Mexican settlers, many of them former residents of the Mesilla Valley, occupied a hilly area south of town which was known as "Chihuahua." Among the new buildings being raised were a new courthouse and jail. On February 17, 1873, just two weeks before the Antrim-McCarty wedding, the *New Mexican* noted, "Grant County is to have a new courthouse and jail. The site has already been selected and work will be commenced in a short time. The courthouse is to be one and a half stories high and built of brick; the jail will be in the basement of the main building."

This was something of an overstatement. The county building, which was on a bench on the east side of Hudson Street between Market and Yankie, was in fact a small one-story adobe structure containing four offices (and no basement). A jail, a small structure separate from the county building and described by Harvey Whitehill as "an adobe affair," was completed just after Christmas, but it would not be until January 1874, when specially built iron doors arrived on Patrick Shanley's freight train and Black Brothers installed them, that it would be described as "one of the strongest places of imprisonment in the country not excepting the guardhouse at Fort Bayard." A little over eighteen months later this building—which was in fact considerably less secure than the glowing press accounts claimed—would figure importantly in the life of young Henry McCarty, or, as he now was, Henry Antrim.

When the Antrims arrived in the early summer of 1873, Silver City was a town with all its hair on, its population a mixture of the most fearless and the most desperate men on the frontier. It was a town where three shifts of bartenders were needed to cope with the round-the-clock thirst of the patrons of saloons like the Blue Goose and the Red Onion or more elegant places like Joseph D. Dyer's recently opened Orleans Club on Main Street, where the high rollers sat all night with their gold and silver stacked in front of them, betting into pots running to thousands of dollars.

On February 24 a correspondent writing to the Santa Fe newspaper reported that "McGary and Dyer, on Main Street, are adding a ten-pin alley to their saloon. Their dance hall is crowded nightly with those eager to trip the light fantastic. Their bar receipts are over a hundred dollars a night. There is money here."

And violence, he might have added: on June 14, 1873, in the arroyo near that same dance hall "an officer"—perhaps the sheriff or one of his deputies, or maybe even a constable—confronted a drunken man named Campbell who refused to surrender his pistol. When the officer grabbed the gun, it discharged, wounding a bystander named Kelly. The following August 6, a William Wilson severely cut saloon keeper Joe Dyer about the face and body with a knife; arrested and hauled in front of the magistrate, he pleaded self-defense and was released. Dyer recovered, although he was scarred for life. A little later in the year David Abraham shot to death an intruder at his home.[3]

Awaiting an opportunity to buy a town plot, the Antrims moved into a thirty-foot-square "simple, gabled log cabin" that had been built near the corner of Main and Broadway, probably by pioneer prospector John Swisshelm. Close by, a Dr. Bailey had just opened up "a first class drug and variety store" in a building formerly owned by Frank Bisby.[4]

They were lucky to have such comparative luxury; many families were liv-

3.3. Mrs. Amanda R. McFarland

Date and photographer unknown. Dept. of History & Records Management Service, Presbyterian Church (USA), Philadelphia, Pennsylvania.

After the death of her husband, Amanda McFarland moved to Portland, where she met Sheldon Jackson, superintendent of the Presbyterian missions. She accompanied him to Alaska and on August 10, 1877, took charge of a school at Fort Wrangell. Jackson left her in charge, the only Christian white woman there. She stayed on as pastor, doctor, and legal consultant to the Indians, settling their political, religious, physical, and moral problems. She became and remained an immense influence in southern Alaska until her death in 1912.

3.4. David Abraham and his family.

Photographer unknown,
San Francisco, ca. 1864–65.
Author's Collection.

David Abraham holds Hyman in his right arm and Louis in his left; Jacob and Abraham are standing; Mrs. Esther Abraham is sitting, holding Sara; Anna is standing; Phoebe is seated holding Sam.

David Abraham was born David Dobrzinsky in Poland, February 27, 1824. His first wife, Esther Leah Julian, died September 4, 1865, in San Francisco; his second wife was Amelia Schaublin (1847–1930). In 1880 he married Emilie Fritz Scholand, the sister of Lincoln County's Emil Fritz, who had two children: Emilie, known as "Mamie" (1872–88) and Anna (1873–?). David Abraham died at Silver City on March 8, 1894. His widow married William McAllister on June 21, 1902, but McAllister lived only two years; she died at Los Angeles on September 7, 1930.

Source: Walter N. Jones, *Tree Branches.*

3.5. The Antrim cabin, corner of Main and Broadway, Silver City.

Photographed by Alfred S. Addis, 1882.
MoNM Negative No. 99054.

This photograph shows the cabin about a decade following the Antrims' occupancy, by which time it had been enlarged to include a dining room with boarding rooms at the rear *(left)*; the original living quarters were at the far end *(right)*.

3.6. Intersection of Main and Broadway, Silver City.

From a photograph by Lucas, Silver City, ca. 1885.
Courtesy of the Silver City Museum.

In this enlarged section of a photograph taken looking northeast from the intersection of Bullard and Broadway, the old Grant County Bank building can be seen on the left. Just beyond it, where the team and wagon are heading north on Main Street, are two buildings. The smaller of these buildings, with a barely sloping gabled roof, appears to be the southern elevation of the Antrim cabin, the end opposite that shown in the Addis photograph (Fig. 3.5).

ing in tents. Immigrants and prospectors were flooding in; a thousand were heading toward Silver City from Utah in June, and by mid-July, with another colony from Colorado expected imminently, the influx had already created a housing and water shortage.

The Antrim family settled in quickly and seem to have made a favorable impression on their neighbors. Mrs. Antrim took in washing, offered bed and board to newcomers, and baked cakes for sale. Her husband did odd jobs of carpentry or worked in a butcher shop while he picked up the ins and outs of silver mining. Mrs. Louis Abraham described them as "very good people and hard working. . . . [Mrs. Antrim] had a little laundry of her own [she was] a hard working woman."[5]

Agnes Meader Snider, with whom he later boarded for a year, remembered Antrim as "a nice appearing fellow, but the report was . . . he wasn't good to his wife." The inference here is none too clear—did he mistreat her, or was he merely a tightwad? Mrs. Snider was emphatic at least on that point. "[A few years] after [his wife] died he left Silver and went to Mogollon . . . and worked in the mines there for about a year. . . . Well, they had some property back in Kansas or Arkansas back then and Billy Antrim was a close stingy man, he saved every dollar he ever made, some of them say he had the first dime he ever made."[6]

Tightwad he may have been, but Antrim certainly seems to have given Catherine plenty of freedom: she regularly attended the dances held three or four times a week in local dance halls. Louis Abraham's description of her as "a jolly Irish lady, full of life, fun and mischief [who] could dance the Highland Fling as well as the best of the dancers," suggests her health was not troubling her unduly at this time.[7]

Ash Upson, who claimed he boarded in her home in the spring of 1874, to some extent confirms this in describing her then. "She was evidently of Irish descent," he wrote, "about the medium height, straight and graceful in form,

3.7. Silver City: south end of Bullard Street, looking north.

Photographer unknown, late 1870s. John Harlan Collection, Silver City Museum.

Taken from Chihuahua Hill, this view shows Main and Hudson Streets to the right and Texas Street less well defined to the left. The location of the Antrim cabin at Main and Broadway would appear to have been adjacent to (but concealed by) the shack to the left of the long building (the Star Hotel) on the extreme right and above center; the Silver City jail is to the right in the background above.

with regular features, light blue eyes, and luxuriant golden hair. She was not a beauty, but what the world calls a fine-looking woman. . . . Her charity and goodness of heart were proverbial."[8]

Subsequent to the completion of a townsite survey in January 1873, residents were able to file claims on city lots; oddly, since the cabin they were living in was on lot 4, William Antrim is recorded as having filed on adjoining lots in block 16.[9] He received the deeds on June 10 of the following year, but by that time any plans he might have had to build on the plots had become redundant, because Catherine was terminally ill.

Meanwhile, Henry and Joe had very quickly gotten to know the local kids—the "Village Arabs," as Owen L. Scott, former Fort Selden government clerk turned editor of the town's newspaper, *Mining Life*, dubbed them. "Street arabs" was a term commonly used to describe wayward urchins in cities as far apart as London and San Francisco and generally understood to mean homeless vagabonds or outcast boys and girls. Silver City's kids were hardly that, but Scott, whose first issue appeared May 17, 1873, remarked early on the need for the city to provide proper educational facilities for them. A local census taken in November of that year would show that Silver City's population of 826 souls included 30 Anglo and 119 Hispanic children between the ages of five and eleven who were eligible for the projected free public school.

Most of the Silver City residents who knew Henry Antrim at that time remembered him affectionately. Louis Abraham, who was seven when he came to Silver City in 1870, recalled Henry "as just an ordinary boy like any other

3.8. The Southern Hotel.

Photograph by White & Graham, ca. 1890s.
R. N. Mullin Collection, HHC.

Built on the site of Cornelius Bennett's store at Broadway and Hudson, a block below the county jail, the hotel was owned and operated for a while by David Abraham and his wife, the former Emilie Fritz, and around the turn of the century by Louis Abraham.

boy and just mischievous." Harry Whitehill, who went to school with him, said Henry "wasn't a bad fellow." Anthony Conner, then ten years old, described him as "undersized, and really girlish looking. I don't think he weighed over 75 pounds." Henry was about twelve years old when he first arrived, Conner remembered. Chauncey Truesdell, another ten-year-old, recalled Henry as "small for his age and kind of skinny."[10]

In January 1874, during what would be remembered as one of the worst winters ever known in Grant County, the first public school was inaugurated; lacking the funds to build a schoolhouse, the commissioners rented McGary's Hall on north Main and hired a Dr. Webster to teach the children for the term which concluded at the end of March. School commenced Friday, January 5; Dr. Webster soon reported that of 140 students eligible for schooling, only 43 had registered, and of those only 32 were actually attending classes. Louis Abraham, Harry Whitehill, and Charley Stevens were among them; all confirmed that Henry also attended. But once school was out, the "arabs" were back on the street and up to their none-too-civilized tricks again.[11]

On February 4, an unidentified thief stole thirty-five dollars from the money drawer of Richard Knight's butcher shop. Scott's *Mining Life* exhorted merchants to "keep a good look-out for these petty thieves. . . . There are a number of them in town." On March 11, a group of youngsters broke into a dance hall and from it burglarized the adjoining Bank Exchange saloon, making off with money from the cash till and several buckets of whiskey. "These thefts are getting to be too common," rumbled Scott. Without naming names, he said the perpetrators were obnoxious kids who ought to be

3.9. Hudson's Hot Springs.

Photographer unknown, spring 1888.
Harlan Collection, Silver City Museum.

Mary and Richard Hudson are second and third from left. Hudson was a witness at the marriage of Daniel Casey and Mary Richards.

put to work sweeping the streets by day and locked up in the new jail at night.[12]

Wayne Whitehill recalled their being one of the targets of editor Scott's ire. "At that time," he recalled, "there wasn't only but just a few white kids, they were mostly Mexicans. . . . There was the Bennett boys [nephews of Judge Cornelius Bennett] and John and Vincent Mays [sons of German-born John Mays, who owned a brewery], . . . the Stevenses [Albert and Charlie, cousins of the Whitehills] and my brother Harry."[13]

Soon after this, Henry started getting into more serious trouble, and it is difficult not to infer some connection between his delinquency and the rapid deterioration of his mother's health—not to mention the fact that his step-father had simply left town, to all intents and purposes abandoning them.

How deep-seated Catherine's tuberculosis may have been, or how she contracted it, can only be guessed. In those days the commonest cause, apart from direct contact with someone already suffering from the disease, was from the consumption of infected meat or milk of cattle, frequently coupled with bad social or environmental conditions. The onset of acute pulmonary tuberculosis is characterized by hemoptysis (spitting blood), the spontaneous collapse of a lung, pneumonia, or bronchopneumonia; the signs of the more insidious variety are a persistent cough, tiredness, loss of weight, and vague "unwellness."

In Catherine's case the decline seems to have been so abrupt that it may well be that a tuberculous lesion had burst into her bloodstream. When this happens the result may be miliary tuberculosis, in which the infection spreads rapidly throughout the body, resulting in inevitable death within two or three months. In addition, March and April were bitterly cold, with some of the severest rain and snowstorms Arizona had ever known, snow two to three feet deep at Pinos Altos, and the thermometer rarely above zero.[14]

Four months before her death, possibly following last-ditch treatment at Hudson's Hot Springs Hotel, twenty-five miles southeast of Silver City, Catherine Antrim became bedridden. It is tellingly revealing of William Antrim's character—and the deterioration of their relationship—that he should have chosen this moment to go prospecting again. As for Henry, with no one to support or feed him, "Well, the first thing he done, he tried to get an uncle of mine named Charlie Stevens to go in with him and rob a little peanut and candy stand an old fellow named Matt Devershire [Derbyshire] had," said Wayne Whitehill. "And so Charlie come and told my father about it and he got Billy and give him a scare about this wantin' to rob a store."[15]

Derbyshire's furniture store—with a sizeable news depot and candy store on the side—had a display of costume jewelry as raffle prizes in the window. Henry's idea, Charlie told his father, was to steal the jewelry and dispose of it in Mexico. Isaac Stevens took his son by the ear and made him confess all to Derbyshire. Asked how he ever got himself involved in such a madcap scheme, Charlie could only offer the explanation, "He had me hypnotized." To circumvent the possibility of Henry's exacting summary retribution on the squealer—as Harvey Whitehill remarked, it was characteristic of Henry that if ever "someone did him dirt then he would seek revenge"—Stevens and Derbyshire hauled both boys over the coals and told them to watch their step. And for almost a year the chastened Henry behaved himself.

On Monday, May 18—commencement had been delayed a week to accommodate repairs to the school quarters—the new teacher, Mrs. Pratt, opened the summer session. It lasted until the morning of Friday, August 7, when heavy rains caused the collapse of the dirt roof, at which point she dismissed class and shortly thereafter left Silver City, never to return. Just five short weeks later, on Wednesday, September 16, 1874, Catherine McCarty Antrim breathed her last in the little cabin on Main Street.

A funeral service was held at the house at two o'clock the following day; the Stevenses, Whitehills, and Truesdells were among those present. Julia Truesdell had prepared the body for burial. According to Louis Abraham's wife, there was "no hearse or carriage or anything of that kind but Mr. Abraham's father [David] had a little express wagon and he took the body to the cemetery [which occupied two blocks bounded by Tenth, Twelfth, West, and Santa Rita Streets] and had it buried. . . . There was no undertaker. I don't think there was any undertaker [here] at that time. They just got her body ready and fixed a box and he took her out." They made a headboard to mark the grave from "a board that was three feet high and two inches thick and twelve inches wide."[16]

For a while after their mother's death Henry and his brother Joe stayed at the home of Richard Hudson and his wife, Mary,[17] who owned the Legal Tender Livery and Feed Stable on the corner of Spring and Hudson; no doubt the boys did their share of chores there. The public school had reopened just two days before Catherine died, and when he and his brother resumed at-

3.10. Catherine McCarty's grave.

Photograph by Maurice G. Fulton, ca. 1942.
R. N. Mullin Collection, HHC.

This was not the original location or marker. In 1882, the city fathers accepted the offer of John Miller, post sutler at Fort Bayard, to move the bodies to a new location northeast of town in exchange for a deed to the property the cemetery now occupied. Miller replaced the original wooden cross marking Catherine's grave with this headboard, which read: "To the Memory of Mrs. Kathrine Antrim, Died September 8th, 1874 AGE 45 YEARS"—her name misspelled, the date of her death incorrect, and perpetuating forever what may have been an error regarding her age.

3.11. Catherine McCarty's grave, Silver City.

Author's photograph, 1994.

Donated to the city by a local funeral parlor in 1947, this is Catherine's marker as it looks today, with the date of her death corrected but otherwise still inaccurate and displaying as well the mindless addenda of modern vandals.

tendance, Henry struck up a good relationship with the new teacher, a willowy twenty-eight-year-old English gentlewoman named Mary Richards. Many years later she would remember him as "a scrawny little fellow with delicate hands and an artistic nature" who was "always quite willing to help with the chores around the school house" and "no more of a problem in school than any other boy growing up in a mining camp."[18]

Mary Phillipa Richards was said to have been fluent in German, Italian, and French and claimed to have been acquainted with such notables in her own country as statesman Benjamin Disraeli, critic John Ruskin, and poet Alfred, Lord Tennyson. For so young a woman she had experienced some remarkable adventures, and a close attachment seems to have developed between young Henry and his elegant teacher; he even fantasized they might be related.

"He thought this because they were both ambidextrous," Mary Richards's daughter Patience said in later years. "My mother could write equally well with either hand, and so could Billy. He noticed this and he used to say to my mother that he was sure they were related because she was the only other person he had ever seen, besides himself, who could do things equally well with either hand."[19]

There were twenty-nine pupils in Henry's class, which *Mining Life* editor Scott—who had recently taken a new partner, O'Neil M. Kechnie, to help him run the newspaper—visited. Miss Richards, he pronounced, "had their interest excited and their advancement was certain."[20] As winter closed in, Billy Antrim made new arrangements for his stepsons which would leave him free to come and go as he pleased—and effectively take them off his hands for good. Henry, now a teenager, would live with Gerald and Clara Truesdell, Chauncey's parents, who had just bought and renovated the old Star Hotel on Hudson Street and had renamed it the Exchange. In return for his bed and board Henry would wait on tables and do whatever chores were assigned to him. Joe would live with and work for Joseph Dyer, proprietor of the Orleans Club, as an errand boy and gofer, placing bets, running numbers, and generally making himself useful.

The question of whether Joe was the older or younger brother has never been satisfactorily resolved. The testimony of his Silver City contemporaries on the subject is conflicting. Compared to his "mild mannered, flaxen-haired, blue eyed" brother he was "larger and very husky," Chauncey Truesdell said. "He looked to be a year and a half or two older than Henry." Anthony Conner also believed that Joe was the older, as did Harvey Whitehill's daughter. But was he?

When Joe died in 1930 in Denver, alone and destitute, his age was recorded on the death certificate as seventy-six, suggesting he was born about 1854. But this date is rendered suspect by the only document known to have actually been completed by Joe himself, a voter's registration form completed on October 13, 1916, on which he gives his age as fifty-three, making the date of his birth 1863. A trio of minor items of evidence suggest that this is the likelier proposition. The first is that on his mother's wedding day his name was given as "Josie"—an unlikely pet name for a nineteen-year-old but not inapposite for a boy of ten. The second is an entry in the 1885 census for Arapahoe County, Colorado (Denver was not yet separated into city and county), listing a Joe Antrimm [*sic*], white, single, age twenty-one, born in Indiana. And the third is an item that appeared in the Silver City newspaper reporting that Joseph Antrim was "among the children who spoke at the Children's Christmas Tree and New Year's Eve Festival held in the City Hall on Thursday evening, December 30, 1875." If Joe really was "among the children" a good three months after his brother Henry escaped from the Silver City jail, only two conclusions are possible: either Joe was appreciably younger than his brother, or at the time Henry went on the run he himself was even younger than anyone has ever imagined.[21]

The season turned from fall to winter. Each evening after school, the "Vil-

3.12. Mary Phillipa Richards.

Photograph by Daniel Früwirth, London, ca. 1868.
Courtesy Mary B. Campbell.

Born in Southampton, England, on April 3, 1846, Mary was the second child of John Edmonds and Mary Ann Davies (Quarrill) Richards; an older brother, Reuben, was born December 19, 1844, and a younger, Edward, on April 12, 1848, both in London. In 1849 the family emigrated to the United States and settled at Brownsville, Texas, where John Richards established a school. On November 13, 1851, another child was born and christened Isabella Louisa Demas Lopez Richards.

Exactly one year later, Mary Ann Richards died following an accidental fall; Isabella was adopted by her godfather and his wife. About 1859, John Richards was murdered by persons unknown at San Fernando de Preces, seventy-five miles from Matamoros; his two sons were taken in by a local family. Mary Phillipa was returned to England late in 1862 and became the ward of Dr. Joseph Baylee, principal of St. Aidan's Theological College in Birkenhead. Educated at a private school, Mary learned Spanish, French, German, and Portuguese, spending a year each in Mannheim, Germany, and Paris, France, before becoming a governess and teacher.

In 1873, Mary returned to the United States and located her brothers on the eight-thousand-acre ranch of James B. L. Primm at the settlement named for his father, Dr. William Primm, (later Kirtley) in Fayette County, Texas. Later that year Mary applied for and was offered the post of teacher in Silver City. She was present when the school opened on September 14, 1874, and continued as teacher until she married Daniel Charles Casey at Silver City on October 5, 1875. In 1880 the family—there were six children—moved to Georgetown, where Mary Phillipa Richards Casey died on the first day of January 1900.

Sources: research by descendants Blanche and Edith Casey and Mary Boulware Campbell.

lage Arabs" staged races on Market Street which Owen Scott noted were "carried on throughout with great hilarity and scarcely a difference [between winner and loser]." According to Harry Whitehill, the boys would have someone be their racehorse and bet for fun. "I could outrun anyone in Silver City until I was 21 years old," he boasted.[22]

Henry also appeared with the other kids in minstrel shows to raise money for the school. In mid-December Mary Richards held open house and staged a party for the children. All of them excelled at recitation, according to indefatigable observer Owen Scott, who praised their teacher for "turning rambunctious kids into attentive scholars." Miss Richards and contractor Robert Black then distributed presents to the pupils.[23]

Out of school and in the absence of any sort of proper parental control, Henry was soon back among the street arabs. Toward the end of 1874, Silver City had acquired its first Chinese immigrant, Charlie Sun, who opened a laundry on north Bullard Street, competition which so unsettled the town's newest laundress, Nellie Johnson (the mining claim lead yielding $140 a ton she had opened up in Pinos Altos in September had obviously petered out), that she placed an ad in the *Mining Life* on November 5 that said, "Boys, that Chinaman can't do as well for you as I can. Bring your washing to Texas Street."[24]

According to Wayne Whitehill, Charlie Sun had come down from Albuquerque, and on the road he was attacked by Indians and wounded fourteen times. "And he used to tell about it, he'd always say, 'He killa me fourteen times, killa me here and killa me here.' When he used to tell it, it sure was funny."

Charlie, twenty-four, was married to a Mexican woman. When she got pregnant, Wayne said, "he was around celebrating around the saloon, treatin' everybody on account of this baby. And when the baby was born it was a nigger. And so he had an old sow out in the backyard and he took that baby out and threw it in there and the sow killed it. No, there wasn't anything done about it."[25]

Around November, Charlie took a new partner into his laundry business. His name was Sam Chung. They were both "westernized" Chinese; that is to say, they no longer wore the distinctive pigtails of their people or burned incense in their establishment (hence the later description "sans cue, [queue] sans joss sticks"). It did not make them any more popular. In fact, the residents of Silver City looked on their presence and their opium dens in Hop Town with undisguised disfavor. It didn't take the "arabs" long to learn that nobody cared what pranks got played on the Asians.

Wayne Whitehill remembered: "[Down near Main Street] there was an adobe building there and the Chinaman had a laundry in there . . . and then the Tremont [Keystone] Hotel was right beyond it. . . . People there gave us orders to chase all the Chinamen out of the town, they didn't want Chinamen there. And they said 'Rock him' every time we [would] see a Chinaman, 'rock him and run him and make him leave.' . . . Manuel [Taylor] got him a rock and peeked around and after awhile he swung and threw it. And when we looked around to see what he'd done with that rock this Chinaman was floppin' around like a chicken with his head cut off. . . . We all took to our heels. God, I was home in no time under the bed. . . . We knew damn well that Chinaman was killed all right. Well, there was never a thing said about it at all." And yes, Wayne confirmed, Henry Antrim was one of the gang who killed the man. "He couldn't have been over ten years old, I don't suppose," he said.[26]

It is difficult to know how much weight to give to Wayne Whitehill's decidedly uneven account: he had no reason to lie, but as he told it, there was no way he could have known for sure that the man died. If, as he indicates, the incident took place in the interregnum between the departure of former Sheriff Charles McIntosh, who skinned out with all the county funds he could

3.13. Harvey Howard Whitehill.

Date and photographer unknown.
John Harlan Collection, Silver City Museum.

The eldest son of David Messmore and Sarah Jane (Perrine) Whitehill, Harvey H. Whitehill was born in Bellefontaine, Logan County, Ohio, on September 2, 1837. Raised in that state, he engaged briefly in railroading, but in 1858 he decided to try his luck mining in Colorado and Nevada. During the Civil War he served as a private in Captain William D. Simpson's Independent Company of New Mexico Mounted Spies and Guides. On December 19, 1865, he married Harriet Margaret Stevens, and they established a home at Virginia City (later renamed Elizabethtown) during the height of the mining activities there. About 1870, Whitehill and his partner Ike Stevens found some promising claims in the San Vicente area of Arizona, and Whitehill was one of those who laid out the townsite which became Silver City. He was to play a leading role in Silver City's civic affairs, first as coroner and then, when in 1874 Sheriff McIntosh absconded with about three thousand dollars of county funds, as sheriff, serving three terms as well as serving on the territorial legislature in 1880. Although Whitehill never killed a man in personal combat, he had "many fights with Apaches" and presided over the executions of at least four men. In 1884 he assisted in capturing the Kit Joy gang of train robbers, and during his last stint as sheriff he put outlaws Broncho Bill Walters and Mike McGinnis in jail.

In later years Whitehill established a ranch on the Mimbres River near Mowry City, where he ran pedigreed cattle. His wife Hattie died on April 20, 1895; on January 30, 1902, Whitehill married Sarah Ann Brown, who was born November 28, 1871, in Hull, Georgia, and who, it was said, he met through a lonely hearts club. He died at Deming, New Mexico, on September 7, 1907.

Sources: pension application; genealogical information from Harvey H. Whitehill III, Albuquerque.

lay his hands on, and Whitehill's April appointment, no record of it exists.[27]

So although Henry can probably be absolved of participating in the stoning to death of the unfortunate Chinese man (if it ever happened), he nonetheless had, as Harvey Whitehill observed, "a proclivity for breaking the Eighth Commandment," and soon after Whitehill became sheriff, he did it again. This time it was "the theft of several pounds of butter from a ranchman named [Abel L.] Webb," the lawman said, "which he disposed of to one of the local merchants. His guilt was easily established, but upon promise of good behavior, he was released."[28]

That summer, Henry's life was again disrupted, this time by domestic difficulties at the Truesdell home. He moved out and found lodgings with a Mrs. Brown—probably Sarah, wife of bartender R. H. Brown—and earned his keep after school in Knight's butcher shop, killing, skinning, gutting, and jointing animals for sale, or pumping the bellows at Levi Miller's smithy. Thanks to Joe, he had access to the Orleans Club, where in typically quick and adept fashion he learned and began to play poker and monte for money. He was sharp, bright, alert. "There was one peculiar facial characteristic that to an experienced man hunter, would have marked him immediately as a bad man," Harvey Whitehill said, "and that was his eyes. They never were at rest, but continually shifted and roved, much like his own rebellious nature."[29]

One of his fellow boarders at Mrs. Brown's was a young stonemason named George Schaefer. "He thought a lot of Billy," Harry Whitehill said, "and Billy used to follow him around." George, whose distinctive choice in headwear had won him the nickname Sombrero Jack, had two loves. He liked to get drunk and he liked to steal. "He had a mania to steal," Whitehill said, "and he was always stealing"—hardly the ideal companion for a youngster as reckless as Henry Antrim, but there it was.

"So the next thing he did [Wayne Whitehill said] was . . . there was a big old log house there [near Main Street] and the Chinaman [Charlie Sun] had a hand laundry in there. He used to get people's clothes and wash them, so he hung a lot of clothes out one evening after he'd washed them . . . and Billy went down there that night [and stole them. The Chinaman] went to my father about it, about somebody stealin' his clothes. So he traced it up some way and found out Billy had done it. . . . Well, he took Billy up and put him in jail and I asked him how long he was gonna keep him there and he said, 'I'll just keep him there just to give him a little scare and I'll turn him out after awhile.'"[30]

This makes it sound like a minor prank, but in fact it was fairly serious larceny. On Saturday, September 4, George Schaefer broke into Charlie Sun's house and stole clothing, two revolvers, and a large bundle of blankets, with a total value between $150 and $200 (a new Colt .45 cost about $12 at that time). Schaefer hid the loot in Georgetown, then offered Henry a cut if he would smuggle some of the clothing into town and keep it for him. Henry made the mistake of hiding the booty in his room, where it was found by Mrs. Brown, who immediately informed Sheriff Whitehill that her lodger was handling stolen goods. When Whitehill picked Henry up on Thursday morning, September 23, Sombrero Jack fled with the rest of the loot before the same thing happened to him.

The *Grant County Herald* had the rest of the story in its September 26 edition:

> Henry McCarty, who was arrested on Thursday and committed to jail to await the action of the grand jury, upon the charge of stealing clothes from Charley Sun and Sam Chung, celestials sans cue, sans joss sticks, escaped from prison yesterday through the chimney. It is believed Henry was simply the tool of "Sombrero Jack" who done the actual stealing whilst Henry done the hiding. Jack has skinned out.

"Sheriff Whitehill just wanted to scare him," Mrs. Abraham said, "so he locked him up in the jail that was here at the time and [it had] a big fireplace and when he went to see him the next day, why he had climbed up the chimney and gotten away and got down to Apache Tejo."[31]

From such evidence as this—and there is plenty more—it seems indisputable that Sheriff Whitehill's intention was to scare Henry sufficiently to deter him once and for all from crime. But Henry did not know that; all he knew was that the district court session would not commence until Decem-

3.14. Daniel Charles Casey.

Date and photographer not known, ca. 1880.
Mary B. Campbell Collection, Silver City Museum.

Casey was born in Plympton township, Port Sarnia, Canada, in 1842 and died at Silver City on December 2, 1912.

ber 13, which meant he would be in jail for nearly three months. On the Friday following his incarceration he told Whitehill that the jailor was keeping him in his cell without any exercise. Whitehill ordered that he be allowed to remain in the corridor for a limited time each morning, then left.

"When we returned and unlocked the heavy oaken [*sic*] doors of the jail," Whitehill recalled in later years, "the Kid was nowhere to be seen. I ran outside around the jail and a Mexican standing on a ridge at the rear asked whom I was hunting. I replied, in Spanish, 'a prisoner.' He came out the chimney, answered the Mexican. I ran back into the jail and looked up into the big, old fashioned chimney and sure enough could see where in an effort to obtain a hold his hands had clawed into the thick layer of black soot which lined the sides of the flue."[32]

Conspicuously filthy, covered with soot, an escaped jailbird without a penny in his pockets, Henry was a fugitive in his own eyes if not in anyone else's. Who could he turn to? Where could he run? Wayne Whitehill said he went first to Manuel Taylor's house. Taylor gave him an old muzzle-loading shotgun, and Henry skipped town and went to Fort Thomas, where he killed a black soldier, took his horse, and left for Lincoln County. Maybe the first part is true; the rest is not. Anyway, Taylor's is only one of perhaps half a dozen names put forward as those who helped the boy after his escape from the jail.[33]

The Truesdells—who do seem the likeliest family to whom Henry would have turned for help—said he did just that: "My mother washed Henry's clothes and dried them by the stove," Chauncey Truesdell averred. "My brother Gideon, Henry and I slept on the floor that night. The next morning mother stopped the stage as it passed our door and asked the driver to take Henry to Globe City [actually, the stage went to Clifton]. Mother gave Henry all the money she had and a little lunch to eat."[34]

But Sarah Brown claimed it was she and a woman named Holson who put the boy on the stagecoach. The Knights claimed he walked fifteen miles to their ranch and stayed with them; Daniel Casey and his wife, the Kid's erstwhile schoolteacher, Mary Richards, told a not dissimilar tale. Mary's daughter related:

> Mother has told me how he showed up at the Knight ranch [where she and her husband were living] and told her what had happened. She and Mrs. Knight put him up in the barn and brought him food for a couple of days and they tried to reason with him. They advised him to go back to Silver City and give himself up, that the penalty for what he had done was in no way as harsh as would be the life he would live in hiding. He agreed to return to Silver City and they loaned him a horse to go back on. But he was afraid to be put back in jail and he went in the opposite direction as soon as he was out of their sight. He went to Arizona, my mother learned later.[35]

Still another story has it that the boy made his way to Chloride Flats, where William Antrim was working. Dan McMillan, one of Antrim's colleagues in the mines, recalled Antrim's being "called out of the mines one day to talk to his son who said the matter was urgent. . . . He told [me] that his boy had gotten himself into a great deal of trouble and he had given him all the money

3.15. The Abraham boys in later years.

Date and photographer unknown. Author's Collection.

Standing, left to right: Louis, Sam, and Hyman. *Seated, left to right:* Abraham and Jacob.

he had on him at that time and told him to leave town." In view of Antrim's attitude toward money—and Henry's attitude toward Antrim—this seems unlikely. And in any case, Antrim was not then at Chloride Flats but in southeastern Arizona.[36]

While it is impossible to be precise about where Henry Antrim went after he escaped from the Silver City jail, there is a commonality in the testimony of all these contemporaries about his general destination. Sarah Brown and the Truesdells said he went to Arizona. Daniel and Mary Phillipa Casey said he went to Arizona. Louis Abraham said the same. So did Harry Whitehill and Anthony Conner. And they were right.

4.1. Herlow's Hotel, San Francisco Street
looking east, Santa Fe.

Photograph by George C. Bennett, ca. 1880.

MoNM Negative No. 11325.

CHAPTER FOUR

The Scotsman

Shortly after his arrival in Santa Fe from San Francisco in October 1872, German-born Paul F. Herlow set up in business at the corner of Ortiz on south San Francisco Street as a butcher—a successful one, if the regular puffs he received in William Manderfield and Thomas Tucker's *Daily New Mexican* are any yardstick. Expanding into the cattle business, Herlow prospered for a couple of years then lost everything when Indians stole a mule herd he had invested in, and "he had to do the first thing that came along to make a raise."

Lower down the street near Sandoval he opened a lodging house, an E-shaped single-story adobe building whose central arm contained an office, bar, dining room, and kitchen, with accommodations in the upper and lower extensions and a corral and feed stables in back opening onto Water Street opposite the jail.

Herlow's, with its mud walls, floor, and roof, was a decidedly no-frills operation intended for "freighters, miners and the public generally"—those whose purse or inclination did not extend to staying at Thomas McDonald's Exchange Hotel on the Plaza, the daily incoming guest list of which appeared regularly in the *New Mexican*. Herlow, "a good honest German," and his wife, Sophie, doubtless served good, honest *gasthof* food with the accent firmly on quantity rather than quality: meat and potatoes, black bread, dumplings, knackwurst, liver.[1]

To Herlow's on Tuesday, August 15, 1876, came a young Englishman, John H. Tunstall, newly arrived after a horrendous 168-hour journey from California. A great many changes had occurred in Tunstall's young life; following the return in 1874 to Victoria, British Columbia, of Elizabeth Turner, his employer's wife, the position in the family firm there Tunstall had held since 1872 had become increasingly untenable. When relations between himself and his father's partner John Turner deteriorated still further, Tunstall convinced first himself, and then his father, that the family fortunes would be better served by his leaving the firm altogether and starting up in the sheep ranching business.

Perhaps fortunately for Tunstall, a planned partnership with a Californian entrepreneur named Martin M. Kimberly to raise sheep on the Aleutian island of Oukamok never got off the ground; instead, the young Englishman decided to spend six months in California learning the business before investing in some land and starting a ranch. He was very soon disabused of that notion by the local men he sought out: former Texas Ranger Captain John Coffee Hays, Santa Barbara land baron William W. Hollister, and

4.2. John Henry Tunstall.

Photograph by Watkins Yosemite Art Gallery, San Francisco, 1876.
Author's Collection.

This is his last known photograph, taken Saturday, February 26, 1876.

John H. Tunstall was born in Hackney, London, on March 6, 1853, the second of five children. He left England in August 1872 to work in the Victoria, British Columbia, branch of the mercantile company of which his father was senior partner. After three years Tunstall quit the firm, persuading his father to finance his going into sheep raising. He left Victoria in February 1876 for California, intending to buy land and raise sheep there, but his six-month tour of inspection persuaded him that New Mexico offered better prospects.

After several months in Santa Fe, he moved to Lincoln late in 1876 to start a cattle ranch and mercantile business. He was killed in what is now called Tunstall Canyon, about twenty miles south of Lincoln, on February 18, 1878; his family never recovered a penny of the small fortune he invested.

Source: Frederick Nolan, *The Life and Death of John Henry Tunstall.*

4.3. Alexander Anderson McSween.

Date and photographer unknown.
Special Collections, University of Arizona Library.

This is a copy of a photograph thought to have been taken originally in Topeka about 1870. Born in Canada in 1843, McSween was educated for the ministry and may even have taken the cloth for a while, but where he spent his early years is unknown. In 1871 he enrolled in the Law Department of Washington University at St. Louis, but he completed only half of the two-year course, perhaps because of health problems.

In the spring of 1872 he moved to Eureka, Kansas, where he taught briefly in a local school; on April 3, 1873, he hung out his shingle as a lawyer. On Saturday, August 23, he was married in Atchison (but not in the church) to Sue E. Homer of that city by the Reverend Edward Cooper, pastor of the First Presbyterian Church.

By the late summer of 1874, the McSweens suffered a reversal of fortunes and left Eureka, leaving no forwarding address. It was their original intention to go to Silver City—McSween had asthma—but following a chance meeting with Miguel Otero, Sr., they decided to try Lincoln, where they arrived on March 5, 1875. McSween was shot dead in his own backyard on July 19, 1878.

Source: J. Evetts Haley, Interview with Susan Barber, August 26, 1927, HHC.

4.4. Saturnino Baca, with his granddaughter.

Date and photographer unknown, ca. 1890.
R. N. Mullin Collection, HHC.

Saturnino Baca was born November 29, 1830, in Cebolleta, then in Mexico, later Valencia County, New Mexico. He served as a U.S. surveyor before the Civil War and enlisted at Cubero on July 26, 1861, as a first lieutenant in Company E, First New Mexico Cavalry. He saw action at Valverde and served at Forts Wingate, Bascom, Defiance, and Stanton before being mustered out of the service with the rank of captain at Santa Fe on September 29, 1866. He was a Socorro County member of the territorial legislature when the bill to create Lincoln County was introduced. He played a not insignificant part in the Lincoln County War and later became a sheep rancher. On the night of July 10, 1889, he was shot while sleeping on his ranch, and his left arm was amputated above the elbow on December 3. He died at Lincoln on March 7, 1925.

Sources: pension application; Harold L. Edwards, "Capt. Saturnino Baca in the Shadow of the Lincoln County War," *Los Amigos* 2, no. 2 (April 1993): 9–14; 2, no. 3 (July 1993): 9–12; 2, no. 4 (October 1993): 10–11.

wealthy sheep ranchers such as James Barron Shaw and Joseph W. Cooper. They all told him the same thing: he was too late to get cheap land in California. The place to look was New Mexico.[2]

Although it was now six weeks since his arrival in Santa Fe, and although he had inspected a number of land grants, considered and rejected a partnership with Taos landowner and rancher Anthony Joseph, and familiarized himself thoroughly with the high and low life of the state capital, the Englishman was still no nearer a decision on how to proceed or where to settle. Then, on October 27, three prominent citizens from the town of Lincoln arrived in Santa Fe: former Lincoln County Sheriff Saturnino Baca, merchant and schoolteacher Juan B. Patrón, and attorney Alexander A. McSween, the latter en route to New York. They took rooms at Herlow's; that evening someone (probably Herlow) introduced the Englishman to McSween.[3]

"There is a very nice fellow here just now from Lincoln County," Tunstall reported, "a lawyer by profession, who has the outward appearance of an honest man (Herlow speaks very highly of him) he has been trying to persuade me to go into stock and not buy land but I have seen too much of California to do so unless I am obliged. But I must say that his plan has a great deal to recommend it."[4]

It most certainly must have, for notwithstanding the cautious reception he claimed to have given McSween's proposition in his account of it to his father, Tunstall was enormously impressed—so much so that the following Thursday, when Saturnino Baca and Juan Patrón left for Lincoln County, Tunstall traveled with them. Perhaps what triggered his excitement was McSween's conviction—Tunstall would repeat it later—that fifty cents of every dollar that was made by anyone in the county was there for the taking.

4.5. Beatriz Labadie and Juan Batista Patrón.

Date and photographer unknown, 1874?
Courtesy Edward S. Phinney, Jr., and Nancy Marxen-Phinney.

Juan Batista Patrón was born in February 1850 in Santa Fe County. He seems to have been looked upon as one of the leading members of the native New Mexican community. He married Beatriz, the daughter of former Indian agent Lorenzo Labadie. He was an unpaid schoolteacher to the Lincoln children soon after his arrival there, about 1872; in 1873 he was one of the leaders of the native New Mexican element in the "Horrell War." In 1876 he served as probate judge. In 1877 he was elected to the territorial legislature and was speaker of the house during the twenty-third assembly in January 1878. He left Lincoln before the climax of the fighting and settled first in Las Vegas and later Santa Rosa. He became a heavy drinker and was reputed to be quarrelsome when drunk. He was killed in dubious circumstances at Puerto de Luna by a man named Michael Maney on April 9, 1884.

Sources: *Las Vegas Daily Optic*, April 12 and 15, 1884.

The proposition the Scotsman had laid before Tunstall was a very simple one: The firm of L. G. Murphy & Co., by controlling the Indian agent at the Mescalero Apache reservation, by having the post trader in their pocket and the contracts for the supply of cattle, food, and other staples to the military establishment at Fort Stanton tied up, had a stranglehold on the economy of Lincoln County. But "the House," as it was known, was in serious financial trouble, mortgaged to the hilt. A man with the means and the determination to meet them in head-on competition, assisted and advised by an attorney who knew every detail of their business arrangements and every trick of their trade, could not only break the Murphy firm's stranglehold but also take over every one of its lucrative monopolies.

L. G. Murphy & Co were the mercantile axis of Lincoln County. The firm had begun operations in the fall of 1866 when two former Regular Army officers, Colonel Emil Fritz and Major Lawrence G. Murphy, formed a partnership and opened a store and a brewery on the edge of the Fort Stanton military reservation. In 1868 they erected a substantial eighteen-room trading post upstream of the fort, together with a branch store, a saloon, and a "sort of hotel" at Placita, a small settlement nine miles downriver mainly inhabited by native New Mexicans and a few Americans.[5]

The firm soon became so well entrenched as de facto Indian agents that in spite of the presence of a series of official appointees, all efforts to loosen their grip on the economics of the Mescalero Apache agency and the local farmers failed. For a decade the entire Bonito Valley was the firm's fiefdom, its inhabitants largely dependent for their living upon and at the mercy of the firm.

4.6. Lawrence Gustave Murphy as a young man.

Date and photographer unknown, 1861?
Rasch Collection, Lincoln County Heritage Trust.

Of L. G. Murphy's early years almost nothing is known; his obituaries stated that he was born in County Wexford, Ireland, and graduated from Maynooth College. A student whose name is given as Laurence Murphy graduated in the Humanities from St. Patrick's College, Maynooth, on August 31, 1849, but was never ordained, which might be considered significant, the more so since Murphy's U.S. Army enlistment papers spell his name the same way. Laurence Murphy came not from Wexford, however, but from Elphin, County Roscommon.

"Laurence" Murphy of Wexford, Ireland, enlisted in the Fifth U.S. Infantry on July 21, 1851, at Buffalo, New York, giving his age as twenty-one and his occupation as laborer; he had blue eyes and red hair, and his height was five feet, eight and one-half inches. He was discharged with the rank of sergeant at Fort McIntosh, Texas; five days later he reenlisted. Murphy then served in the so-called Utah Expedition of 1857–58; that service terminated at Fort Fauntleroy, New Mexico, on April 26, 1861.

Following five years' further service in the First Regiment of New Mexico Volunteers as a quartermaster and regimental adjutant, notably at Forts Sumner and Stanton, he was mustered out at the latter post in the summer of 1866. With backing from merchant-banker Joseph A. LaRue, he and fellow officer Emil Fritz commenced business as L. G. Murphy & Co. For the next eight years their grip on the politics and finances of Lincoln County was comprehensive, but the firm began to go downhill after Fritz's death in 1874.

In 1877, Murphy was diagnosed as having terminal cancer of the bowels; his doctors told him to drink all he wanted to kill the pain, and from that point onward he left the running of the business to his protege, James Dolan, and spent much of his time in an alcoholic stupor. All but destitute, his life's work in ruins, he died at Santa Fe on October 20, 1878.

Sources: ACP file; *Maynooth Students and Ordinations Index, 1795–1895*, St. Patrick's College, Maynooth, Ireland.

In 1873, after having been removed unceremoniously from Fort Stanton by order of the U.S. Army, the firm used the proceeds of the sale of its building there to commence work upon an imposing new headquarters in Placita, recently renamed Lincoln. Emil Fritz meanwhile decided to make what turned out to be his last visit to his family home near Stuttgart. To ensure the financial security of his older brother Charles and their youngest sister Emilie, whom he had brought out to New Mexico and settled on a well-irrigated farm on the lower reaches of the Rio Bonito, Fritz took out a ten-thousand-dollar life insurance policy with the Merchants Life Assurance Company of New York. He had been in Germany only a short time when he died on June 26, 1874.

Into Fritz's place stepped young James Dolan, who had joined the firm as a clerk after being mustered out of the army at Fort Stanton in 1869. Cocky and self-confident even though he stood only five feet, two and one-half

4.7. The Post Trader's building, Fort Stanton, about 1886.

Photograph by J. R. Riddle.
MoNM Negative No. 11677.

The building had eighteen rooms, covering an area of some 6,882 square feet. The windows on the right were the office; the porch fronted a storeroom and the clothing department. Beyond it can be seen the adobe front of the "lager beer saloon."

4.8. Officers and friends, commanding officer's quarters, Fort Stanton.

Photograph by Nicolas Brown, 1871.
MoNM Negative No. 101417.

Left to right: Dr. Charles Styer; Lieutenant Orsemus Bronson Boyd, Eighth Cavalry (seated); Emil Fritz; Lieutenant Casper Hauser Conrad, Fifteenth Infantry; Lieutenant Colonel August Valentine Kautz, Fifteenth Infantry (seated); Captain Chambers McKibbin, Fifteenth Infantry; Mrs. Mary McKibbin (seated); Captain William McCleave, Eighth Cavalry; Mrs. Frances Anne Boyd (seated); Lawrence G. Murphy.

4.9. Commanding officer's quarters, Fort Stanton; the same building today.

Author's photograph, 1996.

4.10. L. G. Murphy & Co. store, Lincoln.

Date and photographer unknown, 1886.
R. G. McCubbin Collection.

This seems to be the earliest known photograph of the building as seen from the street. James Brent, son-in-law of Saturnino Baca and sheriff of Lincoln County, 1886–88, stands sixth from left.

inches in his stocking feet, his character was a volatile mixture of unswerving loyalty and dangerous unpredictability: if you were Jimmy's friend nothing was too good for you, but if you incurred his black enmity or tripped his hair-trigger temper, he was as dangerous as a sidewinder. A good-looking fellow with bright blue eyes, a smart head on his shoulders, and a dynamic, intense, and likeable personality, he had a charm as persuasive as that of any son of Erin who ever kissed the Blarney Stone. And with Lawrence Murphy sinking steadily deeper into alcoholism, Dolan quickly became the House's motivating force.

In dealing with the Mescalero Apaches and the military, the aim of L. G. Murphy & Co. was and had always been to create and maintain a monopoly, supplying the government's requirements at prices no one else could match.

4.11. James Joseph Dolan (*left*) and
L. G. Murphy.

Photograph by Nicolas Brown, 1871.
R. G. McCubbin Collection.

Those needs were beef, flour, beans, sugar, coffee, bacon, and pork for the soldiers and their Apache wards, hay and grain for their horses, charcoal to heat their barracks, and whisky, beer, cards, and credit for their leisure.

To obtain agricultural products, the House controlled and exploited the local native New Mexican population, "mortgaging" land to them and trading goods and services in exchange for their crops and their labor, manipulating the prices at which they bought and sold to ensure their customers became increasingly their pliable debtors. To fulfill their government contracts they bought livestock, "no questions asked," from ranchers in the Seven Rivers area who obtained the animals by stealing shamelessly from the herds of Pecos Valley cattle baron John Simpson Chisum or, on the same basis, from the constant influx of thieves and rustlers who operated in Lincoln County knowing—with Murphy as probate judge and effective alcalde controlling the offices of civil law and his friend and minion William Brady as sheriff—that they were in little danger of being pursued or punished.

Alexander McSween knew the House's business inside out. Almost from the first day of his arrival in Lincoln County eighteen months earlier, he had been employed by them as attorney and debt collector. Only a few months earlier he had severed his relationship with them because he felt his own and their interests were inimical, not least in the matter of Murphy's former partner Emil Fritz, for the executors of whose estate McSween was acting. Although Fritz had been dead two years, the House was in no hurry to see his estate probated, for the simple reason that paying off the dead partner's interest in the firm would ruin them; by appointing William Brady as administrator, Murphy ensured that if there were any settlement, it would be in favor of the House.

The settlement of the estate had become further complicated by the fact that at about the same time Fritz died, the Merchants Life Assurance Company of New York had foundered, and the receiver refused to pay the death benefit. Unable to make any progress with the claim, Brady resigned as ad-

4.12. Charles Philip Fritz.

Photograph by A. W. Wormli, Montrose, Pennsylvania, ca. 1869.
R. G. McCubbin Collection.

Born Carl Phillip Frederick Fritz on January 19, 1831, in Eglosheim, near Stuttgart, Germany, he emigrated with his brother Emil about 1849. Whereas Emil headed for the California gold fields, Charles remained on his seventy-five-acre, two-cow, two-horse farm at Bridgewater township near Montrose, Pennsylvania, where he married Catherine Knebling on May 5, 1856. Catherine Knebling Fritz died January 2, 1884. On July 24, 1885, Charles Fritz married Amelia Bolton Forrest; he died less than six months later on December 2, 1885.

Sources: genealogical research by Walter N. Jones, Pasco, Washington.

4.13. Lincoln, looking west.

Photographed by or for Emerson Hough, 1904.
R. G. McCubbin Collection.

Taken close to the spot where the McSweens stopped when they first arrived, this scene of the town probably looks very much the same as it did that day.

4.14. Juan Patrón's "hotel" in later years.

Photograph by W. A Carrell, 1926.
Carrell Collection, Lincoln County Heritage Trust.

Today, the remodeled building is Casa de Patrón, a gracious bed and breakfast establishment furnished in contemporary style.

ministrator; in September 1876 the probate court appointed Fritz's brother and sister Charles and Emilie in his place. They continued McSween as attorney and assigned to him the responsibility of collecting the policy. It was in this capacity that he was on his way to New York when he met Tunstall. Apart from his disapproval of their methods, McSween's main difference with the House grew out of their claim to the proceeds of the insurance policy as a debt of Fritz to the business, a view McSween strongly disputed.

For a fellow who had spent only a single term in law school and had obtained such experience as he had of the law in the one-horse town of Eureka, Kansas, McSween seems to have had a high opinion of his own abilities. Not everyone agreed; one contemporary referred to him as "a jackleg lawyer, very sharp but not deep."[6] Nor had Lincoln been the El Dorado McSween had believed it might be when he first arrived there in March 1875.

4.15. Susanna Ellen Hummer as a young woman.

Date and photographer unknown.
R. G. McCubbin Collection.

The daughter of Peter Hummer of Adams County, Pennsylvania, Susanna E. Hummer was born December 30, 1845. At the end of the Civil War, "rebelling at the discipline of [her father's] plain sect," she had run away from home and gone to live with one of her sisters in Ohio; her father subsequently disinherited her. According to her own statement, she first met McSween in 1870 in Pekin, Illinois, while she was staying in a hotel and he was a minister en route to Emporia, Kansas. After they became engaged—presumably soon after this meeting—he told her he wanted to study for some other profession before they got married and shortly thereafter enrolled as a student at Washington University.

They were married on August 23, 1873, at Atchison, Kansas, where her name appears as "Sue E. Homer," and moved to Eureka, where McSween practiced law. In the fall of 1874 they left Eureka between dark and dawn, never to return. They arrived in Lincoln on March 5, 1875. "In front of Juan Patron's house was a covered wagon with two black oxen," Amelia Bolton recalled. "A woman got out of the wagon and we saw that she was an Anglo and Mother went out to greet her. She was Mrs. McSween. . . . They both came into our home and told us that they had come to stay; that there was no lawyer there and they had been told it was a good place to start. He was the first one there. She was a nice looking intelligent woman—great pop eyes. She was not beautiful; was pushing and ambitious."

Sources: Frederick Nolan, "The Search for Alexander McSween," *New Mexico Historical Review* 62, no. 2 (July 1987): 287–301; Eve Ball, "Interview with Amelia Bolton Church, December 3, 1951," Lincoln County Historical Society, Lincoln, New Mexico.

Most of his income was derived from commission on debt collections for the House and for legal advice to cattle king John Simpson Chisum during negotiations with Hunter & Evans of St. Louis during the sale of Chisum's ranch and cattle holdings in the summer of 1875. No doubt McSween—and his ambitious wife—saw an association with the (apparently) wealthy Englishman and the piece of the action McSween would get in return for his legal advice as an avenue leading to certain wealth.[7]

Tunstall arrived in Lincoln on Monday afternoon, November 6, 1876, and took a room in Patrón's "hotel." "He was a fine looking chap, very agreeable and the freest, biggest hearted fellow I ever knew," Frank Coe said. "We considered him very much a dude; he had fine tailored clothes, always spick and span, and when he was riding he wore English riding pants and leggins. . . . [When he lived here later] he had a beautiful bay thoroughbred horse that he had brought with him from New York and the finest California saddle and blankets. Those days we always carried a heavy wool California blanket, rolled and tied behind our saddles. Tunstall being better off than the rest of us and not so hardy had two of these blankets."[8]

He was also very much the tenderfoot. Describing the town later, Tunstall told his family it was a small collection of adobe houses scattered up a pretty creek called the Rio Bonito (which means Pretty River) & is in miner's parlance about the "toughest" little spot in America, which means the most lawless; a man can commit murder here with impunity; in talking of a man who had shot another here the other day for calling him a "gringo" (which is the same as calling a frenchman a "frog") & who afterwards rode quietly up the town & told the sheriff "he would like to see the man who could capture him," I said "he is rather bad medicine, I guess." The man I was talking to replied "Who? Ham Mills? (which is his name) No! Not a bit of it! you never saw a better fellow than Ham anywhere; he gets mad quick & shoots quick, but he's a good shot and never cripples; none of his men have ever known what hurt them & I really think he is sorry for it afterwards when he cools off."

That these curious values—the dead man expected to be grateful to his assassin for killing him cleanly and not merely crippling or wounding him badly, the killer himself ruing the deed once he has had time to reflect on it—do not seem to have struck Tunstall as outrageous suggest that he was a lot wider-eyed than he let on. Noting next day that the elections had passed off without anyone getting shot (which had not always been the case, he might have added), he paid a call on Susan McSween and found her to be "a very pleasant woman in every way, she told me as much about the place as any man could have done."[9]

Tall, red-haired, with large, expressive eyes, Susan McSween probably made a much bigger impression on Tunstall than he admitted to his parents, or perhaps even to himself. He said she was the only white woman in town— not quite true—and added that she had a good many enemies in consequence of her husband's profession. Here is another manifestation of his naïveté: did it not occur to him to wonder why? In towns throughout the West there were thousands of lawyers whose wives did not boast that their husbands' work aroused enmity, so what was McSween doing that generated such dislike?

When they renewed their acquaintance on McSween's return after the Christmas holidays, the lawyer told the Englishman that Jimmy Dolan had offered him five thousand dollars to induce Tunstall to buy L. G. Murphy's Fairview Ranch at Carrizo Spring. McSween not only spurned Dolan's bribe, but he also compounded the rebuff by warning Tunstall off, saying that Murphy had no clear title to the place, and instead steering him toward "free" land in the valley of the Feliz about eighty miles south of Lincoln. Once again, McSween's actions rode roughshod over local sensitivities; everyone in Lincoln knew that Hondo Valley rancher Robert Casey, killed two years earlier, had run cattle on that very same land a decade before the Scotsman or his client even knew Lincoln County existed. While they were acting strictly within the letter of the law—Casey had never filed a formal claim on the land—there were those who interpreted McSween and Tunstall's actions as stealing the land from under Casey's widow's nose.

By the end of January, Tunstall had drawn up plans to become a landowning rancher in Lincoln County. In return for acting as his legal adviser and other services, McSween would become a participant in the scheme on a percentage basis, with a full partnership to follow a year or so later. The first step was to file on four thousand acres of land in the Feliz Valley under the Desert Land Act, which was expected to become law in March 1877. As a for-

4.16. Susan McSween as she may have looked in the 1880s.

Date and photographer unknown. Special Collections, University of Arizona Library.

4.17. Robert Adam Casey and his wife Ellen Eveline Shellenbarger Casey.

Date and photographer unknown, 1870s?
Rio Grande Historical Collections, NMSU.

Robert Casey's family placed his birth variously in Ireland or in Lowell, Massachusetts, in July 1828. He married Ellen Eveline Shellenbarger on June 23, 1856, at Waco, in McLennan County, Texas; they had met sometime earlier at Fort McKavett. Casey was fatally wounded by William Wilson in Lincoln on August 1, 1875; he died the following day. His wife, Ellen, died in December, 1912, at age seventy-five. Lily, last of the Caseys, died on May 31, 1946.

Sources: pension application; Lily Klasner, *My Girlhood among Outlaws*; *Roswell Record*, December 24, 1912.

eigner Tunstall was disqualified, so each of the parcels of land would be filed on by proxies, among them Dick Brewer and Samuel Corbet, men who would become Tunstall's staunchest allies in the trying times ahead.

In fact, 1877 was going to be a more dangerous time than any of them could possibly have imagined. Before it was over McSween would be under arrest for embezzlement and Tunstall would be in danger of losing not only every penny of his enormous financial investment in Lincoln County, but also his life. For in the same way they were creating a schism in the loyalties of the citizens of Lincoln County, their friend and ally John Chisum—albeit for different reasons—was doing likewise in the Pecos Valley.

CHAPTER FIVE

Arizona

Hɪsᴛᴏʀʏ ᴅᴏᴇs ɴᴏᴛ ʀᴇᴄᴏʀᴅ ᴡʜᴇʀᴇ Henry McCarty Antrim made his first stop in Arizona, but the odds are it was Clifton, terminus then of the westbound stage, where he surely knew that William Antrim had gone in the wake of the mining discoveries at that place. When he found him, Harry Whitehill said, Henry asked his stepfather for help; Antrim's reply to his stepson's account of his troubles was characteristically unsupportive. "If that's the kind of boy you are," he said, "get out."

Whitehill always believed that if Antrim had taken Henry in then, he would have been all right. But "the boy didn't know what to do, so he went into the old man's room, stole his six-shooter and some clothes, and beat it." He never saw Antrim again.[1]

Alone, homeless, and penniless, the best prospect Henry can have hoped for was to pick up casual work, herding stock or cutting hay on ranches in the Gila Valley until at least he had enough of a stake to set up dealing monte or faro. It must have been the most miserable Christmas of his life. Worse, he did not even have the money to buy himself a horse, and a man afoot in those days was hardly worthy of the name. That perhaps explains why, on March 19, 1876, at the recently decommissioned Camp Goodwin near the San Carlos Apache Reservation, Henry helped himself to a horse belonging to a Private Charles Smith and skinned out for Fort Grant.

This was not the scene of the infamous 1871 Camp Grant Massacre in the environs of old Fort Breckenridge (originally Fort Arivaypa, then Breck, then Stanford), but the "second" Camp Grant, 3,985 feet up in the Pinaleño Mountains southwest of Safford; built at a cost of eighteen thousand dollars and first occupied by troops in 1873, it was designed for three companies of cavalry and one of infantry. Although it was formally renamed Fort Grant the same year, many locals continued to refer to it by its original name.

Henry was no doubt drawn there by news of the settlement known as McDowell's Store, a scatter of gambling and drinking saloons, dance halls, and whorehouses two and three-fourths miles from the fort on the southern perimeter of the military reservation. Frequented by soldiers from the post and cowboys from nearby ranches, it might provide a living for someone adept at cards.

Details of his movements at this time are understandably sparse, but he may have worked briefly on Henry C. Hooker's Sierra Bonita Ranch. William Whelan, Hooker's capable general manager, recalled hiring him, but let him go because he was a "lightweight," physically incapable of handling the grindingly hard work Whelan handed out to his waddies.[2] In view of the

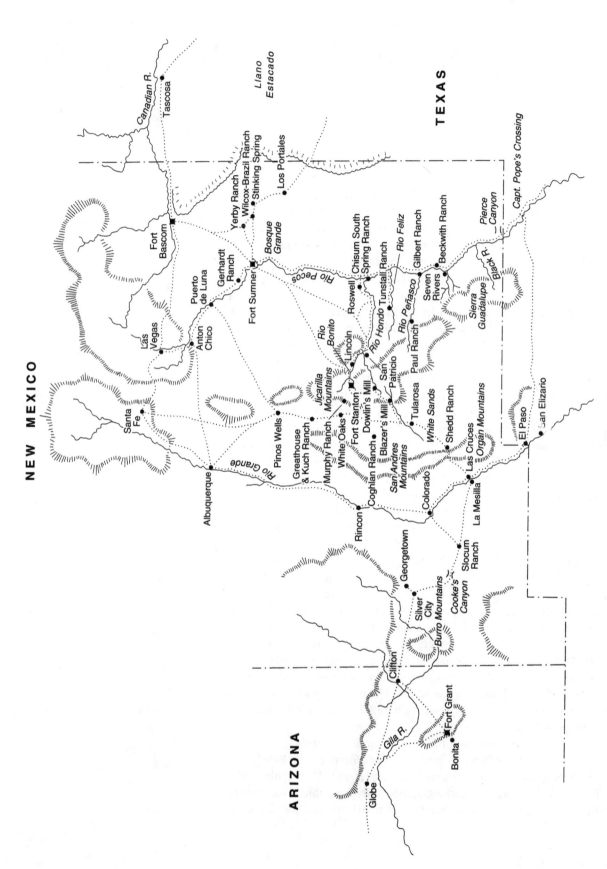

Map 1. The West of Billy the Kid, 1870–81

persistent tradition that he rode for John Chisum, it is possible Henry found work on one of the New Mexico cattle king's several ranches in the region. It is even possible—although the proposition is advanced with considerable diffidence—that the reason no record can be found of his presence in Arizona at this time is because he was revisiting the scene of his childhood, Wichita.

On September 24, 1876, Wichita saloon keeper and former jailbird Walter Beebe was shot and killed in his dance house "across the bridge." According to the *Wichita Weekly Eagle* of four days later a misunderstanding arose between Beebe and a Texas man "which compromised their dignity as chivalrous gentlemen, which had to be settled, so Mr. Texas man came over to the city, to get a pistol, returned and bravely marched up to a knothole in the side of the building, using it for a porthole and shot Beebe, killing him instantly."[3] A few days later a Newton newspaper added the information that the name of the "Texas man" was Ward.[4]

It all seems fairly straightforward, but there is more. Shortly after the Kid's death in 1881, returning to his reminiscence of his having been a "street gamin" in the longhorn days, editor Marsh Murdock of the *Weekly Eagle* had this to say: "We mentioned last week that 'Billy the Kid,' lately executed, was formerly a resident of Wichita. We are reminded, and we expect that it is true, that the shot that killed Walter Bebee [*sic*] in his saloon out on the west end of the bridge, was fired by 'Billy the Kid.'"[5]

No further corroboration, no other details appear ever to have been published. While it is at least feasible that the Kid could have accompanied a trail herd to Kansas, it is difficult to even guess why he would have locked horns with saloon keeper Beebe or what motive he could have had for killing him. In respect of this story, it may be advisable to bear in mind that what appeared in newspapers in those days was often what people believed to have happened but not necessarily what actually took place.

By the fall of 1876, Henry was back in the Bonita area again; along the way he had picked up the nickname "Kid." It appears the only paying job he could find was working as a cook for Miles Wood, a former post butcher now running the Hotel de Luna, a restaurant with sleeping facilities that stood a short distance north of McDowell's store. Not surprisingly, Henry's stint as Wood's short-order cook was brief; it is hard to imagine where he would have learned to rustle up the variety and quantities of food that would have been needed in a busy hash house. "He worked for a few days for [me]," the rancher recalled in 1911, "but he got to running with a gang of rustlers, this place was then the headquarters of the gang."[6]

At about the same time Henry had escaped from Silver City jail, a Scots-born Sixth Cavalry private named John R. Mackie, twenty-seven, had become embroiled in a serious scrape in Milton McDowell's saloon, one of the sprawl of civilian buildings south of the fort that included the Hotel de Luna. On Sunday, September 19, 1874, Private Mackie shot and badly wounded one T. R. Knox in a dispute over cards, the ball striking Knox in the throat and exiting through the shoulder. Mackie was immediately arrested and confined on the military reservation; on October 2, after hearing evidence from witnesses Lewis Elliott, a bartender, and cowboy William A. Wall, the Pima

5.1. Miles Leslie Wood.

Date and photographer unknown, Fort Grant, 1890s?
R. G. McCubbin Collection.

Born in Newbury, Ontario, Canada, on March 27, 1848, the son of John F. and Margaret (McFarland) Wood, Miles L. Wood arrived in Tucson in 1869 and went to work for Henry C. Hooker. That fall he took a herd to Fort Bowie and went from there to old Camp Grant to work as a butcher. He was present at the time of the infamous Camp Grant Massacre. After six years at Fort Bowie he moved to Fort Grant, where he served as notary public and justice of the peace, ran the Hotel de Luna, and later worked as a government contractor for hay and wood. The group of civilian dwellings and ranches in the area did not receive the name Bonita until 1884, taking it from Wood's farm and ranch. Married at Fort Bowie in 1874 to Marie G. Devine, he had eight children. He died at Bonita in 1930.

Sources: Miles Wood, "Life Notes of M. L. Wood," Arizona Historical Society, Tucson.

5.2. The Hotel de Luna, near Fort
Grant.

Date and photographer unknown,
late 1870s.
Courtesy Dorothy DuBois.

County court in Tucson accepted pleas of self-defense from both Mackie and
McDowell, and murder charges were dismissed.[7]

Shortly after this incident, Mackie's army career was terminated; he soon
drifted into petty larceny and thereafter joined a loose-knit bunch of horse
thieves operating in the area between Tucson and the Salt River. He now took
Henry under his wing, educating him in the wilier ways of making a living
without actually working.

"Soldiers would come from Fort Grant to visit the saloons and dance
Houses here," Miles Wood recounted. The soldiers would tie up their horses
outside what they called "the Hog Ranch"—which speaks volumes about the
company to be found there—and go in for a drink, whereupon "Billy and
his chum Macky would steal the saddles and saddle blankets from the horses
and occasionally they would take the horses and hide them out until they
got a chance to dispose of them."

One day, Wood recalled, a lieutenant and a doctor from the fort came
down. "They said they would fix it so no one would steal their horses. They
had long picket ropes on the horses and when they went into the bar carried
the end of the ropes with them. Macky followed the officers into the saloon
and talked to them while Billy cut the ropes from the horses and run off [with
them] leaving the officers holding the pieces of rope."[8]

Not surprisingly, the officers were not amused. Major Charles E. Compton,
commanding, declared the area off-limits and sent his company quartermaster, Captain Gilbert C. Smith, to swear out a complaint against the horse
thieves before Justice of the Peace Miles Wood. "I sent an old man a constable
down to arrest the boy," Wood said. "He came back and said he could not

find them. I sent him down three times but he always said he could not find them. I knew he did not want to find them."[9]

On November 17, Sergeant Louis C. Hartman, disregarding his commanding officer's proscription, rode down to the Hog Ranch, tied his horse outside, and went in for some rest and relaxation. When he came out his horse was gone, together with its saddle, blanket, and bridle, worth in total $150, for which amount Sergeant Hartman knew the U.S. Army would hold him personally responsible. He confessed his sins to his commanding officer, who immediately ordered Hartman, together with four enlisted men—one of them Private Charles Smith, the same soldier whose horse had been stolen by Henry McCarty the preceding March, which suggests Hartman knew perfectly well who the thieves were—in pursuit up the Aravaipa Valley toward Globe.

On November 25, Hartman and his troopers came up on the Kid riding the stolen horse near McMillen's Camp, a newly established settlement that had sprung up (illegally) inside the San Carlos Apache Reservation subsequent to Charlie McMillen's locating the Stonewall Jackson Mine. Lacking an arrest warrant, they simply pulled their guns and reclaimed the animal, leaving Henry afoot. They arrived back at Fort Grant on November 30, having covered some two hundred miles in the pursuit.[10]

Afoot once more, Henry returned to his hand-to-mouth existence. One somewhat unconvincing account has him employed at this time as a civilian teamster on the military reservation and being involved with Frank Cahill in the theft of government mules, some saddles, and a wagon. Even if the writer somehow got the identities of Mackie and Cahill entangled, a number of objections immediately arise: first, that handling a six- or eight-horse team was a highly skilled occupation for which the Kid was totally untrained; second, that anyway, no civilian teamsters were employed by the military at that time; and third, that Major Compton already had one of the mule thieves, a soldier, in custody.[11]

Another traveler, Phoenix photographer George Rothrock, told a picaresque if hardly likely tale of a shoot-out between "the noted 'Billy the Kid'" and a friend in the Fort Grant area at this time. It appeared the Kid mounted the friend's horse, "riding off shooting his pistol at him, and the friend firing his Winchester at him."[12]

In fact, Henry had made his way to McMillen's Camp and from there to Globe, where he again teamed up with Mackie and his gang, who were in turn a part—a very small part—of the major interstate trade in stolen animals carried on by what was known as "the chain gang," a confederacy of opportunists and thieves who supplied the "chain" with its principal resources: horses and cattle. Crude but effective, it was a recognized and reliable channel for disposing of stock stolen anywhere between Texas and California.

The way it worked was simplicity itself: Thieves in the Texas Panhandle would drive stolen stock over into New Mexico and either sell them for cash or exchange them for animals stolen in Arizona or Mexico, which they then drove back to Texas and sold, no questions asked. In New Mexico, rustlers stole stock for sale in either Texas or Arizona. In Arizona, the men who re-

5.3. Charles Elmer Compton.

Date and photographer unknown, 1865?
Roger Davis Collection, U.S. Army Military History Institute.

Charles Elmer Compton was born at Morristown, New Jersey, January 24, 1836, retired from the army with the rank of brigadier general on June 6, 1899, and died at Hollywood, California (in its premovie incarnation), on July 20, 1909. Had he but lived a little longer, what a story he could have told the makers of the 1930 movie *Billy the Kid*.

Source: pension application.

5.4. Officers of the Sixth Cavalry at Pine Ridge Agency, South Dakota.

Photographer unknown, winter 1890.
U.S. Army Military History Institute.

Front row, fourth from left:
Lieutenant Benjamin Harrison Cheever, Jr., officer of the day at Fort Grant when the Kid escaped from the post guardhouse.

ceived that stolen stock in turn sent stock stolen in Arizona back east to New Mexico and Texas or north to Colorado and beyond. L. G. Murphy & Co. in Lincoln County, John Kinney in La Mesilla, and the Clantons in Arizona were major links—receivers, in fact—in this "chain" of supply and demand.

In February 1877, Henry, now widely known as Kid Antrim, joined Mackie in the theft of three army horses from Cottonwood Springs near the headquarters of cattle dealers Norton and Stewart. Officers from Camp Thomas joined Major Compton in requiring Justice of the Peace Wood to swear out a warrant, and on the basis of a statement made by Sergeant Hartman concerning the November theft of his horse and dated February 16, 1877, Wood obliged. They all knew that Henry had probably gone to Globe, so Wood sent the warrant there. "I sent the warrant to the constable in Globe but the kid slipped away from him," Wood related. "The next day the constable arrested him and brought him down as far as Cedar Springs, when he got away again."[13]

For all his lucky escapes, the Kid seems to have been sufficiently chastened by these events to offer to make restitution to the army. Records at Camp Thomas show five horses were actually returned, although they do not say by whom; on the basis of Miles Wood's recollections, it might be safe to assume it was Henry and his wayward friend Mackie, since both of them immediately thereafter returned to their old haunts around McDowell's Store, no doubt ready and willing to pick up where they had left off and once more blissfully oblivious to the fact that the warrant for their arrest sworn out by Wood was still open. They were recognized at once, and word was passed to the justice of the peace.

"The next morning," Wood said, "I saw the two men coming in to breakfast so I told the waiter I would wait on them myself. I had the breakfast for the two placed on a large platter and I carried it in to them. I shoved the platter on the table in front of them and pulled a sixgun from under it and told them to put up their hands and then to go straight out the door."

With local rancher Caleb Martin as backup, Wood marched the two miscreants on foot the two and three-quarters miles up the road to the fort. "I took them to the Guard house and explained to the Sergt. that I would see the Col. and have these men kept until I could notify the sheriff," he said. He then headed for the post hospital, where he was heading an inquest into the shooting of a Chisum cowboy named Jim Lockhart, who had been killed a few days earlier.

"About an hour after this Billy made some excuse and the guard took him out and right in front of several men Billy turned and threw [a] handful of salt in the guards eyes and at the same time grabbed the Guards gun," Wood said, without ever explaining where the Kid could have got hold of enough salt to try so chancy a stratagem. "The guard [called] for the Sergt of the Guard—and several of them ran out and got him and put him back. I then told the blacksmith to make a pair of shackles and rivet them on Billy's ankles."[14]

The blacksmith concerned was an Irishman named Francis P. Cahill, a blustering bully who went by the name of "Windy" because "he was always blowin' about first one thing then another." Burly and gruff, Cahill had a smithy in the civilian settlement outside the military reservation; whenever he would see the Kid he would "rag" him—throw him down, ruffle his hair, slap his face, and humiliate him—in front of the men in the saloon. Apparently Cahill had begun picking on the boy soon after Henry arrived in the Fort Grant area, so no doubt, as he forged the link that closed the shackles, he took advantage of this opportunity to thoroughly rub the Kid's nose in his own misfortune. A less insensitive man might have been more prudent; a youngster as noted for his vengeful nature as Henry was hardly likely to forget—or forgive—such humiliation.[15]

Confident that the prisoner would not be going anywhere until the necessary arrangements could be made to have him transferred to a civilian jail, Wood and his new wife Marie—they had been married the preceding year at Fort Bowie—attended a reception at the home of commanding officer Charles Compton. During the course of the evening, Wood recounts, "the Sergeant of the Guard called the Col. out. [I]n a few minutes he came in and said the Kid was gone shackles and all."

That Miles Wood got the facts a little garbled is perhaps understandable after so many years. The salt-in-the-eyes story was exposed as yet another myth by Charles C. Smith, who heard the story from his father, Captain G. C. Smith, the Fort Grant company quartermaster. The details are sufficiently similar for there to be no doubt it was the same incident. "One night while a social function was in progress at my father's quarters, two or three shots rang out. This did not cause much excitement but when the officer of the day (I believe it was Lieut. Benny Cheever, 6th Cavalry) who had gone out to investigate, returned to the party he announced that the shots were fired by

5.5. Original Fort Grant, Arizona Territory.

From a painting by Bob Boze Bell.
Author's Collection, courtesy of the artist.

In this "aerial view" the commanding officer's quarters are the large building at the top left-hand corner of the parade ground; the U-shaped building on the right-hand side is the hospital, with the chapel behind it. The guardhouse in which the Kid was confined is the small building below the U-shaped commissary on the left-hand side of the parade ground. The road leads off the bottom of the picture toward Bonita.

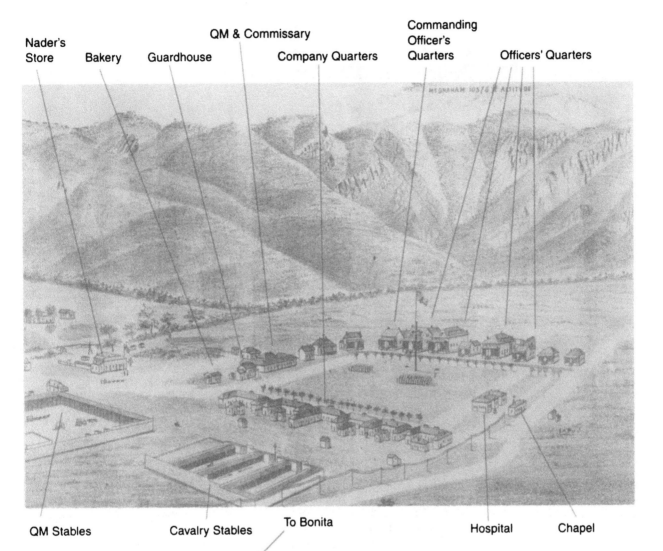

Nader's Store   Bakery   Guardhouse   QM & Commissary   Company Quarters   Commanding Officer's Quarters   Officers' Quarters

QM Stables   Cavalry Stables   To Bonita   Hospital   Chapel

5.6. Fort Grant, Arizona Territory.

Arizona Historical Society Negative No. 20823.

A panorama showing the post after it was rebuilt.

5.7. Fort Grant, the guardhouse.

Photograph by Mitchell and Beer.
Sharlot Hall Museum, Prescott, Photograph No. Mil 137p.

Although captioned "Guard House Where Apache Prisoners Were Kept" and dated ca. 1870, this photograph is clearly of later—perhaps 1880s—vintage. A January 1877 description of the guardhouse by Captain Compton described it as being constructed of overlapping boards standing upright in a foundation of stone and mud mortar, with a dirt floor and a wood shingle roof. This building is clearly identifiable in the panorama (Fig. 5.6).

the sentry at the guardhouse at a man who had escaped; and that the man was later known as Billy the Kid. It has always been believed that the Kid had some soldier help in making his escape."[16]

That this was the case is to some extent confirmed (as is the fact that the Kid was not involved in the theft of the army mules) by the short-tempered telegram sent by Major Compton in reply to an inquiry from Deputy U.S. Marshal W. J. Osborn at Tucson.

Grant, A.T.
August 23rd. 1877

Osborn, W. J.
U.S. Deputy Marshall,
Tucson.

Cahill was not killed on the Military Reservation.
His murderer Antrim, alias "Kid" was allowed to escape and I believe is still at large. Of the mule thieves we have apprehended the soldier and will try him by Court Martial. His accomplices have not yet been arrested.

C. E. Compton
Major, Com'd'g.[17]

All of which suggests—if it happened at all—that rather than the Kid's being involved, the salt-in-the-eyes escape attempt was made by one or more of the soldiers—deserters, actually—being held for stealing government property, and that again, an ingredient from one unrelated story became part of the agenda of another.

Whatever the finer points of the matter, the Kid was at large once more. It may have been immediately after the Fort Grant escape that he sought refuge at H. E. "Sorghum" Smith's hay camp near Fort Thomas. Smith recounted in later years that when the Kid turned up looking for work, he gave him a job helping around camp. "He said he was seventeen," Smith said, "though he didn't look to be fourteen. He hadn't worked very long until he wanted his money. . . . I asked him how much he wanted and tried to get him to take $10 for I thought that was enough for him to spend but he hesitated and asked $40. I gave it to him. He went down to the post trader and bought himself a whole outfit: six shooter, belt, scabbard and cartridges."[18]

On this evidence Henry would have had to have worked at the hay camp for at least a couple of months: a kid doing odd jobs was not going to earn a lot of money when a sunup-to-sundown laborer was paid only a dollar a day. However long he may have been there, it seems clear he was merely "laying out" until it was safe to go back to more lucrative pursuits. It was not long before he was back at Bonita again.

This risky habit of returning to old haunts was to become a familiar pattern in the Kid's life, suggesting a recurrent, almost willful blindness to reality. Experienced probation officers frequently observe the same curious phenomenon. As if lacking any insight into themselves or their environment, young offenders not only seem to become oblivious to the consequences of their actions, but also, even more surprisingly, repeatedly return after a short period to the scene of whatever crime they have committed as if confident all is now forgiven and forgotten. On being arrested, many not only express vast surprise but actually protest at the unfairness of it. There are numerous instances in his life when the Kid seems to have labored under the delusion that escape somehow corresponded with exoneration.

On Friday, August 17, 1877, Gus Gildea recorded, Kid Antrim "came to town, dressed like a 'country jake,' with 'store pants' on and shoes instead of boots." The Kid might have looked like a country jake, but he wasn't any such thing; there was a six-gun stuffed in his trousers.[19] That evening the Kid sat in on a poker game at George Atkins's cantina; at some point he got into an argument and began wrestling with Frank Cahill. Sharp words were exchanged. Cahill called the Kid a pimp—suggesting he may well have had an interest in John Mackie's "arrangement" with the girls at the Hog Ranch—and the Kid replied by calling Cahill a son of a bitch. Cahill grabbed the Kid in a bear hug, and they wrestled each other toward the door.

Locked together, surrounded by a shouting crowd, the two men reeled toward a cattle chute that stood alongside or behind the cantina. According to Miles Wood, who was there, Cahill "threw him down three times which made the Kid mad and he pulled his gun and stuck it in the stomach and fired and killed Cahill." Gus Gildea, who arrived in town the following day, added salient detail. Cahill, he said, "threw the youth to the floor. Pinned his arms

5.8. Gilbert Cole Smith.

Photographer F. Jay Haynes, Fargo, Dakota Territory, ca. 1889. U.S. Army Military History Institute.

5.9. Augustus Montaigne "Gus" Gildea.

Photographer unknown, Eagle Pass, Texas, 1876.
R. N. Mullin Collection. HHC.

Born in DeWitt County, Texas, April 23, 1854, "Gus" Gildea was the son of Mississippi-born John E. and Mary Adelaide (Cashell) Gildea. After attending the "free school" in San Antonio for two years, young Gus became a cowboy at age twelve. In 1868 he was sent to Louisville, Kentucky, to study medicine, but he decamped after a year and did not return to Texas until 1870. He attended St. Mary's College in San Antonio for two years and got a job selling sewing machines. In 1876 he left Texas and went to Arizona with a trail herd; he quit the outfit when it reached the San Simon Valley and went to work for John Chisum. His claims to involvement in the Lincoln County troubles are not altogether convincing, but he was there or thereabouts during the aftermath of the shooting war. In later years he served as a Texas Ranger in Companies D and F, Frontier Battalion, and later still as a law officer at Del Rio, Texas. He is said to have been involved in a gunfight with a Sergeant Harvey of the Tenth Cavalry which resulted in Gus's getting his thumb shot off and another shot through his face which removed part of his tongue and severely affected his speech. He was married in 1885 to Jenny R. Boehmer (Backmer?) and had four daughters. Gildea died at Douglas, Arizona, on August 10, 1935.

Sources: J. Marvin Hunter, comp. and ed., *The Trail Drivers of Texas*, 975–86.

down with his knees and started slapping his face." The Kid's right arm was free from the elbow down. "He started working his hand around and finally managed to grasp his .45. . . . The blacksmith evidently felt the pistol against his side, for he straightened slightly. Then there was a deafening roar. Windy slumped to the side as the Kid squirmed free." And ran.[20]

Tethered to the nearby hitching rail was John Murphey's racing pony Cashaw, well known to be the fastest horse in the valley. The Kid leaped aboard and did not stop until he had put a healthy distance between himself and the scene of the crime. Cahill had been unarmed; even if the Kid had stayed in Bonita to face the music, a plea of self-defense would probably have stood little chance, and there was also the possibility that Cahill's buddies might take matters into their own hands.

There was of course no doctor in the civilian settlement, so Cahill was taken up to the fort, where Assistant Surgeon Fred Crayton Ainsworth did what he could for the wounded man at the post hospital.[21] By the following day it was clear Cahill could not survive. Notary public Miles Wood was summoned to the post to transcribe Cahill's deathbed statement:

> I, Frank Cahill, being convinced that I am about to die, do make the following as my final statement. My name is Frank P. Cahill. I was born in the county and town of Galway, Ireland; yesterday, Aug. 17th, 1877, I had some trouble with Henry Antrem, otherwise known as Kid, during which he shot me. I had called him a pimp and he called me a s——of a b——; we then took hold of each other; I did not hit him, I think; saw him go for

his pistol and tried to get hold of it, but could not and he shot me in the belly; I have a sister named Margaret Flannigan living at East Cambridge, Mass., and another named Kate Conden, living in San Francisco.[22]

Shortly after dictating this testament, Cahill died in what must have been—if he was gutshot as the eyewitness reports seem to indicate—considerable agony. Miles Wood arranged a coroner's inquest, summoning as jurors six citizens from the civilian settlement: Milton McDowell, George Teague, T. McCleary, B. E. Norton, James L. Hunt, and D. H. Smith. Their verdict, predictably, was that the shooting had been "criminal and unjustifiable, and that Henry Antrim alias Kid is guilty thereof." Next day, Sunday, August 19, an "unidentified civilian"—almost certainly Frank Cahill—was buried in plot number 12 of the camp cemetery.[23]

News of the shooting appeared on page three of A. E. Fay's *Arizona Weekly Star* a week later (just below an item noting that John P. Clum, former weatherman for the Signal Corps and more recently Indian agent at the San Carlos Reservation, was setting up a law practice in Florence with H. B. Sommers), and on August 25 it was in Tucson's other newspaper, John C. Clem's *The Citizen*. To the fugitive Kid, such notoriety was to say the very least unwelcome; even the most liberal of prospective employers was unlikely to hire a man wanted for murder. He needed new stamping grounds, and soon.

One thought might have occurred to him: there had been a story in the *Grant County Herald* of June 8 to the effect that cattle king John Chisum was paying four dollars a day for a man and his rifle and planned to use these mercenaries to drive off the rustlers in the Pecos Valley. Everyone knew Chisum never asked questions about a man's past as long as he could handle stock and obey orders. It probably looked like as good an option as any.

6.1. "New Mexico Outlaws"

Photographer Bennett & Burrall, Santa Fe,
ca. 1878–79.
MoNM Negative No. 14264.

Some students of frontier photographs believe
the man standing, center, could be John Kinney.
If so, could the other two be Jesse Evans and
Frank Baker?

CHAPTER SIX

One of the Boys

It was a long, long ride to the Pecos Valley. On the run, homeless, penniless, friendless, there was only one way the Kid could stay alive till he got there: by thieving. And such evidence as exists, explicit and implicit, suggests that soon after he crossed the state line from Arizona into New Mexico, he attached himself to one of the most brazen and rapacious of the bands of thieves who comprised the "chain gang." Known from Socorro to Chihuahua, from the Gila to the Pecos, as "the Boys," led by former Chisum cowboy turned rustler-killer Jesse Evans, they swung a wide and cavalier loop.

"Evans, Baker, Jimmy McDonald [McDaniels] and others would russel the stuff down in this part of the Pecos valley," Lily Casey said,

> and take it up by the Penascos, La Luz, Tuleroso and to The white Sands, and there [at Shedd's ranch or McDaniels's isolated place at San Nicolas Springs] they would be met by a gang from that country who would take the bunch and push them out in to Arizona and then an other one father [sic] out to Colorado. These gangs were well oiled up and in good working order. The Murphy Nolan [sic] Co on the Pecos, the Jessie Evans [gang] between who turned them over to the McKinly [Kinney] gang of Las Cruces, who shoved on out to The Arizona gang and so on, even as far as the Black Hills.[1]

Throughout 1876 and for most of the following year, thumbing its collective nose at any attempt by law enforcement to contain its activities, this loose-knit fraternity of rustlers, rogues, and murderers, using La Mesilla as the hub from which they operated, went where they pleased, stole what they wanted, and terrorized or killed anyone who got in their way. Orchestrating the activities of this central link in the "chain gang" was John Kinney, a former cavalry sergeant whose ranch a few miles west of La Mesilla was the acknowledged "headquarters and rendezvous for all the evildoers in the country."[2]

Acting as an agent and fence for stolen horseflesh and a marketer for rustled cattle behind the front of a ranch, a butcher shop, and later a dressing-out operation, Kinney had himself a sweet racket. The meat—or the horseflesh—was out there on the hoof, easily taken. Control the men who stole it, control the slaughter and dressing out, sell the horses to scratch-ankle farmers or cattlemen who knew better than to ask for bills of sale, the beef to hoteliers and cooks daily feeding hundreds of railroad men and miners who didn't give a hoot in hell where the meat came from as long as it was cheap, and the money rolled in.[3]

Many protested against the racket—and the racketeers—but few dared

6.2. Street scene, Las Cruces.

Photograph by George C. Bennett,
ca. 1882.
MoNM Neg No. 2573.

combat either; Kinney and his Boys were dangerous men to tangle with. On January 1, 1876, a battalion of the Eighth Cavalry commanded by Lieutenant Colonel Thomas Casimer Devin left Fort Selden for Fort Bliss, Texas, camping that night about a mile from Las Cruces. A number of soldiers went to a *baile* nearby and about midnight got into a fight with a gang of what Devin described as "Texas cow boys," among whom were Kinney, Jesse Evans, Charles "Pony Diehl" Ray, and Jim McDaniels. In the fight, Private Matthew Lynch, Company E, was beaten so badly he died four days later of internal hemorrhages.

"The women having run out of the house," Kinney, who was "quite severely injured," was taken outside by his friends while the victorious soldiers went back into the bar to drink. A few minutes later the "cow boys" reappeared at doors and windows, guns blazing. When the smoke cleared, two men were dead—Private John Reovir of Company E shot through the forehead and a Mexican, presumably an innocent bystander, shot through the breast. Three other enlisted men, Privates Benedict Alig of Company A and Hugh McBride and Samuel Spence of Company E, were also seriously wounded.

Lieutenant Colonel Devin noted bitterly in his report to headquarters at Santa Fe that it was "useless to demand any action upon the part of the civil authorities," and he was right. No attempt was ever made to arrest the murderers.[4]

6.3. John Kinney *(left)*.

Photograph by Cuban American Photograph Gallery, Santiago, 1898.
Courtesy George Linn.

Born in Massachusetts in 1853, John Kinney enlisted in the U.S. Army at age seventeen and participated in campaigns in Arizona and Nebraska; he was mustered out as a sergeant at Fort McPherson, Nebraska, on April 13, 1873. By 1875 he was a well-known link in the "chain gang" of stock thieves in the La Mesilla area and was wounded during a brawl with soldiers in Las Cruces on New Year's Eve, 1875.

On November 2, 1877, he shot Ysabel Barela dead in the street of La Mesilla and decamped to Silver City. Upon the outbreak of the El Paso Salt War he raised a posse of "Silver City Rangers" that joined troops and Texas Rangers in the invasion of San Elizario. Soon thereafter he and his men rode under the Dolan flag in the Lincoln County War.

Between May 1879 and the spring of 1881, Kinney scouted for the army; in April 1881 he was one of the deputies who escorted the Kid to Lincoln for his never-to-be-kept date with the hangman. On March 7, 1883, Kinney was arrested on charges of wholesale rustling. He was sentenced to a fine of five hundred dollars and five years' imprisonment in the Kansas State Penitentiary at Lansing. Following an appeal, he was released on February 19, 1886, and sinned no more. He ran a feed lot in Kingman, Arizona, and after service in Cuba during the Spanish-American War he mined successfully at Chaparral Gulch, finally settling at Prescott, where he died on August 25, 1919.

Source: Frederick Nolan, "Boss Rustler: The Life and Crimes of John Kinney," *True West* 43, no. 9 (September 1996): 14–21, and 43, no. 10 (October 1996): 12–19.

6.4. Colonel Albert Jennings Fountain.

Photograph by F. Parker, El Paso, ca. 1890.
R. G. McCubbin Collection.

Colonel Fountain was born on Staten Island, New York, on October 23, 1838, and was killed near Tularosa, New Mexico, April 1, 1896.

The same authorities remained equally supine two weeks later when Jesse Evans, Samuel Blanton (or Blendon), and a man known only as Morris allegedly killed one Quirino Fletcher on the main street of Las Cruces. Fletcher had made the fatal error of boasting publicly that he had escaped from prison in Chihuahua, where he had been imprisoned for killing a man named Mansfield; at about 10:30 on the night of January 19, six bullets were pumped into his body and head by Mansfield's "Texas friends." Nobody was in any doubt who they were, which probably explains why the body lay in the main street until the following morning, when Christian Duper, proprietor of the Montezuma Hotel, had it carried inside. No one wanted to be thought sympathetic to the dead man lest Evans and his cronies take umbrage.[5]

Evans's right-hand men were Frank Baker, robber and murderer; Tom Hill, also known as Tom Chilson, Chelson, or Childron, a stone killer; and Kinney's brother-in-law Nicolas Provencio. All were accomplished horse thieves, brand blotchers, and enforcers. Had the gang consisted only of these four it could have boasted a calendar of robbery and murder second to none, but there were plenty of others who came and went as opportunity presented itself.

The "prime men" of the gang, according to Colonel Albert J. Fountain, included New York–born George "Buffalo Bill" Spawn, who had graduated from soldiering to stealing, and stage robber and murderer Robert Martin. There was Jim McDaniels, involved in the murder of the Mes gang in the San Augustine Pass in February 1876; the rustling fraternity frequently used his ranch at San Nicolas Springs as a holding place for stolen stock. Another sometime member was Bob Nelson, known as "Nelson from the Gila," a fugitive from Arizona justice who had escaped a well-merited hanging there by the skin of his teeth. And there was Ponciano Domingues, who partnered Frank Baker in the robbery of the Martinetti store in Colorado, New Mexico, and the murder of Benito Cruz.

And there were plenty more of the same breed: George Davis, also known as Tom Jones (possibly an alias for Dolly or Dollay or Jesse Graham, brother or cousin of Jesse Evans); Bill Allen; Charles Ray, alias Pony Diehl; Roscoe Burrell, Serafín Aragón, and others known only by surnames—Armstrong and Adams—or aliases—"Buckskin Joe," "Mose." And probably, by early September 1877, there was a young fellow going by the name of "Kid Antrim."[6]

In twos and fours, or sometimes in a band of as many as thirty men, the Boys stole wherever and whenever the mood or the need for fresh funds moved them. That summer of 1877, however, someone stood up for the first time and challenged them. He was Colonel Albert Jennings Fountain, forty, adventurer, newspaper reporter, Indian fighter, veteran of the California Column and of Juarez's Mexican army, former president of the Texas state senate, and former district attorney for the judicial district in which La Mesilla was situated. In the summer of 1877 he was a cofounder, along with Mesilla merchants John S. Crouch and Thomas Casad, of a new newspaper, *The Mesilla Valley Independent*, which produced its first dual-language issue on June 23 with Fountain as editor.

It became immediately apparent that Fountain was going to go after what he called the "banditti"—contemporary usage to describe any gang of outlaws—openly and scathingly in print. On July 14, under the headline "A Fair

Warning," he declared open war on "all persons who make horse and cattle stealing in this country a business. There are twelve of you and if room cannot be found for you in the county jail twelve ropes and twelve cottonwood limbs can be found. You have adroitly succeeded thus far in frustrating the earnest efforts of the district attorney and other officers of law to bring you to justice, you cannot escape swift retribution of an outraged community. *We warn you to beware."*

When Evans and Baker responded to this outrageous attack on their probity by sending word they intended to kill him on sight, Fountain swore warrants for the arrest of John Kinney before Justice of the Peace and Deputy U.S. Marshal Newton Rosencrans. On that same Wednesday, July 18, District Attorney William Rynerson telegraphed Governor Samuel B. Axtell asking him to authorize the calling out of the militia in Doña Ana and Grant Counties.

Axtell acceded, and Sheriff Mariano Barela, who had his own reasons for not pursuing Kinney and the Boys too hotly—spies suggested there could be as many as thirty desperadoes waiting at the ranch—took most of the day to summon a posse of forty men and send them out to Kinney's ranch under the command of Deputy Sheriff Jacinto Armijo. By the time they got there the birds had long since flown. Informed their men might be in Las Cruces, the posse pushed on to that place, but no sign could be found of their quarry. Doubtless relieved, they abandoned the pursuit.[7]

The heat generated by all these activities had the effect of persuading the Boys to seek the safer environs of Lincoln County; late at night on July 20 "some Texans" raided the Mescalero Apache agency at South Fork, stealing thirteen horses; Fountain called them "a party of Dona Ana County thieves," leaving no one in doubt about who he thought they were. His July 28 issue again lambasted the thieves, and two weeks later he offered the proposition that the murder of a well-known stage driver named Hank Dills (who had been killed while tending stock) might as easily be laid at the door of the Boys as the Apaches. In trying to track the movements of the group it quickly becomes clear, as perhaps it was not at the time, that the bandits frequently split up into smaller units, each pursuing its own nefarious ends, with a rendezvous arranged for all to attend at some agreed future date and place.

Thus, on September 9, in the commission of a robbery at Colorado (a settlement founded in 1874 above Fort Selden, now Rodey, New Mexico), Baker and Ponciano Domingues killed Benito Cruz and beat eighty-three-year-old store owner Chaffre Martinetti so badly he never recovered, dying a couple of months later. Not even the promise of a five-hundred-dollar reward posted by Governor Axtell was enough to encourage anyone to try to bring the killers in.[8]

On September 18, 1877, the reunited gang stole horses belonging to John Tunstall, Alexander McSween, and Tunstall's foreman, Dick Brewer, and headed southwest with them toward Jimmy McDaniels's ranch. Among them, according to Lily Casey, was "John H. Tunstal's buggy team he called The Daples Greys them being of a beautiful white tinged with pearly gray, very prettily built and well matched."[9]

A pursuit was mounted by Brewer, Doc Scurlock, and Charlie Bowdre;

6.5. Mariano Barela.

Date and photographer unknown. Rio Grande Historical Collections, NMSU.

6.6. Richard M. Brewer.

Photographer unknown; believed taken at Carthage, Mo., ca. 1870. Author's Collection.

Born at St. Albans, Vermont, on February 19, 1850, Dick Brewer was the oldest son of Rensselaer and Phebe S. (Honsinger) Brewer. He left Wisconsin when he was eighteen because the girl he loved married his cousin; in 1870 he was working for a farmer in Carthage, Missouri, but shortly after that he headed west to New Mexico and settled on a spread in the Peñasco Valley. In 1876 he bought the old Horrell ranch on the Ruidoso and became a friend and supporter of John Tunstall later that year. He was killed in the fight at Blazer's Mill on April 4, 1878.

Source: Frederick Nolan, "Dick Brewer, The Unlikely Gunfighter," *NOLA Quarterly* 15, no. 3 (July–September 1991).

leaving Bowdre and Scurlock to follow the thieves' trail, Brewer pushed on to Las Cruces. Although he stayed three days trying to get Sheriff Mariano Barela to issue warrants or take some sort of action, Barela refused to help. By this time Scurlock and Bowdre had reached town; they told Brewer the Boys—and the horses—were now at Shedd's ranch on the eastern side of San Augustine Pass.[10]

Brewer rode up there, courageously confronting the thieves and demanding the return of the horses, which were in plain sight in the corrals below. Evans sardonically refused to hand them over—not after all the trouble they had gone to get them, he said. But because he admired Brewer's courage, he told him he could have his own horses back. "If you can't give me the Englishman's you can keep them and go to hell," Brewer said. It may have been a great exit line, but it was no way to recover stolen stock.[11]

From Shedd's, eleven of the Evans gang headed west to Santa Barbara, near present-day Hatch. On Thursday, September 27, three of them stole a couple more horses there and headed for Mule Springs, near Apache Tejoe, hotly pursued by a six-man posse led by Deputy Constable Marcial Maes. Coming up on the fugitives, the posse found they had caught a tiger by the tail—not only were they heavily outnumbered, but armed only with pistols, they were forced to retreat before the superior firepower of the better-armed outlaws. Hooting with derision, the Boys moved on, stealing a horse belonging to Silverio Valencia of La Mesilla along the way.[12]

Continuing west—no doubt disposing of the horses to another link in the "chain gang," perhaps the Clantons—they were next spotted stealing more to drive back to Lincoln County for sale there. It was at this point that Henry McCarty, or Kid Antrim, as he was now known, was identified as a member of the gang.

The best available evidence suggests that after he killed Cahill, the Kid had sought temporary sanctuary at Richard Knight's ranch and stage station on the southwestern fringe of the Burro Mountains, from which place, if Gus Gildea's account is to be believed, he sent John Murphey's horse Cashaw back to Bonita. His school friend Anthony Conner, who was working there as a mail rider, recalled that the Kid "remained [at Knight's ranch] about two weeks, but fearing that officers from Arizona might show up any time he left."[13]

From Knight's the boy moved on to Apache Tejoe, a travelers' stopping place built on the ruins of old Fort McLane south of Silver City. He may have joined up there with the Boys (perhaps hoping to share their apparent immunity from the law) as early as mid-September, which doubtless explains why someone claimed to have seen him there with them—and some stolen horses—at the beginning of the following month.

On Monday, October 1, several horses were stolen from the L. F. Pass coal camp in the Burro Mountains about sixteen miles southwest of Silver City. Pursued by the owners of two of the animals—Mounted Inspector of Customs Colonel A. G. Ledbetter and prospector John Swisshelm—the thieves were tracked as far as the road leading to Apache Tejoe, where their trail was lost. The following day Silver City resident C. A. Carpenter passed the ban-

6.7. The San Augustine ranch.

Photographer unknown, ca. 1890.
Rio Grande Historical Collections,
NMSU.

dits on the road through Cooke's Canyon and later informed authorities that
he had recognized one of them: Henry Antrim.[14]

On Wednesday, October 3, according to another report, the bandits exchanged shots with George Williams at his Warm Springs (Ojo Caliente)
ranch; they continued east via the Lower Mimbres toward Fort Cummings,
picking up more horses on the way. Seven miles east of the fort some or all
of this group stopped the westbound stagecoach and made an unsuccessful
attempt to rob it. They then moved on toward what was still referred to as
Mason's ranch (although it was in fact now Slocum's, having changed hands
in the summer) about twenty-five miles west of La Mesilla, and from there
to Shedd's, where they arrived on October 8. On their way through La Mesilla,
Kid Antrim helped himself to a fine-looking pony, not letting on to his companions that it was the property of the daughter of Sheriff Mariano Barela.
That was to prove a significant error of judgment.[15]

7.1. John Simpson Chisum.

Photographer unknown, ca. 1870s.
R. N. Mullin Collection, HHC.

John Simpson Chisum was born in Madison County, Tennessee, on August 15, 1824, the son of Claiborne and Lucy Chisum. He had little or no formal schooling; he spent the first thirteen or so years of his life on his grandfather James Chisum's Tennessee plantation. His parents settled in Lamar County, Texas, in September, 1837; John assisted in the building of the first courthouse there in 1847. At the age of twenty-seven he was selling groceries for M. M. Grant in Paris, Texas, and also served as county clerk.

In 1854 he became the partner of New Yorker Stephen K. Fowler, who financed him in the cattle business for ten years, sharing the profits. By the late 1850s Chisum had located a ranch called the White House, northwest of Bolivar in Denton County, Texas. In 1864, while negotiating beef contracts with the Confederacy, Chisum set up his headquarters on land along the Concho River. By this time he had invented the distinctive branding and ear-lopping techniques known respectively as the Long Rail and the Jinglebob.

The first thousand head of cattle with these unique markings to reach New Mexico were trailed by John Chisum and his brother Pitzer to Bosque Grande on the Pecos about thirty-five miles north of present-day Roswell in the late summer of 1867; they were quickly sold off to the military at Fort Sumner and other interested parties. During the spring of 1868, Chisum formed a partnership with Charles Goodnight. This lasted about three years until Chisum made the decision to settle permanently in New Mexico on land formerly occupied by Goodnight.

During the next five years Chisum became the controlling power in the Pecos Valley. In the spring of 1875 he traded early settler James Patterson twenty-four hundred cattle for forty acres of well-watered land on South Spring River four miles southeast of Roswell, and the headquarters ranch was moved there. Toward the end of the same year Chisum transferred the majority of his stock holdings to Hunter & Evans of Saint Louis. After surgery in Kansas City for a growth on his neck on July 7, 1884, he went to Eureka Springs, Arkansas, in the vain hope the baths would alleviate his illness; he died there on December 22, 1884. Assailed by lawsuits, after his death the Jinglebob empire fell apart; by 1891 it was little more than a memory.

Source: Dan L. Thrapp, *Encyclopedia of Frontier Biography* 1: 264; Mary Whatley Clarke, *John Chisum: Jinglebob King of the Pecos.*

Seven Rivers

By the beginning of John Chisum's tenth year in the Pecos Valley, the frequent raids made by roving bands of Comanches and Apaches upon his cattle and horse herds in the early 1870s were largely a thing of the past. In their place he found himself having to cope not only with the wholesale thievery of the "chain gang" bandits, who had chosen to make Lincoln County, with its vast distances and absence of law enforcement, their theater of operations, but also the smaller but no less significant depredations of a constantly increasing influx of settlers in the region of Seven Rivers. It was a byword of the time, and it was true, that no man could live there who did not steal from Chisum.

The settlement—it could hardly be called a town—had grown up around a trading post run by Heiskell Jones and his wife Barbara, known to every trail herder in the southwest as "Ma'am" Jones. Situated in a sort of No Man's Land not quite over the Texas border but only just inside the Territory of New Mexico, it boasted a scattering of "ranches"—often no more than a dugout, or *chosa*, some corrals and cattle pens—operated by "Texas men" such as Louis Paxton and Milo Pierce, Nathan Underwood and Josiah Nash, the Olinger brothers and "Dutch" Charlie Kruling, William H. Johnson, and the settlement's patriarch, Hugh Mercer Beckwith, none of them too particular about whose brand might be on the mavericks and stray cattle they rounded up for market. With these men John Chisum maintained an odd equilibrium, one moment vilifying them for bleeding him dry, and the next, perforce, hiring them as local range bosses to help round up his herds for market.

Toward the end of 1876, however, thefts from Chisum's herds escalated to an alarming degree, perhaps because of a perception that since the cattle no longer belonged to him—he had sold out to the St. Louis firm of Hunter & Evans a year earlier—he would probably no longer be quite so fierce about protecting them; or perhaps people felt they were no longer stealing from Chisum but from the absentee owners.

Whatever the thieves' self-justification, Chisum had no intention of allowing the rustling to continue, and early in 1877 he went on the warpath. He was in Arizona settling a herd on his new range in the Sulphur Springs area when his "spy," Robert M. Gilbert, who owned a ranch near the confluence of the Peñasco and the Pecos and kept an eye on the movement of cattle up and down the river, tipped him off that the Beckwith ranch might be a good place to check for stolen stock.

Chisum at once ordered his brother Pitzer, ranch foreman Jim Highsaw, and some other cowboys to ride down to investigate; when they got there

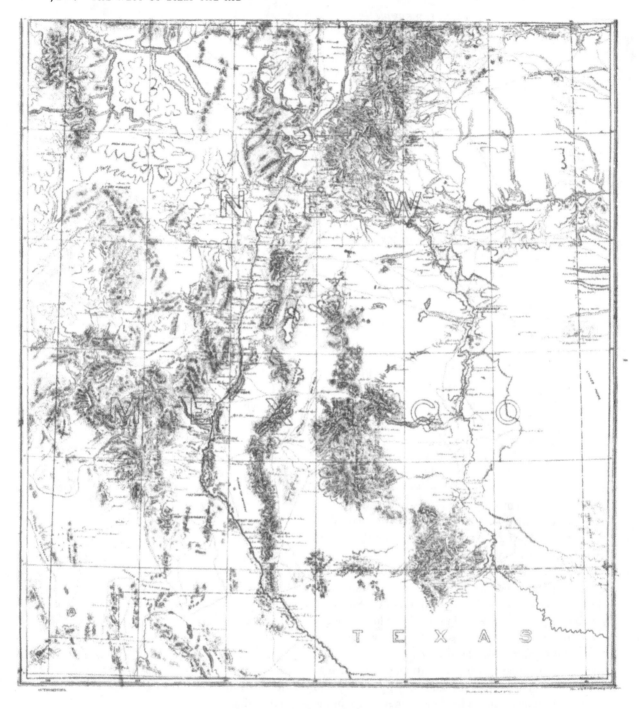

Map 2. District of New Mexico, 1873

7.2. Jinglebob cowboys.

Photographer unknown, 1888.
Lincoln County Heritage Trust.

they found a thousand steers' ears, easily identified as Jinglebobs', buried behind a corral. It was well known that the only way a stolen Jinglebob steer could be sold was to cut off its ears. Therefore, only one conclusion was possible: someone had rounded up, driven away, and sold five hundred head of Chisum cattle.[1]

Chisum was still in Arizona when this news reached him; he immediately saddled up and headed for El Paso. Somehow he not only located the buyer of his cattle, but even obtained a description of the men who had sold them. Accordingly, on March 28, Jim Highsaw rode into a public corral at Loving's Bend on the Pecos, confronted Richard Smith, a sometime foreman for Runnels County, Texas, cattleman Robert K. Wylie, and accused him of the theft. In the heated argument which ensued, Smith was shot to death.

In the Chisum side's account of the encounter, Smith went for his gun and Highsaw beat him to the draw. In a subsequent "report" addressed to U.S. District Attorney Thomas B. Catron of Santa Fe by Seven Rivers rancher Andrew J. Boyle, a former British soldier who held a Doña Ana County deputy sheriff's commission, it was claimed Smith was "shot in the back five times with a Colt's improved .45 cal. six shooter."[2]

This incident, together with Chisum's reported remark on hearing the news of Smith's death, that he had six more Seven Rivers thieves to kill—Nathan Underwood, Louis Paxton, Charlie Woltz, Hugh Beckwith, Bill Johnson, and Buck Powell—was construed by those worthies as an outright declaration of hostilities, Chisum's war to maintain his monopoly on the range and its water. The effect of this "war" would be to align the Seven Riv-

This is the "new" ranch of 1885. The original building was a fortlike eight-roomed adobe structure built around a twenty-four-foot-square patio. It stood on the south bank of the river which, besides good drinking water, offered an abundance of fish. Antelope, fowl, and game of all kinds could be found within half a mile of the house. The place was well equipped with commissary and places to store groceries, dry goods, and so on. No one was ever turned away. Visitors would often arrive without ceremony, stay for days, feeding their horses, eating their fill at the dining table, and then pull out. According to Chisum's wishes, no one ever asked them to pay for their lodging or inquired who they were or where they were going.

7.3. Entrance to South Spring Ranch.

Author's photograph, 1996.

ers ranchers with L. G. Murphy & Co. of Lincoln, who had their own reasons for wishing to frustrate John Chisum's intentions.

The House and its Santa Fe backers were Chisum's direct competitor for army and Indian beef contracts. At the Murphy-Dolan cattle camp on Black River near the Texas border, from which the firm supplied beef when tendering for Indian reservation and army contracts, was their miracle herd—so called because no matter how many cattle they sold, it never grew any smaller.

The miracle herd's existence was a particular thorn in Chisum's side. He knew only too well that the replacement animals that made the miracle possible were being cut from his herds either by rustlers such as Jesse Evans and his gang, from whom the House bought stock at five dollars a head, no questions asked, or by Seven Rivers ranchers supported and encouraged by and sympathetic to Murphy and Dolan, thus placing Chisum in the infuriating position of seeing his competitors beat him out for government contracts with cattle stolen from his own herds and sold on at prices he could not match.

What would have appeared to be proof to John Chisum of their guilt occurred on April 10, 1877, when Jimmy Dolan and cattle dealer Nate Underwood set out from Seven Rivers for Underwood's cow camp on the lower Pecos to bring back a herd to fill an order from the House. En route they saw a group of Chisum riders appear on the road behind them and then disappear into an arroyo. Claiming later they were preempting an anticipated ambush, but far more likely anxious not to let the Jinglebob men get close enough to inspect the brands on the animals they were driving, the Underwood party charged their position and fired a volley of shots in the general direction of Chisum's men before making a run for it.[3]

Choosing to interpret this as a declaration of war, Chisum immediately left his ranch and headed up the valley of the Hondo to Fort Stanton, where he presented his case to the commanding officer, Captain George Purington, and asked him for military assistance in cleaning out the rustlers at Seven Rivers. Purington, a crusty, short-tempered veteran with little love for the locals, told him he had no authority to involve troops in a purely civil matter and advised Chisum to take his problems to the sheriff, William Brady.[4]

Whether the sheriff refused him assistance with a sardonic gleam in his eye we cannot know, but Chisum was certainly left in no doubt about his chances of getting help from Bill Brady, who not only had served in the army with Murphy and Fritz, but also was heavily indebted to the House. Brady anyway could—and did—sidestep involvement by pointing out that the Seven Rivers area was not in his bailiwick but in Doña Ana County (it did not become part of Lincoln County until the spring of 1878), and he advised Chisum to take his problems to Sheriff Mariano Barela in La Mesilla. On the evidence of subsequent events it is clear Chisum decided to kill his own snakes.

Somehow—it is not difficult to guess how—news of his intentions found its way to Seven Rivers, and tensions ran high. How high may be gauged from the recollections of Walter Vail, who traveled in that part of the country in early April en route to South Spring to buy bulls for his Empire Ranch in

7.4. Thomas Benton "Buck" Powell and his wife.

Photographer unknown, believed taken at Eddy, New Mexico, ca. 1904.
R. G. McCubbin Collection.

Thomas Benton "Buck" Powell was born in Mississippi on July 24, 1845, but raised in Texas. A scout for General William R. Shafter against the Comanches in 1869, he came to New Mexico in the 1870s and settled in the Seven Rivers area. He married Eliza Jane Hester, daughter of Rachel Carline Hester of Round Rock, Texas, about 1875 and they had nine children. Powell died on his ranch on the Peñasco on August 31, 1906.

Sources: Philip J. Rasch, "They Fought for the House," in *Portraits in Gunsmoke*, 57.

Arizona. Riding one of John Chisum's horses, Vail "unknowingly rode into the hostile camp; they held him up and were going to shoot him as a spy, when a man known as 'Yanke[e] Miller' stepped out of one of the tents and said, 'I know Vail and all about him and what he is in this country for—I sold a herd of cattle to him in Arizona; he has nothing to do with this fight.'" Vail was allowed to leave; others might have been less lucky.[5]

On April 20 about thirty of Chisum's men, probably led by Pitzer Chisum and Robert Wylie (although Boyle said John Chisum was the leader), left the Wylie cow camp on the lower Pecos and rode upriver to the Hugh Beckwith ranch, a fortlike adobe from which a handful of men could stand off an army of Indians—or anyone else—a few miles north of Seven Rivers near what is now Lakewood. On arrival they surrounded the ranchhouse, rounded up all the horses and mules within sight, and dammed the acequia supplying the house with water. Sporadic shots were exchanged; something of a standoff ensued.

Next morning, upon learning that Buck Powell and Charlie Woltz had slipped through the cordon under cover of night and were on their way to La Mesilla to get help from the law there, the Chisum contingent sent in a local man named Gray under a flag of truce carrying word that the women and children would be allowed to leave before the fighting commenced. The noncombatants—Mrs. Rebecca Stafford, mother of the Olinger brothers, plus Beckwith's daughters Ellen and Elizabeth and their younger brother Nicolas—flatly refused to leave, saying they trusted neither Chisum nor his men.

"April 22," Andrew Boyle reported, still determined to place his enemy on the scene, "Chisum advanced to carry his threats into execution telling his men they would try to take the walls on the other party, and kill them all who were in there. They continued shooting in about 700 or 800 yards distance, the besieged returning the fire. Chisum's men lost courage and would not advance any closer saying they were not going to get killed for $30 a month, that they had hired to herd cattle and not to fight."

It was obvious that "shooting in" at a distance of eight hundred yards was not going to get them very far, so under another flag of truce they requested a parley with Beckwith's son-in-law, William H. Johnson. Johnson declined, saying he could not speak for the others present, many of whom were former Chisum employees to whom Uncle John still owed back wages. This curious reasoning, plus the Chisum riders' disinclination to pursue the fight, seems to have persuaded them to back off. The ditch was cleared, the livestock were released, and the besieging party withdrew.[6]

If the Chisum party thought that was the end of it, however, they were sadly mistaken. Warrants had been sworn by Powell and Woltz at La Mesilla charging Chisum and his men with larceny and rioting. Fifteen days later when Woltz and Powell got back, these warrants were placed for service in the hands of Andy Boyle, who rounded up a posse of fourteen men and headed for Bob Wylie's camp on the lower Pecos, where Chisum was reportedly supervising the spring roundup. When they got there, however, they found only Chisum, sick abed with smallpox and far too ill to be moved. The others had all skedaddled upriver to the safety of the South Spring ranch. Boyle and his posse headed north and reached Jinglebob headquarters on May 10, a Thursday.

"Wylie, seeing we were there, sent out a man by the name of Charles Moore, whom we had seen at the cow camp, with a note stating there were men in there who did not want to fight," Boyle reported, "and if we attempted to take the place some innocent persons might be killed. I sent him an-swer that we did not want to kill any persons, that I had warrants to serve and I was going to serve them, that there was no use resisting."

Wylie offered to meet with Buck Powell and Robert Beckwith and pay them what he owed them. He told Boyle that Jim Highsaw was willing to stand his trial but he would not give himself up to the posse for fear they might kill him; Boyle came up to the house alone, but Highsaw had already skinned out. Wylie accompanied the posse back down the Pecos, where they met Chisum, got their checks, and placed Chisum under bond. Then "every man went home about their business."[7]

Chisum's War, as the Seven Rivers crowd called it, was over, replaced by an uneasy truce. It was into that calm before the storm the Kid now rode. The prospect of earning fighting man's pay at the Jinglebob had evaporated; until he could find work, he would have to ride the grub line. Where and with whom he did so has been a matter of considerable contention; after the fact, everyone was his friend. Whether it was true at the time is another matter.

Frank Coe, for example, claimed the Kid "came up on the Pecos [from Old Mexico] and was arrested at Seven Rivers, a noted camp ground where drov-ers laid over. . . . There was a store there and outlaws galore. He was arrested on suspicion of having stolen horses, but they could not prove that he had done so. Br [?] another smooth-faced boy about the same age, about seventeen, was along with him. They were put in a cellar under an adobe house down at Lincoln, but when nothing could be proved on them they were turned loose. When he got out in the fall of 1877 he came over to my farm on the Ruidoso. . . . The Kid and I hunted that winter and I never lived so good as I did then."[8]

His cousin George told a different tale, in which the Kid helped Billy Morton and Frank Baker to drive some cattle to Lincoln; when they got there they refused to pay him and he would have killed them had Jesse Evans not intervened. Shortly thereafter, Coe concludes, the Kid was hired by John Tunstall.[9]

Not so, argued the Jones family. In their account, Barbara "Ma'am" Jones awoke in the predawn darkness to hear something moving outside her Seven Rivers ranch house. She got a rifle and stuck it through one of the defensive slots in the wall. "Come out of it," she ordered.

And out of it came a slender, nice-looking boy with blue eyes and rather prominent teeth who "stumbled unsteadily" toward the house. Dropping her rifle and unbolting the door, Mrs. Jones half-carried him into the kitchen and sat him down by the fire. He gave his name as Billy Bonney.

She helped him take off his boots—very small boots, she remarked—to find he had no socks and his feet were blistered and swollen. "He'd walked, and he'd walked a long distance," she concluded.

As she got some hot water and a basin to bathe his feet, she asked him when he had last eaten. About three days ago, he told her. She brought milk, heated it, and gave it to him in a cup.

"I don't like milk," he said.

7.5. Barbara Culp "Ma'am" Jones.

Date and photographer unknown.
R. N. Mullin Collection, HHC

7.6. Heiskell Jones.

Date and photographer unknown.
Author's Collection.

Born in Pennsylvania in 1830, William Heiskell Jones emigrated successively to Virginia, Iowa, Colorado, and finally New Mexico, where he arrived with his wife, Barbara, and their sons John and Jim in the summer of 1866. After settling originally at Missouri Plaza, where their son Tom was the first white child born in the Pecos Valley, in 1875 the family had a ranch and trading post near Dowlin's Mill, and Heiskell worked as post butcher at Fort Stanton. About 1876 the family moved to Arizona and then to West Texas, where Jones ran a freighting business. They returned to New Mexico in 1877, and Jones purchased Reed's ranch and trading post near Seven Rivers. His wife, Barbara (born in Pennsylvania on July 2, 1838—and always called "Ma'am") became something of a legend in the Pecos Valley, renowned for her hospitality and her nursing ability. She had nine sons and one daughter. Later the family moved to a location near the head of Rocky Arroyo, where Barbara Jones died December 20, 1905, and Heiskell Jones January 17, 1908.

Source: Eve Ball, *Ma'am Jones of the Pecos.*

Barbara Jones made him drink it anyway and then put him to bed. Next morning, the boy told the family he had walked to the ranch from the top of the Guadalupe Mountains (a distance, incidentally, of between twenty and thirty miles). He and a fellow named O'Keefe had been attacked by Apaches. He "waved O'Keefe to ride out of it," then hid, staying under cover until dark. For three days he had hidden out in the daytime and walked all night.

He stayed with the Joneses for several days, helping about the house and romping with the small children. The story of how he and John Jones practiced their shooting in the yard together is as pretty a picture of male bonding as anyone could want, but whether it is true is another matter.[10]

The tradition in the Brady family is that when the Kid turned up in Lincoln, "tired, hungry, and needing a place to stay," Sheriff Bill Brady "felt sorry for Billy and gave him a job" on his farm below Lincoln. The youngster stayed "only a few days" and then decided to work at a store in town. Later he worked on L. G. Murphy's Carrizo ranch before leaving the Lincoln area, "stopping at farms along the way until he reached the [George] Coe ranch south of Dowlin's Mill. From here, Billy made his way to the Beckwith ranch at Seven Rivers."[11]

Lily Casey, a daughter of the Hondo rancher killed at Lincoln two years earlier, was fourteen years old that fall; she remembered things very differently. While her chronology is as badly garbled as that of the Coe cousins, unlike all the other accounts—apart from the name of the Kid's companion on his arrival—her telling of the events of that October and November owes nothing to Ash Upson's fantasies. In addition, the recollections of her brother Robert Adam Casey, known universally as "Ad," support and even clarify it.

In May 1877, Lily's mother, the widowed Ellen Casey, had spent herself into a financial mess, and a writ was served on her for her debts by Alexander McSween, acting for the plaintiffs. The court ordered Sheriff Brady to impound four hundred head of cattle wearing the KC brand as security and, if Mrs. Casey did not settle, to sell them at a public auction to defray the debt. Acting for Tunstall, McSween then offered Ellen Casey a deal whereby she would receive payment for half of the cattle as an interest-bearing loan. If she paid off the loan she would get her cattle back; if not, Tunstall would keep them. Both the lawyer and Tunstall were confident she would be unable to pay off the loan, which meant Tunstall got the cattle for a fraction under five dollars a head, half their real worth and very nice work indeed.[12]

The cattle were driven down to Tunstall's new Feliz ranch—if the rudimentary building, probably either a chosa or a log hut, that was his headquarters could be so described—on nearly four thousand acres his proxies had filed upon under the new Desert Land Act, by his part-time foreman, Ruidoso rancher Dick Brewer. The cattle more or less looked after themselves on the range; keeping an eye on them while Tunstall was away in St. Louis and Kansas City buying goods for his new store in Lincoln was the job of Tunstall's friend Rob Widenmann, cook Gottfried Gauss, and a local youth.

Things were pretty relaxed during Tunstall's absence, enough at least for Dick Brewer to devote a little time to sparking Charlie Fritz's daughter Carolina, always called Lina. On October 8, John S. Crouch reported ruefully that business had compelled his declining "an invitation to become one of the

7.7. Ellen Casey *(left)* and her children.

Photographer unknown, ca. 1885. Rio Grande Historical Collections, NMSU.

Ellen is standing, John is seated, and Lily Ann is on the right.

fishing party down the Hondo but Col. Rynerson and Dick Brewer in company with the Misses Fritz boasted of having a most enjoyable trip."[13]

Tunstall's possession of the Feliz range rankled with the widow Casey almost as much as his getting her cattle. Long years before the Englishman's arrival, her late husband had claimed "squatter's rights" to, and run cattle on, the land along the river; the fact that these rights had been fairly and legally preempted did nothing to make her any happier. So about the middle of October, discouraged by the troubles besetting her, Ellen Casey placed "old man Turner" in charge of her Hondo property, packed her five children and possessions into a wagon, and with the assistance of family friend Abner McCabe rounded up not only her own cattle but also those she felt still belonged to her on Tunstall's range and headed for Texas.

Her departure coincided with and to some extent triggered a convergence of events that were to have a profound effect upon the life of not only the Kid but also nearly every inhabitant of Lincoln County. During the early part of October, Jesse Evans and the Boys had returned yet again to Lincoln County, first drunkenly shooting up the Tularosa home of a man named

7.8. The Casey ranch on the Hondo.

Photographer unknown, ca. 1890. Rio Grande Historical Collections, NMSU.

The building at right, behind the tree, is the old gristmill. The woman feeding the chickens is believed to be Ellen Casey.

Sylvestre [Silverio Valencia?], who had on an earlier occasion appeared as a witness against one of the gang, and then helping themselves to provisions from the Dolan branch store, managed by Johnny Ryan, at the Mescalero agency. From there they headed into the mountains, where they turned out in mounted formation to welcome the arrival of Dolan's partner, John Riley, and Dolan employee Jim Longwell and to indulge in some rough-humored horseplay before departing a day or so later for Hugh Beckwith's ranch on the lower Pecos.[14]

When word of their whereabouts reached Lincoln, Dick Brewer, appointed a deputy constable on the first of the month, immediately organized a posse, armed and provisioned from Tunstall's store, to pursue the Boys to Seven Rivers. When Sheriff Brady expressed himself disinclined to accompany them out of his own bailiwick, the combined scorn of McSween and Brewer persuaded him to change his mind. On Friday, October 12, the posse thundered out of town and headed south.

John Tunstall, returning from his buying trip to Kansas City and St. Louis, had been forced by illness to remain over three weeks in Las Vegas. There he received word that his horses had been stolen. Sick as he was, he drove nonstop to Lincoln, arriving about midnight on Sunday, October 14. "Dick Brewer [had] left . . . Friday so I was out of the hunt," he wrote his parents.

Rob Widenmann was at Las Cruces [trying to recover a pair of mules stolen by the Boys]; my goods had reached Lincoln at the same time as I did; my new building was not ready to receive them . . . so I stowed them away as best I could unopened. I hardly had any place to sleep, but I rigged up a pallet amongst my effects & slept there as a watchdog. It rained the next day & night & I had the satisfaction of making the discovery that my roof leaked like a sieve. I was up nearly all night moving things from one spot to another. The next day I received an order from Chisum & had to hunt up the goods & fill it & I had to start out on the road again to go & see him on some special matters.[15]

Meanwhile, no doubt, McSween brought him up to speed on events in Lincoln during his three-month absence, which had included the arrival of McSween's brother-in-law and new partner, David Shield, with his wife and five children; the payment by New York bankers Donnell, Lawson & Co. of $7,148.49 in settlement of the Emil Fritz insurance claim; his acquisition of a large piece of real estate on the north side of the street in Lincoln from James Dolan; his filing on 3,840 acres of Feliz Valley land in Tunstall's behalf under the names of nominees Dick Brewer, Avery Clenny, Samuel Corbet, Florencio Gonzales, Dr. Spencer Gurney, and himself; and the depredations of Jesse Evans and the Boys. Tunstall spent the next day putting together an order for John Chisum and left the following morning for South Spring.

After spending a miserable sleety, freezing night stranded ten miles out from his intended stopover—the newly settled home of Jacob Harris near the confluence of the Hondo and Pecos Rivers—Tunstall pushed on toward Chisum's. A few miles down the road he encountered the posse, which had gone down to Seven Rivers, on its way back to Lincoln with a group of prisoners arrested after a sharp exchange of gunfire at or near the Beckwith ranch the preceding morning.

"I looked through the party to see if I could recognize any of the desperadoes (I had seen two of them about 18 months ago)," Tunstall wrote later, "but I failed to recognize them; I finally said, "Why, I thought you boys went out to 'Round up' some wild stock." Dick laughed & the prisoners they had (Jesse Evans, the captain of the desperadoes, Frank Baker, his lieutenant, Tom Hill, who is the hardest nut in all the gang, & a young Texan named Davis) laughed aloud & said, "By Jove, he don't know if Dick has got us or we have got him."

There was some more rough badinage and then the cavalcade moved on; they had been riding all night and were in no mood to linger. Brewer stayed behind long enough to give Tunstall a report on the fight at Beckwith's. In Tunstall's account Brewer said, without elaborating, that the party of desperadoes had numbered seven; apparently only the four named by Tunstall surrendered and were arrested. From this series of negatives can be extrapolated the probability that the Kid was not there but at the Jones ranch.[16]

To which place, although neither Brewer nor Tunstall yet knew it, the widow Casey and her entourage were already making their way. In an unattributed sixteen-page manuscript, Lily Casey set out the "facts" about the Kid she intended to include in her book; as things turned out, she never used them. The following is an attempt—sometimes paraphrasing, sometimes adding supporting evidence from Lily's brother Ad, but mainly quoting Lily directly—to put these into some kind of chronological order. It will

7.9. Robert Adam "Ad" Casey.

Photograph by J. Evetts Haley,
Hondo, N.M., 1937.
J. Evetts Haley Collection, HHC.

be readily apparent that Lily's recollections do not always match either known events or dates, but they are no less believable for that.

"Billy was riding a stolen Chisum horse which he wanted to trade to my mother for a beautiful little bright bay race mare my brother had traded for on the Hondo just before we left," Lily recounted. "The Kid then said 'The mare you have is stolen.'"

"How dare you say I have a stolen animal in my outfit!" Ellen said sharply.

"I guess I ought to know, for I stole her myself," the Kid replied. "I had to make my getaway between two suns. There was no other horse nor time that I could get I had to leave presto-changeo."

Ellen Casey asked who the horse belonged to.

"She belongs to the daughter of Mariano Barela, the sheriff at Las Cruces," the Kid said. "Barela sent me word just the other day by Jesse Evans that if I did not bring the mare back he would come and kill me. He said that the little girl was broken hearted and crying her eyes out for her pet mare."

The fact she might have a stolen horse on her hands made Ellen Casey very uneasy.

"I came by this mare honestly," she protested. "I bought her from Frank McCullum. I have a legal bill of sale for her. . . . I did not know she was stolen. But I do know the one you are riding is stolen because Mr. Chisum never sells horses wearing his brand in this country. If I take the horse I would be an accessory to its theft."[17]

Robert Casey clarified this somewhat:

> When we went to Texas, we passed . . . the old Beckwith ranch and the Kid was there, but I didn't know him from Adam's off ox. He saw the mare and knowed her and wanted to trade for her. He told old man [Hugh] Beckwith she was a race mare and he'd stolen her over at Las Cruces. I didn't know nothing about that. She paced a little.
> He says, "I'll give you two for her."
> Prior to that the Kid had been up with a bunch of Seven Rivers [he means Las Cruces] men and stole Tunstall's saddle horses off the Feliz and taken them down to Seven Rivers. All of them disposed of them except the Kid. He had two he hadn't disposed of and he didn't have gumption enough to dispose of them.
> I says, "That's Tunstall's buggy team, they're stolen."
> He says, "That mare you have is stolen too."[18]

When the Kid could not get the horse, Lily continued, "he made a long pitiful talk to [my] Brother William to get work and go with us on to Texas Will was a very good hearted honest boy and wanted mother to let the Kid go but she feared it was only a ruse and when we got a way down on the Llano Stacado . . . he would run a way and leave us afoot [or] come back stealing not only the mare but all her horses."

"You're just a youngster," Ellen reproved the Kid. "How come you started out stealing?"

"I didn't like going to school," Billy told her.

> I was Idle around town and got in with some bad company and got in a lot of trouble. I knew Jesse Evans was down here and thought I would come over and stay with him awhile and maybe get work. I knew this mare was a

race mare but I was in a hurry. We came through the country to Tularosa
and from there to the Feliz and then over to the Hondo. I stayed with Frank
McCullum; that's when I traded Barela's mare for this horse I'm on. My
partner and I had ridden pretty fast and hard, and she wasn't used to hard
treatment and couldn't stand it. Besides, I knew when I got to Jessie he
would know whose brand it was and want to make me trouble, so I got shut
of her.

Why would Jesse want to make trouble for him? [she asked.]

"You know Jesse has a stand in over there with some of those officers," the
Kid said, "and you have to let their stuff alone."

Elsewhere Lily confirms that "Mariano Burrela, then sheriff of DonAna
County was a particular friend of Jessie Evens; so when the Kid stole this mare
from Barrela and did not bring her back, it caused hard feeling between Evens
and Kid. But Evans let the Kid stay with his crowd."

Ellen Casey asked the Kid when he had come into the country. "It was in
the night when we come down in to the Hondo," he told her. "We lay out in
the hills and rested awhile; we did not want to come down to show ourselves
too much in the daytime. We were looking for a place to sleep and met your
neighbor McCullum. He told us me and my partner Tom O'Keefe we could
stay with him. Next morning the mare was stiff and sorefooted, wanted to
go lame, about given out. McCullum offered to trade me a fresh horse and I
was only too glad because I wanted to get on down the Pecos to catch up with
Jessie."

He went on down to the Seven Rivers country, Lily says, and stopped at
the Murphy-Dolan cattle camp at Blake Springs (Black River). There he had
a run-in with Dolan's foreman, William "Buck" Morton, "cow boss of all the
Murphy Nolan [*sic*] Co cow camps." Morton, who was from Richmond, Virginia, "had run a way from home at the age of fourteen to go West, grow up
with the country, and make a fortune, as many did whether by fair or foul
means, let me tell you Mortin was climbing the ladder of fortune pretty fast
for so young a man, thats what got him killed was to get him out of the way."

"Morton had a girl," Lily continued, "she was a beauty in every way; she
was called the 'Bell' of the Pecos Valley. And the Kid he got to medling in,
and Morton, although a fine man in many ways, yet he was very jealous
hearted, he just could not take good naturedly the Kid's trying to cut in on
him, the Kid then was only considered a little outlaw tramp just hanging
around any where he could get to Stay."

Her brother Will, who was present, told them

how awfully bad [Buck] Mortin abused the Kid telling him to leave, that
he could not hang arround any of his cow camps any longer. The Kid Poor
boy was a stranger in these parts of the country and alone and in trouble,
and he had to take the "cussin out" but told brother Wil[l] "Never you mind
Its a long lane that has no turn I'll just lay for that guy[,"] and he did. My
Brother heard all of this fuss and came back to mother Still begging for her
to let the Kid go with us to Texas. But Mother was afraid of eveil
consequences and stood firm he could not go.[19]

Here, for the first time, are believable details of how the Kid came to be
where he was when Dick Brewer, who had gotten wind of the widow Casey's

departure as he rode up the Hondo Valley, taking Jesse Evans and his side-kicks to the Lincoln jail, "racked out" after her—or, more specifically, Tunstall's cattle—almost immediately with a seven-man posse that included John Middleton, Fred Waite, Sam Corbet, and Florencio Gonzales. At Seven Rivers two of their badly used horses played out, and Brewer sent the other five on to stop the Caseys before they got to the Texas line and beyond the jurisdiction of the Lincoln County court.

Basing the movements of the Casey herd on the accepted cattle driving procedure then in practice throughout the West, it is not too difficult to at least roughly time events. The Caseys quit their ranch on the Hondo on or about October 18—they were certainly gone by the time Brewer learned about it when he and the posse arrived in Lincoln at 2 P.M. on October 20. Because cattle were notoriously reluctant to leave their home range, a trail boss tended to push them between twenty and thirty miles a day for the first few days, after which a day's drive generally averaged about ten miles, depending on the water and grass supply. With no lack of either on the way south, day one would have gotten them halfway to the Pecos, day two to Roswell, day three or four to Gilbert's ranch on the Peñasco, and then they would have continued in easy stages to Beckwith's, the Jones ranch at Seven Rivers, Black River, and the Ramer and Nash cow camp at Pope's Crossing. Given a departure on or about October 18, this would have put them down near the Texas line about October 25.[20]

So on or about Thursday, October 25, Middleton and his men caught up with the Casey caravan and demanded the return of Tunstall's cattle. Faced with this gunpoint ultimatum, Mrs. Casey and her sole adult companion, Abner McCabe, had no choice but to comply. Brewer's crew cut out 209 head to be driven back to the Feliz; the remainder were left at Jim Ramer and Josiah Nash's cow camp while Mrs. Casey returned first to Seven Rivers and then back to her own ranch on the Hondo.

Soon after this, according to Lily Casey's erratic account, Dick Brewer arrived at the ranch with "pretty much the same crowd" who had brought back the cattle and arrested Will and Robert Casey. When her brothers wanted to know why they were being arrested, Brewer would say no more than, "You'll have to go to Lincoln with us and find out."

"Of course Mother would not submit to such treatment of her sons," Lily added. "She was fortunate in catching up with Uncle John [Chisum] who returned with her to Lincoln and used his influence to get Add and Will released." Keeping Lily's cavalier attitude toward dates in mind, it is well within the bounds of possibility that all this happened—if it happened at all, and there is no documentation whatsoever to support it—down the Pecos rather than on the Hondo.[21]

For the moment, then, it appeared Tunstall's "ring" had the situation largely under control. His cattle were back on the Feliz range, Jesse Evans and his gangsters were in jail, the store was stocked and ready for business, and his land scheme was taking shape. In fact, his troubles were only just beginning.

CHAPTER EIGHT
Lincoln

8.1. Lucas Gallegos.

Date and photographer unknown.
Lincoln County Heritage Trust.

As fall turned toward winter, the Kid—now going by the name of Billy Bonney—was still on the Pecos, or at Chisum's South Spring ranch, riding the grub line. Jesse Evans and his Boys were in the Lincoln jail, an adobe built by George Peppin which stood foursquare over a pit dungeon on the north side of the street about opposite the Montaño store. "The cells are entirely underground," reported John Crouch, "and are lined with heavy squared timber substantially put together. I was shown through its 'dungeons' (no rays of daylight reaches its lower precinct) by Sheriff Brady, and from a hasty inspection I should judge that those who are unfortunate enough to become its inmates will find it a rather difficult undertaking to 'go through' it without the consent of those in charge."[1]

From the outset McSween and Tunstall adamantly opposed any possibility of bail for Evans and his partners, so there the Boys suffered each other in close and unsanitary confinement, twenty-three hours out of every twenty-four, for almost a month. Each morning they were brought out for an hour's necessary airing; during one of these, on a Sunday morning, November 4, perhaps, John Tunstall decided to act upon the invitation they had extended when he saw them being taken up the Hondo.

"They asked me if I remember[ed] promising them some whiskey?" he told his parents. "I said, 'Yes' & they chaffed me about the mules, told me they were sold to a priest down in Old Mexico, &c &c. They found that I could joke as well as they could & we laughed a good deal. Some time after that I sent them a bottle of whiskey. I went to see them in gaol after that & joked them a good deal."

If the Englishman really thought he was on kidding-around terms with the likes of Tom Hill, Jesse Evans, and Frank Baker—every one of them a proven cold-blooded killer—he was very badly deluded, as he would all too soon discover.

Still languishing in the *cárcel* were Caterino Romero and Lucas Gallegos, charged with the murder of Gallegos's nephew Sostero García. About a week after Tunstall's visit, Romero somehow managed to escape during the daily one-hour exercise period, in the process letting jailer Juan B. Patrón know (and thereby strongly inferring Patrón's collusion in the escape) that the Boys had filed through their shackles preparatory to their imminent deliverance.

Patrón immediately reported this to Sheriff Brady and also to Alexander McSween. When Brady refused to take remedial action, Patrón quit as jailer, whereupon the sheriff gave the job to a local man named Lucio Archuleta, neglecting either to swear him in or give him the keys. He then stamped

across to the Tunstall store, where, according to Tunstall, "He had the au-
dacity to insinuate that Brewer & I were wishing to go & see the prisoners to
assist them in making their escape. He said, 'he had put them in gaol & they
should stay there in spite of Brewer or anyone else.'"[2]

McSween said, "Mr Tunstall told him 'You know their shackles are filed
and there are holes cut in the logs and take no pains to secure them and do
you dare accuse me who have aided in the arrest of these persons who have
threatened my life, with assisting them to escape?'" At this juncture, Brady
put his hand on the butt of his pistol as if to draw it, but McSween told him
it ill became a peace officer to precipitate a gunfight. "I won't shoot you now,"
Brady growled at the Englishman, "you haven't long to run, I ain't always
agoing to be sheriff."[3]

Brady either believed or chose to believe Tunstall's outrage at his accusations was simulated and that in fact, during one of his visits with the Boys,
perhaps the one during which Tunstall told them they could go to hell and
take his mules with them before he would beg for their return, Evans and
the Englishman had cut some sort of a deal whereby, if Tunstall would drop
all charges and help them escape, Evans would henceforward guarantee
Tunstall's cattle and horses immunity from theft. While such a proposition
indeed might have tempted Tunstall, it is hard to imagine his (and more particularly McSween's) being gullible enough to place any faith in a bargain struck
with a quartet of men who had stated publicly that they intended to kill him.

That is not to say, however, that some arrangement might not have been
arrived at; there were plenty of rumors to that effect. Tunstall was a prag-
matist. He knew the Boys were going to get out of that jail, and there was
nothing he could do about it. Once they were out, he would no longer have
any leverage. He wanted his horses back, and Evans knew who had them. So
a quid pro quo deal—food, arms, and horses awaiting the Boys when they
made their planned breakout in return for the name of the man who had
his "dapple grays"—could well have been struck. It would certainly explain
Evans's otherwise inexplicable expressions of gratitude to Tunstall following the escape and might even explain how, in some accounts, the Kid was
soon thereafter arrested for stealing Tunstall's horses.

To absolutely no one's surprise, the Boys were liberated—the event was
all but advertised in the newspapers—sometime during the Saturday night
of November 16–17 by a large band of men led by none other than Seven
Rivers rancher Andrew Boyle, who had figured so prominently in John
Chisum's earlier troubles on the Pecos.[4]

Also in the "rescue" party—and by their presence effectively scotching any
notion that Tunstall, McSween, or Brewer might have organized the
breakout—were Buck Morton, Billy Mathews, Dick Lloyd, Charlie Crawford,
and—perhaps—the Kid, still looking for a way to get back into Evans's good
books. The Pecos Warriors, as Lily Casey called them, "turned them all out
and told them to 'strike a lit' on a 'B' line for the Lower Pecos country and
not stop until they got beyond old Alcalde Justice Wilson's jurisdiction."[5]

Clearly it was no coincidence, then, that on that day Tunstall scribbled this
hasty note to his parents: "I am still alive & well. Your son John. P.S. You have
no idea of the press of business and annoyance I am staggering under."[6]

8.2. Tully's store, Glencoe, New Mexico.

Photograph by R. N. Mullin, ca. 1940s.
R. N. Mullin Collection, HHC.

This was the original site of the Charlie Bowdre ranch; it looks as if this might well be the original building.

The Boys and their rescuers headed over to the Ruidoso, stopping off long enough to steal a rifle from Charlie Bowdre's place at the mouth of Eagle Creek, then on to Brewer's ranch, where they helped themselves to breakfast and eight of his and Tunstall's played-out horses before heading south. Near Pajarito Canyon they relieved Juan and Francisco Trujillo of their guns and a saddle "for Don Lucas Gallegos" (who had been released, *nolens volens,* in the same deliverance) and rode on to Tunstall's Feliz ranch, where they spent the night before continuing south to Seven Rivers.[7]

Whether they made a trade-off with Tunstall we will never know, but for Billy Bonney, who still had Tunstall's "dapple grey" buggy team, bad news followed hard on the heels of their escape. "The Kid never had sense enough to dispose of those horses," Robert Casey said. "Tunstall sent the Sheriff down there [to Seven Rivers] and arrests Mr. Kid and brings him and his horses up and puts him in jail. . . . Well, there the poor boy lay without a friend to go his bond. Finally, the Kid got tired of staying there [in jail], and didn't know what to do and he sent for Tunstall to come to some agreement with him. The Kid said he was willing to rectify the wrong and told him just how he come to steal the horses, that the Pecos outfit down there had lulled him into it. He touched Tunstall's heart. . . . Either the Kid or Tunstall made the proposal that he'd . . . join his side if he'd get him out of jail. The Kid jumped to it and then he got on his side then."[8]

Lily Casey's interpretation of events was less forgiving:

> McSween and Tunstal courted the Kid's friendship thinking him a young boy and they could get him to turn state's evidence the next court and put a

8.3. Dick Brewer's ranch, Glencoe, New Mexico.

Date and photographer unknown. R. G. McCubbin Collection.

"The house . . . was built in Indian times," Frank Coe said. "It was 100 by 25 feet with the walls twenty inches thick. At first there was a port-hole every four feet. The house was built by Jack Gillam [Gylam] sheriff at Lincoln." In 1873 it became the home of the Horrell clan, and after that of Dick Brewer, who laid claim to 640 acres around it. After his death it became the property of Susan McSween, who sold it to Frank Coe.

Source: J. Evetts Haley, Interview with Frank Coe, March 20, 1927, HHC.

lot of the Murphy Dolan party in the penitentiary or run them out of the country. The Kid saw the wisdom of coming around and he played traitor to the Jesse Evans gang and joined the McLain Hunstal [sic] party. Hunstal pretended he took a great liking to the Kid he being so young and a poor orphan boy in bad company he Hunstal would give him work and a chance to reform and go straight and make a man out of himself. This was [what he said] but the truth was he thought he would get [on] the good side of the Kid and get him to turn state's evidence. . . . He could be a key witness and give lots of information where they could get damning proof of wholesale cattle rustling right there on the Pecos river. . . . This was why this good honest innocent Englishman took such a fancy to the Kid, to use him as a tool, and the Kid was smart enough and crooked enough to change crowdes, but he sure rued it in the end.[9]

That Billy actually did serve a short jail sentence seems indisputable; the "sheriff" who arrested him was probably Dick Brewer, but exactly when, it is impossible to state with any certainty. As we have seen, Frank Coe mentioned his arrest at Seven Rivers; so did his cousin George. "He was arrested [at Seven Rivers] on suspicion of having stolen horses but they could not prove that he had done so," he related.[10]

"I remember how fair and white [he] looked for he had been down in that [Lincoln jail] dungeon," Lily Casey recalled. "Ten feet under ground and just a boy about fifteen past he said he was not sixteen yet."[11] The fact that this statement about the Kid's age is repeated elsewhere in Lily's notes might be read as further evidence supporting the proposition that he was even younger than has hitherto been assumed.

Lacking any documentation, we can only guess where Billy went when he got out of jail, but everything seems to point toward its having been Tunstall's Feliz ranch. If so, it was not a much more cheerful place than the old cárcel, because Tunstall was having a thoroughly miserable time. On December 6, using his newly printed letterhead for the first time, he had written another brief note to his parents. "I am still alive and well," he told them wearily, "the last battle is about over, I can count the dead & the living very nearly exactly, some of the wounded are hard to classify, but the waters are calm enough now for me to settle down & write to you."[12]

Once again Tunstall was badly deceived; the last thing Jimmy Dolan was going to do was let him settle down to count the dead and the living. The very next day—prompted, no doubt, by Dolan's having heard that Alexander McSween and his wife were leaving on an extended trip East in mid-month—Charles Fritz, as administrator of his brother's estate, filed a petition in probate court demanding that McSween be directed to pay over the proceeds of the insurance policy. When court convened on December 10, McSween demurred on the grounds that Emilie Scholand, the other administrator, had failed to appear. He would only pay over the money if she, or her authorized representative, was present. Probate Judge Florencio Gonzales had no choice but to continue the case until the following month.[13]

Choosing to interpret McSween's actions as wilful noncompliance, which they may well have been, Jimmy Dolan left immediately for Las Cruces to huddle with his friend William Rynerson, district attorney for the Third Judicial District. What that worthy's advice was is made apparent by the fact that next Dolan visited Emilie Scholand and without too much difficulty persuaded her that the McSweens were in all probability leaving New Mexico for good and taking the insurance money with them. On December 21 she compliantly signed an affidavit in which she said she had been "informed and verily does believe that Alexander McSween has committed the crime of embezzlement by . . . converting to his own use the sum of ten thousand dollars belonging to the estate of Emil Fritz deceased."

This was a barefaced lie, and all the parties involved knew it; McSween had received $7,148.46 from Donnell Lawson, the balance having been eaten up by their commission and a $700.00 payment to Spiegelberg Bros. Of that $7,148.46, McSween's fees amounted to $2,000.00, his commission on collections for the estate came to another $3,076.90, and he had incurred refundable expenses of $538.60, making a total owed him of $5,115.50 and leaving slightly over $2,000.00 to be paid over to the Fritz heirs—a far cry from the $10,000.00 they were claiming to have been swindled out of.

Anyway, the idea of McSween's throwing away his property, his law practice, the fruits of his intended partnership with Tunstall, and his reputation for such a trifling amount was illogical and absurd. Judge Warren Bristol, of the Third Judicial District Court in La Mesilla, knew that as well as Dolan did, but he signed the papers anyway, and in Santa Fe, Tom Catron started the ponderous wheels of the Ring's legal machine turning.[14]

The McSweens left Lincoln on December 18, rendezvoused with John Chisum at Anton Chico, and went on together to Las Vegas, where they arrived December 22. Catron had meanwhile telegraphed the sheriff of San Miguel County to hold both men pending the arrival of warrants for their

8.4. William Logan Rynerson.

The original is a tintype, date unknown.
R. G. McCubbin Collection.

Born February 22, 1828, in Hardin County, Kentucky, William Logan Rynerson studied briefly at Franklin College, Indiana, before in 1852 crossing on foot to California, where he engaged in mining and also read law in Amador County along with another young lawyer named Samuel B. Axtell. At the outbreak of war he enlisted in the First California Infantry and came to New Mexico with Carleton's California Column. Mustered out at La Mesilla in November 1866, Rynerson took up residence in Las Cruces. On December 15, 1867, he shot and killed John P. Slough, chief justice of New Mexico. He was tried the following March and acquitted on grounds of self-defense; his attorney was Stephen B. Elkins.

On December 22, 1872, Rynerson was married to Luciana Lemon by Father Augustus Morin at La Mesilla. In January 1876, Axtell appointed Rynerson district attorney for the Third Judicial District, encompassing Doña Ana, Grant, and Lincoln Counties; Rynerson was reappointed in 1878. After the Lincoln County troubles ended, Rynerson, partnering with Dolan, Numa Reymond, and John Lemon, established the Feliz Land & Cattle Co. on what would have been Tunstall's range. He died September 26, 1893.

Source: Darlis A. Miller, "William Logan Rynerson in New Mexico."

arrests; when by Christmas Eve these had not arrived, the Las Vegas lawyers the two had retained demanded and were given their release.

Chisum and the McSweens set off for the railhead at El Moro in an ambulance—contemporary usage for any kind of four-wheeled passenger conveyance—but half an hour after their departure they were overtaken by Sheriff Romero and surrounded by a posse armed, according to Chisum, with guns, rocks, and clubs. "Chisum was jerked out head foremost & fell upon his face on the hard road and siezed by the throat," he wrote later. "McSween was also jerked out of the ambulanch and drug off by a lot of the gang & Mrs McSween left siting all alone crying in the ambulanch without a driver or even a protector."[15]

They were taken back to the Vegas, where in due course the San Miguel County court decreed McSween should be taken back to La Mesilla to answer to the complaint. Chisum, however, refused to list his assets as required by the court and was promptly jailed. The old cowman was a canny judge of odds. It is not difficult to believe he had decided it might be prudent to keep some psychological distance between himself and Lincoln County over the next couple of months.

No doubt the news of events in Las Vegas and the other setbacks he had encountered were the reason Tunstall's letters home were full of the blues. "All this stealing has put me back terribly," he complained. "It has cost a lot of money, for men expect to be well paid for going on the war path. I have had to expose myself a great deal in raking over the country, on expeditions arising out of all this, when I was by no means in a fit state to go; I feel pretty badly used up just now."

To make things worse, the weather was bitterly cold; in La Mesilla on December 1 the temperature had fallen to an unheard-of minus 18° F, and snow fell on Christmas Day. If there were any festivities at Tunstall's ranch, he made no mention of them in his letters, only that he was "a good many degrees below par," and although he had a "very fair" dinner, his Christmas Day "was not a success."

"I had a lot of bothering business to attend to," he told his family, "that compelled me to be out in the cold, a great deal, & a careless mexican let all my horses out, & sent me galloping all over creation to fetch them in, when I was not fit to be away from the fire." Things were so bad he "nearly felt home sick (a weakness I never allowed to come over me since I left you) but I had too much fighting on hand, to think about leaving the front."[16]

No mention here of his associate's difficulties with the law, although they must have been at the forefront of Tunstall's mind as he wrote. No doubt he discussed things endlessly with his friend Rob Widenmann, back in the fold after his adventures recovering Tunstall's mules in La Mesilla.[17]

There was still the store to run, the ranch to manage, horses to buy for the new hands who had been taken on—Dick Brewer, acting foreman; Rob Widenmann; John Middleton; Fred Waite; old man Gauss; Henry Brown; and the Kid, now going by the name of William H. Bonney.

How much of their employer's troubles Tunstall's hired hands were aware of is impossible to say. Probably they were not aware at all. The Englishman was not the type to mix with the help, much less confide his plans to them. Their job was simply to "squat" on his Feliz range and tend his cattle until his title was clear—no great responsibility. So while Tunstall and McSween wrestled with their problems, while the range was pretty much shut down by the weather, the Kid spent his days with men like big Dick Brewer, "the handsomest man in Lincoln County, true as steel, as honest and brave as they make them," and the lowering Middleton, who Tunstall described as "just about the most desperate-looking man I ever set eyes on."[18]

Also at the ranch was Henry Brown, a slight, blond Missourian who had worked eighteen months on Murphy's Carrizo ranch and had quit in a dispute over outstanding pay. George Coe remembered him as "a rather short fellow, rather light complected, with blue eyes. He got to be a good warrior." Frank Coe was dismissive. "He was just a kid," he said, "and not half as smart as Billy."[19]

By all accounts, Billy got along especially well with twenty-five-year-old Fred Waite, a college-educated member of a distinguished part-Chickasaw family from Pauls Valley in the Indian Territory; Tunstall's plan was for the two of them to work one of his ranches on the upper Peñasco together in due course. Others included the cook, Gottfried Gauss, and occasional hands such as neighboring rancher "Dutch" Martin Martz and former Mescalero agency teamster and interpreter Bill McCloskey.

It may well have been about this time—if they happened at all—that the Kid went with the Coe cousins on all those winter hunting trips they remembered so well in later years. "There wasn't much entertainment those days, except to hunt," Frank Coe recalled. "We liked to do that and, anyway, we about lived on deer and turkey meat. Then when we wanted sport we hunted

8.5. Gottfried Georg (Godfrey) Gauss.

Date and photographer unknown. R. N. Mullin Collection, HHC.

Gauss was born in Württemberg, Germany, about 1823 and died possibly in Kansas in 1902.

8.6. Fred Waite (*left*) with a man believed to be Henry Brown.

Date and photographer unknown, 1870s.
R. G. McCubbin Collection.

Frederick Tecumseh Waite, who was part Chickasaw Indian, was the son of Thomas and Catherine (McClure) Waite; he was born at Fort Arbuckle, Indian Territory, on September 23, 1853, and educated at Illinois Industrial University in Champaign and in Bentonville, Arkansas, before graduating in the spring of 1874 from Mound City Commercial College, Saint Louis. After working in his father's business at Rush Creek, he went to Colorado and from there to Lincoln County, where he first appears as an employee on the Tunstall ranch in 1877.

After the Lincoln troubles he returned to Indian Territory, moving in 1886 to the Choctaw Nation. He became a model citizen and a distinguished speaker and writer. In 1889 he was elected representative of Pickens County, in the Chickasaw Nation, and became speaker of the Chickasaw house; he was also a member of the tribal police force and a candidate for the senate in 1890. During that year he was elected attorney general of the Chickasaw Nation and later served as its national secretary, an office he was holding at the time of his death on September 24, 1895.

Henry Newton Brown was born in the fall of 1857 at Cold Spring Township near Rolla, Missouri. When Henry was about eighteen he left Missouri and worked as a cowboy and buffalo hunter in Texas, where he may have killed a man.

Brown is said to have worked for the House for about eighteen months and later for Chisum. After the Lincoln County War, Henry worked on the LIT Ranch, later was a deputy sheriff of Oldham County, Texas, then later again, deputy constable of Tascosa. By December 1882, Brown was marshal of Caldwell, Kansas. On March 26, 1884, he married a local girl, Alice Levagood. Barely a month later, on April 30, Brown; his deputy, Ben Wheeler; William Smith; and John Wesley tried to rob the bank at Medicine Lodge, Kansas, killing its president and cashier. They fled empty-handed and were captured by a posse and taken back to town. When a lynch mob stormed the jail the prisoners made a run for it; Brown was shot dead. The badly wounded Wheeler and the other two were hanged without ceremony.

Sources: research by Jean LaReau Miller, Oklahoma Historical Society; Colin W. Rickards, "Better for the World That He Is Gone," *English Westerners Brand Book* 2, no. 3 (April 1960): 2–8; Colin W. Rickards, "More on Henry Newton Brown," *English Westerners Brand Book* 3, no. 1 (October 1960): 8–10.

bear and mountain lion. The first trip out I saw that the Kid, as we had named him, was a fine shot with a rifle; he was very handy in camp, a good cook and good-natured and jolly. He spent all his spare time cleaning his six-shooters and practicing shooting."[20]

There is a consensus in the testimony of all his contemporaries that the Kid was a bright, intelligent, engaging personality. About the average height then of five feet seven, he was slim and dexterous, with hazel-colored eyes and sandy blond hair. He spoke Spanish—or rather the local patois version of it—fluently. Everyone liked him; native New Mexicans especially remembered him with great affection and respect. He was "always nice to the Spanish people and they all liked him," said Lorencita Miranda, "always courteous and a real gentleman" in the words of Guadalupe Baca de Gallegos. He was "brave and loyal to his friends," Carlotta Baca Brent remembered. "I knew this young man to be kind and gentlemanlike with me and all the inhabitants of Lincoln," said Francisco Gómez. "That Billy, *tenía un agilesa in su mente*," said José García y Trujillo—"a quickness of mind," something that everyone who knew the Kid remarked upon.[21]

"I found Billy different from most boys of his age," Frank Coe said:

> He had been thrown on his own resources from early boyhood. From his own statement to me, he hadn't known what it meant to be a boy; at the age of twelve he was associated with men of twenty five and older. Billy was eager to learn everything and had a most active and fertile mind. He was small and of frail physique; his hands and feet were more like a woman's than a man's. He was not the type who could perform heavy labor. . . . Billy explained to me how he became proficient in the use of firearms. He said that his age and frail physique were handicaps in his personal encounters, so he decided to become a good shot with both rifle and six shooter as a means of protection against bodily harm.[22]

On another occasion, Frank Coe said:

> When he got out [of jail] in the fall of 1877, [the Kid] came over to my farm on the Ruidoso, which was fifteen miles above Glencoe. Charlie Bowdre had a farm at the site of Tully's store. The Kid came to Bowdre, who had a good crop of corn laid by, and Bowdre brought him up to my place. I expect he wanted to get rid of him. Bowdre had a Mexican woman and the Kid could talk Mexican better than he could.
> We became staunch friends. I never enjoyed better company. He was humorous and told me many amusing stories. He always found a touch of humor in everything, being naturally full of fun and jollity. Though he was often serious in emergencies, his humor was often apparent even in such situations. He drank very little and smoked in moderation. His disposition was remarkably kind; he rarely thought of his own comfort first.[23]

Despite the Coes' insistence that he bunked with either or both of them throughout that winter, however, it cannot have been so. He had already been hired by Tunstall's foreman, Dick Brewer. "Tunstall had taken a fancy to the Kid," Frank Coe said. "He saw the boy was quick to learn and not afraid of anything, so when he hired him he made Billy a present of a good horse and a nice saddle, and new guns. My, but the boy was proud—said it was the first time in his life he had ever had anything given to him."[24]

"One day I was in Lincoln and met Tunstall and asked him about Billy," George Coe claimed. "'George, that's the finest lad I ever met,' he said. 'He's a revelation to me every day and would do anything on earth to please me. I'm going to make a man out of that boy yet. He has it in him.'"[25]

While all the evidence suggests Billy admired and respected Tunstall, they were scarcely friends; the running of the store, the bank, the ranch; McSween's difficulties; and the machinations of the House left Tunstall little time for socializing during the couple of months the Kid worked for him. As further proof of this, there is not one mention of the Kid in all of Tunstall's volumi-

8.7. Benjamin Franklin "Frank" Coe.

Photograph by Emerson Hough, 1904.
R. G. McCubbin Collection.

The youngest of the four sons of Benjamin and Annie (Kerr) Coe, Frank Coe was born in Moundville, West Virginia, on October 1, 1851. The family settled near Queen City, Missouri, and in 1859, Frank's brother Lou joined a wagon train to New Mexico and farmed for a while in the Raton area and in Lincoln County with a friend, Joe Storms. When Lou returned home to marry his childhood sweetheart, his brothers, especially Frank, got so excited by his tales of the West that they left home to become buffalo hunters and teamsters. In 1871 the clan settled in various locations in Lincoln County, with Frank partnering with Ab Saunders on a farm on the Hondo.

In the summer of 1876, Frank Coe was one of the men who lynched horse thief Jesús Largo; later in the year he and Saunders murdered Nica Meras near Lincoln, and in another encounter they nearly killed Juan Gonzales, a local badman.

After the Lincoln troubles, the Coes went back north to Farmington and soon became embroiled in factional difficulties there. Frank is alleged to have been involved in yet another lynching in February 1880 and was one of the vigilantes who shot it out with Port Stockton, brother of former Lincoln saloon keeper Ike, the following January.

Returning to Lincoln County, Frank married Helena Anne Tully and in 1882 bought the old Dick Brewer ranch. On the night of October 4, 1898, his oldest granddaughter Lesley tried to elope with Irvin Lesnett: Coe killed the young man with a shotgun after Irvin allegedly fired a Winchester at him. Coe was tried and acquitted at Roswell on March 22, 1900. He died September 16, 1931.

Source: Philip J. Rasch, "These Were the Regulators," in *Ho! For the Great West*, 60.

nous correspondence with his family. Nevertheless, Tunstall was clearly aware of the boy's mettle, and from this time forward the Kid is always right there as backup whenever Tunstall confronts his enemies.

Alexander McSween arrived back in Lincoln on January 8 in the custody of San Miguel County Deputy Sheriffs Antonio Campos and Adolph Barrier to learn that word had come up from La Mesilla that Judge Bristol was seriously ill and McSween's preliminary hearing had been postponed. Campos returned to Las Vegas, leaving Barrier to hold McSween under house arrest. Doubtless Tunstall and McSween talked long and late into the night about the options available to them. In the light of their actions, it would seem safe to conclude they decided their best defense was offense.

The following morning at ten, the attorney attended probate court, where L. G. Murphy's substantial claim against the Fritz estate was disallowed by Probate Judge Florencio Gonzales for lack of supporting evidence of any such debt, a bitter pill for Lawrence Murphy, who was dying of cancer, to swallow.[26]

Effectively bankrupt, Dolan and Riley two days later mortgaged everything the House owned—forty acres of land in Lincoln, the Lincoln store building, its entire inventory and all its book accounts, and the cattle and other stock at Black River—for the sum of $10 and Catron's "accommodation endorsement" of their debts and "a certain note this day in the amount of $25,000." The deed was witnessed by Catron's brother-in-law, Edgar Walz, newly arrived from Minnesota, and William S. "Buck" Morton, suggesting, as Lily Casey hinted, that the latter may indeed have had some kind of financial interest in the House.[27]

The new date for McSween's hearing at La Mesilla was fixed for Saturday, February 2; Bristol advised it would be held in private in his home. McSween and Tunstall immediately put their heads together. Before their departure, with their opponents (as they believed) reeling on the ropes, McSween presented to Charles Fritz his suit against the House for $23,376.10 owed to the estate of Emil Fritz, and Tunstall addressed an open letter to the editor of the *Mesilla Valley Independent*:

From Lincoln County: A Taxpayer's Complaint.

Office of John H. Tunstall,
Lincoln, Lincoln County.
January 18, 1878.

"THE PRESENT SHERIFF OF LINCOLN COUNTY HAS PAID NOTHING DURING HIS TERM OF OFFICE."

Governor's Message [to the Legislature] for 1878.

The above extract is a sad and unanswerable comment on the efficiency of Sheriff Brady, and cannot be charged upon "croakers." Major Brady as the records of this County show, collected over *Twenty five hundred dollars,* Territorial funds. Of this sum, Alex. A. McSween Esq. of this place paid him over *Fifteen hundred dollars* by cheque on the First National Bank of Santa Fe, August 23, 1877.

Said cheque was presented for payment by John H. Riley Esq., of the firm of J.J. Dolan & Co., this last amount was paid by the last named gentleman to Underwood and Nash for cattle. Thus passed away over *Fifteen hundred dollars* belonging to the Territory of New Mexico. With the exception of thirty nine dollars, all the Taxes of Lincoln County for 1877 were promptly paid when due.

Let not Lincoln County suffer for the delinquency of one, two or three men.

By the exercise of proper vigilance the tax payer can readily ascertain what has become of what he has paid for the implied protection of the commonwealth. It is not only his privilege but his duty. A delinquent tax payer is bad; a delinquent tax collector is worse.

J.H.T.[28]

8.8. Dowlin's Mill on the Ruidoso.

Date and photographer unknown.
R. G. McCubbin Collection.

It was a master stroke. By simply telling the truth Tunstall was not only clearly identifying the real embezzlers of Lincoln County, but at the same time comprehensively trashing the reputations of Sheriff Brady, John Riley, and his partner, Jimmy Dolan; nobody in the know would be in any doubt at all about who the "one, two, or three men" were. Intended as the coup de grâce, Tunstall's letter was in fact to prove a fatal blunder, turning as it did what had previously been the House's generalized antipathy toward the Englishman into a personal matter between him and Jimmy Dolan, a subtle—and deadly—difference.

At about the same time Tunstall was mailing his letter to the *Independent*, Jesse Evans and two fellow rustlers stole some horses from a rancher in the lower Mimbres Valley. In the pursuit which followed, Jesse was hit in the buttock by a bullet which exited his inner thigh. Somehow—after what must have been an agonizing sixty-mile ride—he made it to the safety of Shedd's ranch.[29]

Meanwhile, Tunstall readied himself for the long journey to the Rio Grande valley. On January 20, the night before he left, he wrote a three-page letter to his "Much Beloved Governor" in London. "I have been up to my neck in worries and aggravations," he said, "but I am feeling somewhat better now. I have to start out tomorrow on a trip 6 days long, it is a hard trip and I dread it. . . . The trip I am about to take is to Mesilla, on some land business, so you can get your map out and trace the route first through the mountains past Dowlin's Sawmill, the indian agency & another sawmill [Blazer's] on to Tularosa, past Lost River the White Sandhills, Shed's ranch, San Augustine Pass, Las Cruces and Mesilla. You can just fancy me nearly perished with cold

8.9. The White Sands.

Author's photograph, 1996.

at the white Sand hills, having a pretty tough time all round, but a *tough* one *there for certain.*"[30]

In addition to McSween and Tunstall, those traveling down included Deputy Barrier; McSween's law partner and brother-in-law, David Shield, who would represent him at the hearing; and bumbling old "Squire" John B. "Green" Wilson, the Lincoln justice of the peace, along for company and protection, with business of his own to attend to in La Mesilla.

The party arrived there January 26, the same day Tunstall's letter appeared in the *Independent;* it must have added appreciably to his pleasure to read about Jesse Evans's misfortunes in the same edition. His hubris was shortlived: a day or two later Jimmy Dolan accosted Tunstall in town and tried to pick a fight with him.[31] Trouble was avoided, temporarily, and on the following day—the *Independent* of the following weekend reported it as Monday, so perhaps the examination extended over two days—McSween attended Bristol's house for his preliminary hearing. Also present were Tunstall, Shield, and Adolph Barrier as well as Dolan and James Longwell, a Dolan employee.

The whole proceeding seems to have been a curious, and at best quasi-legal, affair. No record was taken; McSween was apparently not even sworn as a witness. The questioning, conducted by Bristol and District Attorney Rynerson, was so hostile even the uninvolved bystander Barrier remarked on its partisanship in later testimony. "After the evidence of the prosecution had been taken," the *Independent* reported, "the defense announced that the records of the probate court of Lincoln County were material as evidence on the part of the accused. In view of the time and trouble that would be occasioned by bringing these records, the judge committed the accused to wait the action of the Grand Jury."

The parallel civil case, however, required that McSween post a bond—his surety that he would not flee the country—which was set in the sum of eight thousand dollars. This he offered without delay, but it was categorically refused by District Attorney Rynerson, thus ensuring the termination of

8.10. Corrals of the San Augustine ranch.

Date and photographer unknown. Rio Grande Historical Collections, NMSU

McSween's liberty; upon his return to Lincoln he was to be turned over by Deputy Barrier to the not so tender care of Sheriff William Brady.

The party set out on Tuesday, February 5. Almost immediately following McSween's departure, Judge Bristol—acting on the petition filed by attorney Simon B. Newcomb in behalf of his clients Charles and Emilie Fritz—issued a writ of attachment against the lawyer's (and therefore, since it was contended that testimony had been given at McSween's hearing that they were partners, also against Tunstall's) property. If it concerned him that no such testimony had been given, that no such partnership existed, and that therefore his action was entirely illegal, it gave the learned judge little or no pause. Bristol handed the writ to Jimmy Dolan, who soberly assured him—no doubt grinning from ear to ear—that he would get it to Lincoln fast. He left immediately for Shedd's ranch, accompanied by Charlie Fritz and Jim Longwell, and arrived about midnight.[32]

Next morning, as Tunstall, McSween, and Shield were eating breakfast in the corrals adjacent to the Shedd ranch, they saw two well-armed men coming down toward them: Jimmy Dolan in the lead and Jesse Evans (no doubt

8.11. The Dolan store, formerly the Tunstall store.

Photographer unknown, ca. 1890s.
R. G. McCubbin Collection.

The wooden porch was but one of a number of changes made to the building after the Lincoln County War. The little girl standing near the wagon is Jimmy Dolan's daughter Bessie.

8.12. The Tunstall store, interior, 1996.

Photograph by Dick George, 1996. Courtesy of the photographer.

still limping) as backup. There were angry words as Dolan tongue-lashed the Englishman. "Dolan wished to fight Tunstall," Deputy Barrier testified, "drew his gun on Tunstall three times. Tunstall said he was not a fighting man, did not get his living that way. Dolan as he left the camp said 'Damn you I'll get you yet damned coward,' or words to that effect."

Barrier modestly omitted mentioning the fact that during this angry confrontation he placed himself between Dolan and Tunstall, an act of unthinking courage that can only have been inspired by blissful ignorance. Still fuming, Dolan stalked away, pausing only for a Parthian shot. "You won't fight this morning, you damned coward," he snapped at Tunstall, "but I'll get you soon. When you write to the *Independent* again, say I am with the boys."

He was, too. That afternoon, as the five-man McSween party reached the White Sands, Dolan's ambulance raced past. "On the front seat . . . were Frank Baker and Charles Fritz," Barrier recorded, "Dolan and Jesse Evans on the back seat, Longwell and [John] Long [alias Frank Rivers] on horseback." The reason for their haste became apparent when the party reached Lincoln by back trails on Sunday, January 10. "We found the Sheriff of Lincoln in charge of Mr. Tunstall's Store, also learned that men had laid in wait between Dowling's Mill and Fort Stanton to kill McSween and Tunstall."

"Riley, Dolan and Murphy and Sheriff Brady were in ecstasy over my prospective confinement in the county jail," McSween said later. Johnny Riley had been seen merrily sweeping out the underground jail cell so he might be able to say in future he had readied the room in which McSween was incarcerated; Brady let it be known he might have let Jesse Evans and the Boys escape, but he would make no such mistake in the case of McSween.[33]

McSween did not want to go into that jail. He knew, as everyone in Lincoln knew, that all it took was the "accidental" raising of a few sluices, and water from the irrigation ditches nearby would quickly fill the cellar, drowning any prisoner unfortunate enough to be trapped there. He somehow prevailed upon Barrier not to hand him over to Brady but instead to take him, under arrest, to Chisum's ranch and safety.

Next day, Monday morning, Tunstall took matters into his own hands. Backed by Billy Bonney and Fred Waite, the Englishman marched into his store. In no uncertain terms he told Brady, who was there taking inventory with Jim Longwell, "that he was taking his property for McSween's debts, that he would make all of the party suffer for it and that they had better look out," Longwell said. "Both Tunstall and Widenmann were armed with revolvers, and two of Tunstall's party called 'Kid' and 'Waite' came up to the door with them and stood there with Winchester rifles and pistols and acted in a threatening manner."

It was a tense moment as the two parties glared at each other across the tight confines of Tunstall's store, but Brady knew that although Tunstall was good and mad over what he called a "damned high-handed business," he was not about to precipitate a shooting affray. No matter how much the Englishman huffed and puffed, the attachment of his property was going ahead whether he liked it or not. Brady probably told him just that.[34]

CHAPTER NINE

War to the Knife . . .

Somehow—once again—confrontation ended in compromise rather than combat. "We succeeded in getting all the horses [which belonged to Tunstall] released (2 mules and six horses)," Widenmann reported, "and at once started . . . Gauss with three horses for the ranch and on the afternoon of the same day started William McCloskey & John Middleton for the ranch on two other horses. Subsequently I followed in company with F. T. Waite and William Bonney and arrived at the ranch on the morning of the 12th. R. M. Brewer was there in charge of the ranch, as well as the above-named persons."

It is clear from everything the witnesses say that in the two or three months he had been in Lincoln County, the Kid had grown up fast, no longer Tunstall's frightened rabbit but now his trusty warrior. Widenmann related how, having been informed that Mathews and a posse were "going to round up all the cattle and kill the persons at the ranch, the persons at the ranch cut portholes into the walls of the house and filled sacks with earth" in preparation for the expected attack.

Next morning Mathews arrived "in company with George Hindman, John Hurley, an Indian [Manuel Segovia], [Andrew L.] Roberts, Evans, Baker and [Tom] Hill," Widenmann recounted. "Seeing the last three in the party and knowing they had threatened to kill me on sight, I stepped out and asked the party to stop where they were (which was about fifty yards from the house) and asked Mathews to come forward to state his business."

Mathews told them "he had come to attach the cattle and property of A. A. McSween," the Kid related. On being informed that McSween had no cattle or property there, "Mathews said, that he thought some of the cattle belonging to R. M. Brewer, whose cattle were also at the ranch, . . . belonged to A. A. McSween."[1]

Brewer then told Mathews to round up the cattle and leave a man in charge of them until the courts could settle the question of ownership; clearly uncertain how best to proceed in the face of this unexpected cooperation, Mathews allowed he would first go back to Lincoln and get new instructions. Fine, said Brewer, and invited him in for something to eat, showing himself to be something of a psychologist; men who were eating at your table were unlikely to go to shooting while doing so. Then, just as the situation was neatly defused, the blustering Widenmann, who held a commission as deputy U.S. marshal, announced he was going to arrest Evans, Baker, and Hill.

Appalled, the others told him if he tried that, "all the persons at the ranch would be murdered," the Kid testified. Obviously having heard what Widen-

9.1. Jacob B. "Billy" Mathews and his wife, Dora.

Photographer unknown, ca. 1883.
R. G. McCubbin Collection.

Born in Woodbury, Cannon County, Tennessee, on May 5, 1847, the son of farmer Walter Mathews and his wife Anna (Ashford), Mathews—the spelling with a single *t* is correct—enlisted at McMinnville, Tennessee, in Company M, Fifth Tennessee Cavalry, U.S.A., and was discharged at Pulaski, Tennessee, in August 1865 (other sources give the date as 1867). In 1867 he located in Gilpin County, Colorado, as a miner, and later that year he moved south to Elizabethtown, New Mexico, where he ran a mining claim for an English syndicate. About 1874 he located on land three miles northeast of Roswell, and he farmed there for two years before "squatting" with Frank Freeman on the Peñasco. In 1877 he "bought into" the Dolan business, partnering with Dolan for some years after the war before settling on the Peñasco on the range he had once sold to Tunstall. In 1883 he married Dora Bates; they had three children.

Mathews managed the Peñasco Cattle Co. from 1885 to 1892, in which year both he and Dolan were elected directors of the Peñasco Reservoir & Irrigation Co. As bondsman, Mathews was bankrupted when Frank Lesnett disappeared in February 1893, leaving his accounts ten thousand dollars short; he moved to Roswell and became manager of the Pecos Irrigation & Improvement Co. After further business vicissitudes, he became postmaster at Roswell and was serving in that capacity when he died, of pneumonia, on June 3, 1904.

Source: Elvis E. Fleming, "Deputy J. B. "Billy" Mathews: The Lincoln County War and Other Lives," *New Mexico Historical Review* 72, no. 3 (July, 1997): 239–56.

mann said, "Jesse Evans advanced . . . swinging his gun and catching it cocked and pointed directly at [him]."

"Are you hunting for me?" Evans asked.

"If I'm looking for you, you'll find it out," Widenmann replied.

"Have you got a warrant for me?"

"That's my business," Widenmann said.

"If you ever come to arrest me," Evans told him, "I will pick you as the first man to shoot at."

"That's all right," Widenmann retorted. "Two can play at that game."

Throughout this conversation, reported the Kid, "Frank Baker stood near said Widenmann swinging his pistol on his finger, catching it full cocked at said Widenmann." Widenmann himself said he heard Baker say to Roberts, "What the hell's the use of talking, pitch in and fight and kill the sonsofbitches."[2]

The tension in the little cabin must have been thick enough to cut with a knife, yet again a showdown was avoided by a hair's breadth. After they had eaten, the posse moved out, Mathews, John Hurley, and Segovia heading for Lincoln, the others for Walker Paul's recently completed ranch on the Peñasco.[3] Taking the Kid and Fred Waite along for protection, Widenmann headed for Lincoln to report to Tunstall; they rode part of the way back to Lincoln with Mathews and his men.

9.2. Robert August Herman Widenmann.

Photographer T. Fall, Baker Street, London, 1879.
Courtesy Robert J. Widenmann.

According to a recently discovered baptismal certificate, his name was not Robert Adolph but Robert August Herman; born at Ann Arbor, Michigan, on January 24, 1852, he was the oldest son of Karl August and Pauline (Gärttner) Widenmann.

In 1874, Widenmann quit Ann Arbor and went to Atlanta, where he won the support of a wealthy man named Richard Peters who seems to have funded Widenmann's expedition west, possibly with a view to establishing a goat ranch near Las Animas, Colorado, and later in northern New Mexico. It is possible Widenmann was involved in other difficulties in the South; he had two scars on his back, one from a gunshot wound, the other from a knife.

He was down on his luck when he met John Tunstall in Santa Fe in July, 1876, and followed him to Lincoln, where he made himself indispensable to the Englishman. After he left Lincoln in May 1878 he never returned. He made his way east by way of Las Vegas and Ann Arbor and visited the Tunstall family in London from about Christmas 1878 to June 1879, when he returned to Michigan. He moved to New York and worked in various jobs; on November 23, 1881, he married Albertine Seiler-Lemke; they had four children. In 1892, while working as a piano salesman, he became interested in politics and in 1896 ran for a seat in Congress. Soundly defeated, he abandoned politics and after a couple more unsuccessful stabs at new employment, he quit working and decreed henceforth his children would support him. His wife died in 1905, and his son left home the following year. Elsie stayed with him the rest of his life. They moved to West Haverstraw, New York, where Widenmann died on April 15, 1930.

Sources: research by his grandson, Robert J. Widenmann.

Next day, Tunstall was informed that Murphy, Dolan, and Riley had helped Mathews raise a force of forty-three men from the Seven Rivers area and that Riley had told McSween's house servant George Washington that

> there was no use McSween's and Tunstall's trying to get away from them this time, as they had them completely in their power; that they could not possibly be beat, as they had the District Attorney (meaning Rynerson) the Court, and all the power in Santa Fe to back them; that their plan was to take the cattle ... by sending in two Mexicans ... to make a sham "round up" of the cattle so as to draw the men in Tunstall's house out of it; then the balance of the posse were to take possession of the house and get Tunstall's men.[4]

It would appear the Kid heard this story, too, for next morning, as forty-six-year-old "public grub man" Sam Wortley came down the street with food for the men occupying the Tunstall store, Billy and Fred Waite prevented him from taking it to them. A little later, the Kid drew a bead on Jim Longwell as he stood in the doorway of the store; fortunately for Longwell, Steve Stanley wandered into the firing line, and the target was able to duck inside before the Kid opened up.

"Turn loose now, you sons of bitches!" the Kid yelled at the barred door. We'll give you a game!"

Wisely, nobody replied, and after a while the Kid and his compadre moved away.[5]

The following day, Saturday—perhaps after a "talking to" from Tunstall, who was adamant that nothing be done to give the other side any excuse for violence—Billy accompanied Widenmann, Middleton, Waite, and Henry Brown back down to the Feliz. Tunstall, who left later, rode down to South Spring to ask the Chisums for assistance; perhaps he felt that reinforcements in the shape of Jinglebob riders would deter the posse from attacking his ranch. With John Chisum still in jail in Las Vegas, however, his brothers were disinclined to get involved. Downcast, Tunstall headed for the Feliz, arriving late on Sunday night. He must have been exhausted; he had ridden more than a hundred miles in the last twenty-four hours.

He told his men he would not countenance a pitched battle; everyone must leave in the morning. "We'll leave Gauss here," he told Widenmann. "He's an old man. They won't touch him." At about 3 A.M. he dispatched part-time employee Bill McCloskey, who was friendly with many of the Seven Rivers ranchers, to Paul's ranch with a message for Mathews: although it was made without Tunstall's consent, no resistance would be made to the attachment. McCloskey would also stop off at the neighboring home of "Dutch" Martin Martz, an acknowledged neutral, to ask him to come over and supervise the posse's count of the herd.[6]

Later that same Monday morning, February 18, after a few snatched hours of sleep, they ate a hasty breakfast and started for Lincoln on the road that led up from the Feliz to Casey's ranch on the Hondo, about where Tinnie is today. Fred Waite was driving the wagon, and Tunstall, Widenmann, Brewer, Brown, Middleton, and the Kid were herding the six horses and two mules Sheriff Brady had already exempted from the attachment and a third which "belonged" to Billy—the animal he had traded for Barela's mare.

Mathews's posse reached the ranch to find it deserted except for the two old men. As Mathews vacillated, some of the posse reshod their horses and others helped themselves to food. After a while, Dolan arrived, took charge, and "picked out the men to follow after Tunstall's party to bring them back if they caught them before they reached the Plaza," Gauss said. "From their actions I thought that some of the party of Tunstall's would be killed. I heard, I think it was Morton, cry out 'Hurry up, boys, my knife is sharp, and I feel like scalping someone.' They were all excited and seemed as though they were agoing to kill someone."[7]

"[I] instructed them to overtake the horses and bring them back," Mathews later testified, significantly failing to cite the legal basis upon which he intended to attach horses he knew to be Tunstall's sole property, "and in case there was any resistance, to arrest the men and bring them back too." Buck Morton was deputized to lead the pursuit, accompanied by perhaps twenty-five others. Sam Perry testified that Jesse Evans, Tom Hill, and Frank

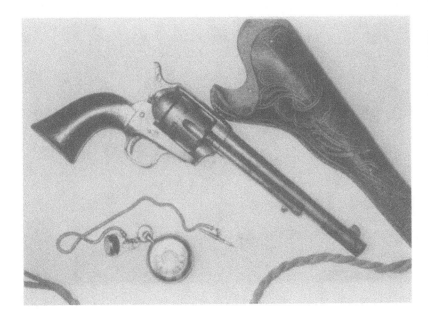

9.3. John Tunstall's gold half-hunter pocket watch, Colt .45, and holster.

Author's photograph, 1996.

Baker "volunteered" to go with the posse because "they had a horse among the horses that Tunstall had taken away . . . and wished to go after it." Thus, the Kid's theft of Barela's mare provided the Boys with the excuse they needed to pursue Tunstall. There can be no question about their purpose in doing so—or at whose instigation they went. Everyone knew who the Boys worked for.[8]

It was about half past five in the afternoon when they caught up with the Tunstall party. "Brewer, Tunstall and I were riding along driving the horses," Widenmann said, "Middleton and Bonney being about 500 yards in the rear, and we three had just come over the brow of the hill [leading down to the Ruidoso] when a flock of turkeys rose to the left of the trail. I offered Tunstall my gun [rifle], he having none, but he declined the use of it, saying I was a better shot than he was. Brewer and I started off after the turkeys, leaving Tunstall with the horses."[9]

"Whilst so hunting," John Middleton said, "we heard yelling, and saw a large crowd of men coming over the hill firing as they were coming. Tunstall and I were on the side of a hill about 700 yards from [the] horses."

Riding drag, the Kid and Middleton "at once rode forward to inform the balance of the party . . . who were some 200 or 300 yards to the left of the trail when the attacking party cleared the brow of the hill and came firing at us." Middleton peeled off to warn Tunstall. "I was within thirty steps of Tunstall when we heard the shooting first," he said. "I sung out to Tunstall to follow me. He was on a good horse; he appeared to be very much excited and confused. I kept singing out to him 'For God's sake, follow me.' His last words were, 'What, John? what, John?'"[10]

9.4. The place where Tunstall was killed.

Author's photograph, 1996.

The cement base and upright of the original Forest Service marker can be seen in the center of the picture. In 1978, to mark the centenary of the murder, a new plaque was placed alongside it by the Lincoln County Historical Society.

9.5. John H. Riley.

Photographer unknown, ca. 1885. R. G. McCubbin Collection.

Riley was born May 12, 1850, at Valentia Island, County Kerry, Ireland; he died at Colorado Springs, Colorado, on February 10, 1916.

Then "I and Widenmann and Middleton and Brewer rode over a hill towards another which was covered with large rocks and trees, in order to defend ourselves and make a stand," the Kid continued. "But the attacking party, undoubtedly seeing Tunstall, left off pursuing us. We heard two or three separate shots and the remark was then made by Middleton that they must have killed Tunstall."[11]

Middleton was right. The best, if admittedly hearsay, evidence is that alone and defenseless, Tunstall turned and rode towards the possemen nearest to him, Buck Morton and Tom Hill. When he saw who they were, he hesitated, but Hill called him to come on up and he would not be hurt. As the Englishman approached, Morton cocked his gun, but Hill said, "Hold on till he comes nearer." When Tunstall was up close, Morton shot him through the upper chest, the bullet severing an internal artery and exiting through the center of the right shoulder blade. Mortally wounded, Tunstall fell face down on the ground, at which point Tom Hill coldly administered the coup de grâce with a shot in the back of the head, the bullet entering behind the right ear and exiting above the left eye.[12]

Whether Morton ever really intended to kill Tunstall, or whether he was urged to do so by Hill, who undoubtedly did, and whether Jesse Evans was also present and involved will never be known and is anyway academic. The cold-blooded execution of the Englishman could be interpreted only one way: it was a declaration of war.

Although Tunstall was killed late in the afternoon and in a remote location, the news of his murder, which Widenmann and Billy Bonney brought to town about ten P.M., spread like wildfire. By midnight a sizeable crowd was assembled in McSween's house. There is no record of who or how many were present or of what was said. Was there angry talk of summary justice, of getting the men responsible for this barbarous crime? More than probably there was, and perhaps word of it reached Johnnie Riley, frightening him enough to send him staggering drunkenly to McSween's house.

"He was bareheaded and seemed very badly scared and was also intoxicated," McSween said. "In order to convince those present that he had no concealed weapons he emptied his pockets of their contents. In so doing he took out of one of his pockets a memorandum book containing some letters, etc. He left the same on the table."

In the book were details of the House's purchases of stolen cattle, a list of code names used by the members of the Santa Fe Ring—McSween's was "Diablo," which suggests the light in which they saw him—and a letter from District Attorney William Rynerson in Las Cruces addressed to "Friends Dolan & Riley" which would later be described as "an incitation to murder." "Shake that McSween outfit up till it shells out and squares up and then shake it out of Lincoln," Rynerson had exhorted the partners just four days before Tunstall was murdered. "I will aid to punish the scoundrels all I can. Get the people with you. Control Juan Patron if possible. You know how to do it. Have good men about to aid Brady and be assured I shall help you all I can for I believe there was never found a more scoundrelly set than that outfit."[13]

Here was proof, if proof were needed, of the district attorney's partisanship; proof that he would never accept McSween's bonds; proof that his friends, Dolan and Riley, could do and get away with whatever they wanted. The question is, and remains, why would Johnnie Riley have allowed such a sensitive document to fall into the hands of the one man who most needed proof of the collusion of law enforcement against himself and Tunstall?

Maybe Riley knew Pandora's box had been thrown open; maybe he wanted out. After this bizarre appearance he disappeared to the safety of Fort Stanton, leaving the conduct of the business to his more aggressive partner. According to some, however, he continued to play a covert role in events; Frank Coe called him the House's confidence man, a smooth talker who "worked in Santa Fe, Albuquerque and Las Cruces and sent in men to help them. He was a damned coward but he gave us more dirt than any of them."[14]

Meanwhile, taking no chances on the mood of the men gathering in the McSween house, Brady requested support from Captain George A. Purington, commanding Fort Stanton, in the shape of "an officer and fifteen mounted men," giving as his reason the fact that he was "unable to find a sufficient number of armed men to assist me in the execution of my duties."

This was hardly surprising; the "armed men" he might otherwise have mustered had not yet returned from the Feliz; without their support Brady doubtless felt exposed. Having little choice in the matter, Purington reluctantly acceded, sending a detachment commanded by Lieutenant Cyrus M. DeLany to guard the Dolan store, an action taken, he reported irritably to his superiors, because "the usual Lincoln County War has broken out."[15]

Purington spoke truer than he knew, but although feelings were running high—hotter heads like Widenmann and the Kid doubtless urging reprisal— there was no immediate confrontation. Alexander McSween was not a fighting man; it was a point of personal pride with him that he never carried anything more dangerous than a penknife. In a situation that cried out for action, McSween counseled caution. The House might have the district at-

9.6. George Augustus Purington.

Photographer unknown, ca. 1861. Civil War Library and Museum, Philadelphia.

Born in Athens, Ohio, on July 21, 1837, George A. Purington spent most of his childhood in Illinois. In 1856 the family moved back to Hudson, Ohio, where Purington entered Western Reserve College; he was a sophomore when war broke out. He enlisted for three months (along with his whole class) in the Nineteenth Ohio Volunteer Infantry on April 22, 1861, and he was mustered as a captain in the Second Ohio on August 27. He had a fine record throughout the war; altogether he participated in more than sixty battles and skirmishes, traveled over twelve thousand miles, was brevetted three times, was never excused from duty for sickness, and had only ten days' furlough. He died at Metropolis, Illinois, on May 31, 1896.

Source: ACP file.

9.7. Cyrus McNeely DeLany.

Photograph by C. M. Bell, Washington, D.C., date unknown.
R. G. McCubbin Collection.

DeLany was born in Ohio about 1845; he died February 27, 1888.

torney and the judge and the sheriff and the power of the Santa Fe Ring behind it, he said, but there was another level of law independent of them all which could be manipulated, and that was the route McSween chose to go.

Consequently, the only positive action taken by anyone that night was his sending Florencio Gonzales, Patricio Trujillo, Lázaro Gallegos, and Ramón Baragón to John Newcomb's farm on the Ruidoso with a note asking him to help them locate Tunstall's body and arrange for it to be brought up to Lincoln for burial.

Next day, however, Widenmann left early for the fort, intending to use his deputy U.S. marshal's commission to formally request military assistance in arresting Evans, Hill, and Baker. At eleven A.M. a wagon rolled into town carrying Presbyterian missionary Taylor Ealy, twenty-nine, and his family, together with schoolteacher Susan Gates. Their five-day journey from the railhead had been a catalog of discomfort and danger: on their arrival at Fort Stanton they were greeted with the news of Tunstall's murder; they were waylaid on the road into Lincoln by Dolan supporters who searched the wagon for arms; and, when they finally reached McSween's, they found themselves "in the center of a battlefield—about 40 men armed in full fighting trim."[16]

McSween offered them temporary accommodation in the east wing of his house, and that evening after dark—about six P.M.—Tunstall's body was brought in. While it was laid out on a table in McSween's parlor, "the Kid walked up, looked at him, and said: 'I'll get some of them before I die' and turned away." Next morning, Dr. Ealy reported, "A coroner's inquest was summoned to view the body. I was present at the inquest. He was run upon and shot in the back."[17]

After hearing the testimony of the Kid, John Middleton, and Dick Brewer, twenty-eight years old that day (it must have been one of the most miserable birthdays he ever had), the coroner's jury assembled by Justice of the Peace Wilson—George Barber (who had arrived in Lincoln just a few days earlier), Frank Coe, John Newcomb, Samuel Smith, and Ben Ellis—agreed and gave it as their verdict that the murder had been committed by Jesse Evans, Frank Baker, Tom Hill, George Hindman, James Dolan, Billy Morton, and others not identified by the witnesses. At the same time, McSween appeared before Wilson to swear a complaint of larceny against Sheriff Brady, who had authorized his deputies to let the troops led by Lieutenant DeLany feed their horses on hay from Tunstall's corral. Later that same Tuesday, assisted by Dr. Ealy, Lieutenant Daniel Appel, post surgeon at Fort Stanton, carried out a post-mortem examination and then embalmed Tunstall's body. There was a significant difference of opinion between the two doctors on the nature and cause of Tunstall's injuries: Appel concluded that the Englishman had been shot twice with a rifle, contradicting Ealy's statement that the head had been badly mutilated, and added that he had found "evidence of venereal disease." It need hardly be said that McSween found Appel's conclusions not only distasteful but also totally unacceptable.[18]

The warrant for Brady's arrest was placed for service, along with those for the murderers of Tunstall, in the hands of Constable Atanacio Martinez, who evinced a distinct lack of enthusiasm for the task, protesting that he might easily get himself killed. "You better take that chance," the Kid told him flatly. "Because if you don't, I'll kill you myself."[19]

On Wednesday morning, accompanied by Fred Waite and the Kid, Martinez went to the Dolan store to make the arrests. He was met at the door by a battery of leveled guns held by Brady and the men he had come after. Brady not only flatly refused to permit the arrest of anyone present, claiming they were all bona fide possemen, but proceeded to place Martinez and his deputies themselves under arrest. Proof, if proof were needed that there was already animosity between the Kid and Brady—and the outcome of this confrontation would exacerbate it to hatred—is offered in George Coe's story that when they got to the Dolan store, Brady "threw down on the Kid, saying: 'You little sonofabitch, give me your gun!'

"'Take it, you old sonofabitch!' the Kid said."[20]

When Brady did just that, and then marched them under ignominious arrest down the length of the street to the old jail in full view of everyone in town, he unwittingly signed his own death warrant; to add insult to injury, that night Brady released Martinez but not the Kid and Waite. As a result, Billy was prevented from attending John Tunstall's funeral, held the following day.[21]

They buried the Englishman beyond the corral wall behind his store; hymns were sung, a lesson read. After the funeral, which was conducted by Dr. Ealy, there was another noisy meeting of citizens, and a committee consisting of Florencio Gonzales, John Newcomb, Isaac Ellis, and José Montaño was delegated to ascertain upon what grounds the sheriff had without warrants arrested a legally empowered constable and his deputies themselves carrying valid arrest warrants. "Brady replied in substance that he kept them prisoners because he had the power [to do so]," testified Gonzales.

On the subject of arresting Jesse Evans, Brady was evasive, but when asked whether he was prepared to accept the committee's bond in double the value of McSween and Tunstall's attached property combined, he was more emphatic. "I will not take a bond of McSween of any kind of amount," he told them. Would he then at least place a value on the property he had already attached? Brady refused; he knew as well as they did the figure was probably three or four times the amount needed to secure the bond, but he was not going to put that in writing. In arresting Martinez he had already compromised his office. He might as well be hung for a sheep as a lamb.[22]

Late that night—perhaps early morning Friday would be more accurate, since they moved into position in the predawn darkness—Deputy U.S. Marshal Widenmann and a military escort led by Lieutenant Millard Goodwin surrounded the Dolan store. Backed up by a sizeable contingent of McSween supporters that included Dick Brewer, the Coe cousins, Scurlock, Sam Corbet, Fred Waite, and the Kid (just released from jail), Widenmann searched the building from top to bottom—the occupants used the word "ransacked"—ostensibly looking for Evans and his sidekicks.

Finding no one there, he led the party down the street to the Tunstall store, where, according to George Peppin, one of those occupying it, Martinez arrested him, commandeered the store keys, and bundled everyone—Peppin, Jack Long, Jim Longwell, Charles Martin, and John Clark—out of the build-

9.8. Daniel Mitchell Appel.

Date and photographer unknown. National Archives Negative No. 111-SC-90540.

Born in Philadelphia, Pennsylvania, on October 28, 1854, Daniel M. Appel graduated from Jefferson Medical College in 1875, was appointed first lieutenant, assistant surgeon, in the Medical Corps on August 5, 1876, and seems to have been almost immediately posted to New Mexico. On February 4, 1878, he was married to Helen Kate Godfroy; they had two children. Kate Godfroy Appel died in Oakland, California, on November 23, 1907. Two years later, on April 15, 1909, Appel, then fifty-four, married the doctor who had attended her, Emma Scribner MacKay, thirty-three. He was found dead at his residence in Honolulu on April 22, 1914, after a lively party at the Young Hotel.

Source: ACP file.

9.9. Jose Montaño and his wife, Josefa.

Date and photographer unknown. Rafaelita Pryor Collection, Lincoln County Heritage Trust, Lincoln, N.M.

ing. It must have given Widenmann and his followers great satisfaction to see Brady fume as he was marched in front of Justice Wilson and made to post a two-hundred-dollar bond for his appearance on the larceny charge; the others were bound over to the grand jury and released.[23]

The following day, McSween in the morning and the triumphant Widenmann that night sat down to write long letters to the Tunstall family informing them of the manner of John's death and events subsequent to it. Their next priority was to ensure McSween's safety; they had heard Jim Dolan was on his way to La Mesilla to obtain an alias warrant that would make it possible for Brady to rearrest McSween and remove him from the protection of Deputy Sheriff Barrier. They also heard, Barrier said, that Dolan had written to Johnnie Riley, who had sought the protection of the military at Fort Stanton, telling him to "have the military ready to assist Brady in arresting McSween & myself, and that he should have Baker, Evans, & company ready to do their part as soon as the military left."[24]

That they somehow became privy to the contents of a personal letter from Dolan to Riley is hard to believe, but there seems no valid reason to doubt the noncombatant deputy's words. On February 24, as Dr. Ealy organized the first evening Sabbath school ever held in Lincoln, someone—no names were ever mentioned—poisoned Robert Widenmann; he later claimed his life was saved only by the fact he had eaten a lot of butter on some batter cakes.[25] Following the service, at another mass meeting of citizens it was resolved that for his own safety McSween should leave town next day.

Still convinced that if they brought the events of the past week to the attention of the right people, swift and decisive executive action would follow, McSween wrote next day to the British ambassador in Washington and also renewed the attack he had begun on Mescalero Apache Indian Agent Frederick C. Godfroy, this time through the head of the Presbyterian Board of Missions in New York. Then, after making his will and having it witnessed by David Shield and Sam Corbet, he left under Barrier's protection for the mountains.[26]

Big, loyal, honest Dick Brewer, who had been heard to swear at Tunstall's funeral that he would not rest until every one of the men who had a hand in the Englishman's death had paid for it with his life, placed no faith in McSween and Widenmann's campaign of letters. If law enforcement in Lincoln County was corrupt, if Brady would not act on legal warrants or permit anyone else to do so, there was only one solution: Brady must be preempted. So on that first day of March, Brewer took control of the situation by appearing before Justice Wilson and having himself appointed a deputy constable.

In turn he deputized a posse that included Middleton, Waite, Scurlock, Bowdre, Smith, Frank MacNab, Henry Brown, Jim French, and the Kid. Calling themselves Regulators, each man bound by an "iron clad" oath never to divulge anything then or in the future that would jeopardize the safety or freedom of any other member of the group, they set out to hunt down Tunstall's murderers.

Although they called themselves by an honorable name inferring honorable intent, it is hard to believe any of them was under any illusions about the real purpose of their crusade. They knew the warrants they held gave them only the power of arrest, nothing more. They knew any prisoner they took, once handed over to Sheriff Brady for trial, would almost certainly walk free. It follows that they knew from the beginning anyone they captured would of necessity have to be executed.[27]

The posse set off down to the Pecos and late in the afternoon of March 6, below Bob Gilbert's ranch at the lower crossing of the Peñasco River south of what is now Artesia, they sighted five men dismounted beneath some trees. Recognizing the approaching posse, the men mounted up and fogged it south toward Beckwith's ranch five miles away, splitting up three-two as they went. The posse pursued the party of three, made up of Dick Lloyd, Frank Baker, and Buck Morton, and in the headlong pursuit which followed over a hundred shots were fired (according to Morton, although how he could have counted while riding flat out for his life for five miles across treacherously broken ground is another matter).

Lloyd's horse gave out, spilling him to the ground. The possemen ignored him, thundering past after Morton and Baker, who, when both their horses could run no further, took cover among some tule reeds bordering the Pecos. The posse's threat to burn them out left them no option but surrender, whereupon "we gave up our arms and were taken prisoners," Morton said. "There was one man in the party who wanted to kill me after I had surrendered, and was restrained with the greatest difficulty by others of the party. The constable himself [Dick Brewer] said he was sorry we gave up as he had not wished to take us alive."[28]

By all accounts the man who wanted to kill Morton was the Kid—yet further evidence of his vengeful streak. Not only had Morton been in charge of the sub-posse that had pursued Tunstall and was widely believed to have fired one of the shots that killed him, Billy had a personal grudge against the man dating back to the Kid's humiliation at the Dolan camp some months earlier. And anyway, if they took Morton and Baker back to Lincoln, he argued, Brady would give them a hearing, post meaningless bail, and set them free. All this Brewer knew as well as Billy did, but that was what he decided to do. He had given his word to the prisoners they would not be harmed, and they would not. Brewer was that kind of man.

The party started back up the Pecos for the Chisum ranch, arriving after dark on Friday, March 8. Chisum's niece Sallie, who had arrived from Texas only the preceding December, gave up her bedroom for the prisoners to sleep in—though it is doubtful they got much sleep—because it was the only one without windows. Somewhere along the way, perhaps at Gilbert's ranch, Bill McCloskey had attached himself to the posse. Doubts about his loyalties—after carrying Tunstall's message to the possemen at Paul's ranch that last night on the Feliz, McCloskey had joined the group pursuing the Englishman—and his friendly acquaintance with Morton did not endear McCloskey to the group, but they let him ride with them anyway.

Sallie Chisum recalled:

> Morton and Baker were as pale as corpses when they came out of the prison room for breakfast in the morning. When they had eaten, Baker came to me and gave me his gold watch, his horsehair bridle, and a letter he had written in the night to his sweetheart.
>
> "I want to make my last request on earth to you, Miss Chisum," he said. "I will never live to get to Lincoln. When you hear of my death, I wish you would send my watch and bridle, which I plaited myself, to my sweetheart and mail this letter to her."

"When Morton told me goodbye, he merely gripped my hand hard," she concluded, "he couldn't talk."[29]

He had, however, used the night hours to compose a four-page letter to a Virginia attorney setting forth his version of the Tunstall killing and naming his captors, including two he claimed as friends: Middleton and McCloskey. "I am not at all afraid of their killing me," he wrote, "but if they should do so I wish that the matter should be investigated."[30]

At about ten o'clock the following morning the posse stopped at the Roswell post office long enough for Postmaster Ash Upson to register and

9.10. Sallie Chisum with her brothers Walter *(left)* and Willie.

Date and photographer unknown, ca. 1877. MoNM Negative No. 91336.

mail the letter. Upson asked Morton if he considered he was in danger; Morton replied he did not, but if anything happened, he wished his people to be informed. Bill McCloskey stepped forward. "Billy, if harm comes to you two," he told Morton, "they will have to kill me first."[31]

The posse pushed on up the hill; later that afternoon merchant Martin Chavez reported to Upson he had seen the posse turn off the main highway below Picacho and take a trail—mainly used by the military to bypass the town of Lincoln—that led through Agua Negra Canyon and around the shoulder of Capitan Mountain. Their reason for doing so, it was later stated, was that they had heard a rescue attempt might be mounted from Lincoln.

According to Frank Coe, who claimed he got the story direct from Brewer:

They had been three days on the road and the horses were near given out and the party was strung out for 200 yards. McCloskey, Baker and Morton were riding almost abreast, talking. The Kid and Bowdre were behind him and I [Brewer] was away back behind. Morton had a pocket pistol he had carried all the time after his capture. He had not been searched. Baker reached over, grabbed McCloskey's pistol and broke to run, shooting back. They thought they might get in the rocks and make a stand. They shot McCloskey as they left right under the jaw. They were killed in a short distance.[32]

This account—and there were several others not dissimilar—raises a number of cogent questions. Would Morton and Baker have killed the one man who had pledged his life to their safety? Would riders as experienced as they have tried to escape on horses that were "near given out"? And even if they had, could they have seriously entertained the hope that armed only with a pocket pistol and one six-gun they could make a stand against a dozen determined and heavily armed men?

There is one other—and more believable—version: Upson claimed he was later told that Frank MacNab put his pistol to Bill McCloskey's head and said, "You are the sonofabitch that's got to die before harm can come to these fellows, are you?" and fired as he spoke. McCloskey fell dead; the terrified prisoners ran for it "as fast as their sorry horses could take them, pursued by the whole party and a shower of harmless lead." Then the Kid spurred his horse around in front; two shots from his revolver and both men fell dead.[33]

Only the last is implausible; the rest has a truer ring than any part of Brewer's lame account. It would be later claimed that when a party which included Sheriff Brady found and buried the bodies there were nine bullets in Morton's body and one in his head; five bullets in Baker. The reliability of this evidence must be weighed with another statement the same writer made, to the effect that "McCloskey [had] objected to shooting them while tied, and said he'd testify to that effect [whereupon] 'Young Kid' Antrim shot him."[34]

Leaving the possemen at what would become their favorite hangout, San Patricio—a little village formerly known as Ruidoso and renamed by the Irish priest who built the church there in 1875—Brewer continued alone up to Lincoln. When he got there, he learned his commission as a lawman had been retroactively revoked by a proclamation issued (on the same day Morton and Baker had been killed) by Governor Samuel B. Axtell. In addition it inter alia removed Justice of the Peace Wilson from office and voided all processes issued by him. As of this moment, Brewer was an outlaw, and so were every one of the Regulators.

CHAPTER TEN
... And the Knife to the Hilt

GOVERNOR AXTELL'S VISIT TO LINCOLN had been prompted by a letter written to U.S. Attorney Thomas B. Catron by Sheriff Brady justifying his actions and those of his posse in the killing of Tunstall and in subsequent events. "Anarchy," he said, "is the only word which would truthfully describe the situation here for the past month. . . . I cannot serve any legal documents or carry out the law if I am not assisted by the military. Please see His Excellency the Governor and ask him to obtain an order from Gen. Hatch to the Post Commander at Fort Stanton to protect me in the discharge of my official duties."[1]

Catron passed the letter to Axtell, who forwarded a summary of it to Washington asking President Rutherford B. Hayes to authorize the use of troops to assist civil law enforcement officers in Lincoln County. When Hayes so ordered, Axtell decided to go directly to Lincoln himself.

Although he remained there only three hours, all of it in the company of Murphy and Dolan, he claimed later to have "conversed with all the citizens of Lincoln County that I could meet" and to have "advised them to seek peace and pursue it, to be in earnest to uphold the law." During his visit he called at the McSween house, where he met David Shield, Dr. Ealy, and Widenmann.

"Someone present requested that he should ascertain the true situation of affairs from the citizens," David Shield stated later.

"God deliver me from such citizens as you have here in Lincoln," Axtell snorted sarcastically.

"The citizens are all right," Widenmann snapped back, "but God deliver me from such executive officers."[2]

Brusquely informing them that he had all the information he needed, Axtell elevated his patrician nose and stalked out. Within the hour he had promulgated a bizarre proclamation that indicated conclusively to both sides that he stood firmly behind the interests of Murphy and Dolan and, by definition, of Thomas B. Catron.

The appointment of Justice of the Peace John B. Wilson by the county commissioners was illegal and void, he decreed, which in turn meant that all processes issued by Wilson were likewise void and that Wilson had no authority to act as a justice of the peace. Robert Widenmann's appointment as deputy U.S. marshal had been revoked; he was no longer a peace officer. From all of which it followed that the only legal writs and processes were those issued by Judge Warren Bristol and the only legal law enforcement officers were Sheriff Brady and his deputies.[3]

10.1. Samuel Beach Axtell.

Photograph by Broadbent & Taylor, ca. 1880.
MoNM Negative No. 8787.

Axtell was born in Franklin County, Ohio, on October 14, 1819; he died at Morristown, New Jersey, on August 6, 1891.

10.2. Montague Richard Leverson.

The original is a tintype, ca. 1872.
Author's Collection (not fully authenticated).

Montague Leverson, who was born in London on March 2, 1830, was the son of Montague and Elizabeth Levyson. A brother, James, was a wealthy diamond merchant. Educated at the University of London and in Germany, Leverson was something of a firebrand in his younger days; he claimed acquaintance with Victor Hugo, the French author-agitator Louis Blanc, and others of similar radical fervor.

In 1848, aged eighteen, he appeared at a Clerkenwell, London, court before Mr. Justice Tyrwhitt on charges of having shot and wounded Priscilla Fitzpatrick. Bailed on personal recognizance of £500 and two sureties of £250, Leverson seems to have successfully avoided further prosecution.

In 1852 he appears in London directories as a patent agent in Bishopsgate, London, remaining there until 1859, when he entered into a partnership under the style Montague Leverson & Hawley, Patent Agents, at the same address. In his lifetime he would produce a great many books, tracts, and papers; all are now long forgotten.

Although he claimed he was invited to Lincoln by Juan Patrón, it seems quite clear Leverson and John Chisum were well acquainted through business, for Leverson attempted unsuccessfully to put up bond for Chisum in January 1878 subsequent to Chisum's arrest in Las Vegas.

He later moved to California, where he served in the legislature, and he was active in the Anti-Vaccination League in New York at the turn of the century. In 1893 he became a doctor of medicine at Baltimore Medical College and a writer on legislative science and law reform, economic science, and education. It has so far proven impossible to establish where or when he died, other than that it was after 1912.

Sources: *Times* (London), May 5, 1848; personal research in London, Paris, and Arbois, France.

A lawyer himself, Axtell was well aware of the flimsy legality of his decree; to rescind Wilson's powers was to invalidate every verdict the justice of the peace had issued since his appointment a year earlier. How many marriages would that nullify, how many repaid debts would have to be refunded, how many prisoners legally jailed now released? And how could he remove Wilson from office without removing the four other still functioning justices of the peace in Lincoln County who had been appointed in precisely the same way?

Nevertheless, the decree stood. Hard on the heels of Axtell's departure, McSween left town accompanied by Deputy Barrier and Dick Brewer, heading for the safety of Chisum's ranch, where his wife was expected back from her extended trip East. There he met and was befriended by a voluble English lawyer, political agitator, and crusader named Montague R. Leverson.

Leverson wasted no time. He wrote to Marshal John Sherman. He wrote to British ambassador Sir Edward Thornton, to Senator H. B. Anthony, and to General Benjamin Butler. He even wrote to the president of the United States. In each letter his tone was hortatory but authoritative; his technique sensational charges, convincingly made. Added to the letters already written by McSween and Widenmann to Secretary of the Interior Carl Schurz and to Sir Edward Thornton in Washington, reinforced by others from Tunstall's family in London to the British Foreign Office, his exhortations may well have been the turning point in McSween's campaign to precipitate intervention by Washington in Lincoln County affairs.

Thornton had contacted William Evarts, secretary of state, who passed the buck to Attorney General Charles Devens. Devens not unnaturally forwarded a copy of the note to the U.S. attorney for the Territory of New Mexico instructing him to make "prompt inquiry into all the circumstances of the murder" of Tunstall "and report fully to me with a statement of what measures have been or can be taken to bring to punishment the parties guilty of this crime."[4]

Not surprisingly, U.S. Attorney Catron put the request on hold, but if he hoped the matter would blow over, he was sadly mistaken. McSween and Widenmann had written again to Thornton updating him on events, and on March 27, Thornton again addressed Evarts, this time apprising him of the charges now being made that the murder had been "incited by the District Attorney of the Third Judicial District and that the murderers are being screened . . . by the Governor of the Territory and the Judge of the District."

Evarts could hardly duck accusations like these; he passed Thornton's note to Devens, who informed him that as well as instructing Catron to "institute a thorough inquiry," he had also "taken other measures to have the subject thoroughly investigated." These "other measures" were the appointment of a special agent of the Justice Department who would go to New Mexico to investigate land frauds, Indian agency graft, the activities of Governor Axtell, and the murder of Tunstall.[5]

During the three weeks following the deaths of Morton, Baker, and McCloskey there were no confrontations between the opposing sides apart from a fracas—the full details of which seem never to have been recorded—in which the Kid and Charlie Bowdre exchanged shots somewhere near San Patricio with Andrew L. Roberts. But there was bloodshed; when it came, ironically enough, it happened a long way from Lincoln.

On March 14, while trying to rob the camp of sheep drover John Wagner, en route from California to Texas, Tom Hill and Jesse Evans shot down but untypically failed to kill Wagner's Cherokee driver, the camp's sole guard. The driver got hold of a Winchester and put a bullet through Hill from stern to stem, killing him instantly. As Jesse Evans leaped on a horse to escape, a second shot drilled through his left elbow, shattering the bone. He made tracks for Shedd's ranch, about ten miles away, only there to run head-on into local rancher and constable David Wood, who arrested him. By the time they arrived at Tularosa, however, Evans needed urgent medical attention, so Wood brought him on up to Fort Stanton.[6]

"The outlaw Jessie Evans is comfortably domiciled at the Post Hospital at Fort Stanton," the *Independent* reported. "He is the lion of the occasion, has many sympathetic friends, and as his wounded wrist is rapidly healing

10.3. William Brady.

Date and photographer unknown, ca. 1860s.
Author's Collection.

The eldest son of John and Catherine (Darby) Brady, William Brady was born August 16, 1829, in Cavan, County Cavan; he left Ireland for America early in 1851. On July 11, 1851, he joined the U.S. Army for a five-year hitch, and he served in Texas; discharged as a sergeant at the end of his first tour of duty Brady reenlisted in the First Regiment of Mounted Rifles for another five years at Fort Duncan, Texas.

Discharged in March 1861 at Fort Craig, he joined the First New Mexico Volunteer Infantry as first lieutenant and adjutant to its commanding officer, Colonel Miguel Pino, and he eventually assumed command of Fort Stanton on May 14, 1864. On August 29, 1866, he applied to remain in the army until the following spring, but he was mustered out on October 31.

On November 16, 1862, Brady married a widow, Maria Bonifacia Chaves Montoya. Bonifacia was pregnant with their ninth child when Brady was assassinated on April 1, 1878.

Source: ACP file; Donald R. Lavash, *William Brady, Tragic Hero of the Lincoln County War.*

Jessie will no doubt soon be on the road again at his old tricks."[7] A few days later, however, Robert Widenmann served his warrant, and Jesse was consigned to the guardhouse to await the sitting of the district court in Lincoln scheduled for Monday, April 8.

On March 29 there was another fracas at Stockton's saloon; Dr. Ealy's breathless recollections are the only record we have of it. "We heard rapid firing downtown," he wrote, "and our house being flat roof[ed] . . . I ran up to get a view of the town & discover if possible what was going on, & before I could discover what it meant someone shot at me from a house near by & my friend Wiednmann was shot at standing upon the ground in front of the house a few minutes later. Afterwards we learned that the firing began at Stockton's saloon & that a young man had been shot through the shoulder." Who the victim was, and what the cause of the affray, history again does not record.[8]

At about noon on March 30, Sheriff Brady and a detachment of troops commanded by Lieutenant George W. Smith rode through Lincoln on their way back from the Chisum ranch, where they had gone to find and if possible arrest McSween. While they were there, Lieutenant Smith exhorted Mrs. McSween to persuade her husband to surrender and avail himself of military protection until court convened. He and his men would escort McSween

10.5. *(On facing page)* The Sheriff's Morning Walk: A Bird's Eye View.

Drawing by Bob Boze Bell.

10.4. Lincoln, looking east.

Photograph by or for Emerson Hough, 1904.
R. G. McCubbin Collection.

Apart from the gabled roof on the Tunstall store, center left, and the Dolan house abutting center right, both postwar additions, the street looks much as it would have that April morning when Brady and his deputies were ambushed.

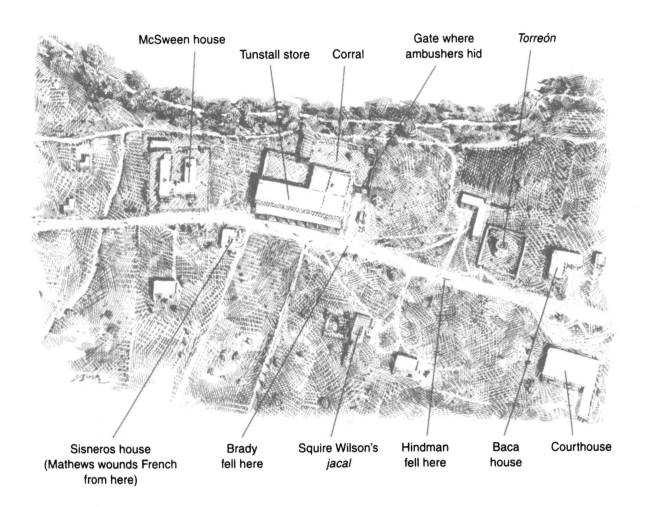

McSween house
Tunstall store   Corral   Gate where ambushers hid   *Torreón*

Sisneros house
(Mathews wounds French from here)   Brady fell here   Squire Wilson's *jacal*   Hindman fell here   Baca house   Courthouse

10.6. Believed to be Isaac T. Stockton and his wife, Ellen.

Date and photographer not known, ca. 1882.
Courtesy Mrs. Pam Birmingham and James S. Peters.

10.7. Jacob Basil "Billy" Mathews.

Photograph by A. M. Parker, Roswell, ca. 1890.
R. G. McCubbin Collection.

safely to the fort, he told her. "You may make a football of my head if a hair of his head is injured," he said, "or if the least insult is given him by word or sign from the highest to the lowest."[9]

Thus encouraged, McSween decided to come in from his hiding place near the Bottomless Lakes. Deputy Barrier, reassured that his charge would have military protection, left for home at once. On Sunday morning, March 31, McSween and his wife, John Chisum, Montague Leverson, Las Vegas drummer Calvin Simpson, and South Fork merchant Albert Howe set off from South Spring in two wagons, expecting to catch up with the military detachment and accompany it to Lincoln as arranged. They never did; heavy rains necessitated their staying overnight at a farm on the Hondo. When they got to Lincoln about eleven the following morning, they found the town in pandemonium; an hour or so earlier the Regulators had assassinated Sheriff Brady and his deputy George Hindman.

•••

At fifty seven hundred feet, spring often comes late to Lincoln; it did in 1878. There was sleet in the wind at about 9:30 that first April morning as Brady set off down the rain-muddied street from the Dolan store. Accompanying him were four deputies: stonemason and builder George Peppin, bartender Billy Mathews, Hondo farmer George Hindman—partially

crippled in an encounter with a bear some years earlier—and former buffalo hunter Jack Long, sometime buddy of the Boys.

On his way down the street Brady stopped for a moment opposite the
McSween home to exchange pleasantries with a woman. The others had
ambled on; huffing from the exertion—he was forty-eight and a heavy
drinker—Brady caught up with them as they reached the Tunstall store, some
four hundred yards east of Dolan's. At the eastern end of the building was a
high wooden gate giving entrance to the corral behind it; as the party drew
level, the gate swung open and a withering hail of lead blasted Brady off his
feet.

"After the firing," Dr. Ealy wrote, "we heard the groans of a wounded man.
After my 1st experience on the house top at such times I kept cool & out of
sight But Miss Gates & my wife looked out & saw the wounded Sheriff lying
in the street. Two or three more shots were fired after he fell. One of Brady's
men named Geo. Hyndman fell just in advance of him. Hyndman begged
for someone to give him water & [Ike] Stocton ran over to him & helped him
up & as he leaned on Stocton's shoulder, he was shot the second time & fell
dead."[10]

Another witness, Gorgonio Wilson, son of the justice, was playing in his
front yard with his sister Juanita. He "looked up to see William Brady fall to
a sitting position. He said, 'Oh Lord' and tried to get up, but there was another round of shots and he fell back."[11] Hit in the head, left side, and back,
Brady collapsed in the mud, dead, as his deputies bolted for the cover of
nearby houses. Up on the hillside a stray shot had sliced through the fleshy
part of old Squire Wilson's thighs as he stood hoeing his onion patch.

The street had emptied. From behind the shelter of the corral door two
figures emerged: the Kid and Jim French. Billy wanted his Winchester back,
the one Brady had confiscated during their February confrontation and
which now lay in the mud beside the sheriff's dead body. What Jim French
was after can only be guessed.

As they scuttled across to where Brady's body lay, Billy Mathews opened
up on them from the Sisneros house, where he had taken cover; one of his
bullets maybe burned Billy's leg but certainly drilled a hole through French's
leg. The Kid skipped back to safety, followed by French; a few minutes later
the door of the corral swung open again and five horsemen galloped out and
down the street, spattering mud. At the lower end of town where the road
curves, John Middleton calmly stopped his horse, dismounted, knelt, and
took aim, returning the fire of the men who had run into the street shooting
at the retreating riders. The citizens scattered; when they came out again the
Regulators had disappeared. Nobody was foolish enough to go after them.[12]

•••

Brady's death polarized the community as completely as Tunstall's death
had done—except that this time it was the Regulators who were the object
of vilification. They knew—they must have known—that this would be the
case. So why did they do it? In the aftermath of the shooting a number of
propositions were advanced. The McSween faction attempted to justify the

10.8. George Warden Peppin.

Photograph by or for Emerson Hough, 1904.
R. G. McCubbin Collection.

George Warden Peppin was born in Chittenden County, Vermont, in 1838. By the time he was twenty, he was in Alleghany, California, where on October 2, 1861, he enlisted as a private in Company A, Fifth Regiment California Infantry. He came to New Mexico with Carleton's Column. Mustered out at La Mesilla on November 30, 1864, Peppin drifted up to Lincoln County, where he pursued the trade of mason and builder. Peppin built or participated in the building of the Murphy store, the McSween house, the Lincoln jail, and residences in Roswell.

He was an important witness at the Dudley Court of Inquiry in 1879 and also at the trial of the Kid at La Mesilla. After a stint as a butcher at Fort Stanton in 1881, he resumed the trade of mason, aided by his son Juan.

Peppin's first wife was Felipe Moya; they had three children. His second wife was Victoriana (Salazar) the widow of Hiraldo Jaramillo, who was killed by James Dolan; there were five children of this second marriage. In August 1887, Peppin lost the use of his left hand when a weight fell on the knife he was using, driving the blade through his wrist and severing all the tendons. In 1893 he was jailer in Lincoln and also served as Sheriff George Curry's deputy. He died of "bowel trouble" at his home in Lincoln on September 18, 1904.

Source: pension application.

killing by claiming Brady, knowing Lieutenant Smith had broken his promise to protect the lawyer, was on his way to arrest McSween, whose arrival in town was imminently expected. Once they had McSween in the jail, it was reasoned, it would be easy for Jesse Evans to "do his part"—and so the Regulators took preemptive action.

The opposition averred that in fact, Brady was on his way to or returning from the building that was used as a courtroom—now the Convento. He was there to inform grand jurors that because of a clerical error they had been summoned to appear a week too early; it was said that the Regulators knew this and planned their ambush accordingly. How they might have found out, or, more important, how they could have been certain Brady would obligingly walk down the street and in front of their guns, was not explained, and anyway, there was no misunderstanding about the date court would open. But even if that had been Brady's intention, it would still not explain why he needed an escort of four well-armed deputies, why he had a warrant for McSween's arrest in his pocket, and why he had a pair of handcuffs on his belt.[13]

Whatever reason—excuse—is offered, killing the sheriff was cold-blooded murder, an outright and unequivocal declaration of hostilities: "Come on,

10.9. The Ellis house, Lincoln.

Author's photograph, 1993.

Attached to the Ellis house and store were a large stable and barn; there was also a freshwater spring in back of the house.

you sonsofbitches, we'll give you a game." It is at least a possibility that the assassination squad—Middleton, Brown, French, MacNab, Waite, and the Kid—had decided that the only way to deal with the crooked law enforcement system that had consigned them to outlawry was to wipe it out.

The two bodies were still lying in the muddy street when the McSween party arrived in town an hour or so later and stopped at the Ellis house. In the meantime, George Peppin, still shaken by his brush with death, had assumed the role of sheriff and had sent a messenger to the fort to summon military assistance. When it arrived, in the shape of Captain Purington, Lieutenant Smith, and twenty-five buffalo soldiers, he began—without warrants and on the most dubious of authority—making arrests.

Escorted by Lieutenant Smith and two troopers, he stormed angrily down the street to the Ellis house, intent on arresting McSween. To his chagrin, McSween coolly refused to recognize his authority—which he considered had died with the sheriff—but agreed to surrender to Lieutenant Smith; with that Peppin had to be satisfied. Next he went to the Tunstall store, and while the soldiers searched for the man Billy Mathews had winged, he arrested Rob Widenmann, who had been seen in the corral when Brady was shot.

From there they went to the McSween house and arrested David Shield

10.10. Samuel Robert Corbet.

Photograph by Furlong & Crispell, Las Vegas, ca. 1883.
R. G. McCubbin Collection.

Born at Rutherfordton, Rutherford County, North Carolina, on August 5, 1851, Samuel Robert Corbet was the second of the eight children of Henry Miller and Carolina (Coleman) Roberts. What brought Corbet to New Mexico is unknown; he became Tunstall's clerk in the summer of 1877 and remained one of his staunchest supporters, particularly in the matter of Dudley's actions during and after the "Big Killing." Shortly after the end of the fighting, Corbet married Teresa Phillipowski, née Padilla, widow of Lyon Phillipowski (killed in a gunfight with William Burns at Lincoln, October 21, 1874); their daughter, Carolina C[oleman?] Corbet, was born July 16, 1880, but died May 13, 1881.

Sam worked briefly for Isaac Ellis as a clerk. He was a witness at the Dudley Court of Inquiry, and from 1879 to 1880 was Lincoln postmaster and in the latter year deputy probate clerk. In the census he gave his occupation as "miner," indicating that he probably joined the gold-strike exodus from Lincoln to White Oaks. Teresa died February 10, 1882; on March 6, her daughter, known as Lola, applied to the probate court to have her stepfather, Sam Corbet, appointed her guardian. In 1883, he married Josefa Baca (born July 4, 1864); she had something of a "reputation," having in June 1882 eloped with George Washington, who had "accidentally" killed his own wife and child in June 1879 while, he claimed, shooting at a dog. The couple were pursued by a posse led by Josefa's father, Saturnino Baca; Washington was hanged in Lincoln town.

Sam and Josefa had a son who died February 28, 1884, at White Oaks, probably while Sam was operating a saloon there. Sometime in the latter part of 1887, and for reasons that remain obscure, Sam left Lincoln County; in January 1888 he and his wife were destitute in Coahuila, Mexico. Of all people, it appears Jimmy Dolan sent him money and did what he could to help him. Two years later Sam was back in New Mexico campaigning to become superintendent of schools in 1890. This would tally with probate records indicating Josefa Corbet died about August 1892, possibly at Las Vegas, possibly of a brain tumor. Shortly thereafter, Sam removed to Texas, where he married yet again, this time to Ola Waddle from Lone Oak. He built his own home and ran a drugstore at Miller Grove, Hopkins County, where he died January 1, 1923.

Source: research by Lewis Ketring, Jr., and Alton Corbet.

and two black servants, George Washington and George Robinson. According to Dr. Ealy they were still "hunting for the wounded man. They searched the house, for they said they tracked him by the blood." Later he learned that Sam Corbet had hidden French, who was unable to ride because of his wound, beneath the floor in the Tunstall store with a pistol in each hand.

Fortunately the searchers never found him; there would have been more dead men if they had.[14]

Meanwhile, Montague Leverson was busybodying himself all over town. First he had hastily composed another letter to President Hayes; when he took it to the post office in the Dolan store, "one of the ruffians, *armed to the teeth*,"

10.11. Colonel Nathan Augustus Monroe Dudley.

Date and photographer unknown, ca. 1861.
U.S. Military History Institute.

Dudley was born at Lexington, Massachusetts (his namesake grandfather fought in the famous Revolutionary War battle there fifty years earlier), on August 20, 1825. The son of John and Esther Eliza (Smith) Dudley, he attended the Eliot School in Roxbury. Brigade major and later division inspector of the Boston division of the state militia for several years, on November 12, 1845, he married Elizabeth Gray Jewett of Roxbury; they had one son, Granville Winthrop Dudley, born in July 1848. Dudley followed "mercantile pursuits" until 1849, when he first crossed the Rocky Mountains to Oregon as chief clerk in the quartermaster's department of the U.S. Mounted Rifles. He went down the coast to California and remained there about six months, returning east via Panama and the West Indies. He visited the Sandwich Islands for about nine months, then in 1852–53 lived in Europe, where he visited military establishments in England, France, and Belgium.

He was rightly seen as one of the stormy petrels of the U.S. Army; his military career was a succession of explosive confrontations with his fellow officers and superiors. After his exoneration by the 1879 Court of Inquiry, he commanded Forts Union and Cummings; in September 1880 he led the cavalry column of Buell's expedition into Mexico, marching 720 miles in the saddle. He became a full colonel of the First Cavalry, joining at Fort Custer and heading the 1885 expedition against the Crows. Dudley retired from the army on August 20, 1889. Bearing the rank of brigadier general, he died at Roxbury, by then a suburb of Boston, on April 29, 1910, and was buried with full military honors at Arlington National Cemetery.

Source: ACP file.

called him a "damned sonofabitch"—which suggests nobody there was harboring any illusions about where Leverson's sympathies lay. When he returned to the McSween house, where Captain Purington was getting ready to leave with the "prisoners," he heard Peppin announce he was going to search McSween's house for weapons; Leverson was appalled.

"Have you or these men a search warrant?" he asked Purington.

"No," Purington replied. "Peppin asked me if he could search, and I told him he could do as he pleased."

"But he purports to do it under your authority!" Leverson protested, and when Purington ignored him, he reminded the colonel that the Constitution provided that no citizen's house could be searched without a warrant.

"Damn the Constitution!" Purington barked, "and you for an ass!"

Turning to the troopers, Leverson warned them that what their officers were permitting was illegal and that they would be liable to criminal prosecution if they followed their orders, whereupon Purington bluntly told him

10.12. Dr. Joseph Hoy Blazer.

Photographer W. H. Cushing, date unknown.
Rio Grande Historical Collections, NMSU.

Joseph H. Blazer, the son of David and Sarah (Hoy) Blazer, was born in Washington County, Pennsylvania, on August 20, 1829. He went to live in Illinois and later in Iowa, where he qualified as a dentist and set up a practice at Mount Pleasant.

Blazer enlisted as a corporal for three years in Company E, First Volunteer Iowa Cavalry, on July 31, 1861, at Davenport, Iowa. He served only eighteen months, suffering a severe hernia when a horse fell on him, and was invalided out at Prairie Grove, Arkansas, December 31, 1862.

Fearing tuberculosis, he came to San Antonio, Texas, and worked as a teamster. He bought a mule train and freighted to Fort Davis and later El Paso. He came to Lincoln County in 1869, located on the Tularosa at a settlement then called Big Fork, and bought in with George Nesmith, a former soldier in the California Column turned local farmer, trading his freight team for a share in Nesmith's ranch and sawmill. Blazer's wife, the former Lucy E. Jobes, died at Mount Pleasant on November 1, 1869.

Dr. Blazer was foreman of the Lincoln County grand jury in October 1874 and again in 1878. As Blazer & Abbott, the company tried to persuade the Bureau of Indian Affairs to buy them out in October 1876 for about twenty thousand dollars. Indian Agent Fred Godfroy recommended against the proposition. On January 7, 1894, the Reverend A. D. Dexter of Monroe, Wisconsin, joined Dr. Blazer in matrimony to Julia M. McWade, daughter of William and Weallby (Wiles) McWade, born 1848 at Buckville, Ohio. Dr. Blazer died at Mescalero, New Mexico, on October 29, 1898.

Source: pension application.

to shut up and quit making such a damned fool of himself. After a few further exchanges, Leverson desisted, afraid he might jeopardize McSween's safety; the soldiers mounted up, and the cavalcade moved off to the fort.[15]

Next day, as Leverson sat in his room at Juan Patrón's composing his longest letter yet to President Hayes, a significant addition to the cast of characters arrived at Fort Stanton: its new commanding officer, Lieutenant Colonel N. A. M. Dudley, Ninth Cavalry. Although Dudley was not officially scheduled to take command until the following Friday, Purington—who was due to depart on extended leave to his home in Ohio—was more than happy to dump the whole mess in the superior officer's lap. So Dudley, in many ways as unfitted by his character and background to handle what was to come as was McSween, was immediately thrown in at the deep end; before very long he would be completely out of his depth.

Even as Dudley took command, the Regulators were in the saddle again, captained once more by Dick Brewer, who, it was said, had heard that several of the men for whom he had warrants were on the Mescalero Apache

Indian Reservation. It was a sizeable hunting party that included the Kid, Middleton, George Coe, Bowdre, Waite, MacNab, Scurlock, "Dirty Steve" Stephens, John Scroggins, Henry Brown, and Ignacio Gonzales. If indeed they had declared war on the crooked law enforcement system, perhaps their real purpose for riding over to that side of the mountains was—as the Dolan side alleged—to ambush the judicial party coming up from La Mesilla which included Judge Bristol and District Attorney Rynerson.[16]

On Wednesday, April 3, Brewer and his men rode up the Ruidoso and over Apache Summit, camping in the heavily timbered mountains; next morning they headed down the Tularosa Creek canyon toward South Fork, or Blazer's Mill, as the little settlement was more widely known.

When the Mescalero reservation had been established five years earlier, the government had leased from mill owner Dr. Joseph Blazer the big two-story adobe house he had built on a bluff overlooking the sawmill. It was now occupied by Indian Agent Frederick Godfroy, his wife Clara, their two daughters, Kate and Louisa, and a cook. Below and to the west of the big house was a scattering of one-story adobes; the sawmill itself was on the other side of the creek, flanked by a large corral.

Soon after her arrival, Clara Godfroy had begun to take in lodgers and serve meals to travelers, all of whom were required to leave their arms outside the house before entering. When they arrived toward noon, Brewer and his men followed the custom, but not without posting a lookout outside: John Middleton drew the short straw. What the Regulators did not know, and no one told them, was that earlier in the day one of the February 18 possemen, Bill Williams, also known as Andrew L. Roberts, had dropped in at the agency; he was selling his farm on the Ruidoso and getting out, and he had hoped the check from the buyer might be at the South Fork post office. Dr. Blazer urged him to leave; an Apache had reported seeing a band of men in the hills the night before, and he suspected they were the Regulators.

It was good advice, and Roberts took it, but on his way west he saw the mail driver's buckboard heading for the mill and retraced his steps. A careful reconnoiter revealed no sign of the Regulators, so he tethered his packhorse up on the hill and started down, unaware of the fact that instead of hitching them outside the agency building the Regulators had given their horses to Dr. Blazer's son Almer and two other boys to put into the high-walled plank corral next to the mill.

Roberts rode down to the agency and tethered his mule near the corner of the house. Hanging his gunbelt with its knife and pistol over the saddle horn, and carrying his Winchester .44, he went into the post office. John Middleton, who had seen the "mighty well-armed man" approaching but did not know him by sight, heard him give his name and slipped inside the house to warn the others. "I've got a warrant for him," Brewer said.

Frank Coe, who later claimed he was not with the posse but happened to be at South Fork on other business, offered to go outside and see if he could talk Roberts, his neighbor on the Ruidoso, into surrendering. He met Roberts as the little man emerged from the post office.

"Come around the house, I want to talk to you," he said.

"I told him we had a warrant for him and [the] others would have to take

10.13. George Washington Coe.

Photograph by J. Evetts Haley, 1927.
J. Evetts Haley Collection, HHC.

Here George Coe shows the extent of the damage to his hand inflicted by Roberts's shot that April day nearly fifty years earlier.

The son of Thomas Coe, who came from Moundsville, West Virginia, and settled at Brighton, Washington County, Iowa, George Coe was born on December 13, 1856. He was just twenty when he arrived in Lincoln County. He farmed with his brother for a while, then moved to his own place on the Ruidoso, with another brother, Jap Coe, farming nearby. George and Doc Scurlock were arrested by Sheriff Brady on suspicion of harboring fugitive Frank Freeman; the treatment George received at Brady's hands put him firmly in the McSween camp. He was as active as his cousin Frank in the Farmington troubles; at the height of them, on November 16, 1879, he married Nebraska-born Phoebe Brown.

George and Phoebe returned to Lincoln County in November, 1884, and thereafter George led a peaceful life; he died at Roswell on November 14, 1941.

Source: George Coe, *Frontier Fighter.*

him. He said: 'No, never alive. The Kid is with you and will kill me on sight.'"

"I told him: 'No, give me your gun and we will walk around to the crowd. I will stand by you.'"

Roberts was adamant; he would never surrender. "I talked to him for half an hour," Coe related. "I begged him to surrender, but the answer was no, no, no."

Meanwhile, the patience of the other Regulators had worn thin; at that moment Charlie Bowdre came around the corner of the house with Middleton, MacNab, Henry Brown, and George Coe right behind him.

"Roberts, throw up your hands!" he yelled.

"He said: 'No,' raised up," Frank Coe said, "brought up his gun and shot from his hip with his Winchester and Bowdre shot him through from one side to the other. The dust flew from his clothes from both sides." Roberts "gave a groan, stepped back to the door. I never saw a man that could handle a Winchester as fast as he could."

Roberts's first shot whacked into Bowdre's belt buckle, putting him out of the fight before ricocheting off to wreck George Coe's gun hand. Another dropped John Middleton with a chest wound close to the heart, another whanged off Doc Scurlock's still-holstered pistol and burned down his leg, and yet another nearly got the Kid. The bullet "just shaved his arm," and the Kid "backed out as if it was too hot in there for him." Black powder smoke drifted; three men were down, the rest running for cover.[17]

10.14. Frederick Charles Godfroy.

Date and photographer unknown.
Author's Collection.

Born May 15, 1827, Fred Godfroy was the third of the eleven children of James Jacques "Jock" and Victoria (Navarre) Godfroy of Monroe, Michigan. Intended by his father for the Catholic priesthood, he attended parochial school in Monroe and partially completed a course of studies at the University of Michigan at Ann Arbor. The death of his father on May 20, 1847, enabled him to avoid going into the church; he instead clerked for many years in the dry goods store of Charles G. Johnson and also in the Wing & Johnson banking office in Monroe; later he worked at Hillsdale in the Mitchell & Waldron bank. He was married to Clara, one of the daughters of Richard Phillips, of Brest. He died of heart disease at the home of his daughter and son-in-law, Kate and Daniel Appel, in Plattsburg Barracks, New York, on May 15, 1885.

Source: research by Chris Kull, Monroe County Historical Commission, Monroe, Michigan.

Early accounts of the fight by members of the Blazer family suggested the fight began outside the agency building, but in the 1920s Frank Coe told J. Evetts Haley that Roberts took shelter not in the "lean-to" that features in most accounts of the shootout but in a single-story adobe. All the photographic evidence indicates that this was probably the same adobe that still stands beside the highway directly opposite the ruins of the old mill. It was at that time Dr. Blazer's house. This in turn suggests that while the confrontation took place outside the agency building, Roberts retreated downhill, firing as he went, until he reached the shelter of the one-story adobe.

His now-empty Winchester useless, and the Regulators between him and the pistol on his saddle horn, Roberts looked frantically around Dr. Blazer's office. On the wall was a single-shot 1873 officer's model .45-70 Springfield rifle. Groaning with pain, he dragged a mattress off the bed to use as both barricade and support while he loaded the rifle. Outside the agency building, Brewer angrily ordered David Easton to go down to the adobe and bring the wounded man out; Easton refused, as also did Dr. Blazer and Fred Godfroy.

"I begged [him] to take his men and go off," Easton recalled. "Brewer replied he would have that man out if he had to pull the house down." He turned away and ran across the footbridge spanning the creek to come around behind a pile of logs near the sawmill below the doorway of the room where Roberts was forted up.

The Blazer's Mill Fight

A Pictorial Essay

10.15. Blazer's Mill, a general view.

Date and photographer unknown, ca. 1893.
MoNM Negative No. 15034.

This view, looking roughly northeast, shows the scattered buildings that formed the settlement. The wooden building center foreground half conceals the actual mill building. Note particularly the single-story adobe beyond and above it, across the road leading up the hill. This would appear to be Dr. Blazer's adobe house (Fig. 10.17), identified by Frank Coe as the building where Roberts made his last stand.

10.16. Blazer's Mill, the mill building.

Date and photographer unknown, ca. 1900.
MoNM Negative No. 104921.

It was believed the lean-to building on the left was Dr. Blazer's office, and that it was in this doorway that Roberts stationed himself; however, since it is clear from Fig. 10.19 that the building faces north, it does not in any way match contemporary accounts of the fight. Note especially the pile of logs to the left of the house in this picture.

10.17. Adobe house at Blazer's Mill.

Photograph by J. Evetts Haley, 1926.
Haley Collection, Haley History Center.

This is the house where Roberts was
killed, identified in 1926 by Frank Coe.
It is clearly visible in Fig. 10.15 above
and facing the mill building downhill.
The ground in front of it is open,
explaining why no one could get a shot
at Roberts. If Brewer came around
behind the mill, as eyewitnesses said
he did, and clambered up behind the
pile of logs, he would have been on the
right-hand side of the mill building
looking uphill and straight into the
doorway of the Blazer adobe. This
topographical detail would seem to
discredit the longstanding belief that
the fight took place around the "big
house" at the top of the hill.

10.18. The same adobe house today.

Author's photograph, 1996.

10.19. Blazer's Mill, ruins.

Date and photographer unknown, ca. 1930s.
Courtesy Cara Mae Coe Marable.

This view of the old mill, taken after the highway was graded, shows how the aspect in Fig. 10.16 faced almost directly north. The Blazer adobe, as shown in this photograph, was (and still is) up on the left-hand side of the road around the corner.

10.20. Blazer's Mill today.

Photograph by Dick George, 1996.

The modern highway was driven right through the battle scene, completely altering the topography. Nevertheless, the ruins of the mill and the adobe opposite can be clearly seen. The agency building stood on the bluff behind the large barn to the right. Roberts and Brewer are buried in the Blazer cemetery just above it.

10.21. John Patten.

Photographer Koch, White Oaks, New Mexico, ca. 1885.
R. G. McCubbin Collection.

Johnny Patten was an eyewitness to the Blazer's Mill fight; his account of it appears in Emerson Hough's *The Story of the Outlaw*. Contradicting the accepted version of events—in which Brewer was buried first and Roberts the next day—he said he made one big coffin, and in this Brewer and Roberts were buried side by side. "I couldn't make a very good coffin," he said, "so I built it in the shape of a big V, with no end piece at the foot. We just put them both in together."

Source: Emerson Hough, *The Story of the Outlaw*, 290.

"He thought he saw Roberts up in the door," Frank Coe said, "and just shaved the door facing with a shot, but missed Roberts; but Roberts saw where the shot came from. He watched for him and when he looked over the next time . . . he just shaved the log and hit him right in the eye and knocked the top of his head off at 125 steps away."[18]

Their leader dead and two of their complement in dire need of medical attention, the Regulators were in complete disarray. If indeed they had ever seriously entertained thoughts of waylaying the Bristol party, Roberts had effectively scotched them. "I took Middleton down to the big spring that furnished water for the mill after he was wounded," Frank Coe said. "He got down and drank until I had to turn him over to keep him from getting into the water. We got an ambulance down there and brought him and George Coe [back to the Ruidoso] in it."[19]

En route they met Lieutenant Daniel Appel, summoned to the agency by Godfroy; he did what he could for Middleton and Coe then hurried on to South Fork. It was nightfall when he got there; Brewer had already been buried in the Blazer cemetery, and Roberts was dying. Bowdre's bullet had entered just above the left hipbone and ranged downward through the groin; there was nothing Appel could do for him. At the end, Roberts "got desperate with pain [and] it took two men to hold him down." He died shortly before noon the following day and they buried him on the hill next to Brewer. For a man who couldn't even lift his Winchester above hip level he had put up one hell of a fight. Even the Kid paid him grudging homage. "Yes, sir," he told his friend John Meadows, "he licked our crowd to a finish."[20]

11.1. José Chávez y Chávez.

Prison photograph, November 23, 1897.
Penitentiary Collection No. 1089, NMRSCA.

Born in Valencia County in 1851, Chávez y Chávez came to Lincoln County when he was about eighteen and was married to María Lenora Lucero at Lincoln on January 10, 1871; he was elected constable of San Patricio Precinct in September, 1874, for a one-year term, and the following year justice of the peace. On February 14, 1877, he was reappointed constable for San Patricio, a position he still held when he joined the Regulators; how many instances where the word "constable" was used to refer to him rather than Lincoln constable Atanacio Martínez, is impossible to say.

Chávez y Chávez was one of those who defended, and escaped from, the McSween house in July 1878. He later served in the short-lived Lincoln County Militia and ran unsuccessfully for constable in the November 1880 elections, perhaps losing the election because he had murdered a prisoner in the Lincoln jail a few months earlier. In 1881, Chávez y Chávez moved to Las Vegas, where he served as a deputy under three sheriffs. On October 22, 1892, he was one of a trio who lynched Patricio Maes and were party to the killing of Gabriel Sandoval by the head of the "Society of Bandits," Jesús Silva. In mid-April Silva killed his own wife; suspecting they might be next, his confederates murdered him. A year later, two of the killers were arrested and imprisoned for life; Chávez y Chávez skinned out. He was apprehended a year later and sentenced to hang in June 1895, but following a great deal of legal maneuvering his sentence was commuted to life imprisonment. He entered the Santa Fe penitentiary on November 23, 1897; he was paroled February 1, 1909, and returned to Las Vegas. In later years he claimed it was he, not the Kid, who shot Sheriff Brady and also bragged of having killed Albert Fountain and his son, perhaps being the only man who ever publicly made that claim. Sometime between 1886 and the turn of the century, Chávez y Chávez married Ruperta Selgado, the former wife of Nicolás Aragón. He died at Milagro, New Mexico, on July 17, 1923.

Source: Frederick Nolan, "A Note on José Chávez y Chávez," *Lincoln County Historical Society Newsletter,* August 1994.

CHAPTER ELEVEN

The Gathering Storm

THE REGULATORS RETREATED to the Ruidoso Valley to lick their wounds. George Coe's right hand was in such bad shape that Dr. Ealy had to amputate his trigger finger. Charlie Bowdre was still hors de combat from the repercussive effect of the slug that had hit his belt buckle, Jim French nursed the hole in his thigh, and the Kid had a burn from the bullet that had so nearly laid him low. As for Middleton, although his wound was less serious than had been feared, it effectively put him out of the shooting war. So once again, there was a lull.

While men like Bowdre, the Coes, and Scurlock kept an eye on their farms, retreating to the safety of nearby hills at any sign of danger, the others made their headquarters among the friendly villagers of San Patricio, where town constable José Chávez y Chávez was a sympathizer. Just another homeless drifter two months earlier, the Kid was now something of a local favorite. He had on several occasions convincingly demonstrated that for all his youth he was as good a fighting man as any of those around him.

They were all young—Bowdre, thirty, and Scurlock, twenty-nine, were the oldest, with the two Franks, MacNab and Coe, next oldest at twenty-seven. Fred Waite was twenty-five; Middleton, twenty-four; George Coe, twenty-two; Henry Brown, twenty; and the Kid, with his slight build and youthful looks, probably seemed a lot younger than all of them. At this time, according to Frank Coe, Billy was about seventeen, "5ft 8in, weight 138 lb[s] stood straight as an Indian, fine looking lad as ever I met. He was a ladys man, the Mex girls were all crazy about him. He spoke their language well. He was a fine dancer, could go all their gaits and was one of them. He was a wonder, you would have been proud to know him."[1]

In addition, he was *simpatico*, relaxed, light-hearted, playful with the children, courteous and gallant to women, respectful of the *viejos*. He danced gravely with the *mamacitas* at the bailes and smiled at their daughters in the *paseo*; everybody liked him, particularly the native New Mexican population. He had spoken their language fluently since he was a street Arab in Silver City. He knew their customs; he not only liked but also shared their life-style.

As a result, Billy soon became "the center of interest everywhere he went, and though heavily armed, he seemed as gentlemanly as a college-bred youth. He quickly became acquainted with everybody, and because of his humorous and pleasing personality grew to be a community favorite. He was a mighty nice dancer and what you call a ladies' man. He talked the Mexican language and was also well liked by the women."[2]

11.2. Carlota Baca Brent and her son, William Joshua.

Date and photographer unknown, ca. 1888.
Rafaelita Pryor Collection, Lincoln County Heritage Trust.

This photograph was probably taken around the same time as the one of Carlota's father, Saturnino Baca (Fig. 4.4). If half of the girls in the Bonito Valley were as beautiful as she, it is hardly surprising the Kid spent as much time as he did with them.

Not all of them liked him; Lily Casey, for example, had little good to say about the Kid (but then, Lily rarely had a good word for anyone outside her immediate family). But even she grudgingly admitted, "The Kid had a great personality, and could ingraciate himself in peoples good graces very quickly[.] he had a laughing blue eye always smiling or laughing, quick and more than acomidating very good hearted, had an inocent timid look all of this took with the girls at once."[3]

While the Regulators "laid out"—and it was not altogether a bad time for it, for the weather was foul, with high winds driving sleety rain and, toward the middle of the month, heavy snowfalls—court convened at Lincoln on the appointed Monday, April 8. Taking no chances on running into an ambush, Judge Warren Bristol and the other attorneys who had come up from La Mesilla were escorted in daily from Fort Stanton and guarded during the court session by a detachment of soldiers.

One of Bristol's first acts was to empower an acting sheriff to serve such warrants as the court might generate—but nothing more. His choice was Kentucky-born John Copeland, thirty-seven, a longtime resident of Lincoln who had a ranch below the fort; later in the month County Commissioners Juan Patrón, Francisco Romero y Lucero, and Will Dowlin confirmed his appointment as sheriff.[4]

By Saturday, April 13, Judge Bristol treated a grand jury of ten citizens, with Dr. Joseph Blazer as foreman, to a lengthy and highly partisan overview of recent events. To indicate just how biased his address was, when the full text of it was printed in the *Las Vegas Gazette*, his remarks on the McSween embezzlement case filled three and one-half columns, while the murder of Tunstall required only a meager sixty words.[5]

On Thursday, April 18, with the town still under snow from a heavy fall two days earlier, the jury completed its deliberations and delivered its findings. Indictments were returned against Jesse Evans, George Davis, Manuel Segovia, and John Long for the murder of Tunstall, with Dolan and Mathews named as accessories. Of the principals only Evans could be found; already under arrest, he was placed under a five-thousand-dollar bond, which sizable sum—the average man's life savings—he seems to have had little trouble raising; neither did Dolan and Mathews, required to post two thousand dollars' bond each.

For the murder of Brady and Hindman the jury fixed responsibility on Middleton, Waite, Brown, and William H. Bonney. These four—the Kid under the more familiar name of Henry Antrim this time—were also indicted for the murder of Roberts at the agency, along with Bowdre, Scurlock, Steve Stephens, John Scroggins, and George Coe. Dolan and Riley were also indicted for cattle theft. The court being unable to locate any of the parties named in the indictments at that time, the warrants were placed in the hands of Acting Sheriff Copeland for service.

In the matter of the Fritz insurance money, the jury fully exonerated Alexander McSween of the charge of embezzlement, expressing regret "that a spirit of persecution has been shown in this matter."[6] This vindication of the McSween cause—with its implicit slap in the face for Judge Bristol—clearly came as no surprise to Dolan and Riley, for on the preceding day they

11.3. The original courthouse building.

Author's photograph, 1996.

Now known as the Convento, this building stands adjacent to the Montaño store, set back a little from the road. This space was the site of the original plaza before the village spread east and west.

wound up their business and made preparations to leave Lincoln, accompanied by the now terminally ill Lawrence Murphy.

On the same day, McSween composed another "card," which, ironically enough, appeared in the territorial newspapers alongside Dolan's announcement of the House's cessation of business.

$5000 REWARD

I am authorized by J. P. Tunstall of London, England, to offer the above reward for the apprehension and conviction of the murderers of his son, J. H. Tunstall, at Lincoln county, New Mexico, on the 18th day of February, 1878. The actual murderers are about twenty in number, and I will pay a proportionate sum for the apprehension and conviction of any of them.[7]

The seat of the judge's chair had scarcely cooled following the adjournment of court when a mass meeting of citizens was held "at an hour's notice" in the same building to discuss the troubles besetting the county. Chaired by Probate Judge Florencio Gonzales, with Saturnino Baca and José Montaño as vice-chairmen and McSween and Ben Ellis as secretaries, a citizens' committee consisting of John Chisum, Avery Clenny, and Juan Patrón drew up a set of resolutions, among which were a condemnation of Axtell's actions during his March visit, an apple-polishing vote of thanks to the new commanding officer at Fort Stanton and to his soldiers, and another to John Copeland for his "important and efficient discharge" of the duties of sheriff.[8]

Incidental to these effusions, McSween saw to it that a petition was signed by everyone present exhorting the members of "the Irish firm" to leave Lin-

11.4. John Hurley.

Photograph by Baker & Johnston, Roswell, N.M., ca. 1882. R. G. McCubbin Collection.

Hurley was born in New York about 1855; he was killed at Chaperito by Nicolás Aragón, January 24, 1884.

11.5. James Albert "Ab" Saunders.

Photograph by A. W. Fell, Lompoc, California, late 1878. Courtesy Cara Mae Coe Marable Smith.

Saunders was born in Mount Pleasant, Iowa, October 14, 1851, and died in San Francisco, February 5, 1883.

coln "for the sake of peace and safety" and return no more. As if all this were not enough of a victory, McSween had received word that a special agent of the Department of Justice was on his way to New Mexico to investigate not only the murder of Tunstall but also the activities of the federal officials. In addition, an inspector of the Interior Department was coming to look into the affairs of the Indian Agency, and an examination of Dolan's handling of the Lincoln post office was also expected.

With McSween offering a $250 reward for any member of the posse and with the new "captain" of the Regulators stating unequivocally that their next field of operations would be Seven Rivers, where quite a few of the men who had served on the Tunstall posse lived, the hard-bitten denizens of that area decided to beat them to the punch. To what degree they were persuaded to adopt this course of action by George Peppin, Billy Mathews, and Johnnie Hurley, who "happened" to be in that area, is uncertain, but it is not difficult to imagine them pointing out to the Seven Rivers settlers that the interests of the McSween crowd were linked with and identical to those of the man against whom most of their grievances were addressed: John Chisum.

Under the aegis of William H. Johnson, a former Brady deputy, thirty or so of them formed a self-styled Seven Rivers Posse and set out for Lincoln, their nominal intent being to "assist" Sheriff Copeland in arresting the murderers of Brady, Hindman, Morton, and Baker—specifically Middleton, Waite, Bowdre, and the Kid.

Although news of their coming reached Lincoln a few days before their actual arrival, it seems not to have deterred Frank Coe and his partner (and cousin) James A. "Ab" Saunders, accompanied by Frank MacNab, from setting off down the Bonito Valley to their ranch on the Hondo the following evening.

It is almost impossible for travelers on the modern highway down the valley today to imagine how vastly different it was in 1878. Descending the Bonito in those days, the road wound "through fine groves of stately walnuts and box elder whose spreading branches in places formed a complete canopy overhead. There is a continuous cornfield from Lincoln to [Fritz's] Spring Ranche broken only by the stream as it winds from side to side of the narrow valley."

Charlie Fritz's ranch was something of a Bonito Valley beauty spot; as well as thoroughbred cattle and hogs, he had an extensive peach orchard and other fruit trees. With not the slightest inkling of the presence of the Seven Rivers Posse, MacNab, Coe, and Saunders stopped off to water their horses where the "fine spring of pure water rises at the base of a hill near the residence," as the same observer wrote, "and plunges down through shady groves of walnut into the valley below."[9]

Frank Coe recalled subsequent events in a latter-day account that probably matches the one he gave his fellow Regulators at the time. "I was riding a race pony and a good saddle animal," he said. "I told the others that we had better whip up a little, but my race pony being so much better [a] saddle animal I had distanced them about a hundred yards when we got near the Fritz ranch."

11.6. The Fritz ranch.

Photograph by or for Emerson
Hough, 1904.
State Historical Society of Iowa.

What they didn't know, Coe went on, was that there were about twenty
men lying in ambush; the rest were at the house of a tenant of Fritz's half a
mile downriver. "I was so far ahead that they let me pass," he said.

> Sanders and McNabb came riding up after I had passed and they opened
> up fire upon them as they reached a point about a hundred yards from the
> house. McNabb's horse went to bucking and threw him. He ran for a mile
> up the cañon. The [Seven Rivers] men . . . ran around the point of the hill
> that McNabb rounded and chased him this distance before they killed him.
> Sanders' horse was killed. . . . He ran over a little knoll and was followed up
> and shot through the hip which disabled him and he was captured. . . .
> When I heard the shooting I tore out on down the cañon. I crowded back
> next to the mountain on the north side of the valley and made for a hill.
> Several of them began shooting at me. Someone shot from the Fritz house
> and killed my horse. A bullet hit her right in the back of the head. She
> stumbled along for thirty feet and fell. I went over her head and jumped up.
> She had fallen on my Winchester. I shot left-handed and carried my
> Winchester on that side. I tried to pull it out but could not.

Pursued by a hail of bullets and armed only with a six-shooter, Coe ran
for the shelter of a canyon about three hundred yards away. The canyon

11.7. The scene of the ambush near the Fritz ranch.

Photograph by Robert Mullin, ca. 1920s.
R. N. Mullin Collection, HHC.

Note the horses watering at the spring.

opened out opposite the rented house where the rest of the posse had stopped; when they saw him they moved to cut him off. He retreated up another canyon, sweating, breathless; his pursuers had a Mexican-raised Apache tracker with them, and they were "damned hard people to contend with," Coe said.

After a further inconclusive exchange of shots, Coe, who had taken cover in a washout, surrendered and was brought back to the Fritz ranch, where he learned that MacNab was dead. Saunders, badly wounded, had been left where he fell.

"I begged them to go get him and bring him in and not let him die out there," Coe said. "They rigged up a buggy of Fritz's and went after him." He also found out why they had pursued him so hard: they had mistaken him for the Kid, who was about the same height and weight; clearly Billy's leading role in the deaths of Morton, Baker, Brady, Hindman, and Roberts had made him one of the posse's prime targets.

At about 10:00 P.M. the posse started for Lincoln, putting Coe on a poor horse so he couldn't make a run for it. "Just around the crack of dawn [on May 1] they gathered around the Ellis house corrals to catch the McSwain party as it came out. The corrals were about sixty yards from the Ellis house on the east. They did not catch anyone there and as their position was too open they backed down the river some 200 yards."[10]

The reason they did not catch the Regulators off guard was because the mail carrier had preceded them into town bringing the news that the posse had killed Frank Coe and two others and was on its way up the hill. When he heard this, George Coe, who was in the Ellis house, got his mad up. "I said

11.8. Frank Coe and his wife, Helena Anne Tully.

Photograph by John Hodges, Durango, Colorado,
February 7, 1882.
MoNM Negative No. 105075.

to [Henry] Brown, my partner there, I said, 'Let's go up on top of the house,'
and old man Ellis said 'Whatever you do, boys, don't fire a gun.' He says,
'Them fellows will come up there and I will be in it,' and I wouldn't have done
it, I don't know what made me, but I did. I was so stirred up that I didn't
care."

When they got up on the roof—Brown carrying a Winchester, Coe with
his Sharps rifle—they saw what looked like a man sitting on a beehive in a
field about four hundred yards downriver. "Each of us got a porthole and
we gave the word and both shot. One shot fell about 200 yards short and I
know it was Henry's, he had a little Carbine. My bullet cut through the flesh
of both the man's legs—they were crossed in front of him—and cut a gash
nearly six inches long through his hip, about 440 steps away."[11]

The man wounded was "Dutch" Charlie Kruling; the two shots opened
the ball. Unfortunately, no satisfactory account of this first, day-long skirmish between the Seven Rivers men and the McSween party exists. According to McSween, the attackers lost six of their men; no one else was injured.
In Widenmann's self-glorifying account the McSween men "poured the lead
into them so rapidly that in less than an hour we had them routed and had
them cut off from their horses. The fighting continued throughout the day,
the murderers trying to regain their horses, while we beat them back at every attempt."[12]

At about 4:30, summoned by an overwrought—others did not hesitate to
say drunken—Sheriff Copeland, a troop of soldiers commanded by Lieutenant George Smith rode into town to the accompaniment of sharp skirmish
fire being exchanged by the two parties. By placing his detachment between

11.9. Millard Fillmore Goodwin.

Graduation photograph, U.S. Military Academy, West Point, 1872.
U.S. Military Academy Archives.

Born in New York State on May 25, 1852, Millard F. Goodwin was admitted to the academy on July 1, 1867, but was court-martialed in October 1870 for "conduct unbecoming an officer and a gentleman." Goodwin altered records to cover up the misconduct of another cadet, Thomas C. Davenport (who was also court-martialed), and was dismissed from the service, with the sentence mitigated to suspension without pay for a year. He was restored on September 11 and graduated from West Point on June 14, 1872, fifty-seventh in a class of fifty-seven.

Goodwin saw extensive service in Texas and Indian Territory before his transfer to Fort Selden, New Mexico, on March 24, 1876. He arrived at Fort Stanton on March 17, 1877, and served there until 1879, receiving his promotion to first lieutenant on April 4 of that year. He appears to have become separated from his wife at this time; she lived in New York while he served at Fort Stanton, where he played a very active role in Lincoln County events. He died in Yonkers, New York, July 19, 1888, exactly ten years to the day after he had served as Dudley's adjutant during the climax of the troubles in Lincoln.

Source: ACP file.

them, Smith quickly defused the situation, accepted the surrender of the Seven Rivers party, and—without relieving them of their arms—took them all to the fort. Amid all the confusion, Frank Coe simply walked out of the Dolan store and rejoined his friends.

Next day, after Dr. Ealy officiated at the burial of Frank MacNab alongside Tunstall, Billy Bonney slipped out of town and headed for San Patricio with Charlie Bowdre and one or two others, thus avoiding involvement in the tit-for-tat legal tussles that took place between the two factions over the next couple of days; had he stayed around, he would probably have been amused. It was as if everybody was arresting everybody.

What happened was that McSween, on hearing the news of MacNab's death, appeared before Justice of the Peace José G. Trujillo in San Patricio—Lincoln, remember, no longer had one—and swore affidavits against the members of the Seven Rivers posse. Copeland took the warrants to the fort, placed the whole crowd under arrest, and asked Colonel Dudley for an escort to take them to San Patricio for their hearing.

Needless to say, the Seven Rivers men were less than keen on this prospect. They need not have worried: Dudley had already chosen sides. During their stay at Stanton under the protection of the military, and before their departure for Santa Fe, Lawrence Murphy and Jim Dolan—fellow military men and, like Dudley himself, heroic drinkers—had exercised their considerable powers of persuasion on Dudley to win him over to their point of view.

Now Dudley—without the support of whose troops Copeland was unable to function—effectively usurped the role of sheriff, giving the hapless Copeland orders he was in no position to question or disregard. To make

11.10. Josiah Gordon "Doc" Scurlock.

Date and photographer unknown, ca. 1920.
R. G. McCubbin Collection.

Scurlock was born in Tallapoosa County, Alabama, on January 11, 1849; his father
was Presley N. Scurlock, a teacher. Doc's nickname was come by honestly: he is
believed to have studied medicine in New Orleans. He was a most unusual feudist:
doctor, farmer, poet, teacher, later a linguist and reader of the classics.

At the age of twenty he went to Mexico; fearing tuberculosis, he returned to the
States in 1871 and worked for John Chisum in Texas and later New Mexico. Subse-
quent to the 1873 killing of his line-riding partner Newt Huggins by Indians,
Scurlock turned his hand to farming in the Ruidoso Valley.

In the summer of 1875, Scurlock was one of the "American posse" that banded
together to wipe out the Mexican horse thieves of Lincoln County. On September
2, 1876, he accidentally killed his friend Mike Harkins while examining a pistol.
Just a few weeks later, on October 19, 1876, Scurlock was married to sixteen-year-
old Antonia Miguela Herrera. They had ten children.

After the Lincoln troubles he left New Mexico for Texas and dissociated himself
from his past. His wife died at Acton, Texas, in 1912; Scurlock moved to Eastland,
Texas, where he died on July 25, 1929.

Source: Rasch, "These Were the Regulators."

quite certain Copeland did as he was bidden, Dudley ordered Lieutenants
Goodwin and Smith to "escort" the sheriff back to San Patricio and there
arrest McSween, Widenmann, and others on tit-for-tat arrest warrants for
riot sworn before South Fork Justice of the Peace David Easton by Dolan's
"affidavit men" Mathews and Peppin.

Copeland and his "escort" rode down to Lincoln, where they arrested Doc
Scurlock, Widenmann, Isaac Ellis and his son Will, John Scroggins, Ignacio
Gonzales, and Sam Corbet; all but the last, who was ill, were sent under guard
to the fort while the sheriff and the soldiers rode on down the river to San
Patricio, where McSween and George Washington were gathered into the
net—the Kid and others having skinned out an hour or so earlier, right after eating dinner with McSween and just before the arrival of the posse.[13]

Justice Trujillo bound the Seven Rivers arrestees over, then the whole caravan returned to the fort, which, as one observer sarcastically remarked, was
by now beginning to look more and more like the Bastille. About this time
George Coe decided to take a "desperate chance" and go with the Kid to the
fort to see how his cousin Ab Saunders was doing. They found Ab in a hospital cot beside "Dutch" Charlie Kruling, "fighting over the war. They couldn't
either one do nothing and [Kruling said] 'You are the one that shot me, aren't
you, George?' and I said, 'I expect so,' and he said, 'I'm glad of it,' he says."
Obviously Kruling thought a nasty wound through both legs was a cheap
price to pay for getting out of the war.[14]

Further affirming Dudley's partisanship, the McSween adherents were
consigned to the guardhouse; the Seven Rivers contingent were allowed the
freedom of the fort. Expressing himself unwilling to be seen "taking parti-

11.11. Frank Warner Angel.

Graduation photograph, 1868.
Courtesy City College of New York.

Angel was born in Watertown,
New York, May 28, 1845; he died in
Jersey City, March 15, 1906.

11.12. Thomas Benton Catron.

Photographer Brands Studios,
Chicago, date unknown.
R. G. McCubbin Collection.

Catron was born in Lafayette
County, Missouri, October 6,
1840; he died in Santa Fe, May 21,
1921.

san sides," David Easton had resigned his office immediately after issuing the warrants, so now the only remaining magistrate before whom the arrestees could appear was Esquire Trujillo at San Patricio. That left Dudley on the horns of a dilemma; he knew if he sent the prisoners down there, Trujillo would free the McSween men and throw the book at the Seven Rivers crowd. His solution was to dump the whole mess back in Copeland's lap; unable without army support to do anything else, Copeland had no option but to set the prisoners free.

The Seven Rivers contingent departed at once for the south, taking along with them not only Saunders's and MacNab's horses, but also six others belonging to Tunstall they had picked up on their way past his ranch. Three days later, Sheriff Copeland returned to the fort to remove the shackled Doc Scurlock from the guardhouse and take him back to Lincoln, where he promptly turned him loose and swore him as a deputy.[15]

Almost at once, Doc took command of the Regulators, and on May 14 they descended on the Dolan-Riley cattle camp at Black River. Driving off the herders, they rounded up all the horses and mules they could find and drove them back to Lincoln, leaving behind two wounded and at least one dead man— "the Indian," Manuel Segovia, who had been a member of the February 18 posse and also the Indian who had pursued Frank Coe after, it was alleged, killing Frank MacNab.[16]

There was no immediate retaliation. "Everything is quiet in Lincoln County," the *Las Vegas Gazette* reported. "A truce seems to have been tacitly agreed upon." Widenmann, in Lincoln preparing to go to La Mesilla to appear as a witness against Evans, who had taken a change of venue in his trial for the murder of Tunstall, confirmed this and suggested the reason. "Everything is quiet here," he wrote the Tunstall family on June 3, "and Mr. Angel, the gentleman sent out here to investigate things, is busily engaged taking testimony."

Angel's appearance on the scene had a necessarily calming effect: neither side wanted to be seen to commence hostilities with Department of Justice investigator Frank Warner Angel watching. But that did not mean wheels were not turning elsewhere. When they made their attack on the Black River camp, the Regulators had overlooked or ignored the fact that it no longer belonged to Dolan and Riley but to Thomas B. Catron, who fired off letters to Governor Axtell and to Colonel Edward Hatch complaining at the lack of law enforcement in Lincoln County and demanding "some steps be taken to disarm all parties there carrying arms."

It may safely be assumed that in both cases these were merely "cover" confirmations of personal representations already forcefully made, for on May 28, Axtell had promulgated yet another proclamation, this time removing Copeland on a technicality from the office of sheriff and appointing in his place one of the most diligent and loyal of all Dolan's partisans, his "affidavit man," George Peppin.[17]

Nobody on either side was in any doubt about what this meant, not even as inexperienced a newcomer to the unpredictable ebbs and flows of Lincoln County sympathies as Frank Angel, who had arrived just a few days before the issue of the proclamation. His task was not an easy one; getting parti-

PROCLAMATION

BY THE GOVERNOR.

For the information of all the citizens of Lincoln County I do hereby make this **Public Proclamation** :

First---John N. Copeland, Esq., appointed Sheriff by the County Commissioners, having failed for more than thirty days to file his bond as Collector of Taxes, is hereby removed from the office of Sheriff, and I have appointed **GEORGE W. PEPPIN**, Esq., Sheriff of Lincoln County. This has been done in compliance with the laws, passed at the twenty-second session of the Legislative Assembly, relating to Sheriffs.

Second---I command all men and bodies of men, now under arms and traveling about the county, to disarm and return to their homes and their usual pursuits, and so long as the present Sheriff has authority to call upon U. S. troops for assistance, not to act as a sheriff's posse.

And, in conclusion, I urge upon all good citizens to submit to the law, remembering that violence begets violence, and that they who take the sword shall perish by the sword.

S. B. AXTELL,
Governor of New Mexico.

11.13. Axtell's second proclamation, May 28, 1878.

Author's Collection.

sans from both sides to testify to the details of Tunstall's death, however informally (none of the depositions was given under oath), was tricky work, but he managed it, and well. Naturally enough those sympathetic to the McSween cause were the most enthusiastic—by the end of the month McSween, Widenmann, Middleton, Gauss, Henry Brown, Sam Corbet, and the Kid had given depositions—but Angel managed nonetheless to persuade Dolan supporters such as Sam Perry, Wallace Olinger, Bob Beckwith, and even Dolan himself to state their cases as well.

Angel was not going to be in Lincoln much longer, however, and George Peppin was already making preparations to take the initiative the moment he left. He swore in as deputies John Long, Marion Turner, Buck Powell, and José Chavez y Baca, the last doubtless in the hope of recruiting some of the locals to his cause, the others an unambiguous earnest of his intentions. Adding to the unease of the McSween faction was the arrival on the scene of a band of about twenty men calling itself the Rio Grande Posse and led by

11.14. Ameredith Robert B. Olinger *(right)* with James Dolan.

Photograph by Bennett & Brown, Santa Fe, ca. 1879. R. G. McCubbin Collection.

Ameredith R. B. Olinger—the name is confirmed in documentation drawn up by his mother—was born in Delphi, Indiana, in April 1850, the son of William C. and Rebecca (Robinson) Olinger. The other children were John Wallace, born a year earlier, and Rosanna Amanda, born in 1854. Sometime prior to 1859 the family moved to Mound City, Linn County, Kansas, where in 1861 William Olinger died. Rebecca and her children may have moved to Cass County, Missouri, where a number of members of her husband's family settled around 1869; at some point she remarried and became Mrs. Stafford. Bob Olinger does not appear in Lincoln County records until 1878, but it is probable that his brother Wallace had preceded him to the Seven Rivers area. Olinger was involved in a number of killings, although documentation of them is sparse; his part in the death of the Kid's friend John Jones may well have influenced the merciless manner in which Billy the Kid killed him in Lincoln on April 28, 1881.

none other than soldier of fortune John Kinney. It was widely understood that Kinney had been sent by William Rynerson to assist the Dolan cause, that Dolan had offered him five hundred dollars if he killed McSween, and that his gang's payoff would be Tunstall's herd of cattle.

Peppin decided to serve his arrest warrants on Tuesday, June 18, and on that day, as ex officio deputy U.S. marshal, he requested an escort of troops from Colonel Dudley, who sent him a detachment of twenty-seven men commanded by Lieutenant Goodwin. The two parties met about halfway between the fort and Lincoln; however, when Goodwin saw the stripe of some of Kinney's "possemen," he flatly refused to have anything to do with the expedition. Only when Peppin promised to get rid of the undesirables as soon as they reached town did the procession move on.[18]

When they got to Lincoln, however, they found that the Regulators, warned of their impending arrival by the "bush telegraph" of local people they used so much more effectively than did their opponents, had departed for the safety of the hills around San Patricio. Peppin and his men were exultant; outnumbered and outgunned, McSween and his Regulators were on the run. All they had to do now was catch them. One big fight and it would all be over.

CHAPTER TWELVE

Catch as Catch Can

12.1. Henry Carroll.

Photographer unknown, ca. 1885.
National Archives Negative No. 111-
SC-90003.

Carroll was born in Copenhagen,
New York, May 20, 1838; he died in
Colorado Springs on February 12,
1908.

Aᴠᴛᴇʀ ᴛʜᴇ Rᴇɢᴜʟᴀᴛᴏʀs ꜰʟᴇᴅ Lɪɴᴄᴏʟɴ, the character of the skirmishing changed, and heavily armed parties began scouring the hills and canyons trying to find them, ready to shoot on sight. From the onset of the rainy season, which traditionally begins on June 24, the feast day of St. John the Baptist, McSween and his men were constantly on the move, camping each night in a different location and living off the land or some friendly farmer's bounty.

About this time, Frank and George Coe started down to Picacho to meet the Kid and some others who were coming up from Chisum's ranch. "The Kid had been down there resting up," Frank said:

> We did not think there was any of the other outfit in the country. About a mile below San Patricio as we were following down the road that led along the valley we were fired upon as we approached some narrows. They had their horses hid. They fired fifteen or twenty shots at us. We were not very far off, but they got just one good shot at us before we got around the point. We whirled our horses and ran back up the river and started across it and make a stand in Gutieres Cañon, almost opposite San Patricio, but we hit a deep hole in the river and our horses went under. We ran on up the river to make a stand and the other bunch backed off. They thought our [whole] party was there. John Kinney, a noted bully from the Rio Grande, led them. Many of his party were Texas outlaws. They heard of this trouble here and flocked in to get into the game.

Possibly this was the "fighting on the Ruidoso" that Dr. Ealy noted in his diary on June 25, adding that "the Sheriff's posse came in at dark."[1]

The following evening, John Long led another posse of six men down to San Patricio; they bivouacked nearby until daybreak, then stormed into the village. A thorough search turned up nobody more dangerous than a frightened George Washington, who surrendered immediately. As Long and his men set out for Lincoln, they flushed McSween, the Kid, and nine other bodyguards—for such the Regulators had now become—but although a short, sharp exchange of fire took place, the only casualty was Long's horse.[2]

A galloper rode to the fort for reinforcements, and Captain Henry Carroll and his troopers joined the posse in its pursuit of the fugitives, up into the mountains south of the Ruidoso, back north to Hondo, and from there north by northwest to the Blue Water road. It was a "toilsome and disagreeable march," Carroll reported, "the most disagreeable duty that can be assigned to either officer or soldier."[3]

He need not have worried: it was to be his last such assignment for some

12.2. Chisum's
South Spring
Ranch.

Photographer
unknown, ca.
1886–90.
MoNM Negative
No. 93148.

This is not the
original adobe
ranch house,
but the enlarged
dwelling which
Chisum built
after the Lin-
coln County
War.

time. Just twenty-four hours after the skirmish at San Pat, word reached Fort Stanton that on June 18 the U.S. Congress had passed a law forbidding the further use of soldiers in civil actions unless by command of the President. Colonel Dudley had no choice but to recall immediately the detachment supporting Peppin. Their absence hardly cramped the posse's style; on July 3, nominally under the leadership of Chavez y Baca, they descended again on San Patricio, this time tearing the town apart and terrorizing its inhabitants.

According to one report they stole $408 from an old woman, ripped the roof off the Dow Bros. store—a hangout of the Regulators—threw goods out into the street, and helped themselves to whatever they wanted. They fired on men working in the nearby fields, broke windows and doors, and killed a tethered horse because its owner was said to be a McSween sympathizer. "Peppin stated that he would turn those who sympathized with the Regulators out of their houses," the report concluded—"that he would take all their property, that he had the power to do as he pleased. Dolan and Kinney enthusiastically endorsed this sentiment."[4]

With their friends in the Hondo Valley now afraid to shelter them, the Regulators found sanctuary at Chisum's ranch. "Ash Upson kept a little store where Roswell now stands," George Coe recalled:

> There was nothing else there. On the morning of the Fourth [of July] . . . the Kid, Henry Brown and I and another one or two went over to buy some few little articles at the store. While there we saw a big outfit of men riding up from the west, probably from the mountains. They had hardly got in

12.3. Sallie Chisum.

Date and photographer unknown, ca. 1880.
J. Evetts Haley Collection.

The matter of whether Sallie and the Kid were "sweethearts" has given rise to plenty of speculation—due especially to her notebook notation, "Two candi hearts given me by Willia[m] Bonney on the 22 of August [1878]." Placed in its proper context, the entry is less romantic. An entry on page 137 notes, "The happiest I ever was on the 29 of Oct. 1879," and repeated, underlined, "Oct. 29, 1879, Tuesday night bid my friend R— goodbye on the 6. of Nov. 1879." Whoever the mystery friend who made Sallie so happy was, it most certainly was not the Kid.

Source: Sallie Chisum Notebook, Historical Center for Southeast New Mexico, Roswell.

shooting distance when we jumped on our horses and pulled for South Spring River ranch. We had the advantage as we had fresh horses and they had tired ones. We fought a running fight for five miles, all the way to the ranch. There were about twenty five of them and only four or five of us. They never got close enough to hit us.

The "big outfit" was a posse of Seven Rivers men led by Buck Powell and Marion Turner. The Kid and his pals outran the pursuit and took shelter at the Chisum ranch. There was a further sporadic exchange of shots, but Powell knew it was hopeless to try to breach the ranch's four-foot-thick adobe walls. "They stayed off on the prairie too far for our bullets to reach them," Coe said. "We stayed up all night but they never charged us."[5]

If being under siege bothered the Regulators, they seem to have given little sign of it. After all, as a later visitor recalled, the Chisum ranch was "a wonderful place, very pretty, fine orchard and garden, big house . . . and best of all, such good, kind, generous people." One of those people was, of course, Uncle John's twenty-year-old niece, Sallie, "a pretty fair-haired girl, full of life and ready for any kind of sport." Billy had made her acquaintance when the Regulators had stayed over at the ranch with Morton and Baker and had gone fishing with her little brother, Will. He seems to have taken advantage of his time under Chisum's roof to improve the relationship—the trip to Upson's store had been to buy her candy. If Sallie had more than her share of swains, if the Kid was just another name to go into her little journal along with those of Sam McAdams and Charlie Pierce and the "very true friend" she never identified, if there was little or no opportunity for the friendship to become anything else, so what? It doubtless beat all hell out of dodging posses in the rain-swept mountains.[6]

It would appear the siege at Chisum's lasted longer than has hitherto been realized. On July 10, Wallace Olinger, with the Seven Rivers party in Roswell, gave a brother living at Denison, Texas, a not-always-precise overview of events: "There is a mob of twenty five in number, now within four miles of us," he wrote:

> We were over there and they fired on us, forcing us to retire. We are only fifteen in number, but we expect to be reinforced in a day or so by the sheriff and a posse of forty five or fifty men and two companies of soldiers.
>
> We have been under arms for three months, and I don't know how much longer we will have to be. My partner, Charlie Kruling, was wounded a short time ago, shot through both legs just above the ankles, but he is getting along very well. He is in the hospital at Fort Stanton.
>
> At the same time he was wounded the sheriff and several others were killed. The mob say they will kill all of us. We will very likely kill several of them first. We were under fire half a day about a month ago—they were in houses and we were in the creek bottom.
>
> The Sheriff's posse had several fights with them in the mountains, and succeeded in killing several of their horses and running the mob out, but they returned yesterday, and are now fortified in J. S. Chisom's house, at the head of South Spring River, four miles from us at Roswell. John S. Chisom and McSween are paying the mob three dollars a day besides giving them all they can make. We cannot either move or stay at home unless we do it in a body. Bob [Olinger] and three others captured one of the mob, but let him go on his promise not to fight us any more; but he is again in arms against us. This will be a bad thing for some one before it is over with, but I hope not for us. We have everything here that we own, and we mean to stay and protect our property, or die in the attempt.
>
> We have the deputy sheriff with us, but we cannot do anything for our posse is too weak to drive them from their present position. This is the old Chisom war renewed with McSween's help. There have been ten or twelve men killed up to the present, most of them being waylaid and shot at from behind adobe walls, that is the way they do their fighting, they won't come out and fight like men, so it is all the worse for us.
>
> Your Brother, J.W.O.[7]

The dateline of Olinger's letter suggests that the Powell posse was maintaining its blockade of the Chisum ranch against the expected arrival of re-inforcements in the shape of Peppin's posse with supporting troops. Meanwhile, another posse, led by John Kinney, sworn in as a deputy by Peppin on June 28 to legalize the activities of his followers, was scouring the hills around Lincoln. On July 8, it was claimed, a band of renegades led by John Selman swooped down on George Coe's ranch near San Patricio and looted it.[8]

All of them were hunting in the wrong forest. McSween and his men were already heading north up the Pecos in a move designed to confuse their nearest pursuers about both their destination and their intentions. At Ciénaga del Macho they turned west and headed cross-country toward San Patricio. All this is to some extent confirmed in a letter written by Bob Beckwith to his sister Josie the following day, July 11. "We arrived here [Lincoln] yesterday in persuit of McSween's mob," he said, "but did not overtake them. We were under the impression that they were coming to recapture the town but they had not been near it. Today we will start to look for them. We do not know where about in the country they are but suppose they are at the Ruidozo or Feliz. they have recruted to twenty five McSween with them in person our party or Sheriff posee numbers about 35 men. the mob are too cowardly to come to us and fight, we have to look for them like indians."[9]

They would not have to "look for them like indians" much longer. McSween was through running; let the heavens fall, he had decided to return to Lincoln. He may have been encouraged to make this decision because he believed the shooting war had been rendered redundant by his other war of words; according to his wife, McSween "received word from Mr. Angel four days before he was killed that the Indian Agent, the governor and the United States District Attorney were [to be] removed for things they did illegally."[10]

On Sunday evening, July 14, the Regulators came down into the Bonito Valley, where they were reinforced by a sizable band of native New Mexicans led by Martin Chavez of Picacho. Quietly and without firing a shot, the sixty or so men occupied Lincoln, completely outnumbering and cutting off from each other the Peppin men quartered in the Wortley and the old stone *torreón*, a tower built by early settlers as a defense against the Apaches.

Guarding McSween in his own home were the Kid and a dozen others. The rest took up strategic positions around town: Henry Brown, George Coe, and Sam Smith holed up in the adobe grain warehouse in back of the Tunstall building, Martin Chavez and perhaps twenty of his men occupied Patrón's and Montaño's, while Bowdre, Scurlock, and another dozen fighting men took over the Ellis store.

Stranded in the torreón—the men in the McSween house and the Tunstall store between them and the Wortley Hotel, the remainder in Patrón's, Montaño's, and Ellis's preventing any escape in the other direction—were Jack Long, Billy Mathews, Sam Perry, Jim McDaniels, George "Roxy" Rose, and a mystery man called "the Dummy" who professed to be deaf and dumb but in fact was not. Up at the Wortley were Jim Dolan, still using a cane to favor the leg broken in a fall from a horse some months earlier, Peppin, Pantaleón Gallegos, Andy Boyle, Lucio Montoya, and a few others. They were outnumbered and outgunned and they knew it. The rattled Peppin sent a messenger at the gallop to locate the Powell-Kinney posse, which was still combing the hills for the Regulators.

Learning that the men in the torreón were drawing food and water from the Baca house, McSween sent a brusque note accusing Baca of allowing the property, which he owned, to be used "by murderers for the purpose of taking my life" and demanding that Baca vacate within three days. Baca, whose wife had given birth to a child only the day before, appealed to Colonel Dudley for protection. Constrained by the new regulations, the best Dudley could do was send Lieutenant Dan Appel into town to see if he could help.

When Appel spoke to McSween, the lawyer told him bluntly that the Bacas were on his ground and harboring his enemies and they would have to leave;

12.4. Robert W. Beckwith.

Date and photographer unknown. R. N. Mullin Collection, HHC.

Beckwith was born October 16, 1850; he died in Lincoln, July 19, 1878.

12.5. Lincoln, from the southeast.

Photographer unknown, ca. 1885.
R. G. McCubbin Collection.

Clearly visible at the center of the picture are the Dolan house and, almost opposite, the flat-roofed Tunstall store. The Montaño store and its attached outbuildings are on the extreme right; it is just possible to discern the ruined torreón (it was rebuilt in 1936) above it at the edge of the picture. Note particularly the scatterings of other placitas still further west.

if they did not, he would burn them out. He said "I've been out in the hills long enough, and now I've returned to my home they won't drive me away again alive."

Appel tried next to talk the torreón's occupants into leaving the "Indian tower," as they referred to it, but they refused to do so unless Appel sent soldiers to occupy and thus neutralize it. After obtaining McSween's permission to do that, the frustrated Appel got back into his ambulance and headed for the fort.

A high wind was blowing dust in clouds that made it difficult to see. Out of them the Powell-Kinney posse appeared; they had been up in Baca Canyon looking for the McSween party. Appel told them McSween's men had occupied the town and that Boyle, Long, and the others were surrounded in the torreón. "There's no way you boys can get in there," he warned them. "They are everywhere except at Murphy Dolan's store and the old restaurant across the street." Unfazed, the posse "rushed on at full galop and I heard shooting as soon as they reached Wortley's hotel," Appel reported.[11]

The storm was about to break.

12.6. Lincoln, looking east.

Photograph by Dick George, winter 1995.

A re-creation of a well-known picture taken ca. 1890, showing how little the town has changed. The Dolan store is below left and the Tunstall store is visible near the center.

13.1. James J. Dolan.

Photograph by Bostwick, New York, ca. 1879.
R. G. McCubbin Collection.

Born at Loughrea, County Galway, Ireland, on April 22 (parish register) or May 2 (family Bible), 1848, Dolan's family emigrated in 1854 to New York, where Jimmy briefly attended a Christian Brothers school before going to work in a "large fancy goods house" at age twelve. In 1863 he enlisted in Company K, Seventeenth Regiment of New York Zouaves, as a drummer boy; he served two years and was discharged at Alexandria, Virginia. In 1866 he reenlisted in the Thirty-seventh Infantry for a further three years, fighting Indians at Fort Riley in Kansas; he was mustered out at Fort Stanton April 3, 1869, and joined L. G. Murphy & Co. as a clerk.

A heavy drinker with a fiery temper, he was arrested for attempted murder at Fort Stanton in 1873 after trying to kill Captain James F. Randlett, Ninth Cavalry. In May 1877 he shot and killed twenty-year-old Hiraldo Jaramillo, an employee, who he claimed attacked him with a knife.

On July 13, 1879, he married Caroline Frances Fritz; their children were Emil, born May 2, 1880 (died at age two); Caroline, born February 19, 1882; Louise, born November 30, 1883 (died at age six); and Bessie, born September 20, 1886. Caroline Fritz died nine days after Bessie was born.

In 1884, Dolan was elected county treasurer and served in that office for four years; in 1888 he was elected to the territorial senate, representing Lincoln, Doña Ana, Sierra, and Grant Counties. That same year he married Maria Eva Whitlock, his children's nurse. On June 3, 1889, he was appointed receiver of the land office at Las Cruces, but he resigned after two years. In partnership with William Rynerson and Numa Reymond, Dolan formed the Feliz Land and Cattle Company, which took over the range Tunstall had never proved up on; in 1894, Dolan built a handsome home there which became known as the Flying H. He died on February 26, 1898.

Source: personal research in Ireland; Jones, *Tree Branches*.

CHAPTER THIRTEEN
The Storm Breaks

S PILLING OFF THEIR HORSES IN THE CORRAL of the Wortley Hotel, Buck Powell's posse announced their arrival with a dozen or so rifle shots which whacked splinters out of the closed shutters on the west side of the McSween house. Hearing this fusillade, a group of Regulators led by the Kid dashed toward it from the Montaño store. As they passed the torreón, Jack Long "hollered at them to halt, they answered me by shooting at me. I returned the fire with the fire of the men I had there with me."[1] A burst of fire from the McSween house scattered the men in the Wortley corral as the Kid and his group reached shelter unscathed.

This is a Billy totally different from the homeless youngster who had arrived in Lincoln County the preceding fall. In the four short months since Tunstall's death he has matured from callow drifter to confident fighting man, in the thick of it every time there is shooting, trusted by his comrades and respected by the opposition. He was "brave and reliable," Frank Coe said, "one of the best soldiers we had. He never pushed his advice or opinions, but he had a wonderful presence of mind; the tighter the place the more he showed his cool nerve and quick brain."[2]

He was going to need both. Up at the Wortley, the Murphys—as the Regulators called Dolan's cohorts—were preparing an all-out assault on the "Modocs"—the contemptuous name given to the McSween faction by a Seven Rivers veteran of the preceding year's Modoc War. Ranged alongside Dolan were some forty fighting men, including George Peppin, Billy Mathews, Jesse Evans—bailed by Judge Bristol and awaiting trial for the murder of Tunstall—Johnnie Hurley, Jim McDaniels, John Kinney, "Roxy" Rose, Charlie "Lollycooler" Crawford, Roscoe "Rustling Bob" Bryant, Sam Perry, Marion Turner, Milo Pierce, Bob and John Beckwith, Bob and Wallace Olinger, Billy Johnson, Andy Boyle, Charlie Hart, Jack Irving, Josiah Nash, Jake Owen, Buck Powell, José Chavez y Baca, Pantaleón Gallegos, Lucio Montoya and another native New Mexican named Eduardo, John, Jim, and Tom Jones, Buck Waters, Jack Thornton, Jim Reese, John Collins, L. R. Parker, John Chambers, and "the Dummy," who "passed as deaf and dumb until about the early fight when he was made to speak."[3]

Against them in McSween's substantial U-shaped adobe mansion stood the Kid, Doc Scurlock, Jim French, Henry Brown, Joe Smith, Tom Cullins, Charlie Bowdre, José Chávez y Chávez, Florencio Chaves, Vicente Romero, Ignacio Gonzales, Francisco Zamora, José María Sánchez, Yginio Salazar, and the Kid's new and inseparable sidekick, Tom O'Folliard. Also in the house were McSween and his wife, Elizabeth Shield (her husband was in Santa Fe

13.2. Milo Lucius Pierce.

Date and photographer unknown, ca. 1880s.
Historical Museum for Southeast New Mexico, Roswell.

Pierce was born in Lincoln, Logan County, Illinois, on August 13, 1839; he died in Roswell, New Mexico, on October 20, 1919.

13.3. *(Left)* William R. "Jake" Owen.

Photograph by Ray V. Davis, ca. 1932. Courtesy Southeastern New Mexico Historical Society.

Owen was born in Wales about 1856 and died in Carlsbad, New Mexico, December 24, 1939.

13.4. *(Right)* John Yeoman Thornton.

Photograph by Baker & Johnston, Roswell, date unknown, ca. 1880s. R. G. McCubbin Collection.

Thornton was born in Danville, Pennsylvania, on January 26, 1856; he died in Roswell on August 16, 1919.

attending court), her five children, and Harvey Morris, thirty, a former resident of New York state who was reading law in the McSween & Shield office.

Forty yards east, behind the stout walls of a grain warehouse in back of the Tunstall store, were Henry Brown, George Coe, and Sam Smith, while safe behind the steel-lined shutters of the store itself were schoolteacher Susan Gates and Dr. and Mrs. Ealy and their two children. On the opposite side and further down the street Martin Chavez, Fernando Herrera, and most of the native New Mexicans—twenty men or more—manned the Montaño store. Also in there were Josefa Montaño, Teresa Phillipowski, and Ellen Bolton.

Others of the group that had come up the valley with Chavez occupied the Patrón building, while a couple of hundred yards further east, Charlie Bowdre, Frank Coe, John Middleton, Steve Stephens, and another eight or ten men invested the Ellis store, making the total McSween force about sixty.

With the battle lines firmly drawn, someone had to make the first move, and that someone was Dolan, who had Peppin send Jack Long to the McSween house with arrest warrants for the Kid and others. His demand for their surrender was greeted with a stutter of shots, and Long ran for cover. "There was a lot of shooting that day," Mary Ealy recorded, "but I don't think anyone was killed."[4]

Night put an end to the fighting; after dark old Green Wilson crept up to the window of the Tunstall store and told Dr. Ealy a man was dying and needed his help. Ealy went with him, but as they passed the torreón its occupants heard them and opened fire. Wilson called out that he was taking the doctor to see a dying man; as it transpired, their mercy dash was futile. Dan Huff, a local carpenter who had been poisoned by one of his relatives,

13.5. Seven Rivers men.

Date and photographer unknown, 1870s; the original is a tintype. R. N. Mullin Collection.

The men were identified by Eve Ball, to whom the photograph was given by the Jones family, as, *rear, left to right:* Jim Jones and Marion F. Turner; *seated, left to right:* Bob Speakes and John Jones. Others believe the man at front left is Buck Powell.

died before morning. His body was brought over to the burial ground east of the Tunstall store, where Sebrian Bates and George Washington had dug a grave; as they were committing the body to the ground, the men in the torreón fired at them. They dumped the body unceremoniously into the grave and ran for their lives.[5]

Tuesday, the two factions kept up sporadic fire at each other all day, but each side knew any kind of direct assault was tantamount to suicide. At this point one of the Dolan crowd had a great idea. A note was written to Colonel Dudley and signed by Peppin (he was at best semiliterate) which said, in part: "If it is within your power to loan me one of your howitzers, I am of the opinion that the parties for whom I have warrants would surrender without a shot being fired. Should it be in your power to do this in favor of the law, you will confer a good favor on the majority of the people of this county, who are being persecuted by a lawless mob."[6]

13.6. Elizabeth (Hummer) Shield.

Date and photographer unknown, ca. 1890.
Author's Collection.

Elizabeth Shield was Susan McSween's older sister. She was born in Adams County, Pennsylvania in 1841, the fourth child of Peter and Elizabeth (Stauffer) Hummer. She had six (possibly seven) children, one of whom died of smallpox in Lincoln soon after the family arrived there. After her husband died, she remained in Las Vegas until the 1890s, then moved to Los Angeles, where she died on December 13, 1916.

Sources: Frederick Nolan, "The Search for Alexander McSween," *New Mexico Historical Review* 62, no. 2 (July 1987): 287–301; pension application of David P. Shield.

The mind boggles at the idea of what havoc Peppin might have wrought had Dudley granted his request, but Dudley, who would have liked to oblige, was constrained by his orders to refuse. At 6:30 P.M. trooper Berry Robinson was dispatched to Lincoln carrying a letter to that effect. As he rode into town, "the men at the McSween house shot at me through portholes on the top," he said. "The sun had not yet set and I am sure they could see I was a soldier."[7]

Stung by this "infamous outrage," as he termed it, Dudley detailed a board of officers—Captains George Purington and Tom Blair and Dr. Appel—to investigate and fix responsibility for the incident. Escorted by five troopers, they arrived in town about noon the next day and checked it from one end to the other. They found "everything closed, every home closed, no one in the street. In one end of town there was a body of 50 men, or such a number, men in the hills to the right [south] of town and these men were keeping up a continuous fire into the town and from the town."[8]

In fact, the morning had begun quietly, so quietly that Charlie Crawford and Lucio Montoya—two of the men Peppin had posted in the hills south of town—were deceived into believing the McSween party had moved out and started down to rejoin the posse. A shot—fired, according to tradition, from a Sharps rifle by Doc Scurlock's father-in-law, a red-headed Basque named Fernando Herrera—tore through Crawford's body from hip to hip, piercing the spinal cord. He fell mortally wounded as Montoya scampered down the hill to safety; he was still lying up there in the broiling midday sun when the officers from Fort Stanton arrived.

As yet unaware of Crawford's plight, they began by questioning Peppin's possemen at the Wortley, where Dolan and Peppin confirmed Robinson's story and added that they had shouted to the men in the McSween house that they were firing at a soldier, but the warning had been ignored. The officers then visited the McSween house and interrogated the lawyer. They concluded, in spite of his denials, that the shots had indeed come from the McSween house.

It was only now they learned that Crawford had been hit. Accompanied by Blair and two enlisted men, the doctor clambered up the slope to where the dying man lay groaning; as they did, they were fired on. "We thought [the shots] came from the Montano house, judging from the direction of the loud whistling they made on the hill," Appel said.[9]

They got Crawford down somehow and took him back to the post hospital; he died there a week later, a long way from his Iowa home. The fighting continued; on Wednesday night, Ben Ellis was shot through the neck while feeding a mule. A couple of men from the Ellis store made their way upriver and begged Dr. Ealy to attend the wounded man, who might otherwise bleed to death. The doctor pluckily went with them, but when a volley of shots smacked into the adobe wall he was sidling along—it was a bright, moonlit night—he scuttled back to the safety of the Tunstall store.

Next morning, however, the good doctor "boldly walked down the middle of the street" to the Ellis house holding his five-year-old daughter Pearl's hand, his wife carrying their baby daughter Ruth beside him, "and there sat Ben waiting for the sergean." The ball had hit him "below the left ear, and passed obliquely between the Aesophagus and trachea," said Dr. Ealy. "It struck the clavicle [and] glanced along the bone to the shoulder," but fortunately it missed the subclavian artery. Ealy recorded irritably that after he stitched the wound up, "The cow boys stole my needle before I finished my work."[10]

If nothing else, Dr. Ealy's boldness confirms the growing confidence of the McSween party. Dudley's report written that day suggests a reason:

> The latest reliable reports give McSween's strength in Lincoln . . . as 63 men. That of the sheriff's posse about 40. Both are thoroughly armed and were supplied with ammunition and I think with 18 days of provisions at least. It is reported that Chisum and some other leader of the party are en route to Lincoln with 35 men and a six pounder. I question the correctness of this report. Still, it may be true, if so the sheriff's posse will have to vacate in a hurry, but whoever thinks this is going to end the war is most seriously mistaken.[11]

13.7. Taylor F. Ealy.

Photographer unknown, ca. 1870.
Author's Collection.

The rumor that reinforcements in such numbers might be on the way would certainly explain why—although all the parties involved vehemently denied any such meeting ever took place—Jimmy Dolan came up to the fort to ask Dudley for help. Teamster Samuel Beard, who, as far as can be ascertained, had no ax to grind, said that on the evening of July 18 he overheard Dudley tell Dolan to "go down and stand them off, and he would be there by twelve o'clock" the following day.

True or not, that same evening Dudley called a meeting of his officers at which it was agreed "for the preservation of the lives of the women and Children" the military would intervene. The following morning, with Captain George Purington leading the column, four officers, a company of cavalry, and another of infantry—a curiously coincidental thirty-five men in all, not to mention a twelve-pound howitzer and a Gatling gun—marched into Lincoln.[12]

If McSween was dismayed by this development there is no sign of foreboding in the jaunty note he wrote that morning to Ash Upson in Roswell, ordering stamps and assuring him that his "School business" would be attended to soon. Perhaps even now he believed the war was won and he the winner.[13]

Outside the Wortley, Dudley halted his command and harangued the possemen assembled there to the effect that he had not come to Lincoln to help them, only to protect women and children. He had no idea which houses were occupied by whom, but if anyone of either party killed or wounded one of his officers or men he would open fire on them with his howitzer.

Peppin must have remonstrated, because Dudley exploded. "God damn you understand me," he snapped, "if one of your men wound one of my men I will blow you above the clouds." That said, he marched his command down the street past the McSween house to some open ground below a partially built adobe structure opposite the Montaño store, where he ordered his detachment to pitch camp.[14]

In spite of the fine words he attributed to himself (and which no one else seems to have recorded), neither now nor at any time later did Dudley make

13.8. Mary M. "Minnie" Shield.

Photograph by Crispell Art Parlors, East Las Vegas, ca. 1886. Rio Grande Historical Collections, NMSU.

Shield was born at Osceola, Missouri, on April 10, 1868; she died in Los Angeles on May 4, 1944.

the slightest attempt to establish where the women and children he had ostensibly come to protect might be. His first action on reaching the campsite was to order the howitzer trained on the Montaño house. If he noticed, or cared, that Dolan's men had used his progress as cover to occupy strategic positions all around the McSween home—Bob Olinger and some others occupying Steve Stanley's house; Johnny Hurley, Green Wilson's hillside jacal; a party led by Andy Boyle moving into the stable in back of the McSween house; Billy Mathews, Sam Perry, and Pantaleón Gallegos in the deserted Schon house—he did nothing to stop them. Peppin decided on the torreón for headquarters; Jimmy Dolan took cover in the Mills house.

Rendered vastly uneasy by the sight of the cannon pointing at them—not to mention Captain Blair's repeating the warning Dudley had given Peppin's party—Martin Chavez and his men abandoned their positions in the Montaño and Patrón houses and retreated down the street to the Ellis house, covering their heads with blankets so the Dolan men could not identify them. A half hour after Dudley's arrival, McSween's hold on the town was broken, and the men in his house were now totally cut off; if they were attacked, not only could they not shoot eastward for fear of hitting soldiers, but also their allies at the Ellis house could not fire at their attackers for the same reason.

As Peppin came up the street flanked by soldiers, Susan McSween stepped out to ask them what was going on. They do not seem to have bothered to reply. "Well, after this we all became alarmed," she said, "all who were in the house seeing Peppin guarded by soldiers."[15]

Perhaps prompted by the sight of Dolan's men hanging a black flag—the old Mexican signal of "no quarter"—McSween's earlier confidence vanished; he scribbled a note to Colonel Dudley on his law practice notepaper and handed it to the Kid to read before giving it to his niece Minnie Shield to deliver:

> Genl Dudley USA. Would you have the kindness to tell me why soldiers surround my house?
> Before blowing up my property, I would like to know the reason. The constable [José Chávez y Chávez] is here and has warrants for the arrest of Sheriff Peppin and posse for murder and larceny.
>
> Respectfully, A. A. McSween.[16]

On Dudley's order his adjutant, Lieutenant Millard Goodwin, tore a page from a notebook and sent this elephantinely sarcastic reply:

> A. A. McSween, Sir. I am directed by the Commanding Officer to inform you that no troops have surrounded your house, and that he desires to hold no correspondence with you. He directed me to say that if you desire to blow up your house he has no objection providing you do not injure any of his command by so doing.[17]

Late in the morning some of the Seven Rivers men, led by Marion Turner, managed to get close enough to the McSween house to pry some of the shutters loose from the windows. Using the butts of their rifles they smashed in

13.9. The Montaño store.

Date and photographer unknown, ca. 1920s.
R. N. Mullin Collection.

This early photograph of the frontage of the Montaño store shows it with the original flat roof and without modern "improvements."

the windows and knocked down the adobe bricks that had been piled up in the window apertures as barricades. Turner yelled out that he wanted to talk to McSween.

"What do you want?" McSween called out.

"I have warrants for you and others in the house," Turner shouted. "Will you surrender?"

"We have warrants for you," McSween replied.

"Show me your warrants," Turner yelled. "Where are they?"

Jim French replied for McSween. "They're in our guns, you cocksucking sons of bitches!"

No further attempt was made after this to solicit the surrender of the men in the McSween house.[18]

At about the same time, Dudley sent for Peppin to tell him the men from the Montaño store had gone down to the Ellis place and suggested Peppin head them off. As Peppin ran down the street accompanied by Bob Beckwith, John Jones, Johnny Hurley, and one or two others, Lieutenant Goodwin positioned the artillery so that the howitzer was pointing down the street and the Gatling gun at the foothills across the Bonito behind the Ellis house. "I might state," said Goodwin, "that the strictest orders were given that under no circumstances would Sgt. Kelsey or Sgt Keefe fire the guns without receiving orders to do so."[19]

Of course; but the men in the Ellis house did not know that. They had already saddled up, and as Peppin and his men approached, they racked out, firing back at the possemen and slightly wounding John Jones. With two-thirds of the McSween force driven away into the hills and powerless to help

13.10. Susan McSween.

Photograph by Fromhart and Benson, Kansas City, ca. 1895. R. G. McCubbin Collection.

their leader, a more confident Peppin led his men back up the street toward the McSween house, Bob Beckwith carrying a bucket of coal oil he had filled at the Ellis place. Near the torreón he was met by a disgruntled Dudley, mightily annoyed because Peppin had allowed his quarry to escape.

Although he had still made no attempt to establish the whereabouts of any of the women and children he had come to protect—there were two women and five children in the McSween house, three women and their children in Montaño's, the Ealys and their two baby daughters in the Tunstall store, and a dozen or so native New Mexican families still in town—Dudley found time to bully timid Green Wilson into issuing a warrant for McSween's arrest, which he handed to Peppin. Peppin deputized the handiest man, Bob Beckwith, and told him to go serve the warrant while he, Peppin, organized a work party consisting of John Kinney and Johnny Hurley, who forced Sebrian Bates and Joe Dixon to help them pile lumber against the east side of the McSween house with a view to setting it on fire.

Frightened by what was happening, Susan McSween determined to make her way to Dudley's camp in the hope of getting him to intervene. Crawling on her hands and knees until she was clear of the house, she hurried down the street. Encountering George Peppin near the torreón, she demanded to know why he was trying to burn down her house. He told her if she didn't want the house burned down she should persuade the men in there to surrender.

"Then I shall go to Colonel Dudley's camp to get protection!" she flared.

"You needn't think you'll get protection from Colonel Dudley or anyone else when you harbor such men in your house!" he retorted angrily.

She hurried past him and down the street to the military encampment and demanded to see Dudley. Her attempt to enlist his support turned into a vituperative slanging match. In the end Dudley ordered the guard to put her out of camp.

"Colonel Dudley, you surely will regret that you would not give me protection, or Mr. McSween," she shrilled. "I see through your whole intention now. I expect nothing less than that they will kill him in his own house, even though they have a warrant for him they will not arrest him, they will kill him!"[20]

Her outburst does not appear to have bothered Dudley unduly; he turned on his heel and disappeared into his tent, leaving her to make her way back to her house to tell those inside what had transpired. When she got there she saw Jack Long and the Dummy splash coal oil against the walls of the kitchen at the northeastern corner of the house and light it; as they scampered through the gate, George Coe, Henry Brown, and Sam Smith opened up on them from the Tunstall store, and the two men took shelter in the only available cover, the privy hole. They remained standing there until well after dark. "It was not a good place to sit down," Long drily remarked.[21]

The first attempt to fire the house failed; Elizabeth Shield and her daughter Minnie extinguished it with water Minnie had brought up from the river. But a short while afterwards Andy Boyle, who had narrowly missed being killed by a bullet that burned his neck, managed to set fire to a pile of kindling and wood shavings laid against the wooden frame of a lean-to used as a summer kitchen. When it began to burn, the men inside the house rushed to staunch the flames only to be driven back by heavy fire from the Peppin men forted up in McSween's stable.

The fire took hold and moved slowly southward along the house, thick smoke coiling upward into the still sky; the defenders retreated from room to room as the heat made occupancy impossible. Sometime late during the afternoon, a keg of gunpowder exploded in the house; after that the flames advanced more rapidly. Begrimed by the oily residue of countless black powder explosions, confined for more than a hundred hours with only the most primitive sanitary arrangements available to them, coughing and retching as they fought the inexorable advance of the leaping flames, the Kid and his compañeros must have been a sorry sight.

"The boys talked to each other and McSween and I were sitting in one corner," Susan McSween recounted. "The boys decided I should leave. They were fighting the fire in my sister's house [the east wing]. McSween said he guessed that was better. The neighbors told me [later] that Dudley got uneasy then. They said he stood on a hill near the store and said: 'My God, why does not that woman come out?' The Kid was lively and McSween was sad. McSween sat with his head down, and the Kid shook him and told him to get up, that they were going to make a break."[22]

Meanwhile, Mary Ealy had persuaded Dudley to give her and her children his protection, and the firing slacked off as Dr. Appel, Captain Blair, and six enlisted men stopped outside the Tunstall store in a wagon to take the family to safety. Susan McSween ran out and begged the officers to extend their protection to herself and her sister; they immediately agreed and stood guard while Susan, Elizabeth Shield, and her five children ran along the street to the wagon, in which they were all taken to the Patrón house.

As darkness closed in, "the house was in a great blaze lighting up the hills on both sides of the town," Dr. Appel recalled. The gunfire increased in intensity; experienced officers estimated that more than two thousand rounds were fired during the evening. The situation inside the McSween house was truly desperate. McSween "sat in a daze and the Kid slapped him and shook him and pulled his hair and told him to pull himself together and make a run for it." Dr. Ealy confirms this. "Two or three men with him . . . said to him now we must break and run for our lives."

"Boys," McSween said, "I have lost my mind!"[23]

No one will ever know for sure what happened in that last hour, other than that as they retreated into the already fire-damaged kitchen, the last unburned room in the house, the Kid took command. Huddled together, the defenders evolved a desperate strategy: the Kid and four others—Chávez y Chávez, Harvey Morris, Jim French, and Tom O'Folliard—would make a break for the gate in the fence bordering the eastern edge of the property and try to get to the Tunstall store, drawing the fire of the attackers. Under cover of this distraction McSween and the others, shielded by the chicken house from the fire of the men in the stable, would run silently in stockinged feet for the gate in the rear adobe wall and down the steep declivity behind it to the river.[24]

They made their move, the Kid said, a little after dark. "The house was burning," he said. "Made it almost as light as day for a short distance around."

13.11. Lieutenant Colonel N. A. M. Dudley, Ninth Cavalry.

Photographer unknown, 1881. Courtesy of Massachusetts Commandery, Military Order of the Loyal Legion, and the U.S. Army Military History Institute.

This portrait of Dudley almost certainly captures the expression he must have been wearing when he had Susan McSween escorted from his camp on July 19, 1878. He looks a lot older than his fifty-six years.

13.12. Tom O'Folliard.

Date and photographer unknown. Author's Collection.

O'Folliard was born in Uvalde, Texas, in 1858; he died at Fort Sumner, New Mexico, on December 19, 1880.

The authenticity of this photograph has been challenged on two grounds: first, that O'Folliard was a big man who weighed about 180 pounds, and second, that the clothing does not appear to be contemporary. Nevertheless, it has been accepted as the only known picture for many years.

Once across that few yards of lighted area, darkness would protect them. The traditional scenario for this event, fueled by a thousand book jackets and a dozen movies, is that they all came out guns blazing, but it appears they first tried to sneak out; it was only when they were seen that the shooting started.[25]

"I came out slowly, tolerably slowly because they were not firing at the time," Chávez y Chávez said. "I went slowly until I saw the soldiers fire, then I went with all my might. . . . There was no firing when I came out until I got to the point in the middle between the two houses [McSween's and Tunstall's.]"[26]

"Some four or five men made a break," Joe Nash testified. "We fired at them as they ran out of the east gate and [across] the space between the McSween and Tunstall premises and until they were out of sight, and could see them pretty plainly by the glare of the light of the McSween building. It being some lighter east of the house."[27]

First to fall in that hail of bullets was Harvey Morris, who got as far as the gate before a single shot killed him. Even as he fell, the Kid was through the gate. Some men he thought were soldiers fired at him from the Tunstall store, turning him toward the river, firing now as he ran, Chávez y Chávez, Frenchy, and Tom O'Folliard close behind. One of the Kid's shots gave John Kinney, sheltering behind the wall at the rear of the house, a nasty moment. "The Kid shot his mustache off . . . . The bullet just cut his lip. He dropped back like he was dead. The Kid thought he had killed him, jumped the fence and ran on. Kinney said he might have killed the Kid as he ran off but he was afraid to raise up as he was afraid the next man coming out of the door would get him."[28]

The second group had meanwhile emerged from the house and was moving stealthily toward the rear wall. "These walls threw their shadows over the space of ground immediately between the gate and the house," Nash said, "and made it almost impossible to distinguish any person when in dark clothes on the grounds. I think that these parties secreted themselves there when the first party made their escape."

Nash, John Jones, Andy Boyle, and Bob Beckwith were guarding the gate in the rear wall. "While we were there someone of the McSween party called out to us to know if we would take them as prisoners. Robert Beckwith replied that he would, that he came for that purpose. . . . Then the man called Dummy come up, walked in to where those parties that asked to be taken [prisoner] were. John Jones, Robert Beckwith, and myself followed."

Two of the McSween men had taken cover in the chicken house; one of them shot Beckwith dead as he stepped forward to serve his warrant. "Then McSween and those on the outside of the chicken house began to fire on John Jones, Dummy and myself," Nash said, "and at the same time run towards the gate trying to make their escape and we returned the fire."[29]

"[T]hen the fire became Promiscuous and that was the time the Big Killing was made," Andy Boyle said. "Robert Beckwith fell first with McSween on top of him and two Mexicans right beside them."

"I came very nearly being hit by someone shooting from the chicken house," Joe Nash said. He and Boyle got a log and punched a hole through the adobe wall with it "and called out to the parties in the house to surrender. They said they would not and had never intended to. Then Andy fired

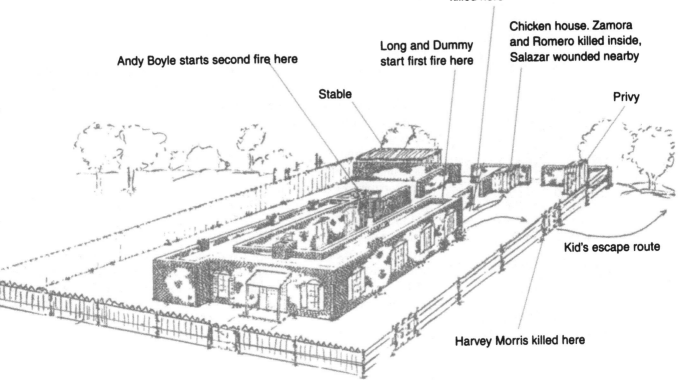

Andy Boyle starts second fire here

Stable

Long and Dummy start first fire here

McSween and Beckwith killed here

Chicken house. Zamora and Romero killed inside, Salazar wounded nearby

Privy

Kid's escape route

Harvey Morris killed here

13.13. The McSween house as it appeared in July 1878.

Courtesy Human Systems Resources and Lincoln County Heritage Trust.

This artist's conception by Linda P. Hart shows the general layout of the house looking north, although it is possible that by the time of the "Big Killing" two extra rooms had been built inside the southern bend of the U to accommodate the Shield family. The two sets of arrows show the escape routes, the successful one followed by the Kid, and the one taken by McSween, Romero, and Zamora, who were driven back in their attempt to reach the rear exit.

two or three shots into the chicken house through the hole. . . . By that time the house was nearly burned up so I dragged McSween out of danger of being burned and some of the boys of our party carried Robert Beckwith away."[30]

It was all over. One man, possibly two, had died inside the house during the fighting. Lying dead near the smoldering ruins were McSween, Harvey Morris, Francisco Zamora, Vicente Romero, and—it appeared—fifteen-year-old Yginio Salazar. John Kinney went over and kicked the recumbent figure; he was about to administer a coup de grâce when Milo Pierce told him not to waste his bullets, the man was as dead as a herring. Later testimony would

13.14. Yginio Salazar.

Photographed from a painting by
Frankie Simons.
Courtesy Joe Salazar.

Salazar was born in Valencia,
February 14, 1863; he died in Lincoln, January 7, 1936.

show that in the confusion Florencio Chaves and José María Sánchez had escaped unhurt and that Ignacio Gonzales had taken a bullet in the arm as he ran.[31]

The victors got liquor and got drunk, firing their guns into the air and whooping it up into the small hours, forcing McSween's servants Bates and Washington to play their fiddles while they caroused. Others broke open the now empty Tunstall store and helped themselves to whatever took their fancy.

After the revelers finally reeled off to their beds, Yginio Salazar, with two bullets in his body and weak from loss of blood, began an agonizing crawl along the riverbank to his sister-in-law's house half a mile away; somehow, almost miraculously, he made it. The Kid and his compañeros, hiding out in the hills, no doubt spent the night torn between elation at their own escape and misery over the fate of their friends.

As for the officers and gentlemen encamped a few hundred yards away, not the slightest attempt was made by any one of them to protest, to intervene, or to see if anyone needed medical assistance; nor was a single word of disapproval expressed at the barbarity of what had taken place that bloodstained day. While they all slept soundly on their cots, the bullet-riddled bodies of McSween, Morris, Zamora, and Romero lay where they had fallen. No one went near them. No one dared.

CHAPTER FOURTEEN

Rustlers

O<small>N THE MORNING OF JULY 20</small> a coroner's jury was assembled and tamely found that McSween, Romero, Zamora, and Morris had come to their deaths "by rifle shots from the hands of the Sheriff's posse." McSween had been shot five times, Zamora eight, Romero three, and Morris once. Friends and family removed the bodies of Zamora and Romero. Even as the attorney and the young New Yorker were unceremoniously buried—there was "no coffin, no hymn, no prayer," as Dr. Ealy recalled—the Tunstall store was being looted again, as it would be several times more in the next twenty-four hours.[1]

By following the bloodstains Yginio Salazar had left in his agonizing half-mile crawl, John Kinney and three other bravos tracked the youth to the home of his sister-in-law and threatened to kill him. Only the presence of Dr. Appel saved Yginio's life: he told Kinney and his men that if they harmed Salazar, he would see them hanged.[2]

"One thing is sure," Dudley reported. "A deep revenge will be sought by the sheriff's posse for the loss of their pet leader *Beckwith*, and a still stronger spirit exists on the part of the McSween men to retaliate for the death of their headman, McSween." In this he was entirely correct; there was not the slightest inclination on the part of the "victors" to allow the "defeated" side to depart in peace: they were to be hunted down, either driven out of the country or killed. By the same token, there was no perception on the part of the "defeated" side that they had lost; vengeance for the death of McSween must now be added to that which had been sought for John Tunstall.

Perhaps fortunately, they seemed unable to locate each other. "From the most reliable information I have," Dudley reported on July 27, "I believe the Sheriff's posse has traced the McSween party to the Pecos; the last report places them only six miles ahead of the sheriff's party. Another fight may be expected anyway. If they will only keep out of towns it matters little how much shooting they do."[3]

The first priority facing the Regulators was finding replacement horses for those that they had perforce abandoned in the Ellis corral and that had been gleefully appropriated by Peppin's possemen. This they did by the simple expedient of stealing what they needed—targeting an unfortunate traveler they encountered on the road and raiding the Casey ranch, and, on August 5, the Mescalero agency, where they killed agency clerk Morris Bernstein.

A cloud of conflicting motives hangs over what at first appears to have been a callous and gratuitous slaying. On the face of it, a band of nineteen men, including the Kid, Tom O'Folliard, Steve Stephens, the Coes, Doc

14.1. The Mescalero Apache Reservation Agency.

Date and photographer unknown, ca. 1880s.
MoNM Negative No. 76123.

This view, looking west, shows buildings that may have been part of the Blazer's Mill settlement. The corrals in which the horses and mules were kept can be plainly seen. Bernstein was probably killed beyond one of the two rises in the near background.

Scurlock, Charlie Bowdre, Henry Brown, Jim French, John Middleton, John Scroggins, Fernando Herrera, Ignacio Gonzales, and Atanacio Martinez, descended upon the agency. As they neared the settlement, the party divided, the Americans heading for a nearby spring while the native New Mexicans continued on down the road.

As they did, the latter group encountered a band of "wild" Indians—that is, Mescaleros so angered by the continued lack of beef and other supplies that they had left the agency to hunt for their own food—and firing broke out between the two parties. At the issue house, where Godfroy and Bernstein were distributing rations, the Apache women nearest the windows "threw back their rations for safe keeping and ran in all directions," Godfroy said. "Mr. Bernstein ran out, going towards the shooting. I councilled him to be very cautious as we did not know who the firing was done by That I was afraid that the wild Indians had just come in had met some of the Indians here and were fighting with them."

As Bernstein galloped off toward the sound of shooting, Godfroy got another horse and followed. "I saw him ride over the crest of the hill, from behind which the shooting was done, and before I got halfway, I saw the horse had been riderless," he said. "I knew then that he was killed, but not by the Indians." How he knew, he was never called upon to explain.

Godfroy retreated toward the safety of the agency, followed by a flurry of shots. "I knew it would be folly to remain there longer, as I would certainly be killed. Knowing that Lieut. Smith and four soldiers were at my house . . . I started to get their assistance."[4]

In the melée on the hillside, four Regulator horses had been spooked, leaving their riders—one of them the Kid—afoot. George Coe pulled Billy up behind him as the soldiers came at the gallop. "I'll bet they shot fifty times at us," George Coe remembered. "We were having to ride on the sides of our horses but they never touched a hair of us."[5]

Having successfully drawn away the guard, the Regulators now swung around to the agency corral, which was full of horses and mules, threw open the gates, and drove every head of them off, the Kid riding one of the ponies bareback. Back on the now deserted hillside Godfroy found the body of Morris Bernstein "lying on its face, with four bullet holes in it. His Winchester rifle, pistol and cartridges were gone, his pockets were turned out and contents gone."[6]

Godfroy's evidence makes it all seem fairly straightforward, if brutal. The Regulators rode in intending to steal horses and instead ran into unexpected opposition; they did not expect Mescaleros to be armed. Bernstein rode headlong into the shooting affray and was shot down. But there was a lot more going on at the agency than any of the official reports and subsequent investigations indicate.

Within a day of that last murderous night in Lincoln, Saturnino Baca, all his professed fears for his own and his family's lives apparently assuaged, was on the road to Manzano with two wagons containing between ten thousand and twelve thousand pounds—over five tons—of merchandise stolen from the Mescalero Apache reservation. Tipped off by Department of Justice investigator Frank Angel, U.S. Marshal John Sherman had the goods—which were found in the possession of Neustadt Brothers, the principal mercantile firm of Los Lunas—impounded.[7]

As a result, all the parties involved in this large-scale (and doubtlessly hugely profitable) conspiracy were edgy and frightened. The ongoing "arrangement"—the Indian agent's turning a blind eye to Dr. Joseph Blazer's illegal exploitation of Mescalero reservation timberland as long as Blazer in turn disregarded their plundering of the agency supplies—seems to have suddenly collapsed, with each at the other's throat.

On August 1, Fred Godfroy, who had business in Lincoln, had asked if he might accompany Captain Blair there, as he was afraid to go alone. At Lincoln, Saturnino Baca, back from his freighting trip to Manzano and claiming his life had been threatened by "Frenchy and Charlie," persuaded Captain Blair to recommend that the military guard protecting him be left in place. Two days later, on August 3, Godfroy again requested a military escort when he returned to the agency from Fort Stanton. "I have reliable information that there are on the road between here and there several men among them 'Kid' and Brown," he said, "the former of whom I know positively intended to kill me and if I went alone I am sure my life would be endangered."[8]

But was it truly the Kid and Henry Brown he feared? It is difficult to imagine what motive either of them might have had for killing him, whereas a lot of other things were happening around Godfroy which constituted a much more immediate threat. Dr. Blazer had been involved a day or two earlier in a fierce row with Morris Bernstein; it can be inferred from the existing documentation that he called Bernstein a thief who, by depriving the

14.2. Lieutenant Millard F. Goodwin.

Photographer unknown, ca. 1880. National Archives Negative No. 111-SC-88218.

This photograph, taken during the Geronimo campaign, shows Goodwin as he must have looked at the time of the Lincoln County War.

Apaches of their supplies, might very well precipitate an Indian war. Bernstein called Blazer a liar; Blazer hit the table with his fist, said no man could call him a liar and live, and threatened he could have fifty Mexicans there within the hour to fight in his corner. He had also been "insinuating and making innuendoes against Maj. Godfroy since the latter refused to discharge Mr. Bernstein."

It is hardly surprising, then, that Blazer said, "A citizen, whose name I will not give [but we can safely guess was Jimmy Dolan] came to me, and told me, he was satisfied from what he had heard, that my life was in danger, that Mr. Bernstein was very much incensed against me." Two or three days later, Bernstein was shot dead. And where was Dr. Blazer when it happened? By his own unconvincing statement he was up in the tower on top of the agency building where no one could see him.

Add to all this the possibility that those "wild Indians" might not have been Apaches at all but white men or native New Mexicans "painted up" and the fact that on the preceding night Jim Reese had been murdered by the Sanches brothers at Tularosa, and it is clear that a lot more was going on than went into the record and that the motives and ensuing actions of all those involved are highly suspect.[9]

What we are left with is the likelihood that Bernstein's death was not by any means the random killing it appeared to be, particularly in view of later developments with the "Indian goods" impounded at Los Lunas. About a month after Bernstein's death, Marshal John Sherman telegraphed his superiors in Washington for instructions because, he reported, "the Administrator of the Estate of the late Mr. Bernstein has stated to me that in case the goods in question are not ordered turned over to him he will cause the same to be replevied."

It has proven impossible to establish the identity of the unnamed administrator of Bernstein's "estate." Whoever he was, he had his share of brass-faced chutzpa, threatening to go to court to recover demonstrably stolen goods from the law enforcement officer who had recovered them. It is certainly possible—taking into account the fact that Bernstein's body was brought to Santa Fe and buried with some ceremony by the Odd Fellows and that U.S. Attorney Thomas B. Catron was throughout kept fully informed of Sherman's progress on the case—to make a fairly informed guess who that individual might have been and what his motive was: dead men tell no tales.[10]

Nevertheless, the killing was attributed to the Regulators, and no doubt there were a number of people who were happy to let it lie that way; later, it would be the Kid who alone and unjustly stood accused of the murder. At the time it all happened, however, Billy and his companions were probably blissfully ignorant of all these undercurrents. They had their horses and more than a few extra head to sell. They effortlessly eluded the pursuit detachment ordered out by Dudley and led by the decidedly pro-Dolan Lieutenant Goodwin and headed up the Pecos, arriving at Bosque Grande on August 13. There they found Jim and Pitzer Chisum—Uncle John was in St. Louis—moving their families and a large herd of cattle north away from the war zone to the new ranges opening up in the Texas Panhandle.

Secure in the anonymity of the slow-moving caravan of wagons, riders,

14.3. The trail to Fort Sumner.

Photograph by Bob Boze Bell, April 1993.

Taken near Vaughn, looking south toward the Capitans, this photo shows the wagon road the Regulators followed on their way up to Fort Sumner in August 1878.

cattle, and horses, the Regulators trailed north with the Chisums. Over the next few days Billy renewed his friendship with Sallie Chisum, who in her diary had recorded his arrival and the fact that on that same day he gave her an "Indian tobacco sack." When they arrived at Fort Sumner four days later, the Kid was still pressing his suit. "Two candi hearts given me by Willie Bonny on the 22nd of August," Sallie recorded. They had also been corresponding; although it seems unbelievable that the mails were still functioning, during the siege of the McSween house he had written her a letter which she noted having received on July 20, the day after "the Big Killing."[11]

Fort Sumner was the largest settlement between Lincoln and Las Vegas, the old military quarters adapted for a variety of civilian uses. Safe from pursuit—they were out of Lincoln County altogether and anyway George Peppin had quit as sheriff and had taken a job as post butcher in the safer environs of Fort Stanton—the Kid and his buddies could and did let down their hair. "The Kid and others had a baile for us," Frank Coe recalled. "All the local girls came; polite and well mannered, they'd never say much upon the floor, but once the tunes started, they would dance all night, with the boys swinging them high."

Doc Scurlock and Charlie Bowdre, both family men, got jobs on the Maxwell ranch and decided to remain at Sumner. The rest headed north to Puerto de Luna, notorious for years as a market for stolen horseflesh. There was another celebratory baile during their two-night stopover, and then, with money jingling in their pockets, they headed upriver to Anton Chico, "the best of the towns this side of Las Vegas," according to Coe.

Trouble awaited them; a posse led by Desiderio Romero, sheriff of San

14.4. Present-day Anton Chico.

Author's photograph, 1995.

14.5. Present-day Anton Chico.

Author's photograph, 1995.

Miguel County, was in Manuel Sánchez's saloon asking questions about the "Lincoln County War party."

"Let's go down and see what they look like," the Kid said, "and not have them hunting us all over town."

With the Kid in the lead, the Regulators went down to the saloon, where they encountered "about eight big burly Mexicans, of all the guns and pistols you ever saw in your life they had them, as they had come down to take us dead or alive."

Undaunted by this array of hardware, the Kid confronted Sheriff Romero. "This is the Lincoln County War party I guess you are looking for right here," he said. "What do you want to do about it?"

It isn't hard to picture the scene, the Kid standing there with those narrowed blue eyes dancing with mischief, a clock ticking somewhere in the silence. Then Sheriff Romero meekly confessed he had no warrants and was not able—or anxious—to make any arrests.

"Come up here and take another drink on the house," the Kid told him. "Then we want you to leave town, right now."

Without a peep of protest, Romero and his posse did just that. "I don't believe I ever saw a man scared worse than that sheriff was," Frank Coe said. It would not be too long before Sheriff Romero gave another vivid display of his lack of gumption.

The Kid and his friends stayed around Anton Chico several more days, holding a dance every night, sleeping in the houses of local people scattered around town. A few nights later they had what Frank Coe called a "war pow-

14.6. The church, Anton Chico.

Author's photograph, 1995.

14.7. Anton Chico.

Photograph by Bob Boze Bell, September 1991.

Many believe the 1880 Pat Garrett–Apolonaria Gutierres and Barney Mason–Juanita Madril double wedding took place in the church, while other sources maintain it was in Plaza Arriba, the upper settlement; still others believe the wedding was celebrated in Fort Sumner.

wow" to decide what they were going to do next. "I told the Kid I was going to Colorado," Coe said. "Things were all broke up and there was nothing at Lincoln for me."

The Kid walked off and said, "It's not all over with me. I'm going to get revenged on that Lincoln County bunch. Who wants to go with me?"

George Coe walked over to stand beside his cousin. "We are going the other way," he said.

"Well, boys, you may do exactly as you please," the Kid said. "As for me, I propose to stay in this country, steal myself a living."

The Coes didn't want any of that. "I told him when it came to stealing horses for a living, I was through," George said.[12]

Everyone else decided to ride with the Kid. They all shook hands around the campfire and wished each other good luck. Nobody needed to be reminded of the "iron clad" oath still binding them to mutual silence. The Coes rode north; the Kid and his partners headed back down the Pecos to Bosque Grande. There, on August 30, John Middleton took the time to reply to a letter he had received from Robert Widenmann, still blockaded at La Mesilla, updating him on Lincoln County events:

The 7 Rivers outfit has stolen your [Tunstall's] cattle. they are at Black River now. We all will start from here day after tomorrow will do the best we can. old man Beckwith killed (Johnson) his son in law so much for him.
If we don't get Tunstall's cattle we will get more in there place.
10 Buffalo men have joined us we are about 36 in number. . . . Old John [Chisum] has gone back on us & Ellis & Son the same, we don't ask no

14.8. Dr. Henry Franklin Hoyt.

Photographer unknown, 1876.
Author's Collection.

Dr. Hoyt was born in Rose, Ramsey County, near St. Paul, Minnesota, January 30, 1854; he died in Yokohama, Japan, on January 21, 1930.

14.9. Howard & McMasters store, Tascosa.

Date and photographer unknown.
John L. McCarty Collection, Amarillo Public Library.

favors of them God dam them. . . . The reason I don't want you to come here is this Everything is stoled out of the country by Pep[pin]s posse, and we intend to play the same game, at this we will back ourselves.[13]

The Kid, now the undisputed leader of what was left of the Regulator group, had meant every word he said. He led them back to Lincoln and they took over the town, defying anyone to do anything about it. Just six nights later, the gang raided the Fritz ranch below Lincoln, driving off fifteen horses and 150 head of cattle. The Kid's plan was to take the animals over into the Texas Panhandle and dispose of them at Tascosa, a raw new cowtown which had sprung up there.

It was a smart move. The word was that Tascosa, just a few years ago an adobe *placita* on a boggy spot at the easy crossing of the Canadian River the natives called Atascosa, was growing like a mushroom. A new country was opening up, with vast ranches operated by the likes of Charles Goodnight and George Littlefield. Although the town consisted only of two stores, a blacksmith shop, and an adobe house, it was already the supply center for the big ranches. Tascosa's cattlemen were not likely to ask too many questions about good horseflesh any more than the town's storekeepers would query the origins of the beef they bought.

About forty miles east of Fort Bascom the group caught up with the Chisum outfit again. "Regulators come up with us at Red River Springs on

14.10. Main street, Tascosa.

Photographer unknown, ca. 1911. John L. McCarty Collection, Amarillo Public Library.

In 1945 what was left of Tascosa—and it was not much—was converted into Cal Farley's Boy's Ranch, a home for underprivileged children.

the 25 Sept 1878," Sallie Chisum noted in her diary. They were driving a sizable remuda of horses, probably swollen by a herd the Kid had decided to appropriate when they were at Puerto de Luna; the idea of stealing horses from horse thieves probably appealed to his often perverse sense of humor.

As they neared their destination they encountered a young fellow riding alone and questioned him about the location of the various ranches in the vicinity; his name was Henry Hoyt, a young doctor "adventuring" in the West much as John Tunstall had done. He and the Kid hit it off at once; Billy told Hoyt they were bringing over a herd of horses to sell.

When the cowmen heard that the Kid and his men were in town, they asked him to meet them. Their spokesman, C. S. "Bill" McCarty—one can almost see the Kid's impish grin when he learned the name of the man he was talking to—asked him what his business was. The Kid answered frankly; cattlemen were always short of horses, so he had brought some over to sell. McCarty told him they wanted no trouble, and Billy gave his word there would not be any.

After that, he and his pals were "part of the town, selling and trading, drinking, gambling, racing horses and shooting at targets."[14]

Temple Houston, son of the Texan hero, outshot the Kid and former Dodge City lawman Bat Masterson in a money match. Billy was "an expert at most western sports," Hoyt observed, "with the exception of drinking." Billy was a handsome youth, he said, "with smooth face, wavy brown hair, an ath-

Toscoso Texas

Thursday Oct 24th
1878

Know all persons by these presents
that I do hereby sell and deliver
to Henry F. Hoyt one Sorrel
Horse Branded BB on left hip
and other indistinct Branded on
Shoulders for the sum of Seventy five
$ dollars in hand received

W H Bonney

Witness
Jas E McMasters
Geo. J. Howard

The above is the handwriting of the
outlaw known as "Billy the Kid"
H.F.H.

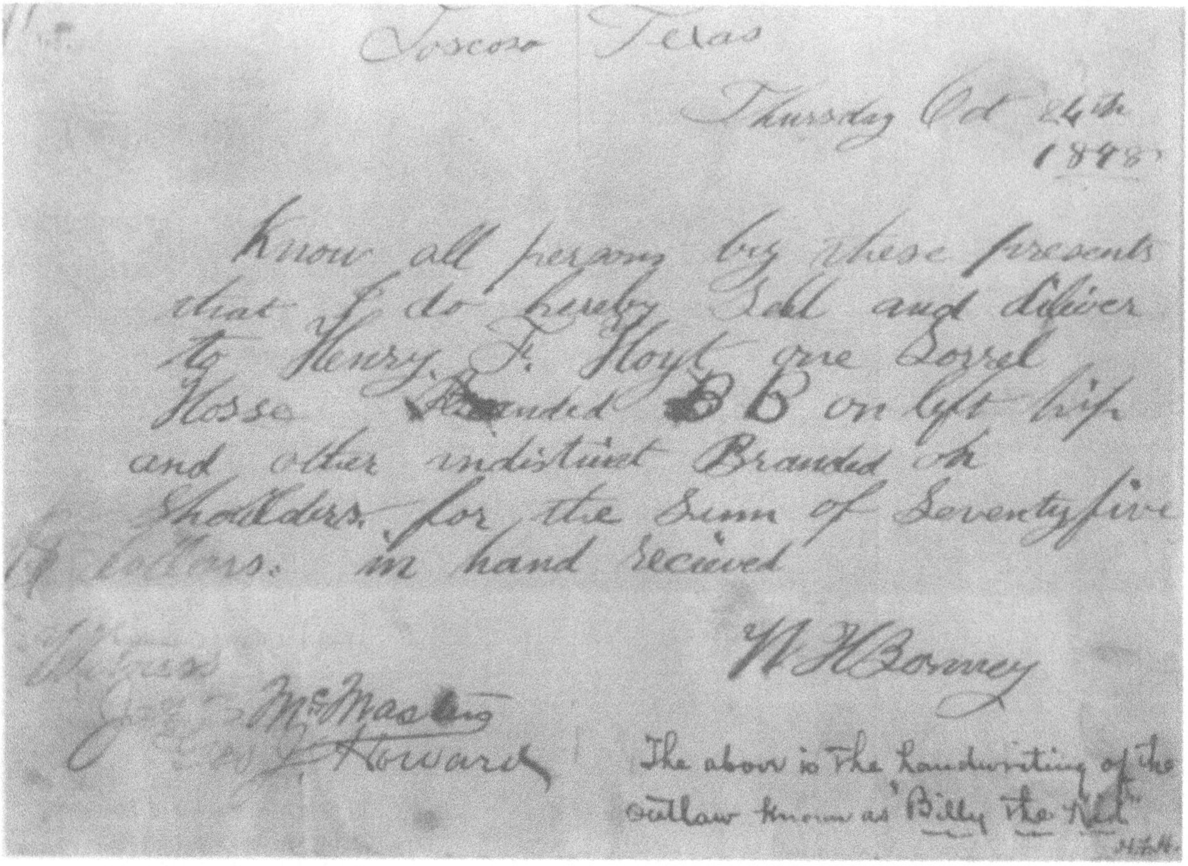

14.11. The Kid's bill of sale.

Panhandle-Plains Historical Museum, Canyon.

"Tascoso, Texas,
Thursday, October 24th
1878.
Know all persons by these presents
that I do hereby sell and deliver
to Henry F. Hoyt one Sorrel
Horse Branded BB on left hip
and other indistinct Branded on
Shoulders for the sum of Seventy five
$dollars in hand received.

W. H. Bonney

Witness
Jas E McMasters
Geo. J. Howard."

letic and symmetrical figure, and clear blue eyes that could look one through and through. Unless angry, he always seemed to have a pleasant expression with a ready smile. . . . He spoke Spanish like a native, and although only a beardless boy, was nevertheless a natural leader of men."

Billy ruled his gang "with a rod of iron," Hoyt related, and went on to tell a hard-to-believe tale of how, one day, while John Middleton was "drinking heavily at Howard & McMasters' store and began to get ugly," the Kid came in.

> In a mild voice that contained, however, a curious note of challenge as well as command, he said,
> "John Middleton, you damned idiot, light out for camp and stay there till I come."
> Wheeling toward him, Middleton, his eyes flashing, replied, "Billy, you'd never talk that way to me if we were alone. You think you're showing off."
> "If that's the way you think just come with me out behind the store, and we *will* be alone," was Billy's quick reply, as he backed toward the door, hand on his gun.
> Middleton's face turned an ashen color, his lower lip dropped, and with a sickly grin he stuttered out, "Aw, Billy, come off [it], can't you take a joke?"
> "You bet I can," said Billy, "but this is no joke. You heard me. Git for camp and git quick." And old John shuffled out the door like a whipped dog.

Was this the response of the man John Tunstall once characterized as "the most desperate-looking man I ever set eyes on"? Well, maybe. However, in spite of the fact that Billy ruled them with a rod of iron, his men "fairly worshipped him," Hoyt said. For instance, one night they all attended the weekly baile at Pedro Romero's store, apparently observing the unwritten law that all weapons must be left at the Howard & McMasters store. During the proceedings, Hoyt and the Kid stepped outside for some air, and Hoyt challenged Billy to a foot race back to the dance hall. As they neared the house, Hoyt slowed, but Billy, going lickety-split, burst in through the door, tripped, and fell headlong in the center of the dance floor.

"Quicker than a flash," Hoyt said, "his prostrate body was surrounded by his four pals, back to back, with a Colt's forty-five in each hand, cocked and ready for business." How or where they had concealed the guns, Hoyt said, was a mystery, as was (and still is) the matter of whom they were defending Billy from. Anyway, the result of this escapade was that in spite of their (professed) contrition, they were thereafter barred from all future dances.

Late in October 1878, just before Hoyt left Tascosa, the Kid rode into town and made the doctor a present of Dandy Dick, the best horse in his remuda, an Arabian sorrel branded BB on the left hip. At the Howard & McMasters store he scribbled out a bill of sale and had it witnessed by the proprietors. Many years later Hoyt learned it was the horse Sheriff William Brady had ridden into town the day he was killed.[15]

After Tascosa, the old Regulator gang broke up for good. Bowdre, Scurlock, and the Coe boys had already bowed out. Following the sale of the horses, John Middleton, Henry Brown, and Fred Waite decided not to return to New Mexico and tried to persuade the Kid and Tom O'Folliard to ride east with them, but Billy was not interested. They said their goodbyes and went their separate ways. None of them would ever meet again.

15.1. John Selman and his son, John, Jr.

Photographer unknown, ca. 1880.
James H. Earle Collection.

The elder Selman was born in Madison
County, Arkansas, November 16, 1839; he
was killed by George Scarborough in El
Paso, Texas, on April 5, 1896.

CHAPTER FIFTEEN

Bloody Murder

WHILE THE KID AND HIS BUDDIES were enjoying themselves in Tascosa, events were in train in New Mexico which would have a profound effect on Billy's future. The first and most important of these was the appointment of a new governor, Lew Wallace. On September 23, 1878, loyal Sam Corbet wrote jubilantly to John Tunstall's father in London:

> The latest and best news I have to tell you is the removal of Governor *Axtell*, United States Attorney T. B. *Catron* Judge *Bristol* United States *Marshall Sherman* and Indian Agent *Godfroy*. All belonging to the Santa [Fe] Ring. I wrote you some time last month about the Sheriff's Posse stealing all the cattle and the Horses from the Felix, for some time I could not get any letters from Mr. Widenmann but for the last 2 weeks I have had several letters from him. He is still at La Mesilla and cannot get back until something is done to get rid of those outlaws who are runing [*sic*] loose in this county headed by Gov Axtell's Pet Sheriff Peppin, those outlaws who stoled the cattle taken them to the Pecos about 150 miles below here and have rebranded them and they say they will have a 1000 head before they leave the county.[1]

Just a few days after Corbet mailed his letter, "the Rustlers"—who for obvious reasons preferred to call themselves "Selman's Scouts"—blazed a three-week trail of havoc from Fort Stanton to the Pecos. It began when Selman's men—among them Gus Gildea, Reason Goble, Rustling Bob Bryant, Charles Snow, and Jack Irving—bought up one thousand rounds of ammunition at Fort Stanton. When news of this transaction reached Colonel Dudley, he confiscated the ammunition and had Selman and his motley crew kicked off the post.

They repaired to Will Hudgens's saloon, where they tried to persuade the owner to go and buy the ammunition for them. When he refused, they wrecked the saloon, abused Hudgens's wife and sister, and pistol-whipped a man named Sheppard who tried to intercede. They then rode down to Lincoln, where they amused themselves by bursting into houses up and down the street, smashing dishes and furniture and generally terrorizing the locals.

At La Junta they smashed up Avery Clenny's little store and stole eight hundred dollars' worth of merchandise. Further downriver they pillaged and burned the Frank Coe–Ab Saunders ranch and at Picacho wantonly killed Clato and Desiderio Chavez y Sanchez and a retarded youth named Lorenzo Lucero, then appropriated the ten horses the boys had been watching. At Martin Sánchez's Picacho farm they shot down and killed his fourteen-year-old son, Gregorio. A few nights later they raped two young women, the wives

15.2. Lew Wallace.

Photographer unknown, ca. 1880.
Author's Collection.

Soldier, writer, and statesman Lewis Wallace was born on April 10, 1827, in Brookville, Indiana. After attending Wabash College he became a newspaperman, then studied law. Following service in the Mexican War, he was admitted to the Indiana bar in 1847, later entering politics and serving as state senator. Named adjutant general at the outbreak of the Civil War, he raised some 130 companies; he became colonel of the Eleventh Indiana Infantry and ended the war a major general of volunteers. He served on the court-martial that tried the suspects in Lincoln's assassination and was chairman of the Andersonville prison inquiry.

His first novel, *The Fair God*, was published in 1873. Following his governorship of New Mexico he became U.S. minister to Turkey, an office he held until 1885. Following the fantastic success of *Ben Hur*, he retired to Crawfordsville, Indiana, where he devoted the rest of his life to writing novels and an autobiography. He died February 15, 1905; his autobiography was completed by his wife, Susan, herself a novelist and artist of considerable merit.

Source: Lew Wallace, *An Autobiography.*

of workers at Bartlett's Mill on the Bonito below Lincoln. When asked who they were, one of them replied, "We are devils just come from Hell!"[2]

With Sam Corbet and Uncle Ike Ellis leading, the citizens responded spiritedly. They "got after them and run them two days and one night nearly to Seven Rivers, but could not get close enough to kill any of them," Corbet reported. "We captured all the loose horses they were driving back[,] animals and all their Blankets and Provisions."[3]

It must have been quite a fight. Fifty years after the event, Gus Gildea, who described himself as Selman's first lieutenant, remembered vividly "the long *all day* fight made by 9 of our men vs. from 25 to 50 or more of the Modocs, both Americans and Mexicans, and we fought them from near the Fritze ranche to the Martin Chavez ranch, about 35 miles as near as I can recollect, through every village on the road and had to take to the mtns, then back to road again and lost several of our horses but no man. We whipped them good and plenty . . . but though they used Buffalo guns on us they did not press us very close."[4]

Even as a new posse was formed in Lincoln to pursue Selman and his men to Seven Rivers, executive action rendered it redundant. Within days of taking office, the new governor, Lew Wallace, was urging President Rutherford B. Hayes to impose martial law in Lincoln County. Mindful of the Posse Comitatus Act, which forbade the use of troops in civil law enforcement, Hayes sidestepped the proposition and instead, on October 7, issued a proclamation admonishing "all good citizens of the United States and especially of the Territory of New Mexico" who had been committing lawless acts "to disperse and return peaceably to their respective abodes on or before noon of the thirteenth day of October, instant."[5]

Coinciding as it did with the departure to the Seven Rivers area of Selman and his thugs, Hayes's proclamation seemed to have the desired effect. There was still crime, still random violence, but for the first time since the murder of John Tunstall some semblance of civil order was reestablished in Lincoln County. It was not by any means an end, but Governor Wallace was encouraged to believe it was a beginning.[6]

Accordingly, on November 13, a month after the expiration of the presidential deadline, "with no report of disturbance or outrage," Wallace promulgated a general declaration of amnesty which pardoned all crimes committed between February 1, 1878, and the date of the proclamation.

This was good news for the men who had stolen or killed or both as members of a sheriff's posse, but where the Kid was concerned—not to mention the men who had fought beside him during the war—the amnesty had a hook in it: it was not to be granted to "any person in bar of conviction under indictment now found and returned for any such crimes or misdemeanors, nor operate the release of any party undergoing pains and penalties consequent upon sentence heretofore had for any crime or misdemeanor."[7]

An incautious, even reckless man might therefore have thought twice before risking a return to an area where all his enemies would have been pardoned while he still remained a criminal, yet—as he had done just a year or so earlier in Arizona—Billy did just that. It may well be he believed, not unreasonably, that others had killed, others had stolen just as he and the Regulators had, but if so his thinking was at best fundamentally naïve. And its effect was to catapult him once more right into the firing line.

Fearing for her life when the Selman gang ransacked Lincoln, Susan McSween had fled to the safety of her sister's home in Las Vegas. There in mid-October Rob Widenmann, en route from La Mesilla to the east—and eventually to London to visit the Tunstall family—stopped off bearing a five-hundred-dollar gift from Tunstall's father.[8]

Thus financed, Susan set out to make war on Dudley. Her first step was to hire as her attorney a relative newcomer to New Mexico named Huston Chapman, an outspoken, energetic, and determined man who immediately began bombarding Governor Wallace with letters calling Dudley a liar and a drunkard, "criminally responsible for the killing of McSween."[9]

Dudley's reaction was, given the man's personality, entirely predictable. Within a week he had eight affidavits from citizens George Peppin, Jack Long, Francisco Gómez, Saturnino Baca, and a John Priest (making his sole appearance in the annals of Lincoln County), plus three officers: Lieutenants George W. Smith and Samuel Pague (both of whom were keeping some dirty laundry of their own safely out of sight) and Dr. Appel. The affidavits attested in sum that Susan McSween was a lewd, licentious, immoral, scandalous, dishonest, and ruthless woman.[10]

Late in November, Chapman and Mrs. McSween came down to Lincoln, where the lawyer continued to press his case against Dudley with Wallace, who was now somewhat more inclined to listen than before. Dudley had contemptuously and publicly rejected Wallace's amnesty by means of an "Open

Letter" to the *Santa Fe New Mexican* signed by himself and all his officers.[11] Although there had never been any intent on Wallace's part to insult him, the unmistakeable hostility of Dudley's reaction told Wallace in no uncertain manner that he need expect neither help nor cooperation from that quarter.

It was at this point that the Kid and Tom O'Folliard rode back into Lincoln, accompanied by Doc Scurlock and Jim French, apparently imbued with an unformed idea that they might somehow avail themselves of Wallace's amnesty; in fact, Billy had written to Sam Corbet telling him he was tired of fighting, that he wanted to stand his trial and quit running from the Dolan crowd and the law.[12]

Hearing they were in town, Sheriff George Peppin, due to attend probate court, got nervous and requested a military escort to accompany him to Lincoln. Accordingly, twenty-seven-year-old Lieutenant James H. French, two noncommissioned officers, and fifteen soldiers met the sheriff at the courthouse and stayed with him until court adjourned at five o'clock. Since the weather was bad and the court had not finished its business, Peppin asked French and his men to remain in town. French agreed, quartered his men, and repaired to Montaño's store, where he talked (and drank) with Peppin, Montaño, and Florencio Gonzales until about 9:00 P.M.

Meanwhile, Peppin learned some of the Regulators were at the lower end of town and reported the fact to Lieutenant French. "He made the remark to me that I ought to go after them," Peppin said. "I told him I would rather not and he said he would go if I would deputize him." Peppin's "I would rather not" neatly underscores not only his healthy respect for the men he was sworn to arrest but also his canny awareness: while they might shoot holes in him if he went after them, they would be a lot more circumspect about doing the same to an army officer.

Thus it was newly sworn Deputy Sheriff French who took three men and went down to the home of former jailer Maximiano de Guevara, a known haunt of the Regulator crowd. He burst into the house, and after some semicoherent questioning, during which he threatened de Guevara and his wife with a drawn pistol, he left. Next, at John Copeland's house, he arrested a young boy carrying a pistol and took him along to the old Baca house near the torreón, now occupied by Mrs. McSween and Huston Chapman.

Once inside, French again started waving his pistol around, declaring loudly that he was a better lawyer than Chapman. There was an argument. French jumped up and cocked his revolver. "Stand back now," he told his men, "God damn him I'll fix him."

Mrs. McSween started crying.

"That will do," French told her. "I don't want any of that strategy. I've seen that played back in the States."

He took off his overcoat and tunic, then called one of the soldiers over to tie one of his arms behind him. "God damn you, sir, you have got to fight me!" he told Chapman.

Chapman refused, whereupon French put on his overcoat, leaving one of the enlisted men to bring along the rest of his clothing, and stalked to the door, where he paused theatrically.

15.3. James Hansell French.

Photographer unknown, June 1874.
U.S. Military Academy Archives.

James Hansell French was born in Philadelphia on March 14, 1851. After graduation from West Point, he served with the Ninth Cavalry in Texas and Colorado until August 31, 1876, when he was allowed to resign because of "ill health" and thus avoid trial for drunkenness.

Reappointed on August 10, 1878, he was assigned to Fort Union and soon began drinking again. He was transferred to Fort Stanton in November 1878.

On January 17, 1880, while serving with Major Albert P. Morrow, Ninth Cavalry, in pursuit of the Apache leader Victorio in the San Mateo Mountains, French was shot through the head. His body was brought to Santa Fe before being sent back to Philadelphia. The funeral procession was one of the largest Santa Fe had ever witnessed.

Source: ACP file.

"My name is Lieutenant French, Company M, Ninth Cavalry, United States Army," he declaimed. "I will see you again, Mr. Chapman."

Some time later that night, John Copeland got into an argument with a local youth, Juan Mes, known as Johnny Mace, which ended with Copeland's shooting the nineteen-year-old in the chest and stomach. Copeland turned himself in to Deputy Sheriff James Tomlinson—he wasn't fool enough to surrender to Peppin—who woke French so Copeland could enlist the protection of the military.

Next morning Chapman and Las Vegas attorney Sidney Wilson, a former law partner of David Shield newly arrived in Lincoln, went down to Montaño's, where Copeland asked them to represent him. When Wilson tried to talk with his client, however, Lieutenant French, either still drunk or drunk again, refused to let him. Later French relented and asked Wilson if he would represent him should charges be brought against him for his actions of the preceding evening. Obviously he already knew or suspected Chapman was going to swear warrants against him, and he was entirely correct.

In yet another collision between the two men a little later at the courthouse, French again challenged Chapman to fight, but although they growled at each other on and off for the rest of the day, Peppin managed to keep them apart. Warrants were sworn by Susan McSween, de Guevara, and Chapman himself charging French with felonious entry and assault with intent to kill. On the young officer's return to the post, Dudley had no option but to place him under arrest while ordering a board of inquiry to convene in Lincoln next day.

The affair fizzled out over the next couple of days as French was acquitted on two charges and bound over to the district court on the third; on December 21, the board of officers recommended no further action be taken. Dudley, who had already expressed his contempt for Judge Wilson as representative of the civil authorities in Lincoln, now went a step further by placing Lincoln off limits to his soldiers and the fort off limits to the citizens, especially Copeland, Chapman, French, Scurlock, the Kid, Brown, the Coes, "and all other parties recognized as the murderers of Roberts, Brady, Tunstall, Bernstein and Beckwith."[13]

For Dudley's proscription the Kid and his buddies clearly did not give a high hoot in hell. Lincoln was theirs again—so much so that on December 27, Jimmy Dolan, Billy Mathews, and Jack Long sought refuge at the fort, claiming that conditions in town made it unsafe to do business, although what "business" the bankrupt Dolan might have had there is unclear. Also finding it unsafe to do business was George Peppin, who decided to turn in his star. Once again, albeit for a short time, Lincoln was completely without law.[14]

That fact in turn renders unlikely the story told by Ash Upson that on December 22 the Kid and Tom O'Folliard submitted to arrest by "George Kimbreel, elected sheriff in November," and were incarcerated in the Lincoln jail, "from whence they easily made their escape and returned to Fort Sumner, where they continued their cattle raids, living in clover; and the Kid by his pleasing manners and open-handed generosity made himself almost universally popular."[15]

Other than this, nothing is known of the Kid's whereabouts over this festive season, neither how he lived or where he went. While Huston Chapman continued his little war with Dudley and assisted Susan McSween in her role as administrator of the estates of her husband, Tunstall, and Dick Brewer, the Kid kept a low profile.

Perhaps it was the Kid, looking for a way out of his troubles but with no money to hire a lawyer even if he risked a trial, whom Huston Chapman had in mind when he wrote to Tunstall's father from Las Vegas on February 10, 1879, interceding on behalf of "the men who fought for your son and done all in their power to avenge his murder." They were "without any means of defending themselves when the trial comes on," he continued. "They were promised by both McSween and Widenmann that they should receive pay for hunting down the murderers of your son, but they do not ask for pay, but think that something should be done to assist them out of their present trouble.... They have asked me to write you and explain their situation, and you can take such action as you may think proper."[16]

Next day he left with David Shield for Santa Fe, where Wallace acceded to Chapman's urging that he come to Lincoln and see for himself what conditions there were like. That achieved, Chapman set out for Lincoln to continue his legal actions against Dudley and French, undeterred by the warnings of his Las Vegas friends that by returning there he was taking his life in his hands.

During his absence, a bizarre peace plan had been drawn up by the two factions. On February 18, Dudley recorded having seen "a letter from Bonny alias 'Kid' the party indicted for the killing of the late Sheriff Brady, addressed to one of the Dolan faction [Jesse Evans], wanting to know whether they proposed peace or fight &c."[17]

A parley was arranged with Evans, Jimmy Dolan, Edgar Walz, Billy Mathews, and Billy Campbell representing one side and the Kid, Tom O'Folliard, Doc Scurlock, Joe Bowers, and José Salazar the other. The date for their meeting could not have been more significant: it was one year to the day since Tunstall had been murdered.

When the two parties met, however (ensconced behind adobe walls for safety, according to at least one report), the opening remarks were not promising, with Evans declaring the Kid "impossible to treat with" and recommending in his hearing that they kill him then.

"I don't care to open negotiations with a fight," the Kid shouted across to them, "but if you'll come at me three at a time, I'll whip the whole damned bunch of you."

Young Edgar Walz, a brother-in-law of Thomas Catron who was supervising Catron's interests in Lincoln, managed to calm them all down and get the leaders to come out and shake hands. They all then repaired to a neutral bar and there hammered out a treaty, in many respects an expanded version of the "iron clad" oath taken by the Regulators and notable for its brazen arrogance. Under its provisos no member of either party would kill a member of the other party without first giving notice of withdrawal from the agreement. All who had acted as "friends" were to be included in the agreement and not molested. No officer or soldier was to be killed for any act carried out before the agreement. No one of either party would appear or give evidence against the other in any civil prosecution. Each party would give individual members of the other party every aid in their power to resist arrest or, if arrested, would endeavor to effect their release. Last, and most significantly, if any member of either party failed to observe the terms of the treaty, he was to be killed on sight.[18]

Their pact effected, the signatories proceeded to celebrate in earnest. Seeing Salazar and the Kid, for both of whom he had warrants, newly appointed Sheriff George Kimbrell slipped out of town to obtain military assistance to arrest them. Their revels growing increasingly raucous, the celebrants reeled into Juan Patrón's place. The moment Billy Campbell laid eyes on Patrón, who had just returned from Santa Fe in the company of Huston Chapman, he yanked out his six-gun, clearly intending to shoot him, but after a scuffle Campbell was persuaded to holster his gun.

The revellers moved on up the street; below the torreón they encountered Huston Chapman, who had just put up his horse and buggy in the corral

15.4. David Pugh Shield.

Date and photographer unknown. Author's Collection.

Shield was born in Reynoldsburg, Ohio, December 5, 1835, and died at Las Vegas, New Mexico, March 6, 1888.

15.5. Where Chapman was shot.

Author's photograph, 1995.

The courthouse (Convento) is out of sight immediately to the left; the church of San Juan Bautista was not built at the time. The torreón is beyond the building with the porch on the right, which now stands where the old Baca house once stood.

behind the old Baca house. The lawyer's face was bandaged against a severe attack of neuralgia; he was on his way to get some bread to make a poultice. He looked up to find Billy Campbell blocking his path.

"Who are you and where are you going?" Campbell demanded.

"My name is Chapman and I am attending to my business," Chapman said brusquely. He had never seen any of these men before.

"Then you dance," Campbell told him, jamming his six-gun into Chapman's belly.

"I don't propose to dance for a drunken mob," Chapman snapped impatiently. "You can't scare me, boys. I know you, and it's no use, you've tried that before. Am I talking to Mr. Dolan?"

"No," Jesse Evans said, "but you're talking to a damned good friend of his."

Two shots rang out, fired almost simultaneously.

"My God, I am killed!" Chapman gasped and collapsed mortally wounded, his clothes set alight by the muzzle flash of the guns.

"I promised my God and General Dudley I'd kill him and I've done it!" Campbell crowed, and he led the party up the street to McCullum's, a new eating house built on the site of the McSween home, where they ordered more drinks and canned oysters.[19]

Jimmy Dolan surreptitiously handed Edgar Walz a pistol and told him to go and put it in the unarmed Chapman's hand; when Walz demurred, the Kid—who had probably been tipped off that Sheriff Kimbrell was on his way back to town with an escort of soldiers—offered to do it. Once out of the saloon, however, he headed down to the Ellis house, where he was joined by Tom O'Folliard, who had slipped away from the McCullum place unnoticed. They saddled up and skinned out for San Patricio, the Kid doubtless filled with dismay and apprehension. He had come to Lincoln hoping to clear his name and start afresh. Instead, he had become an eyewitness to, and was now perhaps even in danger of being named an accessory to yet another bloody murder.

16.1. Byron Dawson
at Fort Duchesne, Utah.

Photographer unknown, 1887.
National Archives, Ref 111-SC-88457.

Dawson was born in Johnson County, Indiana, on August 29, 1838; he died in Washington Township (Indianapolis), Marion County, Indiana, on December 20, 1913.

General George Crook is seated, front row right, next to the two little girls. Dawson is further right, with a saber. Also in the photograph, rear row, fifth from left, is Colonel James F. Randlett, victim of an 1873 assassination attempt by Jimmy Dolan.

CHAPTER SIXTEEN

Going Straight

At about 11:30 p.m. on the night of February 18, 1879, Sheriff George Kimbrell, accompanied by Lieutenant Byron Dawson and a detachment of soldiers, rode into Lincoln intending to find and arrest the Kid and José Salazar. They searched several houses unsuccessfully; sometime after midnight they came across the dead body of H. I. Chapman.

Most of the clothing was burned off the upper portion of the body, Dawson reported, fueling later speculation that whiskey had been poured on Chapman's body and then deliberately set alight. The column was halted as Dawson and Kimbrell went to the nearest residence, Squire Wilson's jacal. When they got there Wilson told them he already knew the body was lying in the road but had not been able to get anyone to help him move it. Dawson had the corpse taken to the courthouse and led his detachment back to the fort, arriving there at 5:30 the following morning.[1]

"Next day, a coroner's jury was held," a witness said, "but the Dolan party was in town armed and the people were so bulldozed no evidence could be brought out."[2] Convinced that the murder of Chapman signaled a recommencement of hostilities, the "bulldozed" male citizens petitioned Dudley to station troops in the town immediately. Less than an hour later, Lieutenant Goodwin and a detachment of soldiers, plus the Gatling gun, were on their way. "I found the people in the Plaza considerably frightened," Goodwin reported, "due to the meeting of the two opposite parties in their town."

Their request that Dudley come to the plaza was conveyed to his commanding officer; Dudley came down to attend a mass meeting that had been called and to address the citizens with a well-received speech. Goodwin also sent six of his men with Kimbrell to San Patricio in an unsuccessful bid to arrest the Kid and Salazar; not the slightest attempt was made to arrest anyone for the murder of Chapman.[3]

What the murder did do, however, was galvanize Governor Wallace into action; he set aside the historical novel-in-progress upon which he was lavishing every moment of his spare time and made plans to visit Lincoln. Coincidentally, Susan McSween decided to pursue her case against Dudley. She entrusted it to a friend of Chapman's, attorney Ira E. Leonard, who immediately drew up a set of charges and specifications against Dudley which included his having aided and abetted the murder of McSween, the burning of his home, and the looting of the Tunstall store, not to mention his threatening to put Justice of the Peace Wilson in irons and slandering Susan McSween. These Leonard forwarded on March 4 to the secretary of war, just

189

16.2. George Kimbrell.

Date and photographer unknown.
Courtesy Andy Gregg.

This is the only known photograph of Kimbrell, reproduced from a newspaper illustration taken about 1910.

Born in Huntsville, Arkansas, on March 31, 1842, seventeen-year-old George Kimbrell came west in the Pike's Peak gold rush of 1859, and he moved to New Mexico the following year. After a short stay at Las Vegas, he moved south to Lincoln County in 1863, working there awhile as a government scout. The following year he squatted on Chaves Flats, about twelve miles east of Lincoln. That same year he married Paulita Romero; they had five children. After a year as sheriff of Lincoln County, Kimbrell was succeeded by Pat Garrett. Kimbrell served as a justice of the peace in his precinct for many years and died at his home in Picacho on March 24, 1925.

Source: Eve Ball, "Charles Ballard, 'Lawman' of the Pecos," *English Westerners Brand Book* 7, no. 4 (July 1965): 1–6.

a day before Wallace arrived in Lincoln with Dudley's mortal enemy, Colonel Edward Hatch. To celebrate the governor's arrival, the citizens of Lincoln announced plans for a ball to be held at the old Murphy store on March 7. A "cordial invitation" signed by George Barber, Allen Ballard, and José Montaño was sent to Colonel Dudley "and ladies" to be present and participate.[4]

Hatch's arrival was bad news for Dudley and his fellow officers, who were frantically trying to keep the lid on a dreadful scandal that had blown up on the very day Huston Chapman was murdered. It had begun when, on Dudley's orders, Lieutenant George Smith—at forty-two possibly one of the oldest lieutenants in the U.S. Army—had been sent on duty to Roswell early in February. On the way downriver he left his wife, Jennie, forty, in the congenial company of the Fritz family at Spring Ranch below Lincoln. There, on several occasions between February 18 and 28, in the presence of Charles Fritz's daughters, and therefore much to Fritz's angry displeasure, Jennie Smith and twenty-three-year-old Lieutenant Samuel Pague consummated an adulterous relationship.

Summoned to appear before Dudley and told his behavior was bringing scandal to the service and ruin to Mrs. Smith and her son and daughter, Pague pledged to cease his attentions. Dr. Appel and Lieutenant Dawson also begged him to mend his ways, but within days the couple were intimate again.

The affair became public knowledge when on March 11, just four days after the Friday night ball and in the wake of their father's complaint to the military, Carolina and Clara Fritz testified to Pague's adultery before Lieutenant Millard F. Goodwin.

16.3. San Patricio, 1996.

Photograph by Dick George, 1996.

In the Kid's time, Frank Coe said, "there were a dozen or fifteen houses in San Patricio. . . . The town had a better street than it has now. It was down next to the river and the smartest of the Mexicans who lived there were gamblers and horse thieves." Today the village is best known for the gallery housing the works of former resident and premier New Mexico artist Peter Hurd, his wife, Henriette Wyeth Hurd, and their son Michael, also a painter.

16.4. Edward Hatch.

Date and photographer unknown.
Author's Collection.

Hatch was born in Bangor, Maine, on April 22, 1831; he died of apoplexy—just as the gun fired for reveille—at Fort Robinson, Nebraska, on April 11, 1889.

16.5. Samuel Speece Pague.

Photographer unknown, 1876.
U.S. Military Academy Archives.

Samuel Speece Pague was born in Ohio on April 14, 1855, graduating forty-third in a class of forty-eight from West Point on June 14, 1876. He was posted immediately to Fort Stanton. In the latter part of 1877 and early 1878 he was on duty in Texas during the San Elizario troubles.

After the Jennie Smith scandal, Pague was posted to Fort Marcy; the affair seems to have continued there. In March 1881 he was court-martialed at Fort Craig, acquitted on the charges of adultery, but found guilty of two of the specifications; he appears to have taken or been sent on a year's leave of absence. His record thereafter is one of general irresponsibility, with many applications for leave and extensions and political support mustered for whatever he wanted.

In or about 1894, Pague took the "chloride of gold cure," also known as the "Keeley cure," for acute alcoholism; it appears to have affected his mind. At about 4:30 P.M. on October 2, 1895, while General Wesley Merritt was reviewing the troops at Fort Sheridan, Pague was drunk on duty; arrested and placed in hospital suffering from "a condition bordering on delirium tremens," he escaped and tried to kill his commanding officer, Colonel R. E. A. Crofton. He was disarmed by Crofton, Mrs. Pague, and two officers and placed in the guardhouse. A court-martial inevitably followed, and Pague was dismissed from the service; his wife divorced him soon thereafter.

On May 26, 1898, he applied to the adjutant general, U.S. Army, for readmission to the service, claiming he was anxious to go to the front in the Spanish-American War. When his application was denied, he obtained work as a draftsman in Chicago, but drifted from job to job, drinking heavily. On July 8, 1899, when he registered at the New Era Hotel in Chicago, he had only ten cents to his name; rooms were fifteen cents, but the clerk trusted him for the other five. Pague repaid him by committing suicide, drinking chloral in the hotel office.

Source: ACP file.

Seventeen-year-old Lina said Pague came to the ranch on February 19 and went to Jennie's room; it was his third visit since she had arrived. He lay on the bed with her head in his lap and she told him she loved him better than her husband. Sixteen-year-old Clara—who slept in the same room—said Jennie sat on Pague's knees and kissed him, and he called her his wife and darling. After checking that Clara was asleep (obviously she was not), Pague undressed Jennie and they had intercourse. Charles Fritz testified that on Pague's last visit, he had found him in bed with Mrs. Smith.

Pague appeared before probate clerk Ben Ellis countercharging perjury, but the weight of the evidence was overwhelming. The affair was the talk of the town; if the list of witnesses is anything to go by, everyone must have known about it. Among them were Will Dowlin, Bonnie Baca, George Barber, Billy Gill, Ben Ellis, Jimmy Dolan (who was "walking out" with Lina Fritz), Mickey Cronin, Mrs. Fritz, and J. A. LaRue, as well as a number of Pague's fellow officers.

16.6. Carolina "Lina" Fritz.

Photographer Bostwick, New York, ca. 1879.
R. G. McCubbin Collection.

Carolina Franzis Fritz was born February 22, 1861, on the family farm near Mont-rose, Pennsylvania, the second daughter of Charles and Catherine (Knebling) Fritz. She was married to James Dolan on July 13, 1879. On December 23, 1879, Jack Winters, who with his partner, John Wilson, had opened up the first quartz mine in White Oaks earlier that year, deeded 350 feet of his North Homestake to Lina. On the same date, the Dolans conveyed half their interest to Joseph A. LaRue. LaRue and Marcus Brunswick, his silent partner, then advanced several thousand dollars to work the mine, which became the leading producer of gold in the district. "Dolan is said to be wealthy," Robert Widenmann wrote enviously to the Tunstall family on February 15, 1881: "He has a half interest in one of the newly discovered mines and has it is said been offered $200,000 for it. The knaves always have the best luck." Ñot always. The Dolans' first child, Emil, born May 2, 1880, died on June 4, 1882. A daughter, Louise, born November 30, 1883, died at the age of six. There were two other children: Caroline, born in September 1881, who married Fred Vorwerk, and Bessie. Lina Dolan herself died on September 29, 1886, following the birth of Bessie.

Source: Jones, *Tree Branches;* R. A. Widenmann to J. P. Tunstall, February 15, 1881, Tunstall Family Papers, copy in author's collection.

Although both Colonel Edward Hatch and Lew Wallace can hardly have been unaware of the scandal, neither appears to have taken part in the proceedings, perhaps because Smith had written to Lew Wallace on March 19 defending Pague as "a good and noble boy." It would appear a decision was made simply to transfer Pague away from trouble. In short order he was relieved of duty and posted to Fort Marcy (Santa Fe).

Nowhere is the full extent of Dudley's hypocrisy and that of every single one of his officers better illustrated than in this sad little episode. Three months earlier at Dudley's behest Smith and Pague had readily taken the statements of half a dozen men blackening the name of Susan McSween, not to mention adding their own smearing depositions, when every one of them knew that Pague was conducting an adulterous affair with Smith's wife and—there seems no doubt of it—that Smith was aware of his wife's infidelity.[5]

Wallace let none of this interfere with what he had come to Lincoln to do. A steady stream of "requests" and "suggestions" streamed from his rooms at Montaño's. "A short interview with the leading citizens satisfied me that it would not be possible in the beginning to obtain affidavits against parties well known to be guilty of crimes," he reported to Carl Schurz, "this on account of the terrorism so general after the brutal assassination of H. J. [H. I.] Chapman."[6]

16.7. A typical Lincoln jacal.

Author's photograph, 1996.

Old Squire Wilson's jacal did not, of course, survive. Very few did; this is a reconstruction located on the grounds of the Lincoln County Heritage Trust.

Next, Wallace persuaded Hatch to suspend Dudley and transfer him to Fort Union, a move to which Dudley strenuously and noisily objected, immediately forwarding to Washington a demand for a court of inquiry to clear his name. Undeterred, Wallace pressed on. He was hopeful once he had a few of the criminals behind bars, testimony against them would be forthcoming. The only way to catch them was to organize the citizens and the military, and so he raised a voluntary militia called the Lincoln County Rifles and appointed as its commander Juan B. Patrón. He drew up a list of thirty-five men he wanted arrested—the Kid, Evans, Dolan, Campbell, and O'Folliard among them—and exhorted Captain Henry Carroll, who was placed temporarily in command at Fort Stanton until the return from compassionate leave of Captain George Purington, to work with the new militia to catch them.

In short order the cavalry rode over to Murphy's old Carrizo ranch and arrested Evans, Campbell, and Dolan. No sooner were they incarcerated in the guardhouse than, as if in answer to Wallace's prayers, a witness—and a potent one—wrote in confidence to the Governor on March 13:

> Dear Sir I have heard that You will give one thousand $dollars for my body which as I can understand it means alive as a Witness. I know it is as a witness against those that Murdered Mr. Chapman, if it was so as that I could appear at Court I could give the desired information, but I have indictments against me for things that happened in the late Lincoln County War and am afraid to give up because my Enemies would kill me. the day Mr. Chapman was murdered [sic] I was in Lincoln, at the request of good Citizens to meet Mr. J. J. Dolan to meet as Friends, so as to be able to lay aside our arms and go to Work. I was present When Mr. Chapman was

murderded and know who did it and if it were not for those indictments I would have made it clear before now. if it is in your power to Annully those indictments I hope you will do so so a[s] to give me a chance to explain. please send me an annser telling me what you can do You can send annser by bearer I have no wish to fight any more indeed I have not raised an arm since Your proclamation. as to my Character I refer [you] to any of the Citizens, for the majority of them are my Friends and have been helping me all they could. I am called Kid Antrim but Antrim is my stepfathers name. Waiting for an annser I remain Your Obedeint Servant,

W. H. Bonney.

Wallace responded with alacrity. It is highly unlikely he had any conception at all of the real danger the Kid was putting himself in by breaking the peace treaty made a month earlier, and it probably would not have made any difference if he had. Here was an eyewitness prepared to turn states' evidence against Dolan, Campbell, and Evans—a veritable gift from the gods. Wallace grabbed it.

"Come to the house of old Squire Wilson, at nine (9) o'clock next Monday night alone," he wrote on March 15. He gave the Kid instructions how to get to the house safely, teaching granny to suck eggs: "I have authority to exempt you from prosecution if you will testify to what you say you know. The object of the meeting at Squire Wilson's is to arrange the matter in a way to make your life safe. To do that the utmost secrecy is to be used.

So come alone. Don't tell anybody—not a living soul—you are coming or the object. If you could trust Jesse Evans, you can trust me."

There seems to have been a considerable amount of dissimulation going on here. Wallace was in fact only interested in one thing: getting credible testimony with which he could indict Dolan and Evans. The Kid was interested in only one thing: getting off the hook. Were it not for the demonstrable fact that when they first met, neither would have known the other had they passed in the street, existing accounts of the episode would be highly suspect. Given the circumstances of their meeting, their actual conversation was probably terse and to the point. Many, many years later, however, when the name of Billy the Kid had acquired legendary status, Wallace endowed it with a glamor it certainly did not have at the time.

"Billy the Kid kept the appointment punctually," he recalled:

At the time designated, I heard a knock at the door, and I called out, "Come in." The door opened somewhat slowly and carefully, and there stood the young fellow generally known as the Kid, his Winchester in his right hand, his revolver in his left.

"I was sent for to meet the Governor here at 9 o'clock," said the Kid. "Is he here?" I rose to my feet, saying, "I am Governor Wallace," and held out my hand. When we had shaken hands I invited the young fellow to be seated so that we might talk together. "Your note gave promise of absolute protection," the young outlaw said warily. "Yes," I replied, "and I have been true to my promise," and then pointing to Squire Wilson, who was the only person in the room with me, I added, "This person, whom of course you know, and I are the only persons in the house."

This seemed to satisfy the Kid, for he lowered his rifle and returned his revolver to its holster. When he had taken his seat, I proceeded to unfold the plan I had in mind to enable him to testify to what he knew about the killing of Chapman at the forthcoming session of court two or three weeks later without endangering his life. I closed with the promise, "In return for your doing this, I will let you go scot-free with a pardon in your pocket for all your misdeeds."

It was an empty promise, but how was the Kid to know? He slipped out into the night, convinced he had found a way—dangerous, but worth the risk—to wipe the slate clean and start over. Wallace, too, was contented with his night's work, but for different and one suspects more pragmatic reasons. So it can have been with considerably less than pleasure that he heard the following day that Jesse Evans and Billy Campbell had persuaded or inveigled the soldier guarding them to desert and help them escape from the Fort Stanton guardhouse.

Made understandably uneasy by this development, the Kid sent a messenger upriver with a note to Wilson:

> Please tell You know who that I do not know what to do, now as those Prisoners have escaped, to send word by bearer a note through You it may be he has made different arrangements if not and he still wants it the same to Send "William Hudgins" as Deputy, to the Junction tomorrow at three o'clock, with some men you know to be all right. Send a note telling me what to do.
>
> W. H. Bonney.
>
> P.S. Do not send soldiers.

Wallace, who was at Fort Stanton, got a note to the Kid:

> The escape makes no difference in arrangements. ~~I will comply with my part, if you will with yours.~~
> To remove all suspicions of ~~arrangement~~ understanding, I think it better to put the arresting party in charge of Sheriff Kimball, who will be instructed to see that no violence is used.
> This will go to you tonight. ~~If you still insist upon Hudgins, let me know.~~ If I don't get ~~receive~~ other word from you the party (all citizens) will be at the junction by three o'clock tomorrow.

Back came the Kid's reply:

> Sir: I will keep the appointment I made but be Sure and have men come that You can depend on. I am not afraid to die like a man fighting but I would not like to be killed like a dog unarmed. tell Kimbal to let his men be placed around the house, and for him to come in alone; and he can arrest us. all I am afraid of is that in the Fort we might be poisioned, or killed through a Window at night. but you can arrange that all right. tell the Commanding Officer to watch)Let. Goodwin(he would not hesitate to do anything there will be danger on the road of Somebody waylaying us to kill us on the road to the Fort.

Evans and Campbell would never be caught on the road, he added. "Watch Fritzes, Captain Bacas ranch [above Lincoln] and the Brewery they will either go to Seven Rivers or to Jicarillo Montians they will stay around close

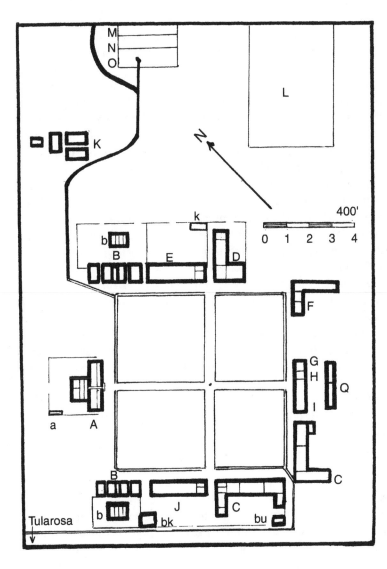

16.8. Fort Stanton map and key to plan.

Author's Collection.

KEY TO THE PLAN
OF FORT STANTON
   A. Commanding Officer's Quarters
      with (a) Stable.
   B. Officers' Quarters with (b) Kitchens,
      (bk) Bakery, and (bu) Butcher
      Shop.
   C. Barracks, each with mess, kitchen,
      and washroom.
   D. Hospital.
   E. Quartermaster's Storehouse.
   F. Unfinished barracks, used as grain
      room and carpentry shop.
   G. Adjutant's Office.
   H. Library.
   I. Guardhouse/Jail.
   J. Commissary/Storehouse.
   K. Laundress' Quarters and (k) tempo-
      rary quarters.
   L. Hay Corral.
   M. and O. Quartermaster's Corrals.
   N. Cavalry Corrals.
   Q. Theatre and Good Templars' Hall
      (private property).

The Rio Bonito lay to the north of the
post. The Post Trader's building, formerly the Murphy-Fritz establishment,
was "upstream some distance, and just
around the point of a little canyon that
led down to the river." A December 21,
1877, map locates it 255 yards (233
meters) due southwest of the commissary (J), on the road to Tularosa. No
church is shown. The L. G. Murphy
saloon/brewery was downstream, on the
way to Lincoln.

untill the scouting parties come in. . . . it is not my place to advise you but I am anxious to have them caught and perhaps know how men hide from Soldiers better than you."

Of course he was anxious for Evans and Campbell to be caught; if they found out what he was up to, they would kill him on sight. He added a postscript changing the location for the arrest to the Gutieres farm a mile below San Patricio "because Sanger and Ballard are or were great friends of Camuls [Campbell's] Ballard told me ~~today~~ yesterday to leave for you were doing everything to catch me. it was a blind to get me to leave."[7]

And so the mock arrest was made on Friday, March 21. The Kid and Tom O'Folliard were brought up from San Patricio and lodged in an outbuilding attached to the Patrón store. Wallace lost no time in going there to debrief the Kid, making copious notes on the Rustlers, their crimes, and their present whereabouts; on local cattle rustlers such as Frank Wheeler, Jake Owen, and "Dutch" Chris Moessner; on the trails the thieves used and the places they hid or sold their cattle; and on the Jones family and Marion Turner, who lived with them and who had "killed a Mexican at Plaiser's Mill [sic] 'just to see him kick.'"[8]

That done, Wallace dismissed the Kid from his mind; there was nothing more he could get from him until district court was in session, and anyway, he felt dealing with such a lowlife was distinctly demeaning, as his March 31 report to Carl Schurz reveals: "A precious specimen named 'The Kid' whom the Sheriff is holding here in the Plaza, is an object of tender regard. I heard singing and music the other night; going to the door I found the minstrels of the village actually serenading the fellow in his prison."[9]

Like practically everyone else since, Wallace completely missed the significance of that serenade. The people singing outside his window were the Kid's people now. Lacking any pretensions himself, Billy loved their lack of pretense. It was their affection that had drawn him to Lincoln, that had made him return now and put his life on the line; it was the only place he had ever *belonged.* To a homeless, rootless boy who had never known permanence, there was something enviable in their unchanging life-style, the way it moved with the seasons. They still cut the grama grass for hay with hand sickles and hoes, they still plowed their fields with an ox team and a forked-stick plow, they still shelled their corn in a wood-framed sieve made with rawhide strings, then flailed it with bent poles the way their fathers and their grandfathers had. Then when they were done the women would shell the corn and make the bread in the outside oven, the *horno,* mix salt and water with the corn to make tortillas, put red chilis in with the beans. Coffee was made carefully, a little water or a little coffee added until it was exactly right. To Billy they were warm, real, the only family he had ever had. To Wallace the native New Mexicans he governed were merely picturesque background, extras in the novel he was writing.

So to his eternal credit, Billy kept his side of the bargain, testifying before the grand jury that began its deliberations on April 14 and that, despite Judge Bristol's stern warnings against partisanship, generated some two hundred indictments, nearly all of them against men who had been opposed to the Tunstall-McSween cause.

The post hospital; again, the porch and gambrel window are later additions.

Original adjutant's office, library, and guardhouse; the arched porch and upper story were added ca. 1890. Quite possibly the Dudley Court of Inquiry sat in this building.

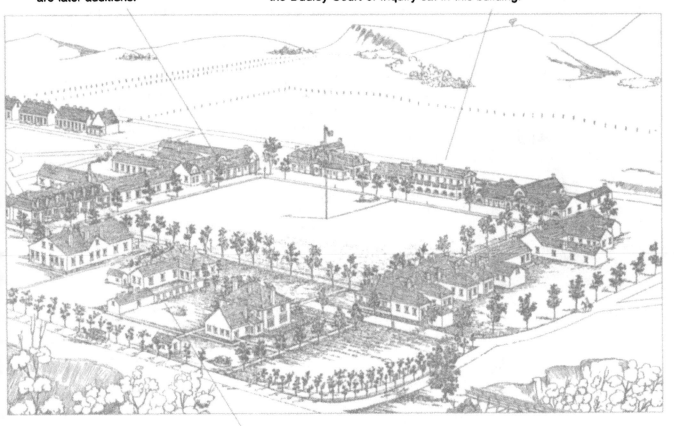

16.9. Fort Stanton, a bird's-eye view.

Drawing by J. Ross Thomas, ca. 1903. Author's Collection.

Commanding Officer's quarters. Like the alteration to the guardhouse and hospital, the buildings on both sides of it were additions dating from the time when the Fort was used as a marine hospital.

16.10. Fort Stanton in its heyday.

Photographer unknown, ca. 1885. National Archives.

The garrison on full-dress parade toward the end of the Apache Wars, with the commanding officer's quarters to the right virtually unchanged from the day Murphy, Fritz, and friends were photographed outside it twelve years earlier (Fig. 4.8).

16.11. Galusha Pennypacker.

Date and photographer unknown. Dickinson College Library Collection, U.S. Army Military History Institute.

Just for the record, Medal of Honor winner Galusha Pennypacker, who presided at the Dudley court of inquiry, was a close personal friend of Dudley's at the time and until his death in 1910.

Marion Turner and John Jones were indicted for the death of McSween, and John Kinney, George Peppin, and Colonel Dudley for burning the McSween house, while—indicating the thrust of the Kid's testimony—Dolan and Campbell were named as the murderers of Huston Chapman, with Jesse Evans as an accessory. Peppin was again indicted, along with some twenty of his possemen, for the murder of Frank MacNab, and John Selman and eight of his Rustlers for the atrocities of the preceding September.

Buck Powell, Jack Long, Billy Mathews, Johnny Hurley, and Tom O'Folliard pleaded and were granted immunity under Wallace's amnesty. Practically everyone else named in the indictments—most notably Dolan and Dudley—applied for and was granted a change of venue to Doña Ana County.

As for Billy Bonney, he expected his own hearing before the court on the charge of murdering Sheriff Brady to be a mere formality in which, in return for his having provided the evidence on which Dolan and Campbell were indicted, the prosecution would decline to proceed. But no such thing happened. Wallace had already returned to the capital, leaving the field wide open to prosecutor William Rynerson, who pressed the charges, challenging Wallace's right to offer anyone immunity.

"I tell you, governor," Ira Leonard wrote Wallace on April 20, "the District Attorney here is no friend of law enforcement. He is bent on going after the Kid. He proposes to distroy [sic] his evidence and influence and is bent on pushing him to the wall. He is a Dolan man and is defending him in every manner possible."[10]

And sure enough, Rynerson won a conviction for murder and a change of venue to Doña Ana County. As Jimmy Dolan's close friend, he knew—both of them knew—that if the Kid were hanged for murder he could scarcely appear as a witness against Dolan. The Kid knew it, too, but his trial would not be held until July, which gave Wallace plenty of time to come through.

A week after the grand jury adjourned, the military court of inquiry into the conduct of Colonel Dudley began at Fort Stanton.

It was not a trial but a hearing to establish whether Dudley should face a court-martial. Three "judges"—Colonel Galusha Pennypacker, Sixteenth Infantry (presiding); Major Nathan W. Osborne; and Captain Henry R. Brinkerhoff—heard evidence adduced by the recorder, Captain Henry H. Humphreys, Fifteenth Infantry, who played a role similar to that of prosecutor, and Dudley's defending counsel, Henry Waldo, a former attorney general and member of the law firm of Catron & Elkins.

It was no contest; Humphreys and Leonard were the equivalent of two modest country lawyers pitched up against one of the sharpest legal brains in New Mexico. They would have been wiped off the map in any courtroom in the territory, and in the totally biased atmosphere of a military court of inquiry they never had a chance. Any competent lawyer today reading the transcript of the hearings, which began on May 9 and heard well over a hundred witnesses, would immediately and accurately describe it as a paradigm of the old adage, "Military justice is to justice as military music is to music."

Humphreys was rarely allowed to ask the most simple factual question without an objection, an adjournment, and (nearly every time) a ruling in

16.13. Henry Lynn Waldo.

Date and photographer unknown.
Author's Collection.

Waldo was born in Jackson
County, Missouri, on January 16,
1844; he died in Kansas City on
July 9, 1915.

16.12. Henry Hollingsworth Humphreys.

Date and photographer unknown.
U.S. Army Military History Institute.

favor of the defendant, while Dudley and the imposing Waldo trashed the
evidence of one after the other of the prosecution witnesses with a mixture
of utter dishonesty and withering contempt. In his closing argument on July
5, for example, Waldo had this to say about the Kid:

> Then was brought forward William Bonney, alias Antrim, alias the Kid, a
> precocious criminal of the worst type, although hardly up to his majority,
> murderer by profession, as records of this court connect him with two
> atrocious murders, that of Roberts and the other of Sheriff Brady. Both of
> them are cowardly and atrocious assassinations. There are warrants enough
> for him on the 19th day of July last to have plastered him from his head to
> his feet, yet he was engaged to do service as a witness and his testimony
> showed that his qualifications do not terminate with blood guiltiness.[11]

He then in measured and contemptuous terms dismissed the Kid's testimony: "A liar once is a liar all the time." It was cruel, but not untypical of the
whole proceeding: anything said in Dudley's defense was the truth; anything
said by a witness for the prosecution was a lie. When the judges retired to
decide which was more probable, no one present doubted what the verdict
would be. "They mean to whitewash and excuse [Dudley's] glaring conduct,"
Leonard wrote Wallace. "There is nothing to be looked for or hoped for from
the tribunal. It is a farce on judicial investigation and ought to be called and
designated 'The Mutual Admiration Inquiry.'"[12]

16.14. Officers of the Fifteenth Infantry, Fort Randall, Dakota Territory.

Date and photographer unknown, ca. 1882.
U.S. Army Military History Institute.

Six of the officers pictured here were involved in Lincoln County events. *Back row, extreme left:* Lieutenant Samuel Pague; *second row, extreme left:* Lieutenant Dillard Hazelrig Clark, sent to protect the army paymaster from the Kid's gang in November 1880; *second row, second from left:* Captain Casper H. Conrad (see Fig. 4.8); *second row, far right:* Captain Henry H. Brinkerhoff, the other judge at the Dudley inquiry; *front row, far right:* Lieutenant Charles Elias Garst, who appeared as a witness for Dudley; *second row, third from left:* Colonel Peter Tyler Swaine, who as judge advocate, Department of the Missouri, found Dudley and his officers guilty of violating the law on July 19, 1878, and concluded they did so "for the purpose of aiding and assisting the Dolan-Riley party, and to further their schemes and objects against the McSween party." His findings were overruled.

On July 18, "after careful investigation and mature deliberation," the court found in favor of Dudley. His actions on July 19 had been prompted by "the most humane and worthy motives and by good military judgment under exceptional circumstances." Proceedings before a court-martial were unnecessary. And with that, apart from a few hiccups further up the chain of command, Dudley was exonerated.

By the time the verdict was rendered, the Kid was long gone. No pardon had come from Wallace, no word that the bargain struck that March night in Squire Wilson's jacal was to be honored. U.S. Marshal John Sherman and his deputy were on their way to Fort Stanton to take him to La Mesilla to stand trial in federal court for the murder of Buckshot Roberts. Even if he did not go down on that count, there was still the territorial case against him for the murder of Brady. That left him only one road to travel. So on the night of June 17 he walked out of his "prison" in the Patrón store, saddled up, and headed out with Tom O'Folliard through the Capitán Gap for Fort Sumner. And if, as they crested the rise, he looked back over his shoulder and said, "The hell with them all," who could blame him?

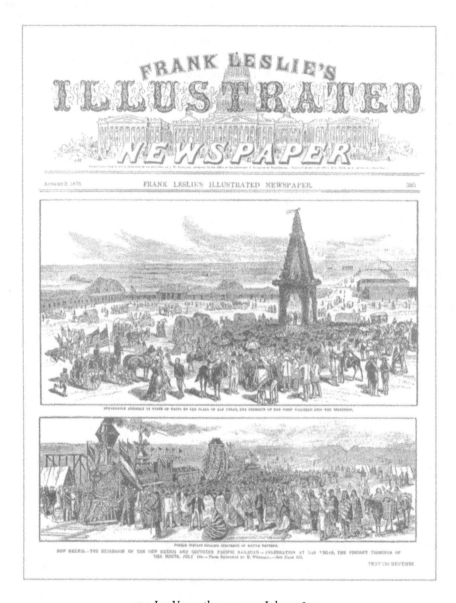

FRANK LESLIE'S ILLUSTRATED NEWSPAPER.

17.1. Las Vegas: the scene on July 4, 1879.

Frank Leslie's Illustrated Newspaper, August 9, 1879.
From sketches by H. Worrall.
Author's Collection.

"New Mexico—The Extension of the New Mexico and Southern Pacific Railroad—Celebration at Las Vegas, the Present Terminus of the Route, July 4th."
  Above: "Remarkable assembly of types of races on the plaza of Las Vegas, the terminus of the first railroad into the territory."
  Below: "Pueblo Indians selling specimens of native pottery."

CHAPTER SEVENTEEN

Outlaws

O<small>N</small> A<small>PRIL</small> 6, 1835, <small>AFTER SUCCESSFULLY</small> petitioning the Mexican government, Juan de Dios Maese, José Antonio Casaus, Miguel Archuleta, and Manuel Durán, on behalf of themselves and twenty-five others from the settlement of San Miguel del Bado took possession of almost half a million acres of grant land in the valley of the Gallinas River. There on the west bank they selected a townsite to which they gave the name Nuestra Señora de los Dolores de las Vegas, Our Lady of Sorrows of the Meadows.

Gradually a town took shape, forming, in the usual New Mexican pattern, around a central plaza, or square, one side of which was a modest church, the other three sides taken up by one-story, flat-roofed adobe buildings. The Vegas, as it became known, quickly established itself as a major stopping place on the Santa Fe Trail, the first settlement reached by wagon trains from Missouri and the last-chance provisioning stop for returning travelers. By 1846, when General Stephen Watts Kearny announced from the roof of a building in the plaza that New Mexico was now part of the United States and its people Americans, the town had something like one hundred dwellings.

Thirty-three years later, Las Vegas was a substantial settlement of more than two thousand inhabitants, with major mercantile houses around its plaza and plenty of saloons and gambling halls. And by the time the first New Mexico & Southern Pacific train steamed in on July 4, 1879, it had a new "addition," a roaring camp on the other side of the river and a mile from the original plaza where the railroad builders had decided to site their depot. The new place was called East Las Vegas, or New Town; the original settlement would eventually become known as Old Town.

To New Town came the track followers, the gamblers, the whores, the bunco men, the enforcers, and the badmen—notable among them Hyman G. Neill, better known as Hoodoo Brown, who got himself elected justice of the peace and took over East Las Vegas the way Al Capone took over Chicago. A tall, thin man with light hair, a small mustache, and a "rakish look," Hoodoo had an idiosyncratic way of dispensing justice. He would lay a double-barreled shotgun on the judicial table and say, "Me and my partner will now open court."[1]

The police force Hoodoo Brown set up to keep East Las Vegas in line boasted as dangerous a complement of hard men as any frontier town in the history of the West; among its members at one time or another were Mysterious Dave Mather, Dave Rudabaugh, John Joshua Webb, Tom Pickett, Joe

17.2. Las Vegas, panorama, looking southwest, 1882.

Published in that year by J. J. Stone, Madison, Wisconsin.
Courtesy Joe and Diana Stein.

East Las Vegas is in the foreground; the Old Town and its plaza are upper center, background. The inset shows the Montezuma Hotel, built on the site of Moore's Hot Springs Hotel in 1881.

17.3. Las Vegas, the old plaza.

Photograph by James N. Furlong, ca. 1879.
MoNM Negative No. 14386.

At the center of the plaza is the notorious "hanging windmill," used on a number of occasions by vigilantes. It was demolished in 1880.

Carson, Jack Lyons, and various other hell-raisers from the Kansas cowtowns. Doc Holliday, who had come to town ahead of the railroad, was keeping a gin mill and gambling hell on Centre Street. Other notable arrivals included Slapjack Bill, the Pockmarked Kid, and Bullshit Jack.

And, quite probably, William H. Bonney was there. Charges later filed in the district court indicate that sometime in July, probably during the month-long bacchanalia that followed the arrival of the railroad, someone known as "The Kid" was keeping an illegal gaming table in Las Vegas. Adding weight to the likelihood of this being Billy is the fact that Dr. Henry Hoyt, formerly of Tascosa, was working in, of all the gin joints in all the towns in all the world, Las Vegas' Exchange Hotel.

One Sunday late in July, Hoyt decided to take dinner up at the handsome Adobe Hotel at the nearby Hot Springs owned and operated by Winfield Scott Moore and his wife, Minnie. In the dining room, to his great surprise, he found his old friend Billy Bonney, who introduced him to his companion, a "Mr. Howard from Tennessee." After dinner, the Kid confided to Hoyt—believe it or not—that Mr. Howard was in fact Jesse James, visiting his old friend Moore, whom he had known as a boy in Missouri. Jesse had suggested they go into business together, but the Kid turned him down because train robbing was not his line.[2]

17.4. Officers at Fort Davis, Texas.

Photographer unknown, 1887. National Archives Negative No. 111-SC-93786.

Front row, second from right: George Purington, looking much as he would have during his sojourn in Lincoln.

On the night of August 9, the Kid was surrounded in a house six miles below Lincoln by Sheriff Kimbrell and a military escort consisting of an officer and fifteen men. Remembering a trick he had used before, Billy eluded arrest, as the exasperated Captain George Purington (once again commanding Fort Stanton) reported, "by climbing up a chimney, leaving his arms behind, and escaping under cover of night."[3]

Evidently the Kid considered being pursued by the military little more than an irritant; as his remarks to Wallace indicate, men as well versed as he in riding the owlhoot trail had no trouble avoiding the noisy pursuit of the pony soldiers. Nor did they, for that matter, have trouble defying it. Frank Coe, down from Colorado to retrieve a haymaking machine, recorded an occasion in which the Kid and Tom O'Folliard came into Lincoln and visited Susan McSween's home. A sergeant from Fort Stanton was dancing with Susan while Coe played the fiddle. The Kid boldly asked the soldier what he was doing there, and the sergeant said if anyone knew that, the Kid ought to.

"Well," said the Kid, "why don't you do something?"

The sergeant mumbled something about not having to do something just because he was sent out to do it. After the Kid, dancing around with his carbine in his hand, crowded him some more by stepping on his feet and making him pull back, the sergeant took the first opportunity he could find to

17.5. Allen J. Ballard.

Date and photographer unknown,
ca. 1870s.
Rio Grande Historical Collections,
NMSU.

17.6. Lucien B. Maxwell *(left)* and
friends.

Date and photographer unknown.
Author's Collection.

skip out the back door. Coe warned Billy that the soldiers were looking for
him. "He said he knew it, but he was tired of dodging and had run from them
about enough."[4]

There was no use his hanging around Lincoln; anyway, it was getting to be
like a ghost town. Early in May gold had been discovered at White Oaks Spring
over in the Jicarillas, and most of the able-bodied men had moved there. Jimmy
Dolan and his supporters were all free on bail, the cases against them continued; on July 13, Jimmy had married Lina Fritz at Allen Ballard's house at La
Junta and had left on a two-month honeymoon. It probably did not seem much
like justice to the Kid, but there it was. It was more than six months since
Wallace had promised him a pardon. Fat chance of that now. The law was still
on his case, and if he was taken, they would give him a fair trial and then hang
him. "I knew I had no show," he said later, "so I skinned out."[5]

17.7. The Maxwell house, Fort Sumner.

Date and photographer unknown, ca. 1882.
Author's Collection.

The place he skinned out to was the area around Fort Sumner, which had proven so hospitable in the aftermath of the Lincoln County War. The old fort buildings, abandoned by the military after the failure of its Navajo concentration camp in 1868, had been purchased by Lucien B. Maxwell from the government in 1871, shortly after he sold his own vast Maxwell Land Grant. About twenty-five families accompanied Maxwell south from Cimarron and formed a settlement that was something between a collective farm and a small town. After Maxwell died in 1875, his wife Doña Luz took his place. Their luxurious home in one of the converted officers' quarters buildings became the social hub of the little town while her son Pedro, known to everyone as Pete, managed the family ranch, sheep herds, and employees.

In the Kid's time there, "Fort Sumner was a gay little place," Paulita Maxwell Jaramillo said in later years. "The weekly dance was an event and pretty girls from Santa Rosa, Puerto de Luna, Anton Chico and from towns and ranches fifty miles away, drove in to attend it. It might surprise you to know that our dances were extremely decorous. Everybody attended them, old and young. We girls at Fort Sumner were not accustomed to dueñas, but with our mothers and grandmothers looking on at our merriment, we were quite well chaperoned. There was no drunkenness, no rowdyism. Our men would not have tolerated anything like that for an instant."

Here at Fort Sumner the Kid had friends, allies, compadres, and sympathizers—not to mention all those pretty señoritas, beautiful girls such as the blonde Celsa Gutierres and Pete Maxwell's sister Paulita. The Kid "fascinated many women," she said. "In every *placita* in the Pecos some little señorita was proud to be known as his *querida*." She recalled the "gallant figure" he

17.8. Peter Menard Maxwell *(sitting)* and his friend Henry J. Lease.

Date and photographer unknown.
MoNM Negative No. 58757.

Pete (Pedro) Maxwell, the oldest son of Lucien and Ana de la Luz (Beaubien) Maxwell, was born at Taos on April 27, 1848. His life was always lived in the shadow of his flamboyant father and his father's famous friends. In 1857, Lucien Maxwell founded the town of Cimarron and made his home there, living in great luxury until a series of ill-advised financial ventures decimated his enormous wealth. When Fort Sumner was abandoned, Lucien Maxwell purchased the site and, after making substantial improvements, moved there in 1871. After his father's death in 1875, Peter became general manager of the business. According to local tradition, after his ignominious flight from the bedroom in which the Kid was killed, he was always referred to as "Don Chootme." He died at Fort Sumner on June 21, 1898.

Source: Jim Berry Pearson, The Maxwell Land Grant; Pauline Jaramillo, *Genealogical and Historical Data of the Jaramillo Family 1598–1989*; research by Don McAlavy, Clovis, New Mexico.

17.9. Enlisted men's barracks, Fort Sumner.

Date and photographer unknown, ca. 1868.
Rio Grande Historical Collections, NMSU.

This is the view the occupants of the Maxwell house would have had looking east across the parade ground. How much of this building was standing in the Kid's time is uncertain.

17.10. Present-day Fort Sumner.

Author's photograph, 1996.

The low wall marks the site of the original enlisted men's barracks (Fig. 17.9). The trees on the right mark the approximate location of the old building in which Saval and Celsa Gutierres made their home.

cut at the weekly dances in Fort Sumner. "He was not handsome but he had a certain sort of boyish good looks. He was always smiling and good-natured and very polite and danced remarkably well, and the little Mexican beauties made eyes at him from behind their fans and used all their coquetries to capture him and were very vain of his attentions"—herself included, it may be added. The Kid's burgeoning relationship with Paulita would become what might be called a fatal attraction.[6]

As fall advanced, the Kid once more became a link in the old chain gang, supplementing his winnings from dealing monte in Beaver Smith's saloon at Fort Sumner by rustling cattle and horses. During his time in Tascosa he had learned that stray stock from the big ranches such as the LX and the XIT would move south across the Llano Estacado before the winter winds until the steeply descending caprock stopped them. All one had to do was ride up there, make sure there were no line riders about, and round them up.

Billy's coworkers in this enterprise were a new and less savory bunch that included former Las Vegas policemen Dave Rudabaugh and Tom Pickett and little Billy Wilson, whose real name was probably David L. Anderson. Rudabaugh, who gloried in the nickname "Dirty Dave," was a ruffian of the worst stripe, a former Kansas train robber turned informer who had more recently held up stagecoaches near Las Vegas under the protection of City Marshal John Joshua Webb. When Webb had been arrested and thrown into the city jail, Rudabaugh tried to break him out, in the process gunning down jailor Lino Valdez. Pickett was a former Texas Ranger who had made himself so unpopular at the Vegas that he had decided to depart for healthier climes before he

17.11. Tom Pickett.

Date and photographer not known. R. N. Mullin Collection, HHC.

Pickett was born at Camp Throckmorton, Wise County, Texas, May 27, 1856; he died in Winslow, Arizona, on May 14, 1934.

17.12. John J. Webb (center, with hands in pockets).

Photographer unknown, Las Vegas, 1880.
Courtesy Andy Gregg.

Webb was born in Keokuk County, Iowa, February 13, 1847; he is said to have died of smallpox in 1882. This photo was taken in 1880 outside the entrance of the Las Vegas jail, in which Billy the Kid was imprisoned just after Christmas 1880. The building, which was on Valencia Street behind the Old Town plaza, appears to have been considerably more substantial than might have been expected.

got shot. Now, like Rudabaugh, he was keeping out of sight by working as a cowboy on the Yerby ranch. When Bowdre rode with the Kid, Rudabaugh and Pickett generally went along.

The gold strike in Lincoln County had spawned a mining camp called White Oaks big enough to constitute a no-questions-asked market for beef. From their "ranch" at Los Portales about seventy miles southeast of Sumner— really little more than a natural holding pen, a hollow in the plains with springs that were one of the few reliable sources of good water on the Llano—the Kid, Bowdre, and O'Folliard could chouse the cattle across to Bosque Grande, where Dan Dedrick now occupied the old Chisum ranch. At the White Oaks camp Dedrick's brother Sam was co-owner of a livery stable; a third brother, Mose, had a place nearby where stolen beef could be butchered and sold to the miners.

To make the return trip pay, the Kid and his boys would steal stock and take it back to the Panhandle, an activity which endeared him to the citizens of neither White Oaks nor anyplace else. Both there and in the Panhandle he and his "gang" came to be increasingly regarded as a scourge about which something, sooner or later, would have to be done. The problem was, in the first place, no one knew where to look for them, and in the second place, no one was too anxious to find them in the first place.

17.13. Thomas G. Yerby.

Date and photographer unknown.
Courtesy Donald Lavash.

A rancher near Fort Sumner, Thomas G. Yerby was probably born in 1847 in the community where he grew up, Stony Hill, Richmond County, Virginia, one of the three children of wealthy farmer A. O. Yerby. The indications are that the father died in the Civil War, because in 1870 a destitute Mrs. Yerby and her daughter Emma had moved in with a Dr. William Douglas and his family; what happened to the older sister, Virginia, is not recorded.

Tom Yerby drifted west, and in 1872 he was employed at Belen, New Mexico, by wholesalers Becker & Co. Later he moved to Las Vegas and became a bookkeeper for Ilfeld & Co. He established a homestead near Bosque Redondo on the Pecos and also acquired land at the head of Arroyo Canadinas. He purchased a lot on the northwestern edge of Las Vegas and in the house he built there he installed sixteen-year-old Nasaria Leyba, who became his common-law wife; they had two children, Juan and Florentina.

Through the years Yerby continued his association with Ilfeld, commuting from Fort Sumner to Las Vegas. In March 1888, Yerby and his partner, Erastus J. Wilcox, left New Mexico to homestead in Montana or Wyoming; Yerby deeded the Las Vegas home to Nasaria, who remained in New Mexico with the children. The family tradition is that Yerby died en route to or shortly after he reached his destination.

Source: Donald R. Lavash, "Thomas G. Yerby and Nasaria," *The Outlaw Gazette* 5, no. 1 (December 1992): 10–11.

Describing his modus operandi, Pat Garrett (or Ash Upson) claimed the Kid, O'Folliard, Bowdre, Scurlock, and two others stole 118 head of Chisum cattle in the Bosque Grande area, drove them to Yerby's ranch, where they rebranded them, and later sold them to some Colorado men at Alexander Grzelachowski's ranch on Alamogordo Creek. This may well be accurate reporting; Chisum herds had reappeared in the Pecos Valley after Hunter & Evans sold them back, or leased them or loaned them or repaid them—the ramifications of Chisum's deals with them were labyrinthine—not to Uncle John but to his brothers, James and Pitzer. They suffered considerable losses to rustlers during the latter part of 1879; rightly or wrongly, the Kid got the credit or the blame, depending on your viewpoint.[7]

Meanwhile, down at Seven Rivers, old scores were still being settled. On August 26 at Joe Nash's chosa in Pierce Canyon—another natural cattle pen like Los Portales—John Jones and John Beckwith got into an argument about which of whose cattle the other had stolen; it ended in gunfire with Beckwith's death.

Three days later, Jones left Seven Rivers to ride up to Lincoln and turn himself in. Stopping off at the Milo Pierce and Louis Paxton cattle camp on the Pecos, he encountered the two partners, Bob Olinger, Buck Powell, Jim Ramer, and Billy Smith. A violent fight ensued. According to Ash Upson,

17.14. Daniel Charles Dedrick.

Date and photographer unknown, ca. 1870s.
Upham Collection, Lincoln County Heritage Trust.

Dan Dedrick was born of Pennsylvanian stock (the original family name was Dietrich) in Indiana about 1848. He was said by Barney Mason to have escaped from a Fort Smith, Arkansas, jail where he was serving time for stealing horses. Later, when things got too warm in the White Oaks area, Dan moved to Socorro and then Arizona. In 1882 he relocated to Trinity, California, and he died at Big Bear, California, in 1937 or 1938.

Samuel Dedrick was also born in Indiana, about 1852. He lost his right arm at the age of twelve or fourteen in a cane crusher. It was he who ran the livery stable at White Oaks in partnership with William H. West. Sam was shot and killed by "a Mexican" on the Rio Verde at Deming, New Mexico, in 1909 for reasons unknown.

Source: Allen Barker, personal correspondence, 1995–97.

17.15. Moses Dedrick and friend, Della Williams.

Photographer unknown, Deming, N.Mex., January 5, 1898.
Upham Collection, Lincoln County Heritage Trust.

Mose Dedrick was born in Kansas about 1860. He was shot by an unidentified assailant about eight miles from Phoenix, Arizona, in 1909. The reason for his death, like that of his brother Sam, remains unexplained.

17.16. *(Left)* John Jones.

Date and photographer unknown, ca. 1870s.
R. N. Mullin Collection. HHC.

Jones was born in Pennsylvania in 1853; he was killed by Bob Olinger on August 29, 1879.

17.17. *(Right)* John M[armaduke?] Beckwith.

Date and photographer unknown, 1870s.
Author's Collection.

Beckwith was born on January 14, 1853; he was killed by John Jones on August 26, 1879.

"John was shot twice in the back and twice in the back of the head. All four of the balls went through, killing him instantly. Pierce was badly shot above the hip, and was taken to Fort Stockton."

It was rumored later that what really happened when Jones reached the cow camp was that Pierce, lying on a cot and faking illness, called him over. When Jones shook hands, Pierce hung on while Bob Olinger shot Jones in the back, one of the bullets going through Jones's body and into Pierce's hip. It was a tradition in the Jones family that the manner in which his friend John was killed fueled the Kid's hatred of Olinger.[8]

Meanwhile, the Kid's notoriety continued to grow; it was widely believed from statements he himself made that he had a personal grudge against John Chisum for failing to pay him for fighting in the McSween corner in the war. According to Will Chisum, the Kid actually cornered John Chisum at Fort Sumner and threatened to kill him if he didn't pay up.

"Billy, you know as well as I do I never hired you to fight in the Lincoln County War," Chisum said. "I always pay my honest debts. I don't owe you anything, and you can kill me but you won't knock me out of many years. I'm an old man now."

"Aw," the Kid said, turning away, "you ain't worth killing."[9]

Thereafter, the story goes, he decided to reimburse himself in kind from Chisum's herds. But the Kid surely knew as well as anyone in the territory that the cattle no longer belonged to Uncle John but to his brothers Jim and Pitzer. Maybe he figured it was the same thing.

One night in January 1880, Jim Chisum and three hands were camped near Fort Sumner, where they had recovered some Jinglebob stock with badly botched brands. They were now driving them back south. Into the camp rode the Kid and two companions; he asked to inspect the brands. Chisum, who

17.18. Pierce Canyon, New Mexico, looking west.

Author's photograph, 1995.

Pierce Canyon, like the Kid's Los Portales "ranch," was simply an easily managed natural holding pen for large quantities of cattle. The U-shaped canyon's steeply sloping sides effectively penned in the animals, making it necessary only to patrol the western, or Pecos, end where it opens up above the river; this was the site of Joe Nash's chosa.

17.19. Pierce Canyon, New Mexico, looking east.

Author's photograph, 1995.

suspected the Kid was himself the brand blotter, let him take a look. No doubt realizing he couldn't hornswoggle Chisum, the Kid invited Jim to bring his boys down to the fort for a drink.

When they got to Bob Hargrove's saloon in the old quartermaster's building on the northeast corner of the parade ground, a Texas man named Joe Grant was being noisily and objectionably drunk. The Kid indicated he'd already had words with Grant, who told him, "I'll bet $25 I kill a man today before you do." Now Grant reeled over to Chisum rider Jack Finan, took Finan's ivory-handed revolver out of its holster, and replaced it with his own. Finan wisely made no protest. After a few minutes, the Kid went over to Grant and pretended to admire the pistol he had just acquired. He knew something Grant didn't know: earlier, Finan had fired three shots from the gun. When Grant allowed him to hold it, the Kid spun the cylinder so that if it were fired the hammer would fall on an empty shell, then gave it back to Grant.

"Texas Red," as Grant was apparently called, got louder and more violent, smashing bottles behind the bar. Finally, shouting that he was going to kill John Chisum, he turned on Jim Chisum.

"Hold on," the Kid said, "you got the wrong sow by the ear, this is Jim Chisum, old Uncle John's brother."

"That's a lie!" Grant shouted as the Kid turned away.

He "squared off at Billy, who when he heard the click [of the hammer on an empty shell] whirled around and 'bang, bang, bang.' Right in the chin—y'could cover all of them with a half dollar."

The Kid looked down at the dead man. "Joe," he said, "I've been there too often for you."[10]

A few days later the Kid was with Charlie Bowdre in the post office at Sunnyside Springs, a mile above the fort. Learning from Bowdre that "another man had turned his toes up at Sumner"—which suggests it was not an unusual occurrence—Postmaster Milnor Rudulph asked the Kid what had happened. "Oh, nothing," Billy said off-handedly. "It was a game of two and I got there first."[11]

A corollary to stealing Panhandle cattle and selling them in Lincoln County was stealing horses in Lincoln County—notably from the Mescalero reservation—and selling them wherever buyers could be found. In February 1880, according to Pat Garrett, the Kid and Mose Dedrick ran off forty-eight horses from the agency. In May, the Kid, Charlie Bowdre, and two others brought fifty-four steers across from the Panhandle and sold them to Tom Cooper in newly platted White Oaks, now a real boomtown. Their hard and dangerous work (for which they earned a little more than seven hundred dollars) would yield the buyer twice that. Cooper was a middleman for Patrick Coghlan, the self-styled "King of the Tularosa," who had just secured a contract to supply beef to Fort Stanton for the year commencing July 1.[12]

That summer was notable, from the Kid's point of view, for two events. The first was the marriage to George B. Barber of Susan McSween, celebrated, if that is the word, on June 20. The second took place in the far-off Texas town of Fort Davis, adjacent to the old fort, where on May 19 Jesse Evans led a gang that robbed the Sender & Siebenborn store, making off with about nine hundred dollars in money and watches and another two hundred dollars'

17.20. John S. Chisum.

Date and photographer unknown, 1880s.
Rio Grande Historical Collections, NMSU.

17.21. Milnor Rudulph.

Photograph by Furlong & Crispell, Las Vegas, ca. 1880s.
Courtesy Michael J. Keleher and Philip Sanchez.

Rudulph was born in Maryland on August 26, 1826; he died in Rociada, New Mexico on November 8, 1887.

17.22. Patrick Coghlan.

Date and photographer unknown, ca. 1890s.
Courtesy C. L. Sonnichsen.

Coghlan was born in Clonakilty, Ireland, March 15, 1822; he died in Tularosa, January 27, 1911.

17.23. George B. Barber.

Photograph by Journeay, date unknown, ca. 1890?
R. G. McCubbin Collection.

Barber was born in Milwaukee, Wisconsin, on May 28, 1846; he died in Carrizozo, New Mexico, October 24, 1928.

worth of merchandise. On the same day they robbed F. W. Rouff, and on the next they ransacked the house of August Diamond.

In response to requests for aid, a party of ten Texas Rangers commanded by Sergeant Ed Sieker was dispatched to Fort Stockton; another of the same size commanded by Sergeant L. B. Caruthers was sent to Fort Davis. Both arrived at their destinations on Sunday, June 6. In his report to Lieutenant Charles Nevill on June 8, Caruthers wrote, "The men who robbed Senders and Seibenborn were two Williamson County men, by the names of Bud Graham alias Ace Carr, and Charlie Graham alias Charlie Graves, also one Jesse Evans." Graham, he said, had been captured; the other two were reported to be at the Horsehead Crossing of the lower Pecos.[13]

The plot thickened. Also in the gang, he revealed, were Dollay Graham, alias George Davis; John Gunter, also known as John Gross; and "their agent," a Captain Tyson, whose real name was John Selman and who Caruthers believed to be the leader of the band. To keep him from leaving town, the Ranger appointed Selman jailor; then a plan was devised to bring Ace Carr to Fort Davis as bait in a trap for the Evans crowd. It might have worked except that Sheriff T. W. Wilson got drunk and spilled the beans; Selman was arrested and put behind bars.

On July 1 a scout of Rangers left Fort Davis; on the Fourth of July they

17.24. Texas Ranger Charles L. Nevill (*right*) with N. O. Reynolds.

Date and photographer unknown, 1870s.
Courtesy Mrs. Beatrice Lear.

came up on a group of men who fled as they approached. A running gun battle ensued until the outlaws dismounted and made a stand. In the ensuing shootout Ranger George "Red" Bingham was killed; when George Graham was shot through the head by Sergeant Sieker, his companions surrendered. The Ranger and Graham were buried by the roadside; the prisoners were then brought back to Fort Davis and thrown into its notorious "Bat Cave" dungeon.

On August 26, Lieutenant Nevill reported having intercepted a letter the prisoners had written "to a friend of Evans in New Mexico called Billy Antrum to cause their rescue, and to use his words he was 'in a damned tight place, only 14 Rangers here any time, ten on a scout and only four in camp right now,' and that Antrum and a few men could take them out very easy and if he could not do it now to meet him on the road to Huntsville [prison] as he was certain to go. I understand this man Antrum is a fugitive from somewhere and a noted desperado. If he comes down and I expect he will, I will enlist him for a while and put him in the same mess with Evans & Co."

Clearly Jesse believed the Kid would ride down to Fort Davis to spring him from jail; that the Kid would have done any such thing defies belief. Yet on September 5, Nevill reported he had heard from a reliable source that "there is a party made up in Lincoln County, N.M. headed by one Billy Antrum alias Kid, for the purpose of releasing Jesse Evans and his gang. If so they may be here in a day or so."

Nevill's intelligence was that after the Kid broke Jesse and his pals out of jail, he planned to round up all the cattle they could find and drive them back to New Mexico to finance the trip, but twelve days of heavy rains and floods— the Pecos was said to be a mile wide at Pecos City and the Van Horn flats— rendered the mission impossible.

17.25. John W. Green, alias Frank Stewart.

Photographer unknown, 1930.
Courtesy Amarillo Public Library.

This, the only known photograph of Stewart, appeared in a Texas newspaper in 1930. Surviving copies of the paper are in poor condition, and this is about the best reproduction that can be made of the picture.

The man known as Frank Stewart was born John W. Green in New York City on October 23, 1852, and by his own (not necessarily truthful) account was a consumptive brought west by his father about 1867 after his mother died of tuberculosis. They both worked in western Kansas until 1870, when the father was killed by Cheyennes. Green turned trail driver and with Charlie Siringo delivered a herd to the LX Ranch in the Panhandle in 1876, returning in 1880 to work there. In 1887, accused of stealing cattle near Liberty, New Mexico, he posted bond signed by some citizens of Las Vegas. Stewart, it was said, appeared before the justice, snatched the bond off the bench, and disappeared. About 1916 he settled in Raton, New Mexico, where he died on May 11, 1935, at age eighty-two.

Source: *Amarillo Sunday News and Globe*, November 30 and December 22, 1930; research by Nancy Robertson, Raton, New Mexico.

Still, Nevill did not dismiss the possibility. Even as late as November 17, when the prison contractors came to take Evans to Huntsville, he reported, "Evans' friends say the contractor will never get to the penitentiary with Evans but I expect they will if they present a fighting appearance. I know Capt. Kidd does not want to fight bad."[14]

Whatever the accuracy of all this, "Capt. Kidd" never went anywhere near Texas. By the time Jesse entered Huntsville, Billy had troubles enough of his own. Unknown to him, a group of Staked Plains ranchers had banded together to form a cattlemen's association; they hired as their detective a capable young cattleman named Frank Stewart to locate and identify the rustlers who were bleeding them dry.

Stewart, whose real name was John W. Green, was a consumptive New Yorker who had come west when he was fifteen after the death of his mother from the same disease. After Cheyennes killed his father in Kansas in 1870, the eighteen-year-old John hired on as a cowboy. Delivering a herd to the LX in 1876 convinced him to return to the Panhandle four years later; there he went to work for Bill Moore. When the cattle association hired him, he adopted the alias of Frank Stewart.[15] At Fort Sumner, Stewart and the four cowboys with him found hides bearing the LIT brand and picked up enough information to suggest that the thieves were the Kid's outfit. When Stewart got back to the Panhandle, the cattlemen agreed to finance and furnish manpower for an expedition into New Mexico to recover their stock and put the Kid out of business—permanently.

CHAPTER EIGHTEEN

Hunters and Hunted

COINCIDENT WITH FRANK STEWART'S INVESTIGATION, although for totally different reasons, the federal government also began to take an interest in Lincoln County again. Letters had reached the Treasury Department—from J. C. Lea, James Dolan, and Ira Leonard, among others—complaining that counterfeit one-hundred-dollar banknotes were being passed in Lincoln and White Oaks. James Brooks, head of the U.S. Secret Service, assigned Azariah Faxon Wild of New Orleans, special operative for the Gulf states, to investigate the case.

After conferring at Santa Fe with U.S. Attorney Sidney M. Barnes, sixty, an erudite Kentucky legislator and Civil War veteran—who made a point of letting Wild know how unimportant he was in the scheme of things—Wild arrived at White Oaks in October, taking the precaution before he went there of buying a miner's suit for $12.50 so he would not stand out in the crowd.

Wild's inquiries quickly established who had done what to whom. On October 4 he met with Ira Leonard and went to LaRue's store—once Tunstall's—where James Dolan showed him a counterfeit hundred-dollar bill he had received from Billy Wilson. José Montaño showed him two more, passed by Sam Cooper and Wilson. A James Patty, alias James Finley, cattle thief, had paid for merchandise at the Dowlin store with another, which Dowlin in turn had used to pay for the schooling of his daughters in Santa Fe.

"In my candid judgement I have struck the worst nest of counterfeiters in the United States and what I believe will lead to the headquarters of the gang and the long looked for [printing] plates if cautiously worked," Wild wrote in his daily report to Brooks. Looking for support, he sent a letter signed by himself, Leonard, Easton, Corbet, Dolan, Ben Ellis, and J. J. LaRue asking Sidney Barnes to arrange for him to have military assistance to make arrests. It would be quite some time before he got any sort of response; the U.S. attorney and his law enforcement arm, Marshal John Sherman, clearly did not think very highly of either Azariah Wild or the Secret Service.

Plunging in with a great deal more enthusiasm than accuracy, Wild reported that the leader of the gang was Billy Wilson:

> In tracing up the history of the character of . . . Wilson, I found he is an
> American who has been in Lincoln County for several years and has the
> name of being engaged with others of his kind in stealing horses and cattle.
> A few weeks ago he and several of his clan stole thirty-eight head of beef
> cattle from a ranch near Fort Bascom and brought them to Lincoln County
> where they found their way into the hands of the United States and are now

18.1. White Oaks, New Mexico.

Photograph by John A. Brown, ca. 1882.
Rio Grande Historical Collections, NMSU.

The mining town of White Oaks sprang up after Missourian John Baxter discovered gold near a spring under a clump of white oaks in the Jicarilla Mountains. At its peak, White Oaks boasted over three thousand inhabitants, but it began to decline when it was bypassed by the railroad and the mines petered out and closed down in 1917. Today only a few residents remain.

18.2. Ghost-town White Oaks.

Author's photograph, 1973.

The Exchange building on White Oaks Street.
William C. McDonald, first governor after statehood in 1912, practiced law here.

18.3. White Oaks.

Author's photograph, 1973.

Two of the ornate houses typical of the boom-town era.

on the Mescalero Indian reservation as I am informed by David Easton, one of the men in charge. The evidence is conclusive against Wilson as being the party who stole them and sold them here.

Cooper and Wilson, he learned, were "both employed in a livery and sales stable at White Oaks kept by one James West, a notorious character recently from Texas." Apparently Wild did not know, and never seems to have found out, that it was from Billy Wilson that W. H. (not James) West and Dedrick had bought the stable, paying him four hundred dollars in counterfeit money, which Billy then unsuspectingly put into circulation.

"There is an outlaw in the mountains here," Wild added, throwing coherence to the winds, "who came here from Arizona after committing a murder there named William Antrom alias William Bonney alias Billy Kid with whom these cattle thieves meet and by many it is believed that they the cattle thieves are shovers of the queer. . . . I have found no evidence this far to support their suspicions."

More interestingly, he indicated that negotiations to obtain the long-promised pardon were again in train between Ira Leonard, acting as the Kid's attorney, and Governor Lew Wallace: "During the Lincoln Co. War he killed men on the Indian Reservation for which he has been indicted in the Territorial and the United States Court," Wild explained:

> Governor Wallace has issued a proclamation granting immunity to those not indicted. The proclamation did not cover his (Antrom's) case and he (Antrom) has been in the mountains as an outlaw ever since, a space of about two years time.
>
> Gov. Wallace has since written Antrom's attorney on the subject saying he should be let go but failed to put it in a shape that satisfied Judge Leonard Antrom's attorney. . . . Antrom has recently written a letter to Judge Leonard which he has showed to me in confidence that leads me to believe that we can use Antrom in these cases provided Gov. Wallace will make good his written promises and the US Attorney will allow the case pending in the US Court to slumber and give him (Antrom) one more chance to reform.

Clearly what Leonard had in mind here was much the same kind of deal for Billy that Wallace had offered him a year earlier: he would testify against the counterfeiters in federal court and in return the charges against him would be dropped.

"I have promised nothing and will not," Wild averred, "except to review any proposition he and his client saw fit to submit to US Attorney Barnes. Judge Leonard has written Antrom to meet him (Leonard) at once for consultation. The chances are that the interview will take place within the next week when I will report fully to you and submit whatever proposition they see fit to make to US Attorney Barnes for such action as he deems proper to take."

That Wild was a Secret Service operative does not seem to have been much of a secret around White Oaks; next, he was approached by Edgar Walz, who asked him if he would pay for information. Yes, if it led to arrests and convictions, Wild said.

> Walz then said: I have a man at my ranch under my employ whose name I am under pledge not to give who states that he was made on one occasion to swear to keep secret what was given him. that he then joined a gang of men whose purpose was to steal cattle, horses, rob and pass counterfeit money. That he knows every sworn man that belongs to the gang which numbers one hundred and sixty one members, that he knows the location of each man and knows just where they get their money and where they keep their bank in this Territory. That they have a pass word and know each other by the means of these pass words.

If the government would pay the man one thousand dollars, Walz said, he would capture the gang and show Wild the cave (probably at Fort Stanton) where the money was kept. After Walz left for his ranch—actually the old Murphy Carrizo ranch, now owned by Thomas Catron—to try to get an agreement in writing, Wild confided in Dowlin, who told him he believed there was "just such a gang working the frontier" and that he believed "Antrom alias Billey Bonney to be one of the gang."

On October 10, Wild reported that West, Sam Dedrick's partner in the White Oaks livery stable, was in Deadwood, Dakota Territory, taking delivery of a herd, and "William Antrom alias Billy Kid is at Fort Sumner. He is a member of the clan[.] I have recently seen a letter written by him [to Ira Leonard] in which he expressed himself as being tired of dodging the officers &c. This letter has been answered. The chances are that I will meet him under circumstances which may bring about good results."

Wild next unsecretly canvassed for the names of men who would support him as deputy U.S. marshals; when Johnny Hurley and Bob Olinger were recommended to him, he forwarded their names to Sherman in Santa Fe for consideration and action. It is an indication of his gullibility that he did so without even pausing to wonder whether, where the Kid was concerned, Olinger or Hurley might have axes of their own to grind. Meanwhile, he used Sunday, October 17 (apparently the Secret Service suspended operations on the Sabbath) to fill in his superior—again with questionable accuracy—on the backgrounds of some of his suspects.

Charlie Bowdre, he said, hailed from Virginia (wrong); William Antrom alias Billie Bonnie alias "Billie Kid," was indicted "for the murder of the Indian Agent. Came from Kansas here" (wrong). Dr. Joseph G. Scurlock, indicted for the same offenses, "claims Georgia as his native place [wrong]. He killed one man each in Louisiana and Texas." Henry Brown was "at present engaged driving buckboard (stage) between Las Vegas and Vinita, Indian Territory." Thomas O'Falliard [sic] had come "From Texas here. He and a man named Joseph Smith robbed a man at White Oaks on or about the 1st day of June 1880 of $700." Jim French, also stated to be from Texas, was wanted for the murder of Brady. And so the list went on. Quite why Brooks needed to know all this is not clear; perhaps Wild wanted him to see he was getting value for the daily four dollars plus expenses Wild was charging.

The following Monday, things began to happen. Edgar Walz came in and revealed the name of the informant: James DeVours, who appears in the 1880 census as a herder, twenty-eight, born in South Carolina. Although he was not prepared to put what he knew in writing, DeVours told Wild there were

18.4. The Carrizo (also Corizozo, Carasosa, Corisoso) ranch.

Woodcut, 1883.
Courtesy R. G. McCubbin.

The former L. G. Murphy ranch near White Oaks as it would have looked in the Kid's time. It passed into the possession of Thomas B. Catron, who in turn sold it in 1882 to an English syndicate headed by J. A. Alcock.

"five persons engaged in making counterfeit national banknotes of $100 and $50. That the press and plates are in this County. That they have nearly $200,000 struck off. That he can point it out. That he has seen the plates and press. That it has recently been moved but that he can find out just where it now is."

This was great news to Wild; he was only ten days into the investigation and already it looked as if he was going to break the counterfeiting ring wide open. Like all of Wild's schemes, however, it was pie in the sky. Two days later he learned that the mail had been robbed twice at Fort Sumner in the last ten days. Several of his reports had been taken, and since the mail carrier claimed—on what evidence is not apparent—to have recognized the thieves as "the Wilson and Kid gang," doubtless by now "the plans of our capture and my mission here is as well known to them as it is to myself." DeVours seems to have thought so, too; he skinned out without leaving a forwarding address.

The state of law enforcement in Lincoln County—in the whole territory for that matter—appalled Wild, who complained bitterly and repeatedly in his reports to Brooks about the apathy of Barnes and Sherman. As it became more and more apparent that he was going to get no support from Santa Fe, Wild determined to conduct his own war against the outlaws and "organized secretly a 'Posse Comitatus' of thirty men here to go and assist in making the arrests not only [of] those who are wanted for passing counterfeit money but those who are wanted for murder, robbing the US Mail, and are indicted in US Courts." The Kid, Wilson, Pickett, and O'Folliard were at a ranch twelve

18.5. Joseph Calloway Lea.

Steel engraving from a photograph.
Author's Collection.

Joseph Calloway Lea was born in Cleveland, Tennessee, on November 8, 1841. His family moved to Missouri, where they settled at a site called Lea's (Lee's) Summit, which figures frequently in the saga of Jesse James and the Younger brothers. After a stint with Quantrill's guerrillas (which he preferred never to discuss), Lea served alongside his close friend Cole Younger in Captain Jarrette's company of the Sixth Missouri under Shelby and rose to the rank of colonel in the Confederate Army. After the war he worked his way back to Mississippi, where, on February 3, 1875, he married Sally Wildy. They moved west to Colfax County in 1876; shortly after their first son, Harry, was born in April 1877, the Leas relocated to Roswell, and Captain Lea bought out the store/post office and hotel, owned by gambler Van C. Smith and his partner Aaron Wilburn, located about a block west of the present-day courthouse. In 1878, Major Wildy, Sally Lea's father, bought the homestead Marion Turner had filed on under Van Smith's nose and deeded it to his daughter. These two purchases became the nucleus of what were eventually to become vast landholdings in the Roswell area.

Lea, the "Father of Roswell," was elected to the territorial legislature in 1889; following the death of his first wife, he married Mabel Day of Coleman, Texas. He was elected the first mayor of Roswell in 1903 and died suddenly, from pneumonia, on February 4, 1904.

Sources: Elvis E. Fleming and Minor S. Huffman, eds., *Roundup on the Pecos*, 279 ff.; Cole Younger, *The Story of Cole Younger, by Himself*, 48, 57.

miles from Fort Sumner, he said; Cooper and Dedrick were at White Oaks and could be taken at any time "unless my reports taken from the mail frighten them away."

If the Kid and his boys were frightened, they gave little sign of it. Two days later, on October 22, Wild reported that "Wilson and gang have within the past few days stole sixty eight head of cattle from a man named Ellis—400 from another party and seven horses from John Chism [*sic*]. They have sent word to John Chism that they have his horses. that if he thought himself a man to come and try to get them."[1]

"Chism" was sick and tired of being stolen from. Along with Joseph C. Lea, a former Quantrill rider who was now a leading citizen and landowner in Roswell, he took steps to deal with their problem. Someone was needed who knew the Kid's country as well as the Kid himself, someone to put a little of the iron into the job of sheriffing Lincoln County that George Kimbrell clearly lacked. Their choice was Patrick F. Garrett, thirty years old, six and a half feet tall, a former buffalo hunter and saloon keeper who had come to New Mexico in 1878 and was now married to a native New Mexican girl, Apolonaria Gutierres from Puerto de Luna, and living at Fort Sumner. Quiet-spoken, determined, and tough, Garrett was persuaded to move to Roswell and run for sheriff.

Because George Kimbrell turned a blind eye to the Kid's movements in and out of White Oaks and even, as Wild noted, played cards with him in Lincoln, the Kid not unnaturally favored Kimbrell over Garrett, who he already knew well. Garrett had probably been one of the ten buffalo hunters who had attached themselves to the Regulator caravan the preceding year at Bosque Grande—and of course the Kid had seen Garrett plenty of times in Sumner. An oft-repeated anecdote has Billy canvassing for Kimbrell among the locals when he encountered future governor George Curry, then a lowly employee of Dowlin & DeLaney. Curry had no idea who he was, of course. "He asked me how I thought the election for sheriff would go in Las Tablas, our voting precinct. I told him our votes would be for Pat Garrett. He asked, bluntly, why I thought Garrett would win, and I replied just as bluntly that Garrett was a brave man who would arrest Billy the Kid or any other outlaw for whom a warrant was outstanding. Mounting a sturdy cow pony, and waving a cheerful "adios," the stranger rode away. It was then that Felipe Miranda, our sheep boss, told me I had been talking with Billy the Kid."[2]

Another version of the story has the Kid telling the future governor, "You're a good cook and a good fellow, but if you think Pat Garrett is going to carry this precinct for sheriff, you are a damn poor politician."[3]

Billy was wrong; on November 2, Garrett carried Las Tablas 39 to 1, and the election by 141 votes over Kimbrell. Because he could not formally take office until January 1, Kimbrell appointed him a deputy; in fact, Garrett acted as sheriff in everything but name. Now Azariah Wild, to whom Marshal John Sherman had finally sent two commissions in the name of Johnny Hurley, crossed out Hurley's name on one of them and wrote in Garrett's, thus—with somewhat dubious authority—appointing Garrett a deputy U.S. marshal.

"I will soon be in readiness to go to Fort Sumner after certain parties," Wild wrote to Lea four days later, "and desire you send Capt. Garrett to lead our party together with as many good citizens as can be found willing to go especially those who have lost stock so that we can make a clean sweep both of the stolen stock and thieves," adding that he intended to pay "some discreet person" two dollars a day to go to Fort Sumner and get the lay of the land.

Lea and Garrett, "old officers in the Army during the war," had "agreed to organise the 'Posse Comitatus' to make a raid on Fort Sumner to arrest counterfeiters. I failed to state in previous reports that we have organised a force in the "Pan Handle" (Texas) to co-opperate [sic] with us on this raid with a view of securing a large number of these outlaws who are from that State."

They left for Roswell on Sunday, November 14, but a heavy snowstorm two days later rendered the roads impassable and necessitated a postponement. Wild was about to leave the Oaks with fifteen men on Friday, November 19, when he got word from Lea that Garrett was on his way up. "He brought with him Barney Mason a man who he and Capt. Lea both agree to vouch for any statement he makes also as to his honesty and fidelity," Wild said.

18.6. George Curry.

Photograph by Baker & Johnston, ca. 1885.
R. G. McCubbin Collection.

Curry was born at Greenwood Plantation, West Feliciana Parish, Louisiana, on April 3, 1861; he died in Albuquerque, New Mexico, on November 24, 1947.

18.8. A replica of Garrett's sheriff's star.

Author's Collection.

Garrett was so proud of his star that he had it gold plated; this copy, also gold plated, was struck from the original.

18.7. Pat Garrett and his wife, Apolonaria.

Photographer unknown (perhaps a wedding photo?), 1880.
Courtesy Leon C. Metz.

Patrick Floyd Jarvis Garrett, the oldest son of John Lumpkin and Elizabeth Ann (Jarvis) Garrett, was born in Claiborne Parish, near Homer, Chambers County, Alabama, on June 5, 1850. Before the Civil War, John Garrett was a prosperous plantation owner, but when his cotton was confiscated after the war, the family fell into debt. Garrett is said to have shot a Northern sympathizer on the steps of the county courthouse; no charges were ever filed. Elizabeth Garrett died March 29, 1867, aged only thirty-seven; John Garrett died of unknown causes less than a year later, February 5, 1868.

Pat, as he was always known, became a trail driver and buffalo hunter near Fort Griffin, Texas. In November 1876 he killed a young skinner named Joe Briscoe for reasons that remain unclear. In 1878 he relocated to Fort Sumner, where he worked in Beaver Smith's saloon and raised hogs. His first marriage, to Juanita, the daughter of Juan José Martínez, ended sadly when his young wife died of unknown causes.

On January 14, 1880, Garrett married Apolonaria, the twenty-two-year-old daughter of Jose D. and Feliciana Gutierres, in a double ceremony in which Barney Mason married Juanita Madril. The Garrett marriage produced eight children, the last of whom, Jarvis, died on May 20, 1991.

In 1880 Garrett was elected sheriff of Lincoln County; after the death of the Kid, he collaborated with M. A. "Ash" Upson on *The Authentic Life of Billy the Kid*, which was published in 1882. He moved to Roswell and became involved in a plan to irrigate the Pecos Valley, but the venture was unsuccessful. After failing to win election as sheriff of the newly formed Chaves County, Garrett moved to Uvalde, Texas, but following the mysterious death of Albert J. Fountain in February 1896, Garrett returned to New Mexico, where he was hired privately to investigate the case. In 1898 warrants were issued for three ranchers—Bill McNew, Jim Gilliland, and Oliver Lee—and in trying to arrest the last two at Wildy's Well, near Orogrande, Garrett was bested in a shootout that saw one man killed. Lee and Gilliland were later tried and acquitted.

On October 7, 1899, as sheriff of Doña Ana County, Garrett was involved in the killing at the San Augustine ranch of an alleged Oklahoma fugitive Norman Newman, alias Billy Reed.

In 1901 Garrett was appointed collector of customs at El Paso by President Theodore Roosevelt, but after a two-year term the appointment was not renewed. He returned to ranching in Doña Ana County; the last two years of his life were fraught with personal and business difficulties. He was shot to death on February 29, 1908, while traveling to Las Cruces with Carl Adamson and Jesse Wayne Brazel; although Brazel confessed to the killing and was acquitted on grounds of self-defense, conspiracy theorists are still arguing over the how, the who, and the whys of the actual shooting.

Source: Leon Metz, *Pat Garrett*.

18.9. Bernard "Barney" Mason and family.

Date and photographer unknown, ca. 1900.
R. G. McCubbin Collection.

Right to left: Richard Mason, Beatrice Mason House, Barney Mason holding Frederick Mason, Katie Mason, Juana "Jennie" Mason, Chestley T. A. House (husband of Beatrice), and Patrick Mason.

Born of Irish parentage in Richmond, Virginia, on October 29, 1848, Barney Mason drifted west to Texas (where he may have been involved in the Mason County War) and from there to New Mexico, where he settled in Fort Sumner. He acted as a spy on the Kid for Pat Garrett and Azariah F. Wild and later became Garrett's deputy. He killed John Farris or Faires, a former participant in Texas' Mason County War, at Fort Sumner on December 29, 1879; it was believed the incident grew out of the earlier conflict. On January 14, 1880, he married Juanita "Jennie" Madril, seventeen, at Anton Chico (or Fort Sumner) with the same witnesses and in the same church as Pat Garrett and Apolonaria Gutierres.

In 1884 Mason worked with Garrett and Jim East hunting rustlers in the Panhandle, and later that year he served as deputy to Lincoln County Sheriff John Poe. On May 1, 1887, he was sentenced to eighteen months' imprisonment for stealing a calf; he entered the New Mexico penitentiary on June 9 but was pardoned the following November.

For a while he homesteaded at Alamogordo near Fort Sumner, then ran a saloon in Portales before moving on with his family to Arizona, where he worked on federal water reclamation projects. In 1908 they relocated to Bakersfield, California, where Barney died of a cerebral hemorrhage on April 11, 1916.

Source: Harold L. Edwards, "Barney Mason: In the Shadow of Pat Garrett and Billy the Kid," *Old West* 26, no. 4 (Summer 1990): 14–19.

18.10. The old Lib Rainbolt ranch near Picacho.

Photograph by M. G. Fulton, ca. 1930.
R. N. Mullin Collection. HHC.

This is one of the oldest ranches in the Hondo Valley, built by the Rainbolts soon after 1860, and a perfect example of what ranch buildings of its day actually looked like. It was here, in 1880, that the Dedrick brothers and W. H. West had their "counterfeit lodge" in which the printing was done.

It appears from the statements of Garrett and Mason that he (Mason) is an experienced stock man and is now and has been for some time past in the employ of a man named [Pete] Maxwell who resides at Fort Sumner. He (Mason) states that a few days ago one Daniel Diedrick who resides at Bosque Grande and who has an interest with his brother Samuel Diedrick and West in a livery stable at White Oaks came to him and proposed as follows.

"I (Daniel Diedrick) want to employ you (Barney Mason) That after a short conversation with Diedrick he (Diedrick) stated that he wanted me (Mason) to take a lot of counterfeit money down to the Rio Grande in Texas and buy up all the cattle I (Mason) could, bring them to a point near New Mexico, turn them over to him (Diedrick) and West, give them a square bill of sale on the same and I (Mason) to then leave the country and go to Mexico and from there wheresoever I pleased." That when West returned a few days since he brought with him $30,000 in counterfeit money which had been made from a new plate and from one which had not yet been "spotted."

Mason goes on to state that Dan Dedrick informed him that when West recently returned to White Oaks that one man who hailed from New York came with him and with them at that time. To the best of his memory he (Diedrick) called the man Duncan and that he was pretending to represent J. W. Hardin of New York.

Mason stated that Diedrick informed him that they could get all the counterfeit money they wanted from West and that he was given to understand that the money came from the New York stranger who came with West on his return to White Oaks.

Mason states that William Wilson boards at his house when at Fort Sumner. that he has seen him counterfeit money at various times. that he (Mason) knows he Wilson passed a $100 on a saloon keeper named [Beaver] Smith at Fort Sumner. that he (Smith) sent it to the bank and had it returned as counterfeit. That Wilson laughed at Smith and agreed to redeem it with some money although Wilson told him (Mason) that he was only letting the old man (Smith) down easy.

That William Wilson and Billy Kid left about the 16th inst with sixty head of stolen horses and went down the Canadian River to be gone two or three weeks. That on their return they would probably return to his house when he would turn them over to Patrick F. Garrett Deputy US Marshal, and Sheriff Steck. Mason says the stranger who was at White Oaks with Diedrick had a business card. That he believed he could get it and give it to me.

Still in the Oaks on November 22, Wild reported excitedly that information had just reached him through a reliable source that the Kid had been driven out of the Canadian River country

and was now at Greathouse's ranch with twenty five armed men and a bunch of seven stolen horses. On Saturday night seven of Kid's men went to White Oaks and attempted to rob one or two places and stole a lot of blankets, overcoats, rifles and provisions. The citizens went out to capture them but they made their escape after about forty shots were exchanged.

This information was conveyed to Gen. [George P.] Buel[l] commanding Post [at Fort Stanton] when he ordered Lt. [Dillard H.] Clark with twelve men to go out to Greathouse's ranch and meet the Paymaster who is expected to be on the road from Santa Fe to Fort Stanton to pay off the troops at that post.

The Kid and his sidekicks had been in Puerto de Luna, where they had stolen sixteen horses belonging to merchant Alexander Grzelachowski, known far and wide as "Padre Polaco" because of his Polish birth and his earlier career in the church. After stopping at Greathouse & Kuch's place to sell four of the animals, they pressed on to the Oaks. With the Kid were Rudabaugh, Joe Cook, Wilson, and Buck Edwards.[4]

"The Sheriff at White Oaks with his Posse went out thirteen miles from town and attempted to arrest Billy Kid, William Wilson and others on Monday the 22nd inst. and had to return to town empty handed," Wild reported next day. In fact, the posse was led by storekeeper Will Hudgens; it included his brother John, James W. Bell, Jim Carlyle, George Neil, J. P. Eaker, Jim Redman, and William Stone. "Kid's force out numbered that of the Sheriff," Wild continued. "Each party had several horses killed. The Sheriff lost no men but whether or not any one was hurt on the other side is not known yet. The Sheriff captured most of their camp equipment and captured two men who left White Oaks in the night to carry Kid's outfit provisions one of whom was Moses Diedrick a brother to the Diedrick who is West and Wilson's partner. there is talk of a 'Judge lynch' trying them at last account."[5]

Three horses were killed: Billy Wilson's, the Kid's—one of those stolen from Grzelachowski—and the one ridden by John Hudgens, which saved his life. If the animal had not raised its head and caught the bullet, they said, it would have killed him. The second of the two men captured was one J. W. Lamper, who was discharged after appearing before Justice of the Peace James Tomlinson, formerly of Lincoln. At the same arraignment Mose Dedrick posted bail, then skipped town lest "Judge Lynch" decide to anticipate the findings of the district court.[6]

18.11. Will Hudgens.

Date and photographer unknown.
Rio Grande Historical Collections,
NMSU.

Interestingly, in view of the fact that the posse was led by Will Hudgens (who a year earlier he had trusted enough to specify as the only man he would surrender to), the Kid perceived the incident as an ambush designed to prevent his consummating his arrangement with Wild. "My business at White Oaks [that day] was to See Judge Leonard who has my case in hand," he said later. "He had written to me to Come up that he thought he could get everything straightened up. I did not find him at the Oaks & Should have gone to Lincoln if I had met with no accident."[7]

Wild was now in Roswell. "We would start from here with a force," he reported on November 26, "only nearly every horse in this section of the country is sick at present with distemper. Deputy US Marshal [Frank] Stewart from Texas is reported to be at Puerta de Luna with forty men and after several of the men who are in this gang for crimes committed in Texas. I shall communicate with him as soon as I can get a reliable man to send, and then press the 'Russlers' from White Oaks back into Fort Sumner and then soround [sic] the place with forces from above and below."

A second posse of White Oaks men, which included the Hudgens brothers, Jim Watt, J. P. Eaker, John Mosby, Ed Bonnell, J. P. Langston, W. B. Dorsey, Charles Kelly, Jim Brent, James W. Bell, and Jim Carlyle, was raised by constable Thomas B. "Pinto Tom" Longworth to pursue the Kid and his gang while the trail was fresh. They pushed north through heavy snow to reach the Greathouse trading post after dark on the evening of November 27 and surrounded it. Longworth returned to White Oaks to get reinforcements and supplies, leaving Carlyle in charge. Wild's account of what happened next is brief and to the point: "One of the Posse name of Carlisle who had lost some mules was one of the leaders of the Posse and after a little talk with the parties on the inside of the house he was induced to go in. Soon as he was inside of the house he was murdered. Soon after Carlisle was murdered William Wilson and his gang made a rush out of the house and made their escape under cover of the night."[8]

According to Greathouse's German cook, Joe Steck, who was first out of the house that bitterly cold gray morning, he was pounced on by the posse and directed to take in a note demanding the Kid's surrender. Billy "read the paper to his compadres, who all laughed," then gave Steck a note inviting whoever was the leader to come in and parley. Carlyle wasn't having any until Greathouse offered himself as a hostage, whereupon Carlyle laid down his weapons and went in.

Notes carried by Greathouse's partner Fred Kuch were traded back and forth until about midday, then "for some reason the White Oaks boys became suspicious; things were not as they should be with their leader and they decided to storm the fort," said Steck, who was inside cooking a meal. "Therefore they sent me word by Mr. Cook [Kuch] to come out as war would commence in earnest." Steck scuttled for a safe place from which to watch events. He had no sooner reached it than "with a crash a man came through a window. Bang, bang, the man's dying yell and poor Carlyle tumbles to the ground, with three bullets in him, dead."

As Kuch and Steck ran away from the house every member of the posse started blazing away. "About 60 or 75 shots were fired at us, bullets flying in

18.12. James R. Brent *(center)* with Pat Garrett *(left)* and John Poe.

Photographer unknown, ca. 1884. R. G. McCubbin Collection.

Brent was born in Brenton, Farquier County, Virginia, on March 17, 1847; he died in Silver City, New Mexico, on June 12, 1928.

all directions," Steck said. The posse told them it was all a mistake, they had thought they were making a diversion to cover the escape of the men in the house. Kuch, Steck, and Greathouse, who had also got clear of the posse, got horses and headed for the safety of the nearby Spencer ranch, where they remained until next morning. When they got back, the posse was gone. "We found poor Carlyle frozen stiff where he fell," Steck said. "We tied a blanket around him and buried him the best we could. He was afterwards taken up and put in a box by the Sheriff's posse."[9]

In the Kid's version of events,

> the house was Surrounded by an outfit led by one Carlyle, who came to the house and Demanded a Surrender.
>
> I asked for their Papers and they had none. So I concluded it amounted to nothing more than a mob and told Carlyle that he would have to Stay in the house and lead the way out that night. Soon after a note was brought in Stating that if Carlyle did not come out inside of five minutes they would Kill the Stationkeeper [Greathouse] who had left the house and was with them. in a short time a shot was fired [by J. P. Eakers] on the outside and Carlyle thinking Greathouse was Killed jumped through the window breaking the Sash as he went and was killed by his own Party they think[ing] it was me trying to make my Escape.
>
> the party then withdrew.
>
> they returned the next day and burned an old man named Spencer's house and Greathouse's, also.[10]

On Monday, November 29, as the Kid and his companions labored through the snowdrifts to the Spencer ranch, where they got food before leaving for Anton Chico, Wild's posse left Roswell "under the command of Deputy US Marshals Olinger and Garrett. The force is made up of the best citizens including a deputy Sheriff, constable and justice of the peace," Wild reported. "We have at the present time between one and two hundred armed men out scouting for this gang of counterfeiters and outlaws. We this day arrested Joseph Cook, one of the parties who were in the fight at White Oaks. He was arrested just outside of [Roswell] between five and six P.M. He had two stolen horses when arrested. He is now chained and now in the same 'Chosa' with me. Cook is a native of Texas and an outlaw."[11]

On Garrett's instructions, Wild took Cook back to Roswell, where in short order he convinced himself he was under siege by men from "Wilson's gang" intent on rescuing Cook. No such event occurred, of course, but Wild made it sound exciting. The Garrett-Olinger posse forged on up the Pecos to the Dedrick ranch, where they found and arrested John Joshua Webb and George Davis, both escapees from the Las Vegas jail. Davis was a small-time horse thief who just happened to bear the same name as the member of the Jesse Evans gang last heard of in Texas.

Apart from the killing by Frank Stewart of a man, name unknown, who tried to commandeer his horse and an abortive pursuit of Tom O'Folliard near the Yerby ranch—the volleys of shots fired at him were ineffectual and on a fresher mount he easily outdistanced the posse's tired horses—the ambitious three-pronged attack on the Kid's supposed strongholds was a total failure, and nothing Wild invented for his reports could conceal that fact. They found neither the Kid, any member of his gang, nor a single head of demonstrably stolen stock at Sumner or at the Los Portales "stronghold."

Ironically, the most lethal blow to the outlaw fraternity was delivered not by Garrett or Wild or any of the "between one hundred and two hundred armed men" he claimed were in pursuit of the outlaws, but by Iowa-born J. H. Koogler, a close friend of Huston Chapman and Ira Leonard and publisher of the *Las Vegas Gazette*.

Angered by the murder of Carlyle and the continuing inability of the law

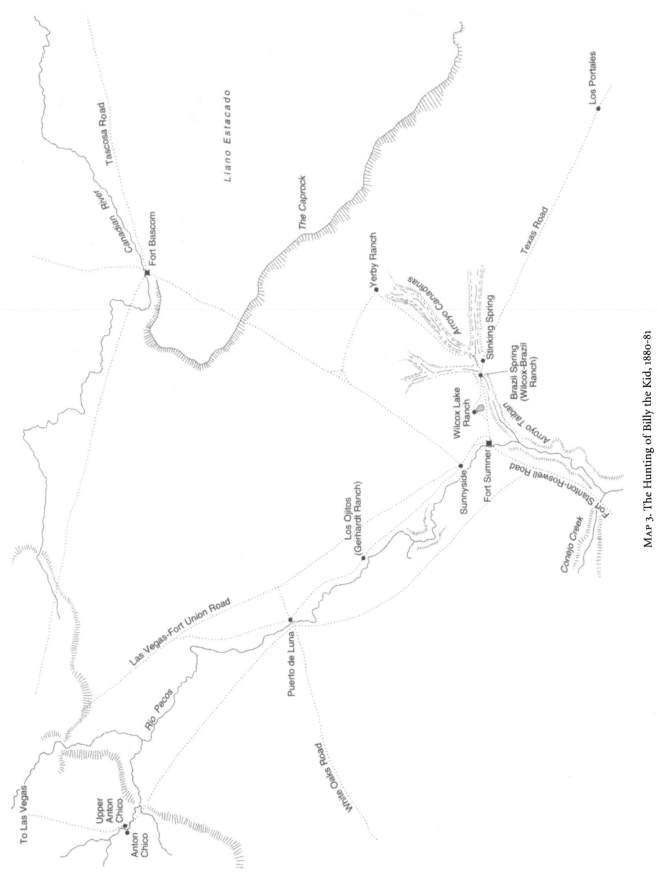

Map 3. The Hunting of Billy the Kid, 1880-81

to terminate the depredations of the outlaws, Koogler launched a campaign in his newspaper against them. Eastern New Mexico, he fumed, had become the fiefdom of "a powerful gang of outlaws harrassing the stockmen of the Pecos and Panhandle country, and terrorizing the people of Fort Sumner and vicinity. The gang includes forty or fifty men, all hard characters, the off-scourings of society, fugitives from justice, and desperadoes by profession.... The gang is under the leadership of 'Billy the Kid,' a desperate cuss, who is eligible for the post of captain of any crowd, no matter how mean or lawless.... Are the people of San Miguel county to stand this any longer?"[12]

Koogler's editorial had an immediate, quadruple effect. First, it gave an identity to the Kid, a sobriquet that immediately set him apart, made him unique. Second, it centered all the attention—and by definition all the responsiblity for the killing and stock theft—on him. Third, and for the first time, it visibly turned public opinion against him. And last, spurred by letters Koogler also wrote to the governor, Lew Wallace took decisive action. Just ten days later, any thoughts he might have entertained about arranging amnesty for the Kid forever banished from his mind, he scribbled a note to his secretary W. G. Ritch: "Be good enough to prepare a draft of proclamation of reward $500. for the capture and delivery of William Bonney, alias The Kid to the Sheriff of the County in which he of Lincoln County."

No use now for the Kid to protest—and he did, by indignant letter direct to Wallace—that although he was known as Kid he was not "the" Kid, nor "the captian of a Band of Outlaws who hold Forth at the Portales." The reward notice was published two days later.

BILLY THE KID

———

$500 REWARD

———

I will pay $500 reward to any person or persons
who will capture William Bonny, alias The Kid, and
deliver him to any sheriff of New Mexico.
Satisfactory proofs of identity will be required.

LEW. WALLACE,
Governor of New Mexico.[13]

Wallace's action was an unequivocal declaration of intent. From this point onward it was no longer a question of whether the Kid would be caught, only when.

CHAPTER NINETEEN

Capture

19.1. Charlie and Manuela Bowdre.

Photograph by Furlong, Las Vegas, ca. 1880.
R. G. McCubbin Collection.

Bowdre was carrying this photograph when he was killed at Stinking Spring (note the bloodstains). It is one of a pair taken at the same sitting; Charlie gave the other to Thomas Yerby.

T HE RELENTLESS IRON GRAY HAND of winter descended on the country, with intermittent blizzards and temperatures rarely above zero even by day.

On December 11 Wild reported, "Deputy Marshal Garrett's posse who went to Fort Sumner some days since in pursuit of the gang of counterfeiters returned with the exception of Garrett and Barney Mason who went on with prisoners [Webb and Davis] to Las Vegas returned this day being compelled to abandon the hunt for the pursuit owing to sickness among their horses."[1]

Earlier in the month Garrett had agreed to a rendezvous with Charlie Bowdre, who had seen the writing on the wall and was looking for a way to quit the owlhoot trail. When they met on December 5 "at the forks of the road, two miles from Sumner," Charlie probably told Garrett pretty much what he had said in a letter to Joseph Lea: "If I don't get clear I intend to leave some time this winter, for I don't intend to take any hand fighting the territory, for it is a different thing from what the Lincoln Co War was. . . . I saw the two Billies [Bonney and Wilson] the other day & they say they are going to leave the country. That was my advice to them for I believe it is the best thing they can do." Garrett told him if he took Lea's advice to "forsake his disreputable associates," every effort would be made to give him an opportunity to redeem himself.

"Bowdre did not seem to place much faith in these promises and evidently thought I was playing a game to get him in my power," Garrett recorded. "I told him if he did not quit them or surrender he would be pretty sure to get captured or killed, as we were after the gang and would sleep on their trail until we took them in, dead or alive. And thus we parted."

Garrett wasted little time in Las Vegas. By December 15 he was back in White Oaks, which place Azariah Wild had left a day before in a wagon driven by Sam Beard—the only person he could find who was willing to brave the weather and take him north. They got eighteen miles before a snowstorm forced them to seek shelter. Nevertheless, even though what the newspapers described as the "polar conditions" enveloping the High Plains seriously restricted movement, the pursuit of the Kid intensified.

Down at Tascosa, each of the Canadian River ranchers had contributed some fighting men to a pursuit party nominally led by Charlie Siringo. Another group under the command of Frank Stewart made the total force fourteen. Together they made their way north to Anton Chico.

19.2. Charles Angelo Siringo.

Photographer unknown, ca. 1886.
R. G. McCubbin Collection.

Siringo was born in Matagorda
County, Texas, February 7, 1855;
he died in Hollywood, California, on October 19, 1928.

Stewart was not by any means the only one working under what Lon Chambers called "a consumed name." Louis Bousman was another. Still another member of the outfit, Frank Clifford— "consumed" name John Francis Wallace, real name John Menham Wightman—had only recently arrived at Tascosa from New Mexico when he heard about the proposed expedition. Rancher Tee Silman, who ran cattle under the E-Cross-E brand, had no one to send and hired Clifford to represent him.[2]

"There were four wagons in the expedition," Clifford wrote,

each with four-up teams, as we called them. That means four horses, or four mules, to a wagon. The wagon I put my war-bags in had mules. It was an LX wagon, with Charley Siringo in charge. There was a combination driver-cook to each wagon and the wagons carried our equipment . . . bedding, war-bags, grub, and anything else we might be likely to need. With the wagons went fourteen riders representing different cattlemen who ran their stock along the Canadian river, either north or south of Tascosa.

The LX had one wagon and five men. Besides Charley Siringo [they sent] Lon Chambers, Lee Hall, a feller known to me only as "Uncle Jimmy," and Cal Polk. . . . The LIT had one wagon, with Bob Roberson [another alias: his real name was Bill Hughes] in charge. Their other men were Tom Emory and Jim East. The Box T wagon had one man, whom we called "The Animal." I can't remember his name [Louis Bousman] or why we called him by that name, but I do remember the man. He was as quiet, well-behaved a man as you could ask for, a fine fellow all the way through.

The E-Cross-E had no wagon and I was the only man, so I was assigned to the LX wagon. Charley Siringo and I doubled our blankets and slept together all the time. We became the best of friends and would have backed each other up in any play. Yet I never revealed to Charley my real name.

In camp on their first night out, Clifford came in for some joshing on account of the size of his feet. "Why," one of the party said, referring to the legendary Texas character, "you might be old 'Big Foot' Wallace himself, or leastways his son."

"Well, the boys called me 'Big Foot Wallace' or 'Foot' or 'Feet' from then on," Clifford said. "None of them, not even Charley Siringo, knew how apt the nickname was, for I never said anything to any of them about it. I've had many a laugh over it to myself, however."

By the time the expedition reached Anton Chico, they were out of food, so Siringo went up to Las Vegas to get supplies. He was gone for a week, during which the boys amused themselves by getting drunk a lot. When he finally came back, he explained that he had got into a monte game and had lost the first draft the association sent him and had to wait for another. They stocked up on bacon, flour, coffee, sugar, and canned tomatoes and corn and started for White Oaks.

"On the morning we left Anton Chico it was snowing," Clifford recalled:

There was already about five inches of snow on the ground. By the time we stopped at noon, snow was from eight to ten inches deep. We made a dry camp, and melted snow to water our horses. Before we could get started again, Pat Garrett, sheriff of Lincoln County, New Mexico, and Frank Stewart, cattle detective for the Canadian Cattle Association, and another man (one of Pat's deputies [Barney Mason]) rode into camp. Pat told us

19.3. Frank Clifford, alias "Big Foot Wallace."

Date and photographer unknown, ca. 1884
Courtesy Michael E. Winter.

Practically every member of the Canadian River posse seems to have been traveling under what Lon Chambers called "a consumed name." Twenty-year-old Frank Clifford, also known as "Big Foot Wallace," was no exception; even the name he later used—John Francis Wallace—was spurious. His real name was John Menham Wightman, and he was born near Pontypool, Wales, on March 18, 1860, the son of coal merchant James Temple and Sarah (Walker) Wightman. After the death of Sarah on October 25, 1866, James Wightman, his daughter Marianne Isabella, and his sons Sinclair W. and John emigrated to America, leaving another daughter, Kate, age thirteen, with family; they eventually settled in Cimarron, New Mexico.

John Menham Wightman later claimed to have been a friend and supporter of Clay Allison, to have been an eyewitness to several of Allison's killings, and also to have participated in the notorious defenestration of the *Cimarron News and Press* in January 1876. After he left Cimarron, Wightman—or John Francis Wallace as he began to call himself—got a job on the Bell Ranch and later at the LX. Subsequent to the events involving the pursuit of the Kid, he settled in Emporia, Kansas, in 1883, and on October 13 of that year he married Sarah Frances Timmons, eighteen. Still using the name Frank Wallace, he died at Little Rock, Arkansas, on September 8, 1946.

Source: John Francis Wallace [Frank Clifford], "Deep Trails in the Old West"; research by Michael E. Winter, Beebe, Arkansas.

19.4. James Henry "Jim" East.

Photographer unknown; early 1880s.
McCarty Collection, Amarillo Public Library.

East was born in Kaskaskia, Illinois, on August 30, 1853; he died in Douglas, Arizona, on June 30, 1930.
Seated, left to right: James H. East, James McMasters, and Pat Garrett. *Standing, left to right:* W. S. Mabry, Frank James, C. B. Vivian, and I. P. Ryland.

19.5. Alexander Grzelachowski.

Photographer unknown, ca. 1880–85.
Courtesy T. Dudley Cramer.

Grzelachowski was born in Graci-
na, Poland, in 1824; he died at
Puerto de Luna, New Mexico, on
May 24, 1896.

that the Kid was down by Fort Sumner, and had a large bunch of Canadian
River cattle that he was aiming to start for Old Mexico with in the morning.
This couldn't be true, as nobody could go any distance through a
snowstorm like that with a big bunch of cattle. There would be nothing for
them to eat. Bob Roberson and Charley Siringo immediately told Pat so.
They really bemeaned [*sic*] him, and didn't mince words, either.

Pat insisted he was telling it straight, and after a long argument, Bob and
Charley agreed to leave it to their men personally to decide who would go
with Pat. We split up exactly even—seven went, and seven wouldn't go. I
was one who didn't.

Clifford's unvarnished account puts a somewhat different spin on the
usual account of Garrett's "organizing" a posse to pursue the Kid; it was more
like Hobson's choice—he took what he could get and acted grateful. So on
December 15, while the rest of the Tascosa contingent sought congenial company in White Oaks, Garrett and a party consisting of Barney Mason, Frank
Stewart, "Poker Tom" Emory, Jim East, Lon Chambers, Lee Hall, Louis "The
Animal" Bousman, "Tenderfoot" Bob Williams, and possibly, although
Garrett does not mention him by name, Cal Polk, set out for Puerto de Luna,
where they arrived the following day, a respectable achievement in such ap-
palling conditions.

At Grzelachowski's they rested, "eating apples and drawing corks," while
Garrett hunted up some local help. None was forthcoming; the locals had
no stomach for a confrontation with the Kid and his friends. To the posse's
disgust, the only volunteer was Juan Roival; however, this suited Garrett perfectly. He needed someone the Kid knew and would not consider a spy; Roival
qualified nicely.

Leaving PdL, as they called it then and still do, at about three in the afternoon, the posse headed downriver for John Gerhardt's ranch at Los Ojitos.
The little settlement had its origin in a suggestion made by Kit Carson in 1864
that pickets be permanently stationed on the road at the point where it entered the reservation, their purpose to "keep out all not having legitimate
business on the Reserve." The army generally referred to the location as Cedar Springs, but the residents—half a dozen households which included those
of Pablo Beaubien and Manuel Abreu, respectively brother-in-law and son-
in-law of Lucien B. Maxwell—just called it "the Springs."[3]

Rancher-physician John Gerhardt had built a stone house and settled at
Los Ojitos soon after the army abandoned Fort Sumner; by ingeniously con-
structing terraced slopes near the sweetwater spring, he was able to irrigate
and develop a lush garden where berries, vines, and pecan trees grew. The
posse got in after a punishing six-hour ride through "a terrible snowstorm
from the northwest" and settled in gratefully for the night. Next morning,
Garrett sent Juan Roival down to Fort Sumner, twenty-five miles below as
the crow flew, to see if the Kid and his cronies were there. They were.

Garrett and Barney Mason now sneaked into town to check the lay of the
land; when they got there they learned the Kid and his gang—doubtless
tipped off by some of his native New Mexican friends that the Garrett posse
was in the vicinity—had moved out and were now at the Tom Wilcox–
Manuel Brazil roadhouse about twenty miles east of town near Taiban Spring.

19.6. Puerto de Luna.

Photographer unknown, ca. 1881.
Author's Collection.

The robust figure with arms akimbo second from right is believed to be Grzela-chowski; his store is to the left of the picture.

Garrett called in the rest of his men, the complement reinforced now by Charlie Rudulph, son of the Sunnyside postmaster, and George Wilson, who had followed them down from PdL. They rode into Fort Sumner and took up station in the old Indian hospital on the eastern side of the fort.

The hospital was a U-shaped building, with the wings facing north-south, where Charlie Bowdre and his wife had quarters and where the Kid and others occasionally bunked. It dated back to about 1868; the army had taken it over when the Navajos, in accordance with tribal custom, refused to use it after one of their people died there, and another Indian hospital was built about three thousand yards to the north of the post.

"Pat hired a Mexican for one hundred dollars to go to the Kid's hideout on the edge of the Staked Plains and tell the Kid that 'the Texans'—that was us—had turned back home, and that it was now safe for him to come on in to Sumner, which the Kid told the Mexican he would do that evening," said Frank Clifford, who although he was not there, claimed he had his information "from the lips of the men who were actually present at the occurrences . . . immediately after the events took place."

19.7. John Gerhardt.

Photographer unknown, ca. 1874.
Author's Collection.

Gerhardt was born in Freisenheim, Germany, in 1830; he died in Los Ojitos, New Mexico, on September 17, 1906.

19.8. Charles Frederick Rudulph.

Photographer Furlong, Las Vegas,
ca. 1882.
Courtesy Louis Leon Branch.

"Lon Chambers was on guard," Jim East recalled. "Our horses were in Pete Maxwell's stable [in the old quartermaster building]. Sheriff Pat Garrett, Tom Emmory, Bob Williams and Barney Mason were playing poker on a blanket on the floor. I had just lain down on my blanket in the corner when Chambers ran in and told us that the 'Kid' and his gang were coming. It was about eleven o'clock at night."[4]

There was a thick fog that night which made it difficult to see anything clearly. The possemen grabbed their guns and waited tensely as the dark shapes of the horsemen loomed ghostlike in the mist, the sound of their hooves muffled by the snow. There were six of them: Charlie Bowdre—doubtless looking forward to seeing his wife and sitting by his own warm fire—Rudabaugh, Wilson, Tom Pickett, O'Folliard, and the Kid. When they were about ten yards away, "Pat Garrett spoke and said throw up your hands," Cal Polk said, "at that moment they jerked their gons out and they big shooting came off."[5]

There was pandemonium, gunflashes lighting the scene like strobe lights, heavy black powder smoke coiling, as the riders wrenched their horses around and thundered off into the darkness. There was a long silence and then out of the fog a horse came walking, its rider sagging in the saddle. It was Tom O'Folliard, shot through the chest near the heart. "His horse went off with him," Louis Bousman said, matter-of-factly, "and then he came back, and we went out and got him and carried him inside."[6]

"I got Tom some water," Jim East said. "He then cussed Garrett and died, in about thirty minutes after being shot." Disinclined to pursue the Kid through the fog into the empty, icy night, Garrett and the others went back to playing poker. Next morning "a big snow storm set in and put out their trail, so we laid over in Sumner and buried Tom O'Phalliard."[7]

The surviving five headed back for the Wilcox-Brazil roadhouse; Rudabaugh's horse, which had been shot, collapsed about a mile east of the fort, and Rudabaugh had to double up behind Billy Wilson. When they got there the Kid prevailed upon Brazil to go back to Sumner and see what he could find out; before they made their run they needed to know where Garrett's posse was.

In fact, Brazil had his own agenda. As soon as he got to the fort he sought out Garrett and told him where the outlaws were. Garrett sent him back with some well-thought-out disinformation to feed the gang if they were still at the roadhouse; if not, he was to come back and let Garrett know.

At about midnight, December 20, just two hours before Garrett's deadline expired, Brazil came back. Half-frozen, his beard full of icicles from the desperate cold, he reported that the Kid and his companions had eaten supper and then departed—where, he did not know. First taking the precaution of sending Brazil ahead to make sure the outlaws had not doubled back to waylay them when they arrived, Garrett immediately got his posse mounted and set off northeast to check the Erastus Wilcox ranch near Red Lake on the off chance his quarry might have gone north, but it was deserted; they rode on to Wilcox's, meeting Brazil on the way. He reported that the outlaws had not come back and showed Garrett their tracks in the snow.[8]

From the direction they had taken, Garrett knew there was only one place

19.9. Fort Sumner, ca. 1868.

Photographer unknown, ca. 1868.
Rio Grande Historical Collections, NMSU.

The building in the foreground is the original post hospital; the building that can just be seen in the far background is the (then) Indian hospital where Charlie Bowdre later lived and Tom O'Folliard was killed.

19.10. Fort Sumner, 1996.

Author's photograph, 1996.

Taken from the corner of the parade ground at about where the man with folded arms is standing in Fig. 19.9, this view looks toward the site of the old Indian hospital, which was to the left of and beyond the gable-roofed building seen here.

19.11. Wilcox-Brazil house from the rear.

Photograph by M. G. Fulton, 1930. Author's Collection.

19.12. Manuel S. Brazil.

Photographer Too Cute Studio, Hot Springs, Arkansas, ca. 1910. Courtesy Joseph Brazil and Armene Brazil Green.

Manuel Silveira Brazil was born June 12, 1850, at Rosais on the island of St. George in the Portuguese Azores. He came to America as a young man and settled at Taiban, about fourteen miles east of Fort Sumner, in 1871. There he ran a ranch and way station in partnership with Thomas Wilcox. Early in the 1880s he was married, but he separated from or divorced his wife. About 1893, Brazil sold out and moved with his young nephew Manuel to Las Vegas, and three years later he went on to Texas, where he had a ranch in Roberts County and served as county commissioner between 1908 and 1914. About this time Brazil remarried; nothing is known about his wife but her first name, Katherine. He spent his last years in Hot Springs, Arkansas, and died there on June 17, 1928, from the after-effects of a fall.

19.13. Rock house near Taiban.

Date and photographer unknown. Courtesy Scott Smith.

This photograph, published as a postcard by J. R. Dumas of Taiban in the 1930s, is purported to be the stone house in which the Kid was captured.

the Kid could be heading: the old stone forage station at Stinking Spring, a boggy waterhole about four miles east of the Brazil-Wilcox place that got its name from the decaying vegetation around it. "We got to the rock house just before daylight," Jim East said. "Our horses were left with Frank Stewart and some of the other boys under guard, while Garrett took Lee Hall, Tom Emory and myself with him. We crawled up the arroyo to within about thirty feet of the door, where we lay down in the snow. There was no window in this house, and only one door, which we would cover with our guns."[9]

The rock house was a stark stone rectangle about thirty feet long and twelve feet wide, with a rough opening—no door—about ten feet from one end at the front. Inside were five men and the Kid's horse; tethered to one of the viga poles outside were the other three horses: Wilson and Rudabaugh were still doubling up.

There are several versions of what happened next; the two most believable, strangely enough, are not Garrett's or even East's, both of which feature one of Ash Upson's fantasies, the Kid telling poor dying Charlie Bowdre to go out and get one of the sons-of-bitches before he dies. If Louis Bousman is to be believed, it was a starker business than that.

"'If Billy goes out to feed the horses,'" Garrett told them, "'he will have on a Mexican hat. You boys cut down and kill him.' Then Bowdre came out to feed the horses, so we all took a shot at him. He fell with his head back in the house. We all thought it was Billy the Kid."[10]

In Cal Polk's version, as Garrett told Bowdre to throw up his hands, Bowdre said, "All right in the minnet as he taken his hands down from the horses head, he jerked out two pistols and fired at us and at the same time we fired. They was three shots hit him one in the leg and too in the body. He dropped his pistols and come realing to worge us. He said something like I wish, I wish, and then said blood is cloging in my mouth and fell across one of our boys, Lee Smith. He roled him over to one side and there he froze in a short time and lay there all day."[11]

The element of surprise was gone now; the outlaws knew there was a posse outside the cabin. Garrett in turn knew that given half a chance the Kid would make a break for it; sure enough, a little while later he saw the tie ropes of the horses moving and realized they were trying to get the horses inside so they could mount up and come out running. He immediately shot one of the horses dead; it fell, partially barricading the outlet. "To prevent another attempt of this kind I shot in two the ropes which held the other horses and they walked away."[12]

He had read the Kid's intentions perfectly. "If it hadn't been for the dead horse," Billy said later, "I would have ridden out on my bay mare and taken my chances of escaping. But I couldn't ride out over that [dead horse], for she would have jumped back, and I would have got it in the head."[13]

"We held a medicine talk with the Kid," East said, "but of course couldn't see him. Garrett asked him to give up, Billy answered, 'Go to H———l, you long-legged s———of a b———!'" Garrett ignored the invective: the Kid and his companions were not going anyplace. If they couldn't drive them out, they would starve them out. He sent a man to the Wilcox-Brazil roadhouse for food, and while they waited they scoured around for wood and built a fire. "While we was warming Billy said Pat have you got anything out there to eat," Cal Polk said. "Pat said yes. Billy said we have got some in here if you will let us come and get wood too. Pat said all right you can all come out after wood if you want too. Billy says you go to H[ell] you cowardly S[on of a] B[itch] and then he hushed."[14]

When the possemen started cooking, the smell of the food was too much for the besieged outlaws. Someone tied a dirty white kerchief to a stick for a flag of truce, and "in a few minets Mr. Ruderbay come out with his hands up," said Cal Polk, "and told Pat that Billy wanted to surrender under sunup." Shortly after sundown, they came out with their hands up. Barney Mason pulled his gun and leveled it at the Kid. "Kill the sonofabitch, he is slippery and may get away," he said. East and Hall promptly "covered Barney and told him to drop his gun, which he did."

According to Clifford, "The first thing the Kid said when he saw the posse was, 'Pat, you so-and-so, they told me there was a hundred Texans here from the Canadian River! If I'd a-known there wasn't no more than this, you'd never have got me!" However, now that it was a fait accompli, the Kid took the surrender philosophically. "I thought it was better to come out and get a good square meal," he said later, "don't you?"[15]

The posse took their prisoners back to the Wilcox-Brazil place; before they settled in for the night a wagon was sent back to bring in Bowdre's body. Early next day, with Brazil driving, the prisoners in the wagon with Bowdre's corpse, the posse headed into Fort Sumner, arriving late on the morning of December 24. There, according to Charles Rudulph, "a deranged, lamenting" Manuela Bowdre "kicked and pummelled Garrett until she had to be pulled away." East said, "As we started in with [the body], she struck me over the head with a branding iron, and I had to drop Charlie at her feet. The poor woman was crazy with grief. I always regretted the death of Charlie Bowdre, for he was a brave man, and true to his friends to the last." Clearly Garrett thought so, too; in spite of the way she had reviled him, he told Manuela to "go over and pick out a suit of clothes to bury her husband in and he would pay for it." He also paid to have the grave dug.[16]

At the blacksmith shop shackles were forged, and the prisoners were chained together, Rudabaugh to the Kid, Pickett to Wilson. During the proceedings, the Kid gave his bay mare to Frank Stewart, telling him he expected he wouldn't have much time for horseback exercise over the next few months. He also gave Jim East his Winchester, "but old Beaver Smith made such an uproar about an account he said 'Billy' owed him, that at the request of 'Billy,' I gave old Beaver the gun," East said. Storekeeper Smith was a one-time Chisum cowboy; some years earlier a gang of Jinglebob riders on a wild drunk had roped and tied him, jinglebobbed his ears, and put a Long Rail brand on his hide. He was something of a "character" around the old fort; it is said it was outside his establishment that the Kid had his only known photograph taken in late 1879 or early 1880.[17]

After the men had eaten, Deluvina Maxwell, a twenty-two-year-old Navajo girl who was Doña Luz Maxwell's house servant, came in and asked if Garrett would consent to the Kid's coming to the house to say a last farewell to Paulita Maxwell. Garrett agreed; after all, it was *pascua de Navidad*, Christmas Eve, with the luminarias in every window and the children tucked up in their beds dreaming of sugarplums.

East and Lee Hall were less sentimental. When they took the Kid and Rudabaugh to the house and Doña Luz asked if Billy could be unshackled so he and Paulita could go into another room and talk awhile, East refused, convinced "it was only a stall of 'Billy's' to make a run for liberty, and the old lady and the girl were willing to further the scheme." Still shackled to Dirty Dave, the Kid and his querida embraced, "and she gave 'Billy' one of those soul kisses the novelists tell us about, till it being time for us to hit the trail for Vegas, we had to pull them apart, much against our wishes, for you know all the world loves a lover."[18]

The party set off upriver for Gerhardt's ranch, something under thirty miles by road. "During the trip the Kid and Rudabaugh were cheerful and gay," Garrett said, "Wilson somewhat dejected, and Pickett was badly frightened."[19] After an overnight stop at Los Ojitos, they plowed on beneath a sky the color of mud to Puerto de Luna, arriving at Grzelachowski's at two o'clock on the afternoon of Christmas Day, just in time for dinner.

This was the Kid's fifth Christmas out in the cold. Not a single one of them had been anything but completely miserable; the first was while on the run after escaping from the Silver City jail, the second God knows where in Arizona, the third either sharing Tunstall's gloom at the Feliz ranch or in the miserable pit jail at Lincoln, the fourth—and maybe the best—somewhere around or in Fort Sumner, and now this: a decent meal of roast wild turkey, to be sure, but then? Yet not once did he fall victim to despair or self-pity; indeed, if Jim East is to be believed, he was already trying to think of a way to make a break for it.

Garrett decided they would eat in two shifts, he and his deputies first. While they ate, East was locked into a long adobe room with a fireplace at one end and a door at the other.

> I sat down on a pile of wood, and the prisoners were at the other end. After we sat there awhile the Kid said, "Jim, do you have anything to smoke?"
> I said, "yes, I have some tobacco."
> He said he had some papers. I said, "Billy, I'll throw you the tobacco."
> He said, "No, I'll come and get it," and he and Dave [Rudabaugh] started across the room toward me. . . .
> I said, "Hold on, Billy, if you make another step I'll shoot you."
> He stopped and said, "You're the most suspicious damn man I ever saw."
> He turned back and I pitched him my tobacco. He threw it back and said he didn't want any of my tobacco.[20]

Two hours later, after partaking of Padre Polaco's "splendid dinner," Garrett and his men pushed on toward Las Vegas, arriving there on December 26 to find the streets thronged with people waiting to see the famous Kid—and maybe hurl verbal insults at the hated Rudabaugh. "People stood on the muddy street corners and in hotel offices and saloons talking of the great event," the *Las Vegas Gazette* reported in a special issue. As the wagon, driven by Manuel Brazil and flanked by Garrett, Stewart, Mason, East, and Emory, rattled into the plaza, "astonishment gave way to joy."

19.14. Deluvina Maxwell.

Date and photographer unknown. Author's Collection.

The story of Deluvina's life was never recorded in detail. Born of Navajo parents in Canyon de Chelly, she was taken as a slave by Apaches when she was nine or ten years old and traded to Lucien B. Maxwell in Cimarron for ten horses. She died in Albuquerque on November 27, 1927.

19.15. Grzelachowski's store, Puerto de Luna.

Photograph by Dick George, 1996.

As for the Kid, he was relishing every minute of his new-found celebrity. Spotting Dr. J. H. Sutfin in the crowd, he called out, "Hello, doc! Thought I jes drop in and see how you fellers in Vegas air behavin' yerselves!" Reporters from the *Optic* and the *Gazette* (could the latter perhaps have been Koogler himself, the man who had given the Kid his immortal sobriquet?) were allowed in to see him. Garrett, disturbed by the hostility shown toward Rudabaugh, posted a heavy guard on the jail building in Valencia Street, but there was no attempt at a lynching.

Next morning, as mail contractor Mike Cosgrove distributed new suits to each of the prisoners, the *Gazette* reported, "A large crowd strained their necks to get a glimpse of the prisoners, who stood in the passageway like children waiting for a Christmas tree distribution." As their shackles were removed so they could change clothes, the Kid was

> light and chipper, and was very communicative, laughing, joking and chatting with the bystanders.
>
> "You appear to take it easy," the reporter said.
>
> "Yes! What's the use of looking on the gloomy side of everything. The laugh's on me this time," he said. Then looking about the placita, he asked "Is the jail at Santa Fe any better than this?"
>
> This seemed to trouble him considerably, for, as he explained "this is a terrible place to put a fellow in." He put the same question to every one who came near him and when he learned that there was nothing better in store for him, he shrugged his shoulders and said something about putting up with what he had to.

19.16. Grzelachowski's store.

Photograph by Dick George, 1996.

This is the room in which the Kid ate his last Christmas dinner.

It is not difficult to picture him standing there in the narrow street behind the plaza, kicking the toes of his boots on the stone pavement to keep his feet warm, looking and acting

like a mere boy. He is about five feet eight or nine inches tall, slightly built and lithe, weighing about 140; a frank, open countenance, looking like a school boy, with the traditional fuzz on his upper lip; clear blue eyes, with a roguish snap about them; light hair and complexion. He is, in all, quite a handsome looking fellow, the only imperfection being two prominent front teeth slightly protruding like squirrel's teeth, and he has agreeable and winning ways.

"There was a big crowd gazing at me, wasn't there," he exclaimed, and then smilingly continued, "Well, perhaps some of them will think me half man now; everyone seems to think I was some kind of animal."

19.17. Las Vegas, the old plaza, looking northeast.

Photograph by F. E. Evans, ca. 1881–82. MoNM Negative No. 50798.

He had already read the *Gazette's* extra, published on their arrival, and expressed indignation at the newspaper's report that he had called his associates cowards. He told the story one more time from his side, as if he still hoped somehow it would be believed. One line attributed to him rings especially true. "I wasn't the leader of any gang," he protested, "I was for Billy all the time."[21]

After the newspaperman left, Garrett, Mason, and Frank Stewart came over to the jail to load the prisoners aboard a wagon and take them from the old town to the railroad depot. Pickett was to be left at Las Vegas; Sheriff Desiderio Romero turned over the Kid and Wilson but refused to hand over Rudabaugh. Rudabaugh had killed jailor Lino Valdez and escaped from this same jail; they wanted to deal with him themselves. Garrett had a pretty shrewd idea what they had in mind and insisted "in no uncertain terms" that his federal warrants took precedence over any charges they might have against the prisoner; Rudabaugh was going to Santa Fe. With ill grace the sheriff consented, and the three men were loaded into the wagon.

Escorted by Garrett, Emory, East, Stewart, and Deputy U.S. Marshal James W. Bell, who had been a member of the posse at the Greathouse ranch when Carlyle was killed, the wagon rolled down the hill to the depot, where they boarded the train without incident. As they waited to leave, however, a crowd of armed and angry citizens began to gather. Realizing they intended to try

19.18. Las Vegas railroad depot, ca. 1880.

Date and photographer unknown, ca. 1880.
MoNM Negative No. 114893.

This single-story building was replaced the following year by a larger two-story
one (see panorama, Fig. 17.2).

19.19. Las Vegas railroad depot, 1996.

Author's photograph, 1996.

and take Rudabaugh by force, Garrett pulled down the shades in the car and warned the other passengers, "Any of you people who don't want to be in it had better get out before I lock the car, as we are liable to have a hell of a fight in a very few minutes." Two drummers beat a hasty retreat, while three miners reached for their weapons and East and Emory each took a window and picked out the men they would kill first. Garrett asked Stewart if he was ready to make a fight of it. Of course he was, Stewart said. Garrett nodded. "Let's make a good one."[22]

As Garrett took one door of the carriage and Stewart the other, Sheriff Romero and five others came toward Garrett flourishing revolvers. "Let's go right in and take him out of there," one of them said, and they pushed forward as if to force their way onto the train.

Garrett shouted, "If you wanted them so badly why didn't you go out and take them?"

"We'll take them now!" they yelled.

"As soon as the first shot is fired we will unloose every man and arm him," Stewart warned them.[23]

"We shoved up the windows," Jim East said, "and Tom Emory took one and I another. . . . We made all the prisoners get down on the floor of the coach so they could not shoot them through the windows."[24]

Garrett told the mob to get down off the steps of the train. Although—or more likely because—he used his "mildest tones," it worked: they backed off, milling around indecisively. Just before the train pulled out, the *Gazette* reporter, who had witnessed the confrontation, asked the Kid how he felt.

"The prospects of a fight exhilarated him, and he bitterly bemoaned being chained. 'If only I had my Winchester, I'd lick the whole crowd,' was his confident comment on the strength of the attacking party. He sighed and sighed again for a chance to take a hand in the fight and the burden of his desire was to be set free to fight on the side of his captors as soon as he should smell powder."

And had he been alarmed? "No!" the Kid said. "We knew to whom we were surrendering when we gave ourselves up. They gave us their word and they'll keep it: they will see us through."

It turned out Sheriff Romero and his toughs had lost their appetite for a fight. Post Office detective J. Fred Morley climbed aboard the engine with a six-shooter in each hand and told the engineer to get rolling. The wheels began to turn, and the mob fell back. As the train rolled out, forty-five minutes late, the Kid lifted his hat and invited the *Gazette* reporter to come and see him in Santa Fe, calling out adios as they pulled away—adios, note, not goodbye.[25]

20.1. Palace of the Governors, Santa Fe.

Photograph by Jesse L. Nusbaum, 1912.
MoNM Negative No. 61544.

This photograph of wood vendors' burro wagons in the old plaza is absolutely timeless; it probably looked much like this when the Kid saw it briefly on his way to jail.

CHAPTER TWENTY

Trials

From the moment he stepped out of the stone shack at Stinking Spring with his hands up, the Kid's agile mind had focused on one thing and one thing only: escape. Somehow, somewhere, he would find a way. Until that opportunity presented itself he did as he had always done and smiled at his own misfortunes. The trip down to Santa Fe was anyway an exciting experience for Billy, quite possibly the first time he had ever ridden in a train. Heavy snowdrifts stalled the locomotive as it reached the summit of Glorieta Pass; in high spirits, Billy amused his captors by clowning with a slice of apple pie, putting it into his mouth in one piece, then removing it again intact.

When the train reached Santa Fe at 7:30 P.M. that Monday, Deputy U.S. Marshal Charles Conklin was waiting at the depot, together with a crowd of kibitzers wanting to see the celebrated outlaws. Once they were safely incarcerated in the miserable hovel on Water Street that passed for the county jail, Garrett and his deputies repaired to the Exchange Hotel to enjoy a drink and the acclaim of the citizens. They would have a little more trouble collecting the promised reward, however; since Garrett was not yet officially sheriff of Lincoln County, Wallace's secretary, W. G. Ritch, declined to pay him the promised five hundred dollars. However, the citizens of Santa Fe rallied 'round and raised the money, which was given to Garrett and Stewart against their promissory note.[1]

Next morning, when he went over to the jail to check on his prisoners, Garrett learned "they had not had a mouthful to eat since they were put in the jail. Whereupon one of the posse went to the keeper of the restaurant who had a contract for feeding the U.S. prisoners and asked why he had not sent down meals to the three. The man said he had done so, and after a little examination it was discovered that Jailer Silva, or some of his henchmen, had eaten the grub themselves. It's pretty rough on prisoners when their jailers eat the meals sent to them."[2]

On January 1, already actively seeking a way out of his impending trial, Billy asked for a pen and ink and wrote a short note to Governor Lew Wallace which said simply, "I would like to See You for a few minutes if you can Spare time." Wallace, however, was not in town; he had asked for and received a twenty-day leave of absence to visit Washington on territorial business and had left by train the day before Billy's arrival.[3]

On January 3, Rudabaugh stood trial on charges of robbing the U.S. mail, was found guilty, and was sentenced to ninety-nine years in jail. This sentence was stayed so that Rudabaugh could be sent back to Las Vegas to stand trial there for the murder of Lino Valdez. Figuring he had nothing to lose,

20.2. County jail, Santa Fe.

Photographer unknown, ca. 1895–99.
MoNM Negative No. 163219.

This view looks west along Water Street and graphically illustrates what a miserable hole the jail must have been. The building stood behind and slightly east of the corral in back of Herlow's Hotel. The actual cell block, which seems to have had six cells, ran south from the portion of the building on the left.

Rudabaugh—probably abetted by fellow prisoner Edward "Choctaw" Kelly, also awaiting trial for murder and probably no keener than Dirty Dave to face the music—determined about halfway through February to try once again to dig his way to freedom and persuaded the Kid and Wilson to pitch in.

By this time Billy was probably ready to try just about anything. In January, Ira Leonard had come to the jail to see him and promised to stop in on his way back to discuss Billy's case; he never turned up. Next, the Kid tried attorney Edgar Caypless, who had defended Rudabaugh and would again represent him and Choctaw Kelly at their forthcoming trials. To retain the lawyer, Billy "sold" him the beautiful bay mare he had been riding at the time of the Stinking Spring capture; the animal was considered to be one of the finest pieces of horseflesh in New Mexico. The problem was, he had already given the horse to Frank Stewart, who had in turn presented it to the wife, Minnie, of hotel proprietor Scott Moore in Las Vegas (she apparently named it "Kid Stewart Moore").[4] To get it back, Caypless would have to file a suit of replevin, and that would take time. Time was the one thing the Kid did not have, so he pitched in with Rudabaugh and Kelly.

The slow, painful task of digging a tunnel beneath the street wall—they can have had nothing much more to do it with than a couple of filched spoons and their bare hands—went on for some time before a "trusty" who had been paid to keep an eye on the quartet blew the whistle on them. On February 28, the sheriff and Deputy U.S. Marshal Tony Neis burst into the cell, where they found "the bed ticking was filled with stones and earth, and removing the mattress, they found a deep hole. . . . By concealing the loose

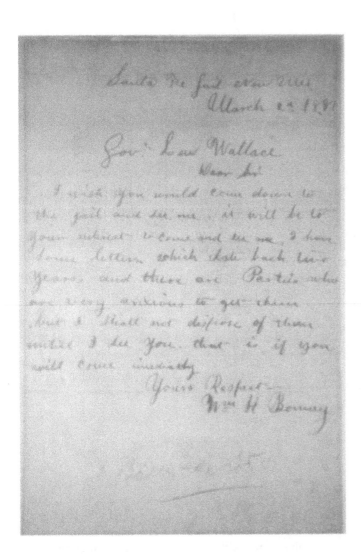

20.3. The Kid's letter from jail.

Courtesy Lincoln County Heritage Trust.

earth in the bed and covering the hole with it, they had almost reached the street without awakening the suspicions of the guard," the *New Mexican* reported.[5]

The result of this was that the prisoners were separated, and Billy, heavily shackled, was placed in solitary confinement; ever the realist, he abandoned all thoughts of escape and concentrated on getting out through the door. Two days later, on March 2, he again asked for writing paper.

> Dear Sir,
>
> I wish you would come down to the jail and see me. it will be to your interest to come and see me. I have some letters which date back two years and there are Parties who are very anxious to get them but I shall not dispose of them until I see you. that is if you will come imediately.
>
> Yours respect.
>
> Wm. H. Bonney

Perhaps Billy thought this unsubtle hint of blackmail would bring Wallace hurrying to his assistance; it did not. After two days, when it was apparent no answer would be forthcoming, he tried yet again.

>   SANTA FE
>   IN JAIL.
>   March 4, 1881.
>
> Gov. Lew Wallace
> Dear Sir
>
>   I wrote You a little note the day before yesterday but have received no answer. I Expect you have forgotten what you promised me, this Month two Years ago, but I have not, and I think You had ought to have come and seen me as I requested you to. I have done everything that I promised you I would, and You have done nothing that You promised me.
>   I think that when You think The matter over, You will come down and See me, and I can then Explain Everything to you.
>   Judge Leonard, Passed through here on his way East, and promised to come and See me on his way back, but he did not fulfil his Promise. it looks to me like I am getting left in the Cold. I am not treated right by [Marshal] Sherman, he lets Every Stranger that comes to See me through Curiosity in to see me, but will not let a Single one of my friends in, not Even an Attorney.
>   I guess they mean to Send me up without giving me any Show but they will have a nice time doing it. I am not intirely without friends.
>   I shall expect to see you some time today.
>
>   Patiently waiting
>   I am Very truly Yours, Respt.
>   Wm. H. Bonney

But wheels were turning of which Billy knew nothing. On March 17, President James A. Garfield accepted Wallace's resignation and took steps to appoint in his place Lionel A. Sheldon, a friend and fellow Ohioan. Edgar Caypless, his hands already full with the defenses of Rudabaugh and Kelly, had run into difficulties when Scott Moore's wife expressed her intention of vigorously contesting his suit to repossess the Kid's horse.[6] Meanwhile the Kid waited in the Stygian darkness for someone, anyone, to come to his aid. No one did.

March 28 was set as the date on which the Kid and Wilson would be taken south to La Mesilla for trial. The day before his departure, stranded somewhere between anger and apprehension, Billy made one last despairing try to contact Wallace. "Dear Sir," he scribbled, "for the *last time* I ask. Will you keep your Promise. I start below tomorrow. Send Answer by Bearer."

To this entreaty, as to all the others, Wallace turned a deaf ear. The Kid's exploits were the subject of newspaper articles throughout the country; he was far too notorious to be given a pardon, even had Wallace ever seriously contemplated granting one. Besides, the governor had other fish to fry. The sales of his novel, *Ben Hur: A Tale of the Christ*, published the preceding year, were beginning to pick up after a faltering start. He considered his work in New Mexico done, and with some very promising mining investments tucked

20.4. Tony Neis *(left)* and Robert Olinger.

Photographer Bennet & Brown, Santa Fe, March 1, 1881.
Harold B. Lee Library, Brigham Young University.

Celebrating their nomination as deputy U.S. marshals to escort the famous Billy the Kid to his trial in La Mesilla, these two constituted what the *New Mexican* dubbed "a heavy team." Eight weeks after this photograph was taken, Billy the Kid killed Olinger at Lincoln.

into his portfolio, he was already actively seeking appointment as an ambassador. His attitude toward the "precious specimen" he had once met in a mud-chinked Lincoln hovel two long years earlier is clearly indicated in an interview he gave in Las Vegas a month later during which

> the conversation drifted into the sentence of "THE KID."
> "It looks as though he would hang, governor."
> "Yes, the chances seem good that the 13th of May would finish him."
> "He appears to look to you to save his neck."
> "Yes," said Gov. Wallace smiling, "but I can't see how a fellow like him should expect any clemency from me."
> Although not committing himself, the general tenor of the governor's remarks indicated that he would resolutely refuse to grant "the Kid" a pardon. It would seem as though "the Kid" had undertaken to bulldoze the governor, which has not helped his chances in the slightest.[7]

20.5. The train depot, Rincon, New Mexico.

Date and photographer unknown, ca. 1883.
R. N. Mullin Collection. HHC.

So on Monday, March 28, Deputy U.S. Marshals Bob Olinger, Tony Neis, and Francisco Chávez took the Kid and Billy Wilson to the Santa Fe train depot, where Ira Leonard was waiting to accompany them downriver. When they reached the end of the track at Rincon, "an ugly crowd" was waiting and "some threats were made," but when the heavily armed deputies got their guns unlimbered and Neis growled, "You don't get them fellows without somebody being killed," the mob dispersed.

The prisoners were kept overnight in a local saloon and taken the rest of the way—a nine-hour journey by stage—the following day. At Las Cruces, "an inquisitive mob gathered around the coach." When someone asked which one of them was Billy the Kid, Billy was unable to restrain his impish sense of mischief. "The Kid himself answered by placing his hand on Judge Leonard's shoulder and saying 'This is the man.'"[8]

His good humor vanished when he learned that "quite a number of Lincoln county men" were on hand to testify against him, among them Jimmy Dolan, Billy Mathews, Bonnie Baca, and Isaac Ellis. He protested "at least two hundred men have been killed in Lincoln county during the past three years, but that he did not kill all of them." His protests were of no avail; he was taken across to La Mesilla and lodged in the filthy little jail opposite La Posta.

Court had been convened on March 28, Judge Warren Bristol presiding. Before him was a crowded docket that included seven criminal indictments for murder; the case of Billy Wilson, charged with counterfeiting; and a series of other crimes ranging from rustling and robbery to rape. The first case to go to trial was that of Pedro Rivera, who was convicted of murder in the fifth degree. The other capital cases Bristol heard—one was stricken for un-

20.6. The plaza, La Mesilla.

Photograph by Stiles & Burke, June 1881.
MoNM Negative No. 14580.

20.7. Courthouse building, La Mesilla.

Photographer unknown, ca. 1881.
R. N. Mullin Collection. HHC.

The building in which the Kid was tried as it probably looked at the time. It was built early in Mesilla history; according to local tradition, the Gadsden Purchase agreement was signed within its walls. It was used as the county courthouse until 1882, incorporating the county jail and a schoolhouse; school was suspended whenever there was a hanging. The building has since gone through a number of other incarnations and is presently a tourist gift shop.

20.8. Warren Bristol.

Date and photographer unknown.
MoNM Negative No. 50340.

stated reasons and two others were granted a continuance—were those of F. C. Clark (an alias), accused of the murder of Robert Mann the preceding January; Santos Barela, accused of the "fiendish" killing of José Jojola and also indicted for raping Jojola's wife; and the Kid, on trial for the murders of Andrew "Buckshot" Roberts and Sheriff Brady.[9]

On Wednesday morning, March 30, Billy was arraigned before Judge Warren Bristol to answer the charge of murdering Roberts at Blazer's Mill. Also named in the docket were Charlie Bowdre, Doc Scurlock, Henry Brown, John Middleton, Stephen Stephens, John Scroggins, Fred Waite, and George Coe, none of whom had been found. Prosecuting counsel was Azariah Wild's bête noir, the six-foot U.S. attorney, Kentuckian Sidney Barnes; defending, Ira Leonard.

The courtroom itself was tiny, crowded, and stuffy, "about fourteen feet wide and twice as long, with whitewashed walls and a wooden floor. At the back end of the room is a small platform on which are a table and chair for the judge. On either side of the platform is a small table with two chairs. In one corner of the back wall is a large bookcase with the glass missing from one door. At the other corner is a stove in front of the fireplace. There is no other furniture in the room except sixteen or eighteen wooden benches without backs."[10]

After the Kid had entered a plea of not guilty, Leonard opened by contending that since the land Blazer's Mill stood on was privately owned, and not federal property, the government had no jurisdiction, while Barnes insisted that the Mescalero reservation was "Indian country" over which the United States had exclusive control. No witnesses seem to have been called, nor, apparently, did the Kid take the stand. On April 6, Bristol cut the Gordian knot with a seven-page opinion that no part of New Mexico was "Indian country" and quashed the indictment. Barnes decided against entering an exception to Bristol's ruling because he "thought it best to let him Kid then be tried & hung and save the United States expense and rid the world of an outlaw."[11]

Barnes was not the only one who didn't like the Kid. Local newspaperman Simeon B. Newman—the Independent once described him as "the spunky, plucky, spicy ex-editor of the defunct 'Las Vegas Mail,' miner, schoolmaster, printer's devil, chief editor, prisoner, martyr of the 'powers that be,' fired life insurance agent, newspaper correspondent, &c &c"—the editor of a short-lived local newspaper called Newman's Semi-Weekly (it had begun publication just a month earlier and ceased publication on April 20), ran an unwittingly prescient piece on April 2 which encapsulated local fears: "[The Kid] is a notoriously dangerous character, has on several occasions before escaped justice where escape appeared even more improbable than now, and has made his brags that he only wants to get free in order to kill three men—one of them being Governor Wallace. Should he break jail now, there is no doubt that he would immediately proceed to execute his threat. . . . We expect every day to hear of his escape and hope that legal technicalities may not be permitted to render escape more probable."[12]

Next day the Kid was back in the dock, this time to answer for the murder of William Brady. On Bristol's instructions Ira Leonard stepped down, and the court appointed John D. Bail and Albert J. Fountain, neither of whom knew the first thing about the Kid or the Lincoln County War, as Billy's attorneys. The prosecution's case was presented by Nova Scotian Simon B. Newcomb, forty-three, a former El Paso district judge who had moved to Las Cruces in 1875 and had become successor to and a close friend of William Rynerson.

How Newcomb presented the case, and what defense Bail and Fountain offered in return, are largely lost to history. It seems astonishing, but not only did the trial receive little or no coverage in the local newspapers, but also the actual court records themselves seem to have disappeared; perhaps had the Kid been able to finance an appeal, a transcript would have been preserved, but he could not. Thus, it is impossible to know what Bonnie Baca and Billy Mathews, eyewitnesses to the murder of Brady, told the jury, what the testimony of Uncle Ike Ellis might have been, or whether (although since the case took only two days to hear, it seems highly unlikely) the Kid's attorneys put him on the witness stand. Not that it would have mattered much had they done so.

"The courtroom was crowded with a motley array of spectators," Court Clerk George Bowman recalled in later years. "In the back of the room sat the judge behind an old fashioned flat-topped desk which was on a raised platform. In front of the desk was a small clearance where the lawyers came to make their pleas. Rough wooden benches were supplied for the spectators. And there, sitting a little to one side of the judge's desk, was Billy the Kid."

He was a "rather pleasant looking" fellow, Bowman said, with "wavy hair, dark eyes, sullen and defiant now. . . . There was the mark of a keen intellect in that forehead, and the clean cut sweep of the jaw, but there was a mark of brutishness in his face, too, a courseness [*sic*] stamped across his features. . . . It looked almost ridiculous, all those armed men sitting around a harmless looking youth with the down still on his chin. As a further precaution, Billy the Kid was kept handcuffed during the trial. He was a dangerous man and the court was taking no chances."[13]

On Saturday, April 9, all the evidence having been heard, Judge Bristol delivered a nine-page summation in English which was translated to a jury comprised solely of native New Mexicans. The defense failed in its attempt to have Bristol instruct the jury on the sole legal theory by which it might have found Bonney either not guilty or guilty of less than first-degree murder. Its basic argument was that to convict, the jury had to find that the Kid had fired the actual shot that killed Sheriff Brady—and no evidence had been offered to show this—or they had to acquit. This "noose or loose" strategy was never more than a pious hope of a defense, and Bristol had no hesitation in shooting it down.

"If he was present—encouraging—inciting—aiding in—abetting—advising or commanding this killing of Brady he is as much guilty as though he fired the fatal shot," he told the jury. "As to what would or would not be a reasonable doubt of guilt I charge you that belief in the guilt of this defendant to the exclusion of every reasonable doubt does not require you to so believe absolutely and to a mathematical certainty. That is, to justify a ver-

20.9. Bonifacio Baca.

Photographer unknown, June 1874.
Courtesy Notre Dame University.

Bonifacio Juan Baca was born April 26, 1857, one of the nine children, and the oldest son, of Saturnino and María Juana Baca. "Bonnie," as he was always known, was educated at the University of Notre Dame, 1872–74; Lawrence G. Murphy paid for his education. Baca emerged as a first honors student.

After he returned to Lincoln he went to work in the new Murphy store. In 1879 he served as a translator at the Dudley court of inquiry and was a witness against the Kid at his trial in 1881.

dict of guilty it is not necessary for you to be as certain that this defendant is guilty as you are that two and two are four, or that two and three are five. Merely a vague conjecture or a bare possibility that the defendant may be innocent is not sufficient to cause a reasonable doubt of his guilt."[14]

Hardly surprising, then, that so instructed, the jury brought in a unanimous verdict of guilty. Bristol set sentencing for the following Wednesday, April 13, and the Kid was returned to the cell he was doubtless sharing with Billy Wilson, Santos Barela, and the mysterious F. C. Clark.

At five o'clock on the appointed day, F. C. Clark was brought before the court. He had from the time of his arrest and throughout his trial steadfastly refused to reveal his identity, admitting only that he had a wife and family and that Clark was not his real name. Bristol reminded him of the verdict and asked him if he had anything to say. When Clark said nothing, Bristol pronounced the mandatory sentence for murder. Clark would be held in the county jail until May 13 and between the hours of 9:00 A.M. and 3:00 P.M. on that day he be hanged by the neck until dead.

A quarter of an hour later it was the Kid's turn to stand as the judge pronounced his sentence. Asked if he had anything to say before sentence was pronounced, Billy made no reply and listened to the judge's words in silence. Unlike Clark, who would be held in the Doña Ana County jail until his execution, he was to be returned by the sheriff to the jurisdiction of the county in which he had committed his crimes and confined in prison until May 13. There, on the same day and between the same hours designated for the execution of Clark, he was to be taken out and "hanged by the neck until his body be dead."[15]

Many a man would have given up hope, but not the Kid. Such evidence as there is suggests that if anything, he felt he had been badly treated. Simeon H. Newman had given Billy what he considered "a rough deal" in his April 7 article; he "had created prejudice against me, and is trying to incite a mob to lynch me. . . . I think it is a dirty mean advantage to take of me, considering my situation and knowing I could not defend myself by word or act. But I suppose he thought he would give me a kick down hill."

As for Wallace, "Considering the active part [he] took on our side and the friendly relations that existed between him and me, and the promises he made me, I think he ought to pardon me," Billy continued. "Don't know that he will do it. . . . Think it hard that I should be the only one to suffer the extreme penalty of the law."[16]

No use hoping for a miracle; two days after he was sentenced, Billy wrote again to lawyer Edgar Caypless in Las Vegas. Fountain had done his best for him, he said, and "is willing to carry the case further if I can raise the money to bear his expense. The mare is about all I can depend on at present so hope you will settle the case right away and give him the money you get for her. . . . I shall be taken to Lincoln tomorrow. Please write and direct care of Garrett, sheriff. Excuse bad writing. I have my handcuffs on."[17]

The following night at about ten o'clock—the time of departure had been kept secret and a report circulated that in fact the party would not leave for Lincoln until the middle of the week—the Kid was taken out of his cell and bundled into a Dougherty wagon to be taken to Lincoln. Billy had said he

20.10. Stagecoach.

Date and photographer unknown. Author's Collection.

Probably it was in just such a vehicle that the Kid was brought from Rincon to La Mesilla and later taken from there up to Lincoln.

expected to be lynched on the way to Lincoln by White Oaks parties seeking to avenge Jimmy Carlyle; there were other mutterings to the effect that a rescue attempt might be mounted. To ensure that nothing of the sort happened, Doña Ana County Sheriff James M. Southwick had the Kid cuffed and shackled, then chained to the back seat of the wagon. He had deputized a heavy crew to escort it; in addition to his deputy Dave Wood and Wood's ranching partner D. M. Reede, it included Bob Olinger, Billy Mathews, John Kinney, Tom Williams, and W. A. Lockhart. All were heavily armed; it was understood that if there was any trouble, the first one to be shot would be the Kid.[18]

So on April 21, after stopovers at Pat Coghlan's Tularosa ranch and Blazer's Mill—where Billy humorously reenacted the shootout with Buckshot Roberts for the possemen—the Kid was handed over to Sheriff Pat Garrett at Fort Stanton and escorted by him and Olinger to Lincoln. Because the town had never had a jail that would hold a cripple, to quote Pat Garrett, the Kid was to be held in the old Dolan store, bought just a few months earlier by the county and now serving as its courthouse, in which Garrett had an office on the second floor.

The layout of the building was largely unaltered since the days when it had been the home of Lawrence G. Murphy; the Kid was taken to what had once been Murphy's bedroom, a large square room on the northeastern corner of the building. It had two large windows, one looking down into the street and

20.11. Blazer's Mill.

Author's photograph, 1996.

This is the old Blazer home, now abandoned, in which the Kid and his guards spent a night on their way to Lincoln and where Billy acted out the shootout with Roberts for their amusement, which might be seen as further support for the proposition that it was indeed in this house that Roberts made his last stand.

20.12. The Lincoln County Courthouse.

Photographer T. Dudley Cramer, 1936.
Author's Collection.

The Kid was held in the room on the nearest corner. In 1881 the stairs on each side of the balcony had not yet been added.

north, the other on the east side directly above the entrance to the post office. Across the hall in what had been the quarters of Eliza Lloyd, the hard-swearing Irishwoman who had been Murphy's housekeeper, were five civil prisoners arrested for their part in disturbances on Tularosa Creek a little while earlier.

The men Garrett had picked to guard the Kid were well chosen. Neither Bob Olinger nor Jimmy Bell had any reason to like or trust him. So the Kid was kept handcuffed and shackled day and night. In addition, a chalk line bisected the room into two halves, a true "deadline" in every sense of the word: they told him if he even attempted to cross it he would be killed on the spot.

The tradition has grown through the years that Bell treated the Kid decently but that Olinger taunted him every chance he got. But Bell had been a close friend of Jimmy Carlyle's and knew that the Kid had been one of those who shot Carlyle. It is unlikely his attitude toward Billy was at best anything warmer than neutral.[19]

Olinger, however, was unashamedly partisan. He had been with the Seven Rivers posse that killed Frank MacNab, and he later fought for the House; his friend Bob Beckwith had died in the last fight at McSween's. He had been a member of the posse that scoured the upper Pecos country looking for the Kid. He had killed the Kid's friend John Jones—treacherously, by all accounts. He liked to poke the Kid with the barrel of his shotgun and invite him to make a run for it so he could have the pleasure of blowing him apart. "There existed a reciprocal hatred between these two," Garrett said, "and neither attempted to disguise or conceal his antipathy for the other."[20]

Before leaving on April 27 for a two-day trip to the Oaks that would include a stop at Las Tablas, or "Board Town" (where he probably went to order the timber for the Kid's gallows), Garrett warned his deputies against giving the Kid any chance to make a break. His admonition probably echoed what a friend of Olinger's had said just a few days earlier: "You think yourself an old hand at this business. You have guarded many prisoners, and faced danger many a time in apprehending them, and you think you are invincible and can get away with anything. But I tell you, as good a man as you are, that if that man is shown the slightest chance on earth, if he is allowed the use of one hand, or if he is not watched every moment from now until the moment he is executed, he will effect some plan by which he will murder the whole lot of you before you even have time to suspect that he has any such intention."[21]

Olinger, who made no secret of his contempt for the Kid—he said the Kid was a cur and that every man he had killed had been murdered in cold blood—just smiled and replied that there was no more chance of the Kid's escape than there was of his going to Heaven.

He could not have been more wrong.

21.1. The Kid's window.

Photograph by W. A. Carrell, 1926.
Carrell Collection, LCHT.

This moody photograph almost conjures up an image of the Kid sitting, watching, waiting. Walter Noble Burns wrote, "It is one of the most attractive pictures . . . I have ever seen. So simple. But so effective. The two sunlit windows; the chair and its shadow in the oblong of sunshine on the floor; the rest black shadow. It's beautiful."

CHAPTER TWENTY ONE

Adios, Boys!

IT WAS THURSDAY, APRIL 28. The Kid had been in Lincoln a week now, and a sort of routine had been established. At the noon hour each day, Sam Wortley would send food over, just as he had done every day since the Kid arrived; later on—at a time referred to in contemporary usage as "evening" but meaning about 5:00 P.M.—the other prisoners would be taken over to the Wortley for supper while the Kid, as usual, ate alone.

He spent much of his time sitting by his upstairs window watching the little world of Lincoln go by on the street below. It seems unlikely he would have been allowed visitors, although it is not hard to imagine acquaintances stopping beneath his window to exchange pleasantries. One visitor who did not quite make it was the Kid's stepfather, William Antrim, who "started across ahorseback over to see Billy the Kid before they hung him and he was delayed on the road, his horse got sick or something, and he didn't get there . . . till the next day." One wonders what they might have had to say to one another.[1]

At about the usual time on this routine Thursday, Bob Olinger escorted the five Tularosa prisoners across the street to the Wortley, leaving Deputy James Bell in charge of the Kid. There was no one else in the building, although old Gottfried Gauss had quarters and a little vegetable patch in a building in back of the store, as did Sam Wortley.

Endless theories have been advanced about what happened next; the fact of the matter is, nobody knows. All that can be truthfully said is that in a daring series of swift and decisive moves, Billy the Kid somehow got hold of a pistol and with it shot and mortally wounded James Bell. Gauss, out in the courtyard to the rear of the building, "heard a shot fired, then a tussle upstairs in the courthouse, somebody hurrying downstairs, and Deputy Sheriff Bell emerging from the door running toward me. He ran right into my arms, expired the same moment, and I laid him down, dead."[2]

A report in the *Las Vegas Gazette* on May 10 suggested (on what evidence is not known) that "the handcuffs had been taken from his left hand, to allow him to eat supper. Watching an opportunity, he dealt J. W. Bell a blow with the irons on his right hand. This broke his skull and as he fell, the Kid grabbed his pistol and finished the work." It is a persuasive story, but it fails to explain how Bell got outside or why, if Gauss's account is correct, a shot was fired first and was followed by a "tussle."

A second and marginally more convincing hypothesis, based on the postmortem findings of Pat Garrett and an account supposedly given by the Kid to J. P. Meadows, has it that Billy asked to be taken to the privy outside the

21.2. Wortley Hotel and Whelan store, Lincoln.

Photographer unknown, ca. 1890.
MoNM Negative No. 11657.

This is the earliest known picture of the Wortley, to the left
and behind the Whelan, later Aragón, store.

21.3. The Wortley Hotel.

Author's photograph, 1996.

The Wortley building today, seen
from approximately the same
spot.

courthouse building. On the way back upstairs, Bell carelessly lagged behind. The Kid got to the top of the stairs and around the corner where he was out of Bell's sight, slipped the cuffs off one wrist, and as Bell came up, lashed him over the head. There was a scuffle between the dazed deputy and Billy in which the Kid got Bell's gun. Bell broke loose and dashed down the stairway trying to escape, leaving the Kid no option but to kill him, which he did.

"Kid told me exactly how it was done," Meadows said. "He said he was lying on the floor on his stomach, and shot Bell as he ran down the stairs. Kid said of this killing, 'I did not want to kill Bell, but I had to do so in order to save my own life.'"[3]

This theory has much to commend it, notably the "tussle" Gauss heard and the fact that Bell had a cut on his head; it may well be the gun went off as the two men struggled. And it has been proven by recent experiment in Lincoln that a fit young man, although shackled and handcuffed, could indeed race up the staircase in under fifteen seconds, outdistancing someone moving at normal walking pace, and grab a gun. What is wrong with the proposition is that it asks us to believe that Bell, an experienced and wary lawman, saw the Kid doing all of this yet failed to perceive it as threatening.[4]

A third and more plausible story has it that a pistol had been hidden in the outside privy and a signal given to the Kid that it was there. When he got to the top of the stairs, he turned around and told Bell to come up with his hands raised. Bell turned and ran, trying to get around the right angle at the bottom of the stairs that would shield him from the Kid's sight, but Billy fired twice, one shot missing completely, the other ricocheting off the wall and tearing through Bell's body from right to left. He staggered out into the yard, where he died in Gauss's arms. But where is the "tussle" in this version?[5]

Not that it matters: the Kid had killed Bell, and now he was free. Heart pounding, he shuffled his way across to the armory, once Jim Dolan's quarters, and grabbed the Whitneyville shotgun Bob Olinger had left propped against the wall. Then he hurried back to his former cell and squatted or knelt by the open window—the sill is only about two feet off the floor—and waited.

Over in the Wortley Hotel, Bob Olinger heard the shots and scrambled to his feet, exclaiming (does one only imagine vexation in his words at having missed the chance to kill Bonney himself?), "The Kid has tried to escape and Bell has shot him!" Why he should have jumped to such a conclusion is hard to understand. Olinger was an experienced peace officer. He knew perfectly well that given half a chance, the Kid would make a break. The minute he heard those shots he should have deputized backup and approached the courthouse warily, taking no chances until he knew for sure who had shot whom. Olinger did none of this: alone and unready, he ran straight into a kill zone. Billy the Kid was waiting for him at the open window, the shotgun cocked.

"Hello, Bob," he said and fired both barrels.

The big man went down dead, his right shoulder, chest, and side riddled with thirty-six buckshot, something like a quarter of a pound of lead fired at a range of less than ten feet. Above, the Kid smashed the weapon over the sill, breaking the stock, and threw the broken gun down at Olinger's body.

"You damned sonofabitch!" he snarled. "You won't corral me with that again!"

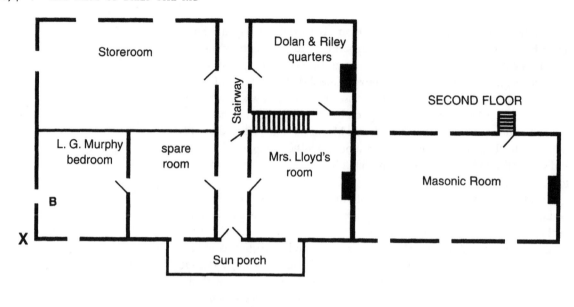

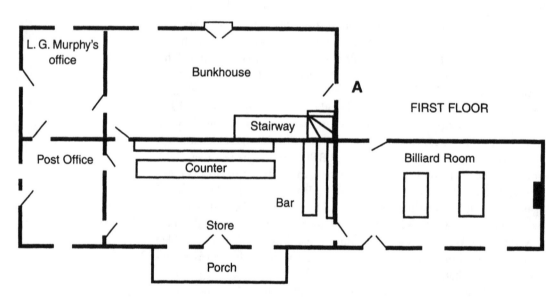

21.4. Ground plan of the courthouse (L. G. Murphy & Co. Building), 1881.

Author's collection.

The building was largely unaltered at the time the Kid was a prisoner. He was kept in what had been Murphy's bedroom; the spare room next to it was Garrett's office. The other prisoners taken across to the Wortley by Olinger were held in what had been the room occupied by Mrs. Lloyd (Murphy's housekeeper).

On April 28, 1881, the Kid and Deputy James Bell walked down the stairway and out through door *A* to the privy; on the way back, the Kid made his break. The mortally wounded Bell staggered back out through the door they had just entered and fell dead in the yard. The Kid hobbled to the armory (Dolan and Riley's old quarters), got Bob Olinger's shotgun, and returned via Garrett's office to window *B*, from which he shot Olinger. The *X* marks the spot where Olinger fell.

A minute or two later, armed with a Winchester and two six-shooters from Garrett's gun store, the Kid came out onto the balcony, where he held the whole town of Lincoln in thrall for more than an hour. It was said afterwards that Lilly, the manager of the Wortley, and merchant J. A. LaRue had both got down their guns but were restrained from action, Lilly by two friends, LaRue by his wife. In another account, local stonemason Bob Brookshire, who hewed tombstones in exchange for bed and board, started across the street; the Kid told him to go back to the Wortley or he would kill him. Other than this, not a soul lifted a finger to contest Billy's domination. Garrett later ascribed this to terror, but the Kid had enough friends in Lincoln for it to have been at least passive encouragement, or even admiration.

Addressing the crowd from the upper balcony like a politician soliciting votes, Billy "told the people that he did not want to kill Bell, but, as he ran, he had to. He said he grabbed Bell's revolver and told him to hold up his hands and surrender; that Bell decided to run and he had to kill him. He declared he was 'standing pat' against the world, and while he did not wish to kill anybody, if anybody interfered with his attempt to escape, he would kill him."[6]

Nobody, least of all Gottfried Gauss, doubted that if provoked, he would do it, so when the Kid ordered Gauss to saddle one of Judge Leonard's horses and promised to "clear out as soon as I can have the shackles loosened from my legs," Gauss found a prospector's pick, which he tossed in through the window, and bustled off to round up a mount. No one interfered as the Kid worked on the shackles until he had one leg free; then he tied the loose chain to his belt and went down to the rear of the courthouse, where Gauss had saddled the only available horse, a skittish little pony named Collie that belonged to County Clerk Billy Burt.

"When Billy went down stairs at last," Gauss recounted, "on passing the body of Bell he said, 'I'm sorry I had to kill him but couldn't help it.' On passing the body of Olinger he gave him a tip with his boot, saying 'You are not going to round me up again.'"[7]

The first time the Kid tried to mount, Billy Burt's pony, spooked by the clanking shackles, bucked him off. Billy ordered Alexander Nunnelly, one of the Tularosa prisoners, to catch it up and bring it back. Nunnelly protested, concerned not to be an accomplice.

"Well, you can tell them I made you do it," the Kid said. Nunnelly got the horse and the Kid swung aboard.

"Tell Billy Burt I'll send his pony back," he said. "And don't bother to look for me this side of Ireland. Adios, boys!"

Kicking the pony into a run, he headed west out of town. Some people say he was singing.[8]

***

If Billy read half of the things written about him in the next few weeks he might have been forgiven for thinking himself a cross between Satan and Superman. Thrilled by accounts of his cool, reckless, daring escape, readers—not only throughout the territory but also as far apart as San Francisco and

21.5. Bob Olinger's shotgun.

Author's Collection.

This is the gun with which Billy the Kid killed Bob Olinger. It is the property of publisher James H. Earle and is on display at the Texas Ranger Hall of Fame in Waco, Texas.

21.6. The old courthouse.

Author's photograph, 1996.

The appearance of a "Kid" on the balcony was just a happy coincidence.

New York—waited with bated breath for his next daredevil exploit. There were reports of him here, there, everywhere. It was said he had been killed in El Paso by City Marshal Dallas Stoudenmire. It was said he had met Billy Mathews on the road and "quietly shot him" and another man. Two days later he was supposedly at Fort Sumner. There was a story that he rode into a Chisum cow camp near Roswell and killed three of Chisum's men. It was reported he was in Las Vegas, at Seven Rivers, on his way to Mexico with twenty-five cowboys.[9]

He wasn't.

In a short interview with the *Las Vegas Gazette*, Barney Mason, who had been trailing him (at a respectable distance, let it be added), set out a convincingly believable account of the Kid's movements following his escape from Lincoln. "He went first," Barney told the paper, "to or about the Agua Azul [in the Capitan mountains] where he lost the horse taken from Lincoln."[10]

This is confirmed by the Kid's friend Yginio Salazar, who said Billy came to Las Tablas (just a few miles from Agua Azul) and "laid off there for three or four days. He laid out in the hills and came to my house to eat. I told him to leave this place and go to old Mexico." While he was at Las Tablas, Billy Burt's pony got loose from its tether and found its way back to Lincoln.[11]

"He went from there down about Newcomb's cow camp [on the Feliz]," Mason continued. "There he took a horse from one of his men and rode from there to Consios [Conejos] Springs [about twenty miles southwest of Fort Sumner]. There he slept again."

Again, this correlates more or less with John Meadows's claim that the Kid came to see him at his Peñasco Ranch and gave him his account of the escape. Meadows urged him to go south to old Mexico, but the Kid was determined to head north to Fort Sumner, to lay over there awhile until he had enough money to leave the country.

"Sure as you do, Garrett will get you," Meadows said, "or you will have to kill him."

"Don't you worry," Billy said, "I've got too many friends up there."

"Currington [Jim Cureton] was rounding up cattle [at Conejos Spring]," Mason said, "and some of his hands rode past the sleeping Billy. The latter became frightened and jumping up, scared his horse, which again broke away. He then footed it to Buffalo Arroyo about twelve miles where he was furnished with another horse. From there he made his way to Fort Sumner by the west side of the river. He staid above Fort Sumner that evening."

Mason got into Sumner late Saturday night (June 11) the newspaper reported, "and [black freedman Montgomery] Bell came early Sunday and stated that one of his horses had been stolen as he thought by a Mexican." Barney and Jim Cureton located the horse, the Kid and four other men at the head of Buffalo Arroyo. Outnumbered, they retreated to Sumner for reinforcements, but Mason could find no one to serve on a posse. Thoroughly unnerved—he knew the Kid hadn't forgotten Mason's trying to kill him at Stinking Spring— Mason packed his family into a wagon and hit the road for Roswell. About six miles from Sumner near Arroyo Taiban they met the Kid, but he let them pass without incident.[12]

In Santa Fe, Lew Wallace, who only a day or two earlier had signed the Kid's death warrant, now reinstated the five-hundred-dollar reward "to any person or persons who will capture William Bonny, alias the Kid, and deliver him to any Sheriff of New Mexico." Easier said than done: nobody knew where he was. Barney Mason was confident the Kid was staying on a sheep ranch north of Sumner, where he was reported to have dyed his skin and let his beard grow so he looked more native New Mexican than the natives. Once again, Barney seems to have been right on the money.

"Billy the Kid had been stopping with me for several weeks," said sheep-herder Francisco Lovato. "He came to me after he had escaped from jail at Lincoln, thinking my camp was a safe place. He was with me nearly all the time Pat Garrett was seeking him."[13]

In another, admittedly undocumented account, when the Kid came to Fort Sumner after his escape, the Maxwell family were away; finding the house open, he made his way to one of the rooms on the second floor. He had been there a couple of days when Antonia Molina, the Maxwells' housekeeper, walked into the room and found him sitting in a chair by the window. She started screaming, thinking he was a ghost—he was supposed to have been hanged some days earlier—whereupon Billy grabbed her, covering her mouth with his hand. "I'm not dead," he said, "I'm very much alive and am here in hiding. You fool, shut your mouth and get me something to eat, I'm starving."[14]

Numerous other reports reached Garrett that the Kid was in the Sumner

21.7. John Meadows.

Date and photographer unknown.
Author's Collection.

BILLY THE KID.

$500 REWARD.

I will pay $500 reward to any person or persons who will capture William Bonny, alias The Kid, and deliver him to any sheriff of New Mexico. Satisfactory proofs of identity will be required.

LEW. WALLACE,
Governor of New Mexico.

21.8. Wallace's reward notice.

Daily New Mexican (Santa Fe), May 3 1881.

21.9. Pat Garrett.

Photographer Furlong, Las Vegas, 1881.
R. G. McCubbin Collection.

area, but he could not believe Billy was foolhardy enough to have remained in New Mexico. In his usual methodical way, Garrett put out feelers. He wrote to Manuel Brazil at Taiban asking him if he had seen the Kid. Early in July he received a note from Brazil which stated that he was hiding out because he was afraid the Kid knew of his part in his capture at Stinking Spring; he was confident the Kid was around but had no hard information on his whereabouts. Garrett wrote again to Brazil proposing a meeting at the mouth of Arroyo Taiban after dark on July 13.

Confirmation of Brazil's hunch came from John W. Poe, a thirty-year-old Kentuckian and an experienced law enforcement officer who had replaced Frank Stewart as the Panhandle Stock Association's detective. Poe, who had agreed to serve as Garrett's deputy, had been in White Oaks since March checking up on the shadier cattle-dealing activities of Pat Coghlan. A friend sleeping off a binge in the loft of the Dedrick & West sales stable overheard a conversation between the two men which indicated the Kid was in the Sumner area; Poe reported it to Garrett. His story and Brazil's hunch persuaded Garrett, although he remained skeptical, to ride up to the old fort.[15]

On the way, he stopped off at Roswell to pick up another deputy, Thomas C. "Kip" McKinney, and on July 11 the three of them headed north up the Pecos, reaching the rendezvous at Taiban Creek on the night of the thirteenth. They waited all night, but Brazil did not show. It was agreed that since Poe was completely unknown in Sumner, it was safer for him to ride in and reconnoiter than the other two. If unsuccessful, he was to go to Sunnyside

21.10. John William Poe and his wife, Sophie.

Date and photographer unknown, ca. 1883.
R. G. McCubbin Collection.

Born in Mason County, Kentucky, on October 17, 1851, John
Poe left home at seventeen and became a buffalo hunter and
town marshal of Fort Griffin, Texas, and later deputy U.S.
marshal; in 1879 he went to Wheeler County, where he succeeded Frank Stewart (q.v.) as a detective for the Canadian
River Cattlemen's Association. On May 5, 1883, he married
Sophia Alberding at Roswell; in that same year he succeeded
Pat Garrett as sheriff of Lincoln County. Leader of the posse
that arrested convicted killer and escapee Nicolás Aragón at
Chaperito after a gunfight that resulted in the death of Johnny
Hurley in 1884, Poe turned in his badge in 1885 to concentrate
on banking and business interests. He was one of the founders
of the Bank of Roswell in 1890, became its president in 1893,
and resigned when it became the First National Bank in 1899.
Almost immediately he helped found and became president of
Citizens Bank. He died at Battle Creek, Michigan, on July 17,
1923, allegedly a suicide.

Source: Sophie A. Poe, *Buckboard Days*.

and try to get some information from Milnor Rudulph. They would all meet
after dark north of the fort at a spot called Punta de la Glorieta, where the
road to Fort Union crossed the *acequia madre*.

"There was a very tense situation in Fort Sumner that day," Poe wrote later,
"as the Kid was at that very time hiding in one of the natives' houses there."
Not surprisingly, therefore, any mention of the Kid created an edgy silence.
Poe managed to convince the locals that he lived at the Oaks and was on his
way home to the Panhandle for a visit. He had a couple of drinks, ate a meal,
and, having learned absolutely nothing, headed for Sunnyside, where he
found postmaster Rudulph too frightened of reprisals to say anything useful.[16]

While Poe was at Sunnyside, a man who went by the name John Collins,
a former member of the Kid's gang, headed for the sheep camp where the
Kid was hiding out to warn him that the law was in the area. On the way out
he met the Kid coming in.

"Billy," he warned, "don't go down there. I just saw Poe and no doubt
Garrett and a posse are around town looking for you."

The Kid laughed it off. "Oh, that's O.K., I'll be all right," he said, and rode
on, leaving Collins bewildered—didn't he care he might get killed?[17]

When they met at Punta de la Glorieta late that brightly moonlit night,
Poe sensed that Garrett "seemed to have but little confidence in our being
able to accomplish the object of our trip, but said he knew the location of a
certain house occupied by a woman in Fort Sumner which the Kid had for-

21.11. Thomas Christopher "Kip" McKinney and family.

Date and photographer unknown. Historical Museum for Southeast New Mexico, Roswell.

Left to right: Thomas Newton McKinney, Letitia McKinney, Clifton Leslie "Cliff" McKinney, Alvareta Letitia "Alva" McKinney, Thomas Christopher "Kip" McKinney, Otto Augustus McKinney, baby Lewis Thalis McKinney with Pearl Arizona McKinney, and Mary Minerva "May" McKinney.

Kip McKinney was born March 19, 1856, at Birdville, Tarrant County, Texas, a member of a family of Texas patriots, one of whom had died at the Alamo. He was with his father John McKinney when the latter drove a herd from the Palo Duro to Seven Rivers in the late 1870s, and he was involved in that area with the group led by Andy Boyle and known as the Seven Rivers Warriors. He served as a Texas Ranger and later became a deputy U.S. marshal and traveled through New Mexico and Arizona.

On May 8, 1881, while serving as Garrett's deputy before the hunting of the Kid, McKinney killed Bob Edwards, said to be a horse thief. On July 24, 1882, he married Letitia Teresa Smith, who was fostered by Kip's parents and had lived in the same home at Uvalde, Texas. Later the U.S. Army hired Kip as a scout for wagon trains. In 1891 he worked for the army at Fort Huachuca, and he served in the Spanish-American War as a guide. McKinney died of lung cancer on September 20, 1915.

Source: Calvin McKinney, Notes on "Kip" McKinney, June 1990, Lincoln County Historical Society, Lincoln, N.M.; *Carlsbad Current*, September 24, 1915.

merly frequented, and that if he was in or about Fort Sumner, he would most likely be found entering or leaving this house some time during the night."[18]

Poe and McKinney were complete strangers to Fort Sumner. They knew nothing about the people and even less about the Kid. Not so Garrett. He knew where the Kid would be if he was in Sumner—somewhere near his sweetheart, Paulita Maxwell, who, if the gossip Garrett's wife Apolonaria had doubtless heard from her sister Celsa was true, was pregnant with Billy's child. He would have known, or surely anyway guessed, that Paulita had told Billy about her condition during their Christmas meeting; this was the reason the Kid had gone to Sumner, this the reason he was still there.

21.12. Paulita Maxwell and her husband, José Jaramillo.

Photographer unknown, probably a wedding photo, 1882.
Courtesy Pauline Jaramillo.

Born in Mora in 1864, Paula (Spanish: Pabla) Maxwell was the eighth of nine children born to Lucien Bonaparte and Ana María de la Luz (Beaubien) Maxwell, the oldest of whom was Peter Maxwell (q.v.). Paulita, as she was always known, married José Jaramillo (1861–1935), son of a wealthy Los Lunas stock raiser, in January 1882. It was an unhappy match; he is said to have been a heavy drinker and eventually left her for another woman. There were three children: Adelina (Welborn), Luz (Flanner), and Telesfor. Paulita died of nephritis at Fort Sumner on Tuesday, December 17, 1929, and was buried next day in the old military cemetery beside her brother Peter and close to the Kid's grave. Contrary to tradition, she was not a native New Mexican but half French and one-quarter Irish on her father's side and one-quarter Hispanic on her mother's.

Source: Jaramillo, *Genealogical and Historical Data; Fort Sumner Leader*, December 20, 1929.

21.13. Telesfor Jaramillo.

Date and photographer unknown, ca. 1899.
Courtesy Pauline Jaramillo.

Telesfor was Paulita Maxwell Jaramillo's son.

"I concluded to go and have a talk with Pete Maxwell," is the way Garrett put it, but if Poe is to be believed, he had to be pushed into it. He led the way to town; on their way in, they encountered a man named Jacobs whom Poe knew slightly. Stopping at his camp to drink coffee, they left their horses with him and proceeded the rest of the way on foot, concealing themselves in the peach orchard. According to Poe, they kept "fruitless watch" until after eleven o'clock, at which point Garrett suggested they leave without letting anyone know they had been in town.[19]

But why did Garrett want to quit? He had lived in Sumner, he knew everyone in town, he was married to a Puerto de Luna girl. Why did he not go, for example, to the home of his sister-in-law to ask if she had seen the Kid? He had two well-armed and experienced law enforcement officers backing him. The Kid was one man alone. Why was Garrett so anxious to sneak away without letting anyone know of his presence? Reading between the lines of Poe's account, it is not too difficult to decide.

Garrett had seen the dead bodies of his two best deputies laid stiff and stark in a shed behind the Dolan store. He had heard the story of how the Kid smiled and said, "Hello, Bob," as he shot Olinger down like a dog. The Kid was here, somewhere in the darkness, escaped from the hangman with nothing to lose. He might at any moment step out from behind a tree or a building, appear in a doorway with a gun in his hand, smile that cold and wicked smile and say, "Hello, Pat." Garrett had seen the old man with the scythe, and it had unnerved him. He did not want five hundred dollars badly enough to die for it.

As they were about to leave the orchard they heard muffled voices. "Soon

21.14. Peter Maxwell and friends.

Date and photographer unknown,
ca. 1882.
Courtesy Edward S. Phinney, Jr.,
and Nancy Marxen-Phinney.

Seated, left: Juan B. Patrón. The
man on the right is thought to be
A. P. "Paco" Analla.

a man arose from the ground," Garrett said, "in full view, but too far away to recognize. He wore a broad-brimmed hat, a dark vest and pants, and was in his shirt sleeves." They did not recognize the man, who went indoors; only later did they learn it was the Kid, who had come down out of the hills and was staying in the home of Garrett's sister-in-law, Celsa Gutierres.

By now it was nearly midnight; everything was silent and still beneath the full and watching moon. The three men moved in the shadows toward the Maxwell house, an imposing twelve-unit adobe sheltered by porches on three sides, standing on the west side of the parade ground surrounded by a white picket fence with a little gate. Pete Maxwell's bedroom was on the southeastern corner. In the warmth of the July night the doors and windows stood open.

"You fellows wait here while I go in and talk to him," Garrett said. McKinney nodded and squatted on the ground; Poe sat on the porch. A hundred yards away in Celsa Gutierres's kitchen, Billy the Kid picked up a worn old butcher knife and set out to get some meat from Maxwell's meat house.

21.15. The Maxwell house.

Date and photographer unknown, ca. 1883.
R. G. McCubbin Collection.

The building in the foreground is the ruin of the old quartermaster building; Saval and Celsa Gutierres lived a little further west. The improvements made by the Maxwell family to the old officers' quarters can be compared to the earlier, single-story buildings used by the military. The building to the far left was a sort of community center where the weekly bailes were held.

When Poe and McKinney saw the slight figure approaching along the inside of the fence, they not unnaturally assumed it might be Maxwell or one of his employees. The man was partially dressed, bareheaded, and barefooted, walking briskly. "He came on until he was almost within arm's length of where I sat," Poe recounted, "before he saw me, as I was partially concealed from his view by the post of the gate. Upon his seeing me he covered me with his six-shooter as quick as lightning, sprang onto the porch, calling out in Spanish 'Quien es?' (Who is it?)—at the same time backing away from me toward the door through which Garrett only a few second before had passed, repeating his query, 'Who is it?' in Spanish several times."

Inside, Garrett had just wakened Pete Maxwell and asked him if the Kid was in Fort Sumner. At that moment the Kid came into the room, backlit in the doorway.

"¿Pedro," he hissed, his voice tight with tension, "quiénes son estos hombres afuera?" (Who are those men outside?).

In the same moment he sensed the presence of someone beside Maxwell's bed. "¿Quien es?" he asked, and then in English, "Who is it?"

"El es," Maxwell whispered to Garrett, "it's him!"[20]

Garrett jerked out his gun and fired. In that fraction of time, Billy must, *must* have heard the swift triple click of the hammer going back, a despairing NO! forming in his mind as the gun blazed and the shocking impact of the bullet put him down. Half blinded by the gunflash, Garrett dived to one side to avoid return fire. Seeing the faint gleam of the washstand and fearing it was the Kid getting up, he fired off a panicked shot that ricocheted and buried itself in the headboard of Maxwell's bed. Even as he fired, Garrett was

21.16. Room the Kid was killed in.

Author's Collection.

The doorway through which the Kid came can be seen clearly between the two porch pillars on the left. McKinney was inside the fence, Poe on the porch near the gate. The window through which they saw the Kid's body is visible between the porch pillars to the left of the gate. (Compare with Fig. 17.7, which shows the whole building.)

21.17. Present-day Fort Sumner.

Author's photograph, 1996.

Taken from approximately the same spot as Fig. 17.7, this photograph looks northwest toward the site of the Maxwell house, the remains of which were washed away when the Rio Pecos changed course; it stood beyond the flagpole and extended back toward where the brush lining the riverbank now is.

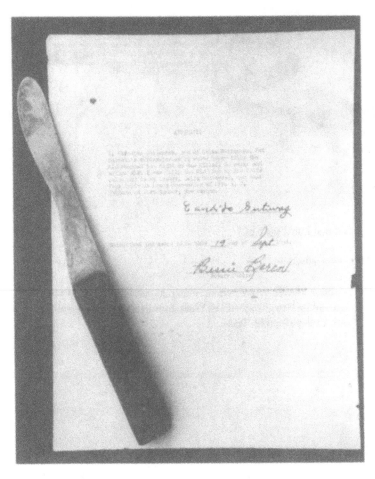

21.18. The butcher knife the Kid was carrying when he was killed.

Author's Collection.

The knife lies on a notarized affidavit made in 1951 by Celsa Gutiérres's son Candido, who identified it; the affidavit also confirms that the Kid was indeed staying at the Gutiérres house that night. The fact that the knife has survived leads one to wonder why—if indeed he was carrying one, as Garrett and Poe said he was—the Kid's gun was not also preserved by either one of them or the Maxwell family.

scrambling to his feet and on his way to the door; he got there just in time to prevent Poe and McKinney from shooting the terrified Maxwell, who had bolted from the bedroom in a tangle of bedclothes.

"What the hell happened in there?" Poe barked.

Back to the wall, pistol ready, Garrett panted "That was the Kid, and I think I got him!"

"Pat, the Kid would not have come here," Poe said, "you've shot the wrong man."

Garrett shook his head. "I'm sure it was him. I know his voice too well to be mistaken."[21]

There was no sound now inside Maxwell's bedroom, but none of them ventured inside. Lights were going on, people coming out of their houses to find out what the shooting was about. Pete Maxwell went down the porch to Doña Luz's room and came back with a lighted candle, which he put on the windowsill. Peering inside, they could see the body of a man lying on the floor. The story is always told that Deluvina Maxwell went inside and after a moment or two came out again to tell them the Kid was dead. "I did not do it," she said. "Pete took a candle and held it around in the window and Pat

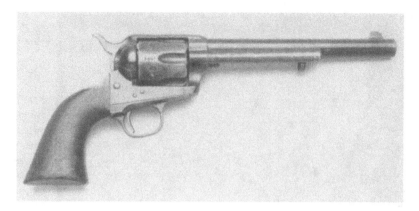

21.19. The gun that killed the Kid.

R. G. McCubbin Collection.

Blued steel Frontier Model, single-action, caliber .44-40, serial number 55093, originally supplied by Houghton's of Las Vegas, now part of the collection of James H. Earle, College Station, Texas.

21.20. Quartermaster's corral, Fort Sumner.

Date and photographer unknown, ca. 1868.
Rio Grande Historical Collections, NMSU.

The building on the left housed Maxwell's carpenter shop, where the Kid's body was taken the morning after he was killed.

21.21. The table on which the Kid's body was laid out.

Date and photographer unknown. R. N. Mullin Collection. HHC.

21.22. Jesus Silva.

Date and photographer unknown, ca. 1910. R. G. McCubbin Collection.

Jesús Silva, who died at Fort Sumner at age ninety-eight in 1940, claimed he made the Kid's coffin and also dug his grave.

stood back in the dark where he could see into the room. When they saw that he was dead, they both went in."[22]

The body was examined and found to be that of the Kid. Garrett's first shot had struck him in the left breast just above the heart; death would have been more or less instantaneous. By now a large crowd had gathered; when she learned the kid was dead, a sobbing Deluvina Maxwell cursed Garrett and pounded his chest. "You pisspot!" she raged, "you sonofabitch!" Other young women of the town consoled the equally desolated Paulita Maxwell. Armed young men of the town shook their fists and hurled insults at the lawmen, who retreated into the Maxwell house for safety, "keeping constantly on our guard," Poe said, "as we were expecting to be attacked."[23]

Nothing happened, and the rest of night passed without incident. In accordance with custom, the women lit candles in the bedroom where the Kid lay, and people took turns staying with the body and reciting prayers. The following morning a coroner's jury was convened by Justice of the Peace Alejandro Seguro with Milnor Rudulph, who had come down from Sunnyside with his son Charles on hearing the news, as president. After viewing the body and hearing Garrett and Maxwell's testimony, the jury concluded that William Bonney, alias "Kid," had been killed by Garrett. In flowing longhand Rudulph added that the jurors—Antonio Saavedra, Pedro Lucero, Jose Silva, Saval Gutierres, and Lorenzo Jaramillo—were "unanimous in the opinion that the gratitude of the whole community is owed to said Garrett for his deed, and that he deserves to be rewarded," phrasing which most certainly did not describe the sentiments abroad in Fort Sumner that day.[24]

The corpse was taken to Maxwell's carpenter shop in the old quartermaster's buildings on the east side of the fort and laid on a workbench, where the women washed the body. A rag was stuffed into the hole in the Kid's back, and Pete Maxwell donated a clean white shirt for a shroud. A coffin was made

21.23. The Kid's grave.

Author's photograph, 1971.

In 1882 a reporter from the *Las Vegas Daily Optic* described entering the cemetery "over the remains of the once handsome gate" on the north. "To the right of the entrance," he reported, "lies the grave of Billy, the Kid, marked by a plain board, with the stenciled letters "Billy the Kid." . . . The southwest part of the little burying ground is filled with graves of soldiers who were killed by Indians near the fort as the few legible headboards read 'July 7, 1866.' Over in the southwest corner lies the grave of Lucien B. Maxwell, once so famous in New Mexico."

The original military cemetery was at first unenclosed. In 1867 an adobe wall 5 feet high and 27 inches wide at the bottom, sloping to an edge at the top, was built around the plot—154 feet east-west and 146 feet north-south (which explains why it later became known as "Hell's Half-acre"). Trees were planted and headboards placed on every military grave.

Between January 2, 1863, and February 1, 1868, twenty-two military burials were recorded, the last being that of Private William Epple, Third Cavalry. On September 30, 1904, the Pecos broke its banks and the entire area was flooded for a week to a depth of four feet, washing away or moving most of the markers and stones. In 1906 all the bodies in the military graves, which were "on the western side of the cemetery," were disinterred and reburied at Santa Fe National Cemetery; it is not entirely impossible that the Kid's remains were moved at the same time.

In 1932 local residents Charlie Foor, Jesús Silva, Paco Analla, and Vicente Otero determined the location of the grave and placed the "Pals" tombstone on the spot. Sometime later a second stone was placed nearby; stolen in August, 1950, it was recovered at Granbury, Texas, in 1976. In the meantime, tourists began chipping pieces off the "Pals" gravestone, so a storm fence was erected around it. After the recovery of the stone from Granbury, sterner measures were taken to protect both (see Fig. 21.24).

Today the cemetery is some 187 feet across; the north wall is about 30 feet further north than it was in 1872, whereas the south wall is in the same place. Taken in conjunction with the details provided by the *Optic* reporter in 1882, all this suggests that the stone marking the Kid's grave is a lot nearer the right place than anyone had any right to expect.

Sources: Cemeterial Files, Fort Sumner, 1863–68, RG 92, NA; *Las Vegas Daily Optic*, January 16, 1882; research by Gregory Scott Smith, Museum of New Mexico, Fort Sumner.

21.24. The Kid's grave, 1996.

Author's photograph, 1996.

The steel cage was added after the smaller tombstone, stolen and taken to Texas, was recovered. It is the only prison that ever held Billy the Kid.

by Domingo Swabacker; Jesús Silva dug a grave close to the north wall of the old military cemetery near the graves of Charlie Bowdre, Tom O'Folliard, and John Farris, killed by Barney Mason two years earlier.

The women meanwhile had placed lighted candles around the body "according to their ideas of properly conducting a 'wake' for the dead."[25] Then, neatly and properly dressed, the body was placed in the coffin and taken to the cemetery in Vicente Otero's wagon. Practically the whole population attended the funeral, although who conducted the service—there was no priest—is not known for certain.[26] After the burial a rough wooden cross was erected and the crowd dispersed. For many years, they say, Deluvina left flowers on the grave in the summertime.

22.1. "Patsey Garrett" on the crest of the wave.

Date and photographer unknown, perhaps ca. 1900.
Rio Grande Historical Collections, NMSU.

CHAPTER TWENTY-TWO

The Men Who Made the Myth

Wɪᴛʜɪɴ ᴅᴀʏs ᴏғ ʜɪs ʙᴇɪɴɢ ᴋɪʟʟᴇᴅ, newspapers across the entire country were vying with each other to produce the most sensational accounts of Billy the Kid and his bloodthirsty career—not just in the major cities, but also in isolated hamlets where one might never have expected to encounter an awareness of his existence, such as Longview, Texas, about 120 miles east of Dallas. There, on August 26, 1881, the *Longview Democrat* ran a three-column reprint of the *St. Louis Globe-Democrat*'s "True History of the Boy-Devil's Exploits," which, in consigning him to "A Bloody and Dare-Devilish Immortality," contained some glosses even the wildest romancers of Lincoln County epic have never dared incorporate into their stories: "Mrs. McSwain's" playing inspiring airs and battle songs on her piano until the besieging posse got the range and shot it to bits with their buffalo rifles; Tom O'Folliard's stopping in flight from the burning house "amid a perfect storm of balls and buckshot" in a vain attempt to succor his friend Harvey Morris; the Kid's being dissuaded by Ira Leonard and John McPherson, chief of Las Vegas police, from assassinating Colonel Dudley. Already, within weeks of his death, he is Billy the Kid the avenger, the outlaw, the cold-blooded killer. "How many men he killed, how many deeds of daring deviltry and cruelty he perpetrated will probably never be known until the record books of damnation are opened," the story concluded. The Kid—not the real young man so recently dead but a new, improved, special-ingredient Kid who never existed—was already on his way to becoming a legend.

"The hero of the hour in New Mexico now, the king lion in the Territorial menagerie, is PATSEY GARRETT," the same reporter blathered, but in this instance it was not overstatement. Pat Garrett had indeed become famous overnight. For a man as essentially disingenuous and simple as he, such fame must have been a burden, but he bore it, both then and later, with considerable dignity. Famous or not, he experienced considerable difficulty collecting the reward; Acting Governor William Ritch dragged his feet, and not until February 1882 did the territory finally stump up. (In 1883, in a further belated burst of admiration, the citizens of Grant County resolved to have a cane made for Pat with wood from the Silver City home of Billy the Kid, topped with "a gold head with appropriate inscriptions.")[1]

Although eight books purporting to tell the Kid's life story had already appeared, Garrett—assisted by "Ash" Upson, who had moved in with the Garretts at their new Roswell home in August 1881—decided to write a book about Billy, most probably to spur the territory into paying the overdue reward, but which he claimed was intended to "correct the thousand false state-

22.2. Marshall Ashmun "Ash" Upson.

Photograph by R. G. McCubbin from a portrait, 1996. Courtesy Frontier Times Museum, Bandera, Texas.

ments which have appeared in the public newspapers and in yellow covered cheap novels."

With Upson on board, however, that ambition was never more than a pious hope, for Ash could resist hyperbole no more than he could Hostetter's Bitters. Forty-four years old when he came to the Lincoln County's Hondo Valley in 1872 from Las Vegas, and before that from Santa Fe, Marshall Ashmun Upson was born in South Carolina on November 23, 1828, a birth date he would later confer upon Billy the Kid. His parents (his father was from Georgia and his mother from New York) moved to Wolcott, Connecticut, when he was a small child, and there he learned the printing trade and became what they called in those days a "jour." Later, he moved to New York. Said to have been at one time a reporter for the *New York Tribune* (although many prefer to believe it was the *New York Sun*, to which he often sent news items) Upson truly was, as he sometimes signed himself, "A Rolling Stone."

Upson worked for a while on James Gordon Bennett's *New York Herald*, made a name for himself on the *Cincinnati Enquirer*, set up the *Leavenworth Herald*, and during the next seven years may or may not (his testimony is less than trustworthy) have wandered around Colorado, Utah, New Mexico, and Indian Territory; served as an assistant quartermaster in the Federal army; sojourned in Old Mexico; and later joined the Arkells in establishing the *Rocky Mountain News*.

"I have longed to see the regions of gold," he wrote in February 1866. "I have seen them. I pined to live among the dark-eyed senoritas of Mexico to judge of their beauty compared to my native country-women. In this I was more than satisfied—I was disgusted. The wild life of the Indians tempted me to trust my precious carcass (!) among the Navajos," implying that he tried that, too. He was now in Kansas City, on the staff of A. W. Simpson's *Daily, Weekly and Tri-Weekly Commercial Advertiser*.

The Mexican sojourn of which he spoke took place between the years 1853 and 1860. At some point thereafter he also found time to run a small-town newspaper in Louisiana, Missouri. He got his nose smashed at "The Dirty Woman's Ranche" in the South Pass of the Rockies—exactly when is uncertain, but sometime about 1864. On another occasion a few years later he got shot in the left cheek and the breast, an experience that left him scarred in more ways than one.

By his own unreliable account he was appointed acting adjutant general of New Mexico in 1869; although no record of this appointment can be found in the appropriate archives, it is known that he spent five weeks in Santa Fe trying to persuade the legislature to pass a law funding the territorial debt, then something over eight hundred thousand dollars. His efforts were hardly disinterested; apparently he had acquired twenty-five thousand territorial warrants at ten cents on the dollar, and if Congress could have been persuaded to make an appropriation, they would have quadruped in value.

Small, frail, a heavy drinker, he worked a small mining claim at Tuerto, New Mexico, that went bust, leaving him six hundred dollars in debt. He then filled in as a reporter on the *Elizabethtown Argus*, at which low ebb in his fortunes and at the suggestion of Calvin Simpson, a Las Vegas drummer, he moved down to Lincoln. His plan was to open a store there or a newspaper, or both, in partnership with Alec Duval, who claimed to have an arrangement with the sutlers of Forts Union, Bliss, and Stanton whereby they would give him a stock of goods on commission. This turned out to be somewhat optimistic, and early in February 1872, Ash found himself instead teaching school at the Casey ranch.

In 1874 he once more tried mining, this time in the Silver City area, where he claimed to have boarded for a while at the home of Mrs. Catherine Antrim. He had no luck mining, and by the following year Ash was working for the *Mesilla News*. In 1876 he returned for a while to the Casey ranch and then moved to Roswell, where he got friendly with Van C. Smith and became storekeeper, postmaster, stagecoach agent, notary public, justice of the peace, hog raiser, and farmer.

He wrote to his father in Connecticut:

> The causes which brought me here were the following: In the first place Mrs. Casey is harvesting her crops and has kept her children employed in planting, herding cattle, building new houses, etc., since last April. Since the first of April I have not had 3 weeks school. Nothing to do but keep her books and write a few letters, except attending to chickens and suchlike trifling employment. I became very much *ennuyed* as the French say. John S. Chism [*sic*] the cattle-king, of whom I wrote you, wanted me to survey 320 acres of land for him, four miles from here [at South Spring] where his store is. He went to Arizona some six weeks ago, with two large herds of cattle—some 4000 or 5000 head, and is daily expected back. . . . This place, Roswell, is only four miles from Chism's principal ranch, and there is no one living here except F[ollett] G. Christie, the acting, deputy postmaster. He is an old California miner, and is very much dissatisfied here, all alone, and making nothing except a small salary for looking out for the property.

Christie had promised him the position of postmaster and wrote to Van Smith, who was in Santa Fe, "to find out what he says in the matter." Ash expected to find himself—with the backing of local farmer Alberding H. Smith, not related to Van Smith—in charge of the post office, store, government agency, and stage business "besides looking out for Van's property" at Roswell. "Better than the idle life I led at Mrs. Casey's and a chance to make a start—always providing we get the consent of Van, of which I have no doubt."[2]

Unfortunately for Ash, a series of local misunderstandings, beginning with John Chisum's "war" on the smaller ranchers of the Seven Rivers area and culminating in the Lincoln County War, got in the way of his plans. He stayed on at Roswell as postmaster—he was officially appointed in 1877—and notary public, running his 160-acre ranch and raising hogs while trying to remain neutral in the bloody factional fighting swirling around him.

When the Lincoln County troubles ended, Ash moved back to Roswell; the 1880 census shows him living adjacent to, if not with, Rebecca Stafford, mother of the two Olinger brothers. It was at this time he became acquainted with Pat Garrett and agreed to ghost-write his book, which was completed in a two-month blaze of work.

The end result, *The Authentic Life of Billy the Kid, the Noted Desperado of the Southwest, Whose Deeds of Daring and Blood Made His Name a Terror in New Mexico, Arizona and Northern Mexico*, was printed and published in

22.3. A reproduction of an advertisement for *The Authentic Life of Billy the Kid*, from the Santa Fe *Daily New Mexican*, July 18, 1882.

R. G. McCubbin Collection.

The book was issued in paper wrappers with 137 pages, three plates, and a frontispiece portrait of Garrett which also appears on the back wrapper. Page 113 is misnumbered 121, and all the pages thereafter are incorrectly numbered. It is now exceedingly rare.

IS NOW READY! AND ON SALE.

Billy gave a vague account of the result of this enterprise yet uncompromising as it sounds, it leaves little to surmise, said he:—

"It was a ground-hog case. Here were twelve good ponies, four or five saddles, a good supply of blankets and five pony loads of pelts. Here were three blood-thirsty savages revelling in all this luxury, and refusing succor to two free-born, white American citizens, foot-sore and hungry. The plunder had to change hands there was no alternative—and as one live Indian could place a hundred United States troops on our trail in two hours, and as a dead Indian would be likely to take some other route, our resolves were taken. In three minutes there were three "good Injuns" lying around there, careless like, and with ponies and plunder we skipped. There was no fight. It was about the softest thing I ever struck."

Price 50 cents. By mail post paid.
Address Chas. W. Green, Manager.

February or March 1882 by Charles W. Greene, editor of the *Santa Fe New Mexican* and paid-up member of the "Santa Fe Ring." With its first part full of Upson's grandiloquence and fabrications and its second—written or anyway dictated by Garrett—the first's plain and unadorned antithesis, the book was a dismal failure. Blind to its faults, Upson blamed Garrett, the publisher, everyone but himself. It had been "bungled in the publication," he wrote a relative. "The Santa Fe publishers took five months to do a month's job, and then made a poor one. Pat F. Garrett, Sheriff of the County, who killed the 'Kid' and whose name appears as author of the work (though I wrote every word of it) as it would make it sell, insisted on taking it to Santa Fe, and was swindled badly in his contract. . . . The publisher does not know how to put the book on the market."[3]

On March 22, 1882, the *Las Vegas Daily Optic* had these sardonic words to offer on the subject: "Pat Garrett is sick at Roswell. Probably the 'Life of Billy the Kid' in print as executed by the *New Mexican* gave him gangrene of the bowels." Paradoxically, as the years went by the book would become a bestseller and also the foundation for the legend of Billy the Kid, but by that time Garrett and Upson were no longer around to reap the fortune in royalties they had hoped for.[4]

In a way, Garrett's bad luck was a harbinger of the rest of his life, which became a succession of brilliant beginnings ending in disappointing failures; he was canny and tough, but as his biographer noted, "his business methods were thoroughly inept." He stepped down as sheriff in 1882 and backed candidate Jimmy Dolan; the office went to John Poe. He tried raising cattle; it was not his métier. He organized and led a special antirustler unit called the LS Rangers in the Panhandle but quit when he discovered he was expected to kill the thieves, not arrest them. He had the brilliant idea of irrigating the Pecos Valley; the scheme flourished, but, lacking investment capital, Garrett was unable to share in its success. He ran for sheriff in newly formed Chaves County; when he lost, he gave up on Roswell and moved to Uvalde. In 1896 he returned to New Mexico to become sheriff of Doña Ana County; despite his successes, his term of office ended in bitter feelings. The high point of his career came in 1901 when President Theodore Roosevelt appointed him collector of customs at El Paso, but his handling of the post was so slipshod he was not reappointed. He ended up on a scratch-ankle ranch near Organ on the eastern side of the San Augustine Pass and died a dismal death, shot in the back of the head on a lonely trail between the ranch and Las Cruces on February 29, 1908.

Within a couple of decades of Garrett's death, Billy the Kid was largely forgotten; "Who remembers Billy the Kid?" Harvey Fergusson asked rhetorically in an *American Mercury* article in the summer of 1925. The Kid's fame had not persisted, he observed, and he wondered why. The answer was not long in coming. It had been awaiting the arrival in New Mexico of a Chicago newspaperman named Walter Noble Burns. The son of Colonel Thomas Edgar and Chris Ella (Noble) Burns, he was born in Lebanon, Kentucky, on October 24, 1872, and educated at schools in Louisville. In 1890 he became a junior reporter on that city's *Evening Post*. After serving in the First Kentucky Infantry during the Spanish-American War, he worked on the *St. Louis*

Post-Dispatch, the *Kansas City Times*, the *Denver Republican,* and the *San Francisco Examiner.*

On November 10, 1902, he married Rose Marie Hoke in Chicago and thereafter made that city his home. From 1908 to 1914 he was first a contributor of personal stories and a literary column and later Sunday editor of the *Chicago Inter-Ocean*, moving to the *Chicago Examiner* the following year and three years later to the *Chicago Tribune*. In the late 1890s he made a whaling voyage in the brigantine *Alexander* from the South Pacific to the Arctic Ocean, out of which experience he wrote his first book, *A Year with a Whaler*, which was published in 1913; it was not a success (Burns described it as "not worth reading").

It was not until 1923, while he was working for the *Chicago Tribune*, that he first visited New Mexico and found the story that would make him rich and famous. He came, originally, in search of a magazine story; in those days, apart from the good money it paid, a byline in mass-circulation magazines like *Colliers* or the *Saturday Evening Post* almost always led to book publication.

Familiar only with the legend as propagated in guide books and the "facts" as set forth in Garrett's *Authentic Life*, Burns interviewed Frank Coe, Paulita Maxwell Jaramillo, Yginio Salazar, Sallie Chisum Robert, Susan McSween Barber, Charlie Foor, and perhaps others, gathering material for his book. Although his transcriptions of what they said may not always be totally reliable, they are probably in some cases—like Paulita Maxwell's—perhaps even more revealing to us now than they were to Burns at the time.

Following the appearance of a short trailer article by Burns titled "Billy the Kid," in their magazine *Frontier* in December 1925, *The Saga of Billy the Kid* was published by Doubleday, Page & Co. in 1926 and simultaneously as a main selection of the newly formed Book of the Month Club, whose judges—among them Dorothy Canfield, Heywood Broun, and William Allen White—proclaimed it to be full of "the vivid reality of the moving pictures without the infusion of false sentiment and . . . melodrama." It was, they felt, "a chronicle such as the Elizabethans wrote and read."

With such a send-off it was hardly surprising that the book immediately became a popular bestseller, in the process bringing Billy the Kid, like some long-buried vampire from whose heart the stake has been unwittingly removed, suddenly and irresistibly back to life. The motion picture rights were purchased by Metro-Goldwyn-Mayer, and King Vidor was eventually assigned to direct the movie, with top cowboy star Johnny Mack Brown playing the part of Billy the Kid and Wallace Beery that of Pat Garrett.

It is difficult—almost impossible—to classify Burns's style: Was he a historical romanticist or a fictional historian? His approach aped that of the historian (his last chapter, for example, is replete with verifiable data), yet the very titles of his books suggest the romantic spirit rather than the questioning skepticism of the careful historian. He wrote in the tradition of the romantic novelist, sometimes even the dime novelist; bibliographer Ramon F. Adams said all his work should be in the fiction section of the library.

There are advantages to this approach, of course; as a fictional historian Burns seldom bothers—or needs—to separate fact from legend. Anyway,

22.4. Walter Noble Burns.

Date and photographer unknown, ca. 1926.
Special Collections, University of Arizona.

This snapshot, found among his papers, is believed to be a photo of Burns, standing near the entrance to the OK Corral at Tombstone, that was taken during his trip there to research the book *Tombstone: An Iliad of the Southwest*, published in 1927.

writing down cold facts was not what he had set out to do. His Kid was a new take on a figure formerly seen as a black-hearted villain, "the boy who never grew old . . . a sort of symbol of frontier knight-errantry," cool, daring, self-possessed, handsome, generous, a brave boy fighting corruption, first in the form of Murphy, then Dudley, and lastly the Santa Fe Ring, "a figure of eternal youth riding forever through a purple glamor of romance."

Of course Burns knew he had taken liberties with history. "Mrs Barbour [*sic*] said she did not play the Star Spangled Banner nor anything else on her piano during the fire," he admitted to a correspondent. "The Star Spangled story however is still current in that country and it was simply too good for a good dramatist to leave out. Neither did McSween have a bible in his hand except the one I put there—also for dramatic effect." Consciously or otherwise he was writing romantic folklore—note how many incidences of the word *tragic* the book contains—and it is extremely doubtful that even though it was nominally biography, he ever expected his readers to treat his "drama of Death and the Boy, . . . a little cyclone of deadliness whirling furiously, purposelessly, vainly between two eternities," as history. But that is what they did.

"Mrs Barbour said my picture of McSween, her husband, was a caricature," he wrote later. "Miss Klasner will hate me all her life for my portrait of Ollinger. Yet I wonder how far from the truth I was in my attempts to portray these two men. In writing of anything on which there is a difference of opinion, I have found it next to impossible to please any one much less every one. But I will admit I am a partisan. If I were not a partisan of my hero, I would find it difficult to write about him entertainingly or even to write about him at all. My partisanship is my enthusiastic interest in my subject."

The success of Burns's book—especially its sale to the movies—excited anger and envy in about equal parts in Lincoln County. Jimmy Dolan's wife Maria, "Mamie," was so incensed by the picture it painted of her late husband that she took all of Dolan's papers out of storage and burned them so no one would ever get their hands on them and write any more distortions and untruths about him. Because it preempted her plan to write the "true" story as she believed only she could, Susan McSween hated it, too; so, for not dissimilar reasons, did Lily Casey Klasner, while J. Evetts Haley, who had interviewed practically everyone still alive who had been associated with the Lincoln County War and who, had he persisted, might have written a great book on the subject, abandoned the project.

In fact, a major effect of the *Saga* was to convince people who "knew" the "real" story, and a lot more who did not, that if Burns could get rich on retelling the story of Billy the Kid, maybe they could, too. In its wake came not only a freshet of "biographies" of outlaws and gunfighters—Burns's own book on the Earps and Tombstone, Robertus Love's on Jesse James, and F. J. Wilstach's on Wild Bill Hickok—but also a whole new generation of books about Billy the Kid.

George Coe's was one of the first, then one by one everybody who had "known" the Kid began to put their recollections into print. And slowly the avalanche—of books and magazines and articles, of films and TV plays and dramatic works, each feeding off the other, all celebrating the "noble bandit"—began. Books by Emerson Hough and Charlie Siringo were notably influential in shaping the legend. Yet none of them—not a single one—has had one-tenth of the influence upon our perception of Billy the Kid that Burns's had. Burns truly was a mythmaker; how sad it was that he should have died in 1932, just six short years after the book was published, without ever having known how lasting a contribution to the subject his *Saga* would continue to be.[5]

To his contemporaries, the Kid's death had been a consummation most devoutly to be wished—"good riddance" being then the consensus of practically everyone who wrote about it. Burns totally altered that perception of Billy, transforming him from a dangerous cattle thief who had met a well-deserved end into a sort of Robin Hood, *caballero muy simpático*, a young, brave, determined boy fighting a corrupt system that might have killed him but never could defeat him.

The mostly legendary exploits attributed to Billy the Kid, first by Upson and then so much more persuasively by Burns, have since been perpetuated in a seven-decade procession which includes "true-life" accounts by three governors of New Mexico and a hundred other writers as well as articles by authors as different as Emerson Hough, Eugene Manlove Rhodes, J. Frank Dobie, Dee Brown, and J. Evetts Haley and poetry by S. Omar Barker, Michael Ondaatje, Jack Spicer, and Henry Knibbs. The Kid's adventures, his prowess as a gunfighter and a lover, his boyhood, and even his ghost have provided inspiration for fiction by Zane Grey, Edwin Corle, Fred N. Kimmel, Nelson C. Nye, Allen Barker, Will Henry, William McLeod Raine, Charles Neider, Rebecca Ore, Larry McMurtry, and Preston Lewis. There have been many, many attempts to tell the story truly, and there will doubtless be many, many more. I add my own small contribution without apology.

Adios, boys!

Notes

Abbreviations

Much of the official documentation of the Lincoln County War and Billy the Kid's part in it is found in one of three archives. Because of the frequency with which they occur, I have taken the liberty of using a number of abbreviations for these sources when they are cited in the notes. The first is Records of the Adjutant General of the U.S. Army, Record Group 94, National Archives, consisting of related correspondence, military reports, and other documentation of the "civil disturbances" in Lincoln County, assembled in Consolidated File 1405 AGO 1878. Its official National Archives classification is Microfilm M666, Rolls 397–98. It is referred to in these notes as File 1405 AGO 1878.

The second source is the Records Relating to the Dudley Court of Inquiry (DCOI) in the office of the Judge Advocate General, CQ 1284, Record Group 153, National Archives. Present-day researchers are forever indebted to the late Bob Barron of El Paso, who—at what cost to his sanity and his eyesight no one will ever know—transcribed, printed out, and published the complete record as *Lieutenant Colonel N. A. M. Dudley Court of Inquiry, Fort Stanton, New Mexico, 1879*, Lincoln County War Series, vols. 1–4 (El Paso, 1995). It is referred to in the notes as DCOI, followed by the volume and page reference.

The third indispensable source is officially classified as Frank W. Angel, "In The Matter of the Cause and Circumstances of the Death of J. H. Tunstall, a British Subject," file number 44-4-8-3, Records of the U.S. Department of Justice, Record Group 75, National Archives. It is cited in the notes as Angel Report.

Further equally valuable material is found in the series of interviews conducted in the late 1920s by J. Evetts Haley and now on file in the History Center of the Nita Stewart Haley Memorial Library in Midland, Texas. It is abbreviated in the notes as HHC.

The letters and diaries of John H. Tunstall and correspondence addressed to his family from New Mexico subsequent to his death are not available to general researchers. Those cited are copies in the author's collection.

Other frequently used abbreviations include:

AAAG	Assistant Acting Adjutant General
AGO	Adjutant General's Office
DNM	[Military] District of New Mexico
NMSRCA	State Records Center and Archive, Santa Fe, New Mexico

Chapter 1. The Kid from Nowhere

1. Santa Fe, Las Vegas, Las Cruces, and Silver City newspapers published within days of his death stated that the Kid's real name was McCarty or McCarthy and that he was born in New York. On July 18, Indianapolis papers blazoned the story. Chicago and Denver had similar information five days after the event, as did Boston, Portland, Salt Lake City, and Tombstone, Arizona. In New York, newspapers headlined the story on July 20, in Minneapolis and Seattle the following day, and in San Francisco two days later. Atlanta, Mobile, Montgomery, and New Orleans got the news on July 20 and Kansas City on July 27. It is hardly surprising, then, that so many people "knew" the Kid was born in New York and that his name was McCarty or McCarthy—even before Upson wrote the *Authentic Life*, which then "confirmed" it. For a selection of some of the newspaper accounts of the Kid's death, see Edwards, *Goodbye Billy the Kid.*

2. U.S. Department of the Interior, Bureau of Pensions, Pension Application of William H. H. Antrim, April 2, 1915, El Paso, Texas.

3. Whether Juan Patrón's brother-in-law Lorenzo Labadie (who might well have been understandably diffident about doing so) ever went anywhere near the old post hospital where Bonney was occupying quarters adjacent to those of Charlie Bowdre and his wife Manuela is another matter. Census taking was a little more informal in those days than today.

4. From 1865 on, William H. Antrim lived at various addresses in Indianapolis—at 58 Cherry Street and 70 Plum Street—while working as a laborer, a teamster, or an express company clerk. During 1867 a Catherine McCarty resided at 199 North East Street, in the same general area as Antrim. These facts, together with a statement made in Kansas on March 25, 1871, in which Antrim testified he had "known Catherine McCarty for 6 years last past," and the fact that they both appeared in Wichita at or about the same time, would seem reasonable confirmation that he met her in Indianapolis.

5. The information in this paragraph is based upon research in Indiana census and marriage records by Lee Cotten, Sacramento, California.

6. J. Evetts Haley, Interview with George Coe, June 12, 1932, HHC; Interview with Frank Coe, February 20, 1928, HHC.

Chapter 2. Wichita

1. "I was told in Silver City in the 1950s that 'everybody knew' Billy was an illegitimate child. . . . Antrim's family told me he became very upset when anyone mentioned his wife and promptly changed the subject. I am convinced there is some scandal in her past" (Philip J. Rasch, personal communication, August 17, 1990. See also "A Man Named Antrim," in Philip J. Rasch, *Trailing Billy the Kid,* 38–45).

2. In fact, Wichita already existed and had done so since April 1868, when James R. Mead, state senator for Butler County, had helped Governor Samuel J. Crawford, W. H. Lawrence, Darius S. Munger, and A. F. Horner promote a Wichita town and land company (after rejecting the names of Beecher and Hamilton). It was decided that Munger would locate a claim on the site that would include the two-river junction. Munger, aided by a Mr. Fenn, surveyed and platted the first townsite and built what would be the first residence, a two-story building of squared cottonwood logs with floors of walnut and cottonwood boards. Plaster

for the gables was made from sand from the Little Arkansas River and lime by burning mussel shells and buffalo hair.

3. *Wichita Eagle*, March 1, 1890; James R. Mead, "Reminiscences of Frontier Life," Kansas State Historical Society, Topeka, 75.

4. U.S. Department of the Interior, Bureau of Land Management, "Application and Proof of Catherine McCarty," RG 49, NA.

5. List of 124 signatories reproduced in H. Craig Miner, *Wichita: The Early Years, 1865–80*, 28. Much of the material on the growth of Wichita which follows is from the same source.

6. *Wichita Tribune*, March 15, 1871. Two doors south of Catherine's laundry was the Green Front Store and news depot, and diagonally opposite further up the street blacksmith J. B. Albaugh had his wagon and carriage shop. Further up Main was the Hess & Getto grocery store.

7. Bureau of Land Management, "Application and Proof of Catherine McCarty."

8. U.S. Bureau of the Census, Sedgwick County, Kansas, 1870.

9. Pauline Kimmerle, "Date: July 1870. Place: Wichita" (Reminiscences of Mrs. Pauline Kimmerle), Wichita-Sedgwick County Historical Museum Collections, Wichita, Kansas.

10. Miner, *Wichita*, 49.

11. Mary Weeks, "Date 1870–71. Place: 12 miles northeast of Wichita, section 24" (Reminiscences of Mrs. Mary Weeks), Wichita-Sedgwick County Historical Museum Collections, Wichita, Kansas.

12. Bertha Germen, "First Experience on a Prairie Farm" (Reminiscences of Mrs. Bertha Germen), Wichita-Sedgwick County Historical Museum Collections, Wichita, Kansas.

13. Daisy Denton Cantillion, "Mrs. Amanda Ballard" (Reminiscences of Daisy Denton Cantillion), Wichita-Sedgwick County Historical Museum Collections, Wichita, Kansas.

14. *Wichita Vidette* quote and details of life in Wichita from Miner, *Wichita*.

15. George Anderson, cited in Miner, *Wichita*, 55.

16. *Wichita Weekly Eagle*, August 18, 1881.

17. Nyle H. Miller and Joseph W. Snell, *Great Gunfighters of the Kansas Cowtowns, 1867–1886*, 33–35.

18. Sedgwick County, Kans., Deed Records, Book B, 165.

19. Sedgwick County, Kans., Deed Records, Book A, 478.

20. Sedgwick County, Kans., Deed Records, Book B, 168; Book A, 129. In 1919, Antrim sold the farm, which had been rented ever since he left Wichita, for sixteen thousand dollars.

21. Sedgwick County, Kans., Deed Records, Book B, 168.

22. Bureau of Pensions, Pension Application of William H. H. Antrim, April 2, 1915; *Denver Post*, April 1, 1928.

Chapter 3. Silver City

1. Santa Fe County, N.M., Libra de Matrimonios [Marriage Book] A, 35–36. On that same day of March, photographer W. T. Heister opened his new shop on the Plaza; it is tempting to wonder whether the newlyweds took advantage of Heister's special opening-day, reduced-price offer and stopped in to have their picture taken.

2. Bureau of Pensions, Pension Application of William H. H. Antrim, April 2,

1915; *Denver Post*, April 1, 1928; J. Evetts Haley, Interview with Frank Coe, March 20, 1927, HHC.

3. *Daily New Mexican* (Santa Fe), March 6, 1873; *Silver City Mining Life*, June 21 and August 9, 1873.

4. *Daily New Mexican* (Santa Fe), March 6, 1873; Susan Berry and Sharman Apt Russell, *Built To Last: An Architectural History of Silver City*, 18. The cabin was demolished in 1894 after serving for several years as a shoe repair shop.

5. Lou Blachly, Interview with Mrs. Louis Abraham, Tape No. 2 [1952], MSS 123B, Folder 2, Special Collections, University of New Mexico General Library, Albuquerque.

6. Lou Blachly, Interview with Agnes Meader Snider, March 29, 1952, MSS 123B, Folder 273, Special Collections, University of New Mexico General Library, Albuquerque.

7. *Silver City Independent*, June 12, 1917.

8. Pat F. Garrett, *The Authentic Life of Billy the Kid*, 8. For the purpose of these notes I have used the 1954 University of Oklahoma Press edition edited by J. C. Dykes.

9. Grant County Deed Book 2, Grant County Courthouse, Silver City, N.M., 14. On January 24, 1873, the *Daily New Mexican* noted, "Mr. Kidder has finished his survey of the Silver City townsite."

10. These and other recollections of Henry are cited in Robert N. Mullin, *The Boyhood of Billy the Kid*, and Jerry Weddle, *Antrim Is My Stepfather's Name*.

11. *Silver City Mining Life*, February 21, 1874.

12. Ibid., February 7, March 14, 1874.

13. Lou Blachly, Interview with Wayne Whitehill, March 23, 1952, MSS 123B, Folder 503, Special Collections, University of New Mexico General Library, Albuquerque.

14. *Mesilla News*, March 7, 28, 1874.

15. Blachly, Interview with Wayne Whitehill.

16. Blachly, Interview with Mrs. Louis Abraham.

17. California Column veteran Richard Hudson was a founding father; he had established a farm at San Vicente, south of Pinos Altos, in 1868, and he was at the meeting in June 1870 to rename the area Silver City. He built the Hudson Hot Springs in 1872, "hacienda-style around a courtyard, [a] gable-roofed adobe . . . wrapped with ornate frame veranda" (Berry and Russell, *Built To Last*, 9, 10, 37).

18. *Mesilla News*, September 19, 1874; Bill McGaw, "Out of the West: Billy the Kid's Teacher Saw Him as Sensitive, Effeminate, Fearful Youth," *El Paso Times*, December 17, 1960.

19. McGaw, "Out of the West."

20. *Mesilla News*, September 19, 1874; *Silver City Mining Life*, September 26, 1874.

21. U.S. Census, Arapahoe County, Colo., 1885; *Grant County Herald* (Silver City), December 31, 1875. If the "Joe Antrimm" in the census is the right one, the entry would indicate that the McCarty family was in Indiana as early as 1863 or 1864 and offer the possibility either that the Kid was also born there or that the reports suggesting the boys were half-brothers were correct.

22. Helen Wheaton, Interview with Harry Whitehill, September 3–4, 1928, Historical Files, Silver City Museum, N.M. When reading his recollections, it is well to remember that Harry was only two or three years old when Henry McCarty was running with the street arabs.

23. *Silver City Mining Life*, December 19, 1874.

24. *Silver City Mining Life*, November 5, 1874; *Mesilla News*, September 19, 1874.

25. Wheaton, Interview with Harry Whitehill. On July 22, 1876, the *Grant*

County Herald of Silver City noted that the dead body of an infant had been found in a sack near the Catholic church. "The discoloration of the throat and the fracture of the skull marks it as a case of infanticide," said the report. The following issue, July 29, said, "Charley Sun, knight of the tub and sad iron, took to himself a wife, thereby 'dividing his cares and doubling his pleasures,' and in the course of time his better and gentler half became 'as ladies wish to be who love their lords,' and Charley, anxiously looked forward to the auspicious day when the tendril of their loves would suck its little thumb in their united presence, but it came not to brighten the current of domestic life, for it had passed the portal of death." Charley disposed of the body in a sack, the report continued, whereupon town gossips concocted theories "various and dire" as to the cause of death. A warrant was issued and Charley was "brought before Judge Rilea, who, upon a hearing of the case, discharged him and gave him a clear certificate."

26. Wheaton, Interview with Harry Whitehill.

27. The first recorded death of a Chinese in Silver City appeared in the *Grant County Herald* on August 23, 1879, which reported, "A Chinaman, name unknown to us, came here sick a few days since, and died last Sunday [August 17]."

28. H. H. Whitehill, "Billy the Kid: The Subject of an Interview with H. H. Whitehill of This City," *Silver City Enterprise*, January 3, 1902.

29. Ibid.

30. Blachly, Interview with Wayne Whitehill.

31. Blachly, Interview with Mrs. Louis Abraham.

32. Whitehill, "Billy the Kid."

33. Blachly, Interview with Wayne Whitehill.

34. Chauncey O. Truesdell, Reminiscence, September 29, 1950, Biographical File, Silver City Museum, N.M. Truesdell did not explain why they had to sleep on the floor when they must have had a perfectly good bed they could have shared.

35. McGaw, "Out of the West." The fact that Mary Richards and Daniel Casey did not marry until Sunday, October 5, 1875, casts some doubt on this account. Immediately after their marriage, Daniel Casey became severely ill, and he had a slow recovery; the couple were living in Silver City at least as late as December 1875. Perhaps the Knight ranch incident took place later, after Henry was on the run; he was in and out of the area periodically following his escape.

36. *The Mustang*, April 14, 1950, cited in Philip J. Rasch and Robert N. Mullin, "New Light on the Legend of Billy the Kid," *New Mexico Folklore Record* 7 (1952–53): 4.

Chapter 4. The Scotsman

1. *Daily New Mexican* (Santa Fe), November 16, 1872, inter alia.

2. Fuller accounts of Tunstall's adventures may be found in Frederick Nolan, *The Life and Death of John Henry Tunstall*, and *The Lincoln County War: A Documentary History*.

3. *Weekly New Mexican* (Santa Fe), November 7, 1876.

4. John Tunstall to My Much Beloved Governor, October 28, 1876, Tunstall Family Papers. Originals in the private family collection; copies in the author's collection.

5. A military report on the post trader's building prepared in 1870 indicates it was a substantial one of adobe, "160 feet long in front with wings running back 81 feet at each end with sundry buildings in the rear. The building has 18 rooms,

covering an area of some 6882 square feet (under roof) leaving out of the calculation the General Ware Room and Lager Beer Room" (U.S. Department of the Interior, Bureau of Indian Affairs, Selected Documents Relating to the Mescalero Apache Indian Agency, Microfilm E99 M45 U55x, University of New Mexico General Library, Albuquerque).

6. Lily Casey Klasner, "The Kid," Lillian Klasner Collection, Harold B. Lee Library, Brigham Young University, Provo, Utah.

7. A fuller biographical study of the McSweens is in Frederick Nolan, "The Search for Alexander McSween," *New Mexico Historical Review* 62, no. 2 (July 1987): 287–301.

8. Frank Coe, "A Friend Comes to the Defense of Notorious Billy the Kid," *El Paso Times*, September 16, 1923.

9. John H. Tunstall to My Much Beloved Trinity, November 16, 1876, Tunstall Family Papers. The fact that the fracas Tunstall refers to, in which former sheriff Ham Mills shot and killed Gregorio Valenzuela, had happened a whole year earlier, on October 10, 1875, suggests someone was twisting the Englishman's tail. The story had resurfaced because after spending a year in Texas, Mills had returned to face the music. A petition raised by L. G. Murphy and signed by practically everyone in town was submitted to Governor Axtell, who pardoned Mills.

Chapter 5. Arizona

1. Wheaton, Interview with Harry Whitehill.

2. In the 1876 census for Pima County, Arizona, enumerated sometime before July 1, 1876, a "William Kidd" appears in the list of Camp Grant residents five names above that of H. C. Hooker.

3. *Wichita Weekly Eagle*, September 28, 1876.

4. *Newton Kansan*, October 5, 1876.

5. *Wichita Weekly Eagle*, August 18, 1881.

6. *Arizona Citizen* (Tucson), December 23, 1901. On June 30, 1911, Miles L. Wood completed a form sent to him by the Arizona historian asking for a biographical sketch; it prompted him to begin writing down his reminiscences about the Kid, first in a penciled draft and later in a fuller, pen-and-ink version. In 1923 he completed a third account entitled "Memories of Old Bonita," and still later, an unfinished memoir entitled "Life Notes of M. L. Wood." All tell more or less the same story about the Kid, although the details vary in each. I have used the first two, referred to hereafter as Wood, Reminiscences.

7. *Arizona Citizen*, September 25 and October 29, 1875. John R. Mackie was born in Glasgow, Scotland, on July 21, 1849. His real name was McAckey. He was still a fourteen-year-old schoolboy when he enlisted on June 15, 1862, at Harper's Ferry in the 1st P.H.B. Maryland Volunteers, later the 13th Maryland Infantry. Serving as a musician, he was captured at Harper's Ferry on September 15, 1862, and paroled the same day. Discharged at Baltimore, Maryland, on May 29, 1865, he reenlisted at Harrisburg, Pennsylvania, on December 30, 1871. After service in Kansas and New Mexico he was discharged at Camp Grant, Arizona, on January 4, 1876. Subsequent to his adventures with the Kid, he wandered all over the country— California, Tennessee, Illinois, Idaho, Nevada, Washington Territory, and Montana. In 1894 he entered the National Home for Disabled Volunteers in Milwaukee, Wisconsin, where he died July 21, 1920 (his 71st birthday), of 'lung disease, rheumatism and general debility.'

8. Wood, *Reminiscences*.

9. Ibid.

10. Record of Events register, Fort Grant, Returns from RA Cavalry Regiments, 1833–1916: 6th Cavalry, 1875–1880, Microcopy 744, Roll 63, RG 94, NA.

11. Anton Mazzanovich, "Tony Tells about the Kid," *Tombstone Epitaph*, March 9, 1933; Colonel C. C. Smith, "Concerning the Capture of Billy the Kid," *Tombstone Epitaph*, March 30, 1933.

12. Richard Dillon, "Adventures of an Army Post Photographer," *Old West*, Fall, 1977.

13. Record of Events register, Co. F, 6th Cavalry, Fort Thomas, February 1877, Microcopy M617, Roll 1265, RG 94, NA; Wood, *Reminiscences*. Five horses were reported stolen.

14. Wood, *Reminiscences*.

15. J. Fred Denton, "Billy the Kid's Friend Tells for the First Time of Thrilling Incidents," *Arizona Daily Citizen* (Tucson), March 28, 1931.

16. Smith, "Concerning the Capture."

17. Wood, *Reminiscences*; telegram cited in Donald Cline, *Alias Billy the Kid: The Man Behind the Legend*, 51.

18. *Arizona Daily Citizen*, February 4, 1932.

19. Denton, "Thrilling Incidents."

20. Wood, *Reminiscences*; Denton, "Thrilling Incidents."

21. Assistant Surgeon Fred Crayton Ainsworth, born in Vermont, was appointed assistant surgeon on November 10, 1874; major and surgeon in 1891; and colonel and chief of the Pension and Record Office in 1892. He retired with the rank of brigadier general on March 2, 1899.

22. Miles Wood sent Cahill's deathbed statement to the *Arizona Weekly Star* (Tucson); it was published on August 23, 1877.

23. Philip J. Rasch and Allan Radbourne, "The Story of 'Windy' Cahill," *Real West* 28 (August 1985): 22–27. The "Record of Interments Made in the Post Cemetery" show that "a citizen," description unknown, was buried in grave no. 12 on August 19. It would seem likely this could have been Cahill.

Chapter 6. One of the Boys

1. Klasner, "The Kid."

2. *Mesilla Valley Independent*, July 21, 1877.

3. Frederick Nolan, "Boss Rustler: The Life and Crimes of John Kinney." *True West* 43, no. 9 (September 1996): 14–21, and 43 no. 10 (October 1996): 12–19.

4. *Mesilla News*, January 8, 11, 1876; Lt. Col. Thomas C. Devin to Asst. Adj. General, Headquarters, District of New Mexico, January 5, 1876, Returns of the 8th Regt. of Cavalry, January, 1876, Letters Received, HQ, District of New Mexico, Microfilm M1088, Roll 38, RG 94, NA.

5. *Weekly New Mexican* (Santa Fe), January 22, 1876.

6. *Mesilla Valley Independent*, July 21, 1877. The newspaper also alleged the gang had murdered Juan and Jesús Mes, "left their bones to bleach near the Palo Chino," and also killed Rosas Olguín "in the back alleys of Las Cruces." Biographical sketches of these individuals are in Frederick Nolan, "Lesser Lights: A Note on Some of 'The Boys,'" *Los Amigos*, July and October 1995; January, April, and July 1997.

7. *Grant County Herald* (Silver City), July 21, 1877. It might be pertinent to note here that in the 1880 census for La Mesilla the occupant of the house next to that

of John Kinney was Jacinto Armijo, Sheriff Mariano Barela's deputy.

8. The reward was posted October 4. It was published in the *Mesilla Valley Independent* on October 6, 1877.

9. Klasner, "The Kid."

10. Shedd's ranch was really a small settlement where travelers often made extended stops; in the nine-month period between January and September of 1874, more than thirty-two hundred people passed through its portals. *Mesilla News*, October 16, 1874.

11. *Mesilla Valley Independent*, September 22, 1877; Nolan, *John Henry Tunstall*, 243–44.

12. *Mesilla Valley Independent*, September 29, 1877.

13. Denton, "Thrilling Incidents"; Anthony Conner, Letter to *Silver City Independent*, March 22, 1932.

14. *Grant County Herald*, October 6, 1877; *Mesilla Valley Independent*, October 13, 1877. The identification of Henry Antrim at this meeting has been questioned, but there seems no reason to doubt the Kid was involved with the Boys as early as September. Lily Casey Klasner confirms his theft of the Barela mare and also that he had Tunstall's "dapple grey" horses. Klasner, "The Kid."

15. *Mesilla Valley Independent*, October 6, 1877; Klasner, "The Kid."

Chapter 7. Seven Rivers

1. Still the best and most reliable short overview of Chisum's activities at this time is Harwood P. Hinton, Jr., "John Simpson Chisum," *New Mexico Historical Review* 31, no. 3 (July 1956): 177–205; 31, no. 4 (October 1956): 310–37; and 32, no. 1 (January 1957): 53–65. There is also much valuable information in Lily Klasner, *My Girlhood among Outlaws*, 254–55. The best single short work is David King, "The Pecos War," *True West* 43, no. 12 (December 1996): 19–22; 44, no. 1 (January 1997): 12–16.

2. Andrew J. Boyle, "Report to Thomas B. Catron," *Mesilla Valley Independent*, June 23, 1877. The indictment shows William R. "Jake" Owen and Charlie Perry as witnesses. They testified that Smith was killed "by revolver shots in the head, back and breasts." Doña Ana County Criminal Case no. 451, NMSRCA.

3. Boyle, "Report."

4. Ibid.

5. Edward Vail, "Reminiscences," and Walter L. Vail to Edward Vail, March 24, 1877, Vail Collection, Manuscript 827, Box 2, Arizona Historical Society, Tucson.

6. Boyle, "Report."

7. Boyle "Report." Robert K. Wylie returned to Texas and died on July 11, 1910, after falling from a train near Trinidad, Colorado; he left an estate in excess of $250,000. Highsaw, too, returned to his native heath and is said to have spent his later years operating a saloon in Merkel, Texas.

8. J. Evetts Haley, Interview with Frank Coe, April 20, 1927, HHC.

9. George Coe, *Frontier Fighter*, 58.

10. Eve Ball, *Ma'am Jones of the Pecos*, 116–20.

11. Donald R. Lavash, *William Brady, Tragic Hero of the Lincoln County War*, 66–67

12. Nolan, *Lincoln County War*, 129–30.

13. *Mesilla Valley Independent*, October 20, 1877.

14. Ibid., October 13, 1877.

15. John Tunstall to My Much Beloved Parents, November 29, 1877, Tunstall

Family Papers. The "special matters" Tunstall referred to probably included Chisum's investment of funds received from Hunter & Evans for his cattle into the recently founded Lincoln County Bank.

16. Ibid., 164. Quite how Tunstall could have encountered two of the "desperadoes" eighteen months earlier is unclear; he had been in Lincoln County less than a year.

17. Klasner, "The Kid."

18. J. Evetts Haley, Interview with Robert Casey, June 25, 1937, HHC. Interestingly, although he described many of his purchases of horseflesh to his father, Tunstall had never made any mention in his letters home of the fine horses he owned.

19. Klasner, "The Kid."

20. Wayne Gard, *The Chisholm Trail*, 110 ff. The date the Caseys left is extrapolated from the fact that the posse was reported to have reached Lincoln at 2:00 P.M. on October 20. *Mesilla Valley Independent*, October 27, 1877.

21. Klasner, "The Kid."

Chapter 8. Lincoln

1. *Mesilla Valley Independent*, October 13, 1877.

2. John Tunstall to My Much Beloved Parents, November 29, 1877 [not finished and mailed until January 9, 1878], Tunstall Family Papers.

3. A. A. McSween deposition, Angel Report.

4. Joseph Boyle to H. C. Smith, February 18, 1878, Hank Smith Collection, File 41, Panhandle-Plains Historical Museum, Canyon, Texas. Boyle clearly saw himself as something of a hero in this episode. His brother reported, "I heard from Andy lately. He was doing glorious work in New Mexico. He led a band of ten who freed four Texan prisoners from jail, when guarded by 100 Mexicans."

5. Klasner, "The Kid."

6. John Tunstall to My Dear Parents, November 17, 1877, Tunstall Family Papers.

7. "The liberators took [Lucas Gallegos] along to keep him from telling on them. At Seven Rivers where there were no Mexicans they were talking about rigging up some escuse [*sic*] to kill him to get him out of the way, saying dead men tell no tales. We all knew this old Mexican so when Will came and told us what they were talking about doing, mother interceeded and offered to take him a way down in Texas where she was going, to save his life and she did. I relate this to show how hardened this Banditi was and how little they regarded a humane life. Or even their own" (Klasner, "The Kid").

8. Haley, Interview with Robert Casey, June 25, 1937, HHC.

9. Klasner, "The Kid."

10. Haley, Interview with Frank Coe, March 27, 1927, HHC.

11. Upson said when the Kid was put in jail a year or so later, he wrote on the door, "William Bonney was incarcerated first time, December 22, 1878; Second time, March 21, 1879, and hope I never will be again. W. H. Bonney." Either the story is pure invention or, in his customary slipshod fashion, Upson misdated the event by a year. Garrett, *Authentic Life*, 85.

12. Tunstall to My Dear Parents, December 6, 1877.

13. Probate Court Journal, Lincoln County, N.M., December 1, 1876–March 24, 1881, 50; James J. Dolan deposition, Angel Report.

14. *Fritz and Scholand* vs. *McSween*, Civil Case no. 141, Lincoln County, N.M. The use of the words 'is informed and does verily believe' usually indicates that

the witness has or had no personal knowledge of the facts, suggesting that Mrs. Scholand—whose command of English was limited—simply signed whatever piece of paper was placed under her nose. No matter: on the basis of it, Judge Bristol could—and did—knowingly and willingly violate McSween's constitutional rights by issuing and signing a warrant for his arrest.

Ironically, McSween's insistence upon correct legal protocol was his downfall; Dolan *wanted* him to keep the money. The legal trap that was being set, although ostensibly aimed at McSween, was actually designed to bring down the real target: Tunstall. That was why Jimmy Dolan had leaned so heavily on his booze-fuddled father-in-law-to-be not to accept any money from the lawyer.

15. Klasner, *Girlhood*, 274.

16. John Tunstall to My Much Beloved Parents, November 29, 1877. Tunstall Family Papers.

17. A full examination of Widenmann's adventures trying to recover Tunstall's stolen mules in La Mesilla is in Nolan, "Boss Rustler."

18. Miguel Antonio Otero, *The Real Billy the Kid*, 145–50; Tunstall, Letter to My Much Beloved Parents, November 29, 1877. Tunstall Family Papers.

19. Haley, Interview with George Coe, June 12, 1932; Interview with Frank Coe, March 27, 1927, HHC.

20. *El Paso Times,* September 16, 1923. The problem with both George and Frank Coe's reminiscences is that they kindle the uneasy feeling that they "knew" the Kid a lot better after he was dead than they ever did while he was alive. Frank Coe, in particular, went to great lengths in later years to convince anyone who would listen that he and the Kid had been bosom buddies. Yet neither of them so much as opened his mouth on the subject until anyone who might have been able to contradict them was either dead or long departed from the scene.

Worse, both frequently contradict themselves. Frank Coe tells us in one breath that the Kid "drank very little and smoked in moderation" and in the next that he "never saw him drink a drop, and he never used tobacco in any form." George Coe relates over and over the hoary falsehood of the Kid's betting him a pearl-handled revolver against five cents that he would kill Sheriff Brady before Coe did. Frank Coe one minute says he escaped from the burning McSween house—"The Kid led the way out with a six-shooter in each hand. We came running through fire and bullets"—and in the next breath says, "I was at the Ellis hotel and George Coe was in the store between." He recalls that he and George stayed out of trouble "until they burned our ranch at La Junta," while George dates it from his being arrested by Sheriff Brady toward the end of March. Such "memories" are clearly a combination of faulty recollection, hearsay, and what both men had read elsewhere after the fact. However, they are the nearest thing to eyewitness accounts that we have, and better faulty recollections than none at all.

21. These and many more similar reminiscences may be found in Robert F. Kadlec, *They "Knew" Billy the Kid.*

22. Otero, *Billy the Kid.*

23. *El Paso Times*, September 16, 1923; Otero, *Billy the Kid.*

24. *El Paso Times*, September 16, 1923.

25. Coe, *Frontier Fighter*, 53.

26. Probate Court Journal, 58–59.

27. Dolan deposition, Angel Report.

28. *Mesilla Valley Independent*, January 26, 1878.

29. Ibid.

30. John Tunstall to My Much Beloved Parents, January 20, 1878. Tunstall Family Papers. The route the caravan would follow took them on their first day 26 miles

to Dowlin's Mill and on the second day down past Blazer's Mill and on to Tularosa, about 35 miles. Instructions issued to patrols leaving Fort Stanton warned, "Lost River water very bad; should not be used." Next day they would skirt the White Sands, about 25 miles away ("Water very alkaline," say the military manuals, "if necessary dry camp can be made"), and go on up to Shedd's ranch, a further 32 miles. On the sixth and final day they would drop down to La Mesilla, a distance of 22 miles, having covered about 140 miles in all.

31. R. A. Widenmann deposition, Angel Report.

32. Depositions of McSween, Dolan, Barrier, Shield, and Longwell, Angel Report.

33. Depositions of Barrier and McSween, Angel Report.

34. Depositions of Widenmann and Longwell, Angel Report.

Chapter 9. War to the Knife . . .

1. Depositions of R. A. Widenmann and W. H. Bonney, Angel Report.

2. Ibid.

3. Other than that he was one of the earliest ranchers in the Peñasco Valley and an acknowledged noncombatant, little is known about William Walker Paul. On December 13, 1877, the *Mesilla Valley Independent* reported: "Mr. Paul the pioneer settler and U.S. Forage Agent has the material on the ground for the construction of a commodious two story residence, he heartily agrees with the apostle of his name 'it is not good for man to be alone'; hence these costly preparations for coming events, *i.e., little Pauls.*"

4. Deposition of McSween, Angel Report.

5. Deposition of James Longwell, Angel Report.

6. Deposition of Widenmann, Angel Report.

7. Deposition of Godfrey Gauss, Angel Report.

8. Deposition of J. B. Mathews, Angel Report.

9. Deposition of Widenmann, Angel Report.

10. Deposition of John Middleton, Angel Report.

11. Deposition of Bonney, Angel Report.

12. Depositions of George F. Kitt and Albert Howe, Angel Report. The details of Tunstall's wounds are from Assistant Surgeon D. M. Appel's post-mortem report dated February 20 and 21, 1878, sent to the Tunstall family by Robert Widenmann in May 1878 and cited in Nolan, *Lincoln County War*, 286.

13. Deposition of McSween, Angel Report; a copy of Rynerson's letter is exhibit no. 19 in the Angel Report.

14. Haley Interview with Frank Coe, February 20, 1928, HHC.

15. Angel Report; Purington to AAAG, Santa Fe, February 21, 1878, File 1405 AGO 1878.

16. Mary Ealy, "The Lincoln County War," Special Collections, University of Arizona Library, Tucson.

17. Haley, Interview with Frank Coe, February 28, 1927, HHC; Ealy, "Lincoln County War."

18. Deposition of D. M. Appel, Angel Report.

19. Deposition of M. F. Goodwin, Angel Report. Goodwin actually said the threats were made by "'Kid' Antrim and others at the McSween house," but given the Kid's vengeful mood I imagine he would have used something like these words.

20. Haley, Interview with George Coe, August 18, 1927, HHC.

21. The date of Tunstall's burial is and has been a matter of some contention. Dr. Ealy, who conducted the service, dated it both February 21 and 22. I am inclined after mature reflection—and taking into account the fact that the Kid and Waite were held in custody only thirty hours—to conclude it took place on Thursday, February 21.

22. Deposition of Florencio Gonzales, Angel Report.

23. Deposition of George W. Peppin, Angel Report.

24. Deposition of A. P. Barrier, Angel Report.

25. Taylor F. Ealy to Dear Father [John C. Ealy], February 25, 1878, in Lawrence O. Ealy, Correspondence, diaries, and memoirs of Taylor F. and Mary Ealy, Special Collections, University of Arizona Library, Tucson; Widenmann to J. P. Tunstall, February 28, 1878, Tunstall Family Papers.

26. McSween to Sir Edward Thornton, February 24, 1878, "Correspondence Respecting the Murder of Mr. J. H. Tunstall on the 18th February, 1878, in Lincoln County, New Mexico, United States, 1878–86," British Foreign Office, File FO5 1964, Public Record Office, Kew, England; McSween to John C. Lowrie, February 25, 1878, Bureau of Indian Affairs, Letters Received, 1878, RG 75, NA; McSween Probate File, Lincoln County, N.M.

The timing of McSween's fresh assault on Godfroy may well have been prompted by a report in the *Mesilla Valley Independent* on January 19 to the effect that subsequent to the publication by a board of inquiry on Indian affairs of a lengthy report containing startling disclosures of swindling the Indians, Secretary of the Interior Carl Schurz—to whom McSween had written earlier on the same subject—had dismissed S. A. Galpin, chief clerk of the Indian Bureau, "for neglect of duty in not reporting knowledge of fraudulent practices by Indian Agents."

27. Haley, Interview with Frank Coe, February 20, 1928, HHC.

28. *Mesilla Valley Independent,* April 13, 1878. The original letter from Morton to H. H. Marshall, dated "South Spring River, March 8, 1878," is in Robert G. McCubbin's private collection.

29. Sallie Chisum, quoted in Walter Noble Burns, *The Saga of Billy the Kid,* 88.

30. Morton to H. H. Marshall.

31. Garrett, *Authentic Life,* 55.

32. Haley, Interview with Frank Coe, August 14, 1927, HHC.

33. Garrett, *Authentic Life,* 56–57. There is no reason to doubt that here, as in the earlier scene in Roswell, these words or something like them were what was actually said. In all probability Ash Upson heard the story directly from one of the possemen.

34. "XYZ" letter to *Albuquerque Review,* March 30, 1878. Ash Upson, who was in a position to know, said the bodies were buried by sheepherders; in 1955, M. G. Fulton told this writer he had talked to one of them, Francisco Gutiérrez, who confirmed it.

Chapter 10. . . . And the Knife to the Hilt

1. File 1405 AGO 1878.

2. Depositions of S. B. Axtell and D. P. Shield, Angel Report.

3. The full text of the proclamation is in Nolan, *John Henry Tunstall,* 294–95.

4. Phillips (acting attorney general) to Catron, March 18, 1878, Angel Report.

5. Thornton to Evarts, March 27, and Phillips to Evarts, April 9, 1878, Angel Report.

6. *Cimarron News & Press,* March 28, 1878. David Wood was a veteran of the

California Column who became a prominent citizen of Las Cruces and a substantial Doña Ana County cattleman in partnership with D. M. Reede.

In respect of Evans's wound, it has been the convention to accept newspaper reports that said his wrist was shattered in this incident. However, his prison records stipulate the scars were "above and below his left elbow." Ed Bartholomew, *Jesse Evans, A Texas Hide-burner*, 70.

7. *Mesilla Valley Independent*, April 6, 1878.

8. Ealy, "Lincoln County War." Ealy remarked on another shooting incident in his diary for Thursday, March 28. "At 9 A.M. firing began down town," he said. "I went up on the house top to see what it meant. I was shot at. Did not see who did it. But I know it was one of three men."

Writing to President Hayes on Tuesday, April 2, Montague Leverson observed that "a few days ago, one of the constables who had been deputed by Justice Wilson to arrest the murderers of Mr. Tunstall rode into town in company with a young boy about 16; Peppin called to the constable to stop as he had a warrant to arrest him; the latter said, 'all right come and read it to me.' Peppin's answer and that of his ruffians with him was a volley from revolvers and rifles. The 2 boys turned on them and the 7 fled!" (M. R. Leverson to Rutherford B. Hayes, April 2, 1878, British Foreign Office File Fo5 1964, Public Record Office, Kew, England).

The details of this affray strongly suggest the constable and his youthful friend were Dick Brewer and the Kid. Added to the undisputed fact that the Kid threw down on the unarmed Billy Mathews in the plaza on March 28, these confrontations clearly challenge the proposition that the Regulators did not return to Lincoln until the night before Brady's murder—not to mention all the conspiracy theories attached thereto—and suggest that at least some of them were in town, defying arrest and using their guns, two or three days before Brady was killed.

9. Leverson to Hayes, April 2, 1878.

10. Ealy, "Lincoln County War."

11. Kadlec, *They "Knew,"* 20. In this version Brady, Mathews, John Hurley, and Florencio Chaves were taking a prisoner to the courthouse when the ambush took place.

12. Ealy, "Lincoln County War."

13. Taylor Ealy said the Sheriff "intended to meet McSween who was just entering town in front of the jail, an ugly building of adobe mostly underground where water could be run in, & put him into the jail. I was told that the handcuffs were actually in his pocket when he was carried back to Riley & Dolan's house." Lawrence O. Ealy, Correspondence, diaries, and memoirs of Taylor F. and Mary Ealy, Special Collections, University of Arizona Library, Tucson.

14. There has been considerable argument about whether French, the Kid, or both of them were shot. Ealy was quite specific about it; in one of his several versions of these events he named French. As for the Kid, in Ealy's personal copy of Garrett's *Authentic Life* he wrote, alongside the sequence in which the Kid is wounded in the thigh, "Was not hit." Frank Coe implicitly confirms this. "The Kid and his crowd rode out of town," he said. "Jim French could not ride. . . . About two days later the Kid's party went back and got him and brought him down to my place. There was an American, a good old fellow with a Mexican wife who lived across the river in a brushy *rincon* of a place you could not find without a search warrant. I took French over to his place. His name was Tom Weatherhead. French stayed there for three weeks before he was able to ride" (Haley, Interview with Frank Coe, March 20, 1927, HHC).

15. Leverson to Hayes, April 2, 1878.

16. L. G. Murphy wrote to Colonel Dudley on April 6 warning him of the

ambush plan; Dudley was sufficiently concerned to send a troop of cavalry to escort the Bristol party to the fort. If nothing else, the fact that they were leaving Las Cruces only on April 6 provides conclusive proof that there was no misunderstanding about the date district court would open in Lincoln.

17. Frank Coe, Letter to *New Mexico State Tribune* (Albuquerque), July 23, 1928; Haley, Interview with Frank Coe, March 20, 1927, HHC.

18. Haley, Interview with Frank Coe, March 20, 1927, HHC; deposition of David M. Easton, DCOI 2:276.

19. Haley, Interview with Frank Coe, August 14, 1927, HHC.

20. *New Mexico State Tribune*, July 23, 1928; J. P. Meadows, "Billy the Kid As I Knew Him," Rasch Collection, Lincoln County Heritage Trust, Lincoln, N.M.

Chapter 11. The Gathering Storm

1. Frank Coe to William Steele Dean, August 3, 1926, Museum of New Mexico History Library, Santa Fe.

2. Coe, *Frontier Fighter*, 49.

3. Klasner, "The Kid."

4. Lincoln County Commission Records, April 10, 1878, NMSRCA.

5. *Las Vegas Gazette*, May 4, 1878, Angel Report.

6. Ibid.

7. *Mesilla Valley Independent*, May 4, 1878.

8. Ibid.

9. Ibid., October 20, 1877.

10. Haley, Interview with Frank Coe, August 14, 1927, HHC.

11. "Public Meeting Held at Mescalero, New Mexico, June 12, 1932, under the auspices of the Alamogordo Chamber of Commerce," unsigned typescript, Historical Center for Southeast New Mexico, Roswell.

12. When a list of the possemen known to have come up from Seven Rivers is compared with a list of those who asked to be examined before Easton, the names missing are those of Jim Patterson, Tom Green, John Galvin, and Charles Martin or Marshall. Could any or all of these, together with Charlie Kruling, have been the men said to have been injured or killed in the May 1 fight?

13. Deposition of D. M. Easton, DCOI 1: 103; Dudley to AAAG, May 4, 1878, in File 1405 AGO 1878; deposition of M. F. Goodwin, Angel Report.

14. Haley, Interview with George Coe, March 20, 1927, HHC; "Public Meeting."

15. Easton to Dudley, May 1; Dudley to AAAG, May 4, 1878, in File 1405 AGO 1878.

16. J. Evetts Haley, Interview with Florencio Chaves, August 15, 1927, HHC; John H. Riley to Dudley, May 14 and 17, 1878, in File 1405 AGO 1878; *Cimarron News & Press*, May 4, 1878.

17. Thomas B. Catron to Axtell, Axtell to Hatch, May 30, 1878, and a specimen of the proclamation in File 1405 AGO 1878.

18. Peppin to Dudley, June 18; Dudley to AAAG, DNM, June 22, 1878, in File 1405 AGO 1878.

Chapter 12. Catch as Catch Can

1. Haley, Interview with Frank Coe, August 14, 1927, HHC; Norman J. Bender, *Missionaries, Outlaws and Indians: Taylor F. Ealy at Lincoln and Zuni, 1878–1881*, 48.

2. *Weekly New Mexican* (Santa Fe), July 6, 1878.

3. H. Carroll to Post Adjutant, July 1, 1878, in File 1405 AGO 1878.

4. Dudley to AAAG, DNM, June 29; to G. W. Peppin, July 3, 1878, in File 1405 AGO 1878; *Cimarron News & Press,* July 25, 1878.

5. Haley, Interview with George Coe, March 20, 1927, HHC.

6. William A. Keleher, *Violence in Lincoln County, 1869–1881,* 59; William Hunter McLean, *From Ayr to Thurber: Three Hunter Brothers and the Winning of the West,* 84.

7. *Denison* (Texas) *Daily News,* July 26, 1878. Courtesy Chuck Parsons.

8. Coe, *Frontier Fighter,* 150. Coe is the only person who ever placed Selman in Lincoln County this early. It is possible he confused two incidents: Selman unquestionably led "the Rustlers" when they burned the Frank Coe–Ab Saunders ranch on the Hondo during the anarchy of late September 1878, but it seems far likelier it would have been Kinney and his new "deputies" who looted George Coe's ranch on the upper Ruidoso in July.

9. Robert Beckwith to Dear Sister, July 11, 1878, in Philip J. Rasch and Lee Myers, "The Tragedy of the Beckwiths." *English Westerners Brand Book* 5, no. 4 (July 1963): 1–6.

10. Susan E. Barber, "Notes of Correction on the Saga of Billy the Kid," undated manuscript [1926], Fulton Papers, Special Collections, University of Arizona Library, Tucson.

11. Haley, Interview with W. R. "Jake" Owen, March 2, 1933, HHC; McSween to Baca, July 14, and D. M. Appel to Post Adjutant, July 15, 1878, in File 1405 AGO 1878.

Chapter 13. The Storm Breaks

1. Testimony of John Long, DCOI 2: 333.

2. *El Paso Times,* September 16, 1923.

3. Testimony of Long, DCOI 2: 340; George Peppin, 2: 321; and David Easton, 1: 109.

4. Ealy, "Lincoln County War."

5. Ealy, "Lincoln County War."

6. Exhibit 78, DCOI 4: 839

7. Deposition of Pvt. Berry Robinson, File 1405 AGO 1878.

8. Testimony of G. A. Purington, DCOI 2: 461.

9. Testimony of D. M. Appel, DCOI 2: 472.

10. Ealy, "Lincoln County War."

11. Dudley to AAAG, DNM, July 18, 1878, DCOI 4: 844.

12. Testimony of Samuel G. Beard, DCOI 1: 77.

13. McSween Probate File.

14. Testimony of Peppin, DCOI 2: 305.

15. Testimony of Susan McSween, DCOI 1: 128.

16. Exhibit 56, DCOI 4: 735.

17. Testimony of M. F. Goodwin, DCOI 2: 452.

18. Testimony of Marion Turner, DCOI 2: 394.

19. Testimony of Goodwin, DCOI 2: 447.

20. Testimonies of Susan McSween, N. A. M. Dudley, Purington, Goodwin, Sgt. A. Keefe, Pvt. T. Baker, Mrs. Teresa Phillipowski, DCOI.

21. Testimony of Long, DCOI 2: 343.

22. J. Evetts Haley, Interview with Susan E. Barber, August 26, 1927, HHC.

23. Notes of D. M. Appel, Exhibit B6, DCOI 3:653 (microfilm); Walter Noble Burns to W. A. Carrell, February 16, 1930, Lincoln County Heritage Trust, Lincoln, New Mexico; Ealy, "Lincoln County War."

24. Haley, Interview with W. R. "Jake" Owen, March 2, 1933, HHC. "It was 9 P.M. when they came out," Owen recalled, "and all those that fell had their shoes and boots off, and I don't know why."

25. Testimony of William H. Bonney, DCOI 1: 191.

26. Testimony of José Chávez y Chávez, DCOI 1: 194

27. Testimony of Joseph [Josiah] Nash, DCOI 2: 378–79.

28. Haley, Interview with Frank Coe, March 20, 1927, HHC. According to the testimony of Milo Pierce, some of Peppin's posse were wearing army surplus clothing, among them Jesse Evans, Andy Boyle, Jim Reese, and one of the Jones boys.

29. Testimony of Nash, DCOI 2: 379–80, 383.

30. Testimony of Andrew J. Boyle, DCOI 2: 361–62; testimony of Nash.

31. J. Evetts Haley, Interview with Yginio Salazar, August 17, 1927, HHC.

Chapter 14. Rustlers

1. Proceedings of the Coroner's Jury, in DCOI 4: 850; Ealy "Lincoln County War."

2. Testimony of D. M. Appel, DCOI 2: 477.

3. Dudley to AAAG, DNM, July 27, 1878, File 1405 AGO 1878.

4. Testimony of F. C. Godfroy, File 1405 AGO 1878.

5. Haley, Interview with George Coe, March 20, 1927, HHC.

6. Testimony of Godfroy, File 1405 AGO 1878.

7. Sherman to Attorney General, September 10, 1878.

8. Godfroy to Post Adjutant and Dudley to AAAG, DNM, August 3, 1878, File 1405 AGO 1878.

9. Testimony of J. H. Blazer and Thomas Blair to Post Adjutant, August 9, 1878, File 1405 AGO 1878.

10. Sherman to Attorney General, October 16, 1878; *Weekly New Mexican*, October 5, 1878. The unnamed administrator of Bernstein's estate did indeed sue for replevin, that is, restitution; Sherman said the writ was returnable Monday, October 21, in Valencia County. Unfortunately the attorney general's reply and instructions to Sherman do not seem to have survived, so the outcome of the case is unknown.

11. Sallie Chisum, Notebook, Historical Center for Southeast New Mexico, Roswell.

12. The details of events at Fort Sumner and Anton Chico are compiled from three sources: Haley, Interview with Frank Coe, February 20, 1928, HHC; Haley, Interview with George Coe, March 20, 1927, HHC; and Coe, *Frontier Fighter*, 200. I have put the various conversations into what seems logical order.

13. Middleton to R. A. Widenmann, August 30, 1878. There was no longer any civil law enforcement in Lincoln County; what Middleton referred to as "Pep's posse" was in fact a motley crowd of desperados led by John Selman and including many of the men who had come up from Las Cruces with John Kinney. They embarked upon a pitiless two-month campaign of theft and violence in which children were shot for target practice and women gang-raped by the roadside. It was not so much a part of the Lincoln County War as a by-product of it. Terrified settlers abandoned their farms and left the country; by late August,

Roswell and Seven Rivers had virtually become ghost towns.

Tunstall's cattle were stolen from the Feliz ranch on Sunday, August 18; just a day earlier, Hugh Beckwith, who blamed his son-in-law Bill Johnson for the death of his son Robert in the last fight at Lincoln, shotgunned Johnson—one-time leader of the Seven Rivers Posse that had killed MacNab—to death and was himself badly wounded by Wallace Olinger.

14. John L. McCarty, *Maverick Town: The Story of Old Tascosa*, 78–80.

15. Henry Hoyt, *A Frontier Doctor*, 148–56. He in turn, Hoyt said, gave the Kid a little gold lady's watch he had won in a card game. He knew the Kid wanted it for "Señorita Lolita" in Fort Sumner. Attached to this watch was "a handsome long chain of braided hair," which Hoyt claims can be clearly seen crossing the Kid's shirt front in the famous tintype. In fact what can be seen is not a watch chain but part of the pattern of the Kid's shirt.

Chapter 15. Bloody Murder

1. Corbet to J. P. Tunstall, September 23, 1878. Corbet's elation was a little premature; although Axtell, Catron, and Godfroy were indeed suspended in the wake of Frank Angel's investigations, neither Bristol nor Sherman was removed from office.

2. The best source of information on the depredations of the Selman gang is Dudley's weekly reports. Dudley to AAAG, DNM, September 28 and 29, October 3, 5, 10, and 19, 1878; S. B. Axtell to His Excellency the President, August 20, 1878, all in File 1405 AGO 1878.

3. Corbet to J. P. Tunstall, October 1, 1878.

4. A. M. Gildea to M. G. Fulton, December 14, 1929. Most sources seem to agree that the gang consisted of about ten men, although perhaps not always the same ones: Selman; his brother Tom, alias Tom Cat; Gus Gildea; Charles Snow; V. S. Whitaker; Bob Speakes; John Nelson (from the Gila); Jim Irvin[g]; Reese Gobley; John Collins, alias the Prowler; and Jake Owen. Selman was killed in El Paso by George Scarborough; his brother was probably lynched in 1882. Bob Speakes, also wanted for the murder of a man named Beatty near Albuquerque in 1878, may have been the man who enlisted in the Texas Rangers at Fort Stockton in 1880, was found to be under indictment, and was discharged. "Rustling Bob" Bryant was killed by his fellow Rustlers en route to Seven Rivers. John Collins, real name Caleb Hall, went to Texas, lived for a while in Silver City, and died at Cripple Creek, Colorado, on March 12, 1935. Charles Snow, alias Johnson, was one of the Clanton gang of rustlers wiped out at Guadalupe Canyon on August 12, 1881. After killing a sheepherder named William Thompson in Uvalde County, Texas, in 1879, Arkansas-born Reese Gobley, real name Reason Goble, convicted rapist of a ten-year-old girl, seems to have vanished off the face of the earth. Along with Charlie Moore, sometimes called Windy, John Irving, "age about 36" and a "veteran" of the Salt Wars, was shot and killed by unknown assailants near the White Sands in December 1879. Jake Owens died of natural causes on December 24, 1939.

5. Lew Wallace was at his home in Crawfordsville, Indiana, when he received the news of his appointment on September 4, 1878. Before taking office he visited Washington, where he read Dudley's reports and the correspondence received by Secretary Schurz and the President. Special Agent Frank Angel gave Wallace a small notebook in which he had recorded his impressions of the principals involved in the Lincoln troubles. So Wallace was not entirely unprepared for the events awaiting him.

6. According to Dudley's report of October 10, two men had been killed and one hanged by a party led by Juan Patrón somewhere between Lloyd's Crossing on the Pecos and Fort Sumner, and "three other parties," assumed to be members of the Selman gang, had been killed at Puerto de Luna. On October 19 Dudley noted that sixty-five head of horses belonging to the Jicarilla Apaches had been driven off and some four hundred sheep stolen by seven Americans; the three men herding the sheep had disappeared. A small herd of cattle had been stolen near Tularosa. The post offices at Roswell, Seven Rivers, and Lloyds Crossing had been abandoned. Dudley to AAAG, DNM, October 10 and 19, 1878, File 1405 AGO 1878.

There was one other significant event at this time: on October 20, 1878, Lawrence G. Murphy died of cancer in Santa Fe.

7. The Wallace proclamation appears as part of Exhibit No. 3, DCOI 3: 632–33.

8. Widenmann appeared as a witness for the prosecution in the preliminary hearing of Jesse Evans before Judge Bristol for the murder of Tunstall. His testimony was ridiculed and Evans was released on bail. Conspicuously avoiding Lincoln County, Widenmann fled La Mesilla as soon as it was safe to do so and never returned to New Mexico again.

9. H. I. Chapman to Governor Wallace, October 24, 1878, Exhibit No.4, DCOI, 3: 634–35.

10. The affidavits appear as Exhibits 7–12B, DCOI, 3: 638–52.

11. *Daily New Mexican* (Santa Fe), December 14, 1878.

12. Corbet to John Middleton, February 3, 1880.

13. The details of the events involving Lieutenant French and Chapman in Lincoln are drawn from Proceedings of a Board of Officers, December 14, 1878, which appears as Exhibit No. 28, DCOI 3: 685–706. Dudley's ban, promulgated as General Orders No. 62, December 20, 1878, appears as Exhibit No. 45, DCOI 3: 724.

14. Dudley to AAAG, DNM, December 7, 1878, File 1405 AGO 1878. Conditions did not favor holding elections any more than they had permitted the sitting of the district court in October. As a result, Peppin remained nominally sheriff until about the middle of January; exactly when George Kimbrell was elected to succeed him is uncertain.

15. Garrett, *Authentic Life*, 82. Further evidence that the Kid was not ready for jail was provided by Dudley, who recorded that "'Kid' told the Sheriff [Kimbrell] if the warrant for him was for murder that he would not be taken alive." Dudley to AAAG, DNM, February 19, 1879, File 1405 AGO 1878.

16. Chapman to J. P. Tunstall, February 10, 1878. The question of what McSween and Widenmann planned to use for money to fulfil these promises is answered in one of John Middleton's letters to J. P. Tunstall from Kansas; he indicated that McSween gave him a note for five hundred dollars against the Tunstall estate. Yet no claim was ever lodged with administratrix Susan McSween Barber by any of the former Regulators. Of course it is possible they realized it would be a waste of time: the only person who got any money out of the Tunstall estate was Susan McSween.

17. Dudley to AAAG, DNM, February 19, 1878, File 1405 AGO 1878.

18. Ibid., February 21, 1879.

19. Events and conversations described are drawn from two sources: a letter signed "Max" in the *Las Cruces Thirty Four*, March 5, 1879, and a report in the *Mesilla Valley Independent*, July 5, 1879. I have put them into what seems logical order.

Chapter 16. Going Straight

1. Dawson to Post Adjutant, February 19, 1879, File 1405 AGO 1878.

2. "Max" to *Las Cruces Thirty Four*, March 5, 1879.

3. Goodwin to Post Adjutant, February 23, 1879, File 1405 AGO 1878.

4. Exhibit No. 60, DCOI 3: 739.

5. Copies of all the testimony taken are in Samuel Speece Pague, Appointments, Commissions, and Promotions Files, 3690 ACP 1876.

6. L. Wallace to Carl Schurz, March 21, 1879, Wallace Collection, William Henry Smith Memorial Library, Indiana State Historical Society, Indianapolis.

7. The Kid's letters and Wallace's replies are, with the exception of the first, all in the Wallace Collection. The interview appeared in the *Indianapolis World*, June 8, 1902.

"A scouting party from the post yesterday in Dowlins ran across the trio who so successfully escaped from the post guardhouse on the night of the 19th of March," the *Mesilla Valley Independent* reported on April 5. "Evans and Campbell abandoned their horses and took to the mountains, but unlucky 'Texas Jack' was not quick enough and now languishes in the Stanton calaboose." Evans and Campbell were later reported seen at Seven Rivers and still later near Tucson. Neither ever returned to New Mexico.

In April 1881, Governor Wallace posted rewards for a number of men wanted in connection with the Coe-Stockton feud in Rio Arriba County, among them Ike Stockton, formerly of Lincoln, and a man named Wilson Slough, alias "Texas Jack." *Daily New Mexican*, May 3, 1881.

8. "Statement by the Kid," March 23, 1879, Wallace Collection.

9. L. Wallace to Carl Schurz, March 31, 1879, Wallace Collection.

10. Ira E. Leonard to Lew Wallace, May 19, 1879, Wallace Collection.

11. All the details of the court of inquiry proceedings are from DCOI. Waldo's remarks about the Kid are in DCOI 3: 552–53.

12. Ira E. Leonard to Lew Wallace, June 6, 1879, Wallace Collection.

Chapter 17. Outlaws

1. The growth of Las Vegas and the careers of its badmen are chronicled in Howard Bryan, *Wildest of the Wild West*. The Hoodoo Brown anecdote is on p. 109.

2. *Territory* vs. *The Kid*, Criminal Case No. 1005, District Court Records, San Miguel County, N.M., NMSRCA; Hoyt, *Frontier Doctor*, 183–87. On December 6, 1879, the *Las Vegas Optic* noted, "Jessie James was a guest at Las Vegas Hot Springs, July 26th to 29th. Of course it was not generally known." There is no way of confirming whether the meeting between the Kid and Jesse ever took place or whether Hoyt—and Miguel Otero, who also reported it—saw the newspaper item at the time and later "remembered" it happening.

3. G. A. Purington to AAAG, DNM, August 17, 1879, Letters Received, Headquarters, District of New Mexico, Microfilm 1088, Roll 38, NA.

4. Haley, Interview with Frank Coe, February 20, 1928, HHC.

5. *Las Vegas Gazette*, December 28, 1880.

6. Burns, Saga, 180–90.

8. M. A. Upson to Ad Casey, September 9, 1879, Klasner Collection. A fuller examination of these events is in Nolan, *Lincoln County War*, 394–95.

9. Allen Erwin, Interview with Will Chisum, 1952, Arizona Historical Society, Tucson.

10. Ibid. Will was Jim Chisum's son and heard these stories directly from his father, who was an eyewitness. Some of the details may have been influenced by later "knowledge," but they complement, enhance, and enlarge upon what Upson said; there is no reason to question their integrity.

11. *Las Vegas Daily Optic*, n.d., cited in Peter Hertzog, *Little Known Facts*, 10.

12. *Daily New Mexican*, April 22, 1880.

13. The citations are from Bartholomew, *Jesse Evans*.

14. Ibid.

15. *Amarillo Sunday News and Globe,* November 30, 1930.

Chapter 18. Hunters and Hunted

1. Reports of Azariah F. Wild, New Orleans District, Secret Service Division, U.S. Treasury Department, in Records of U.S. Secret Service Agents, 1875–1936, Microfilm T915, Roll 308, RG 87, NA [hereafter cited as Wild Reports].

2. George Curry, *George Curry, 1861–1947: An Autobiography*, 18–20.

3. William A. Keleher, *The Fabulous Frontier*, 72–73.

4. Garrett, *Authentic Life*, 91. Beginning at chapter 16, the tone of the narrative changes completely. Gone, with one or two minor exceptions, are Upson's inventions and embellishments; the rest of the *Authentic Life* is pretty well all Garrett, a flat and factual—and more to the point, reliable—account of a long and thankless manhunt. If it also at times makes Garrett look smarter, tougher, and braver than anyone else around, well, it was his book.

5. Wild Reports.

6. Garrett, *Authentic Life*, 94.

7. Bonney to Wallace, December 12, 1880, published in *Las Vegas Gazette,* December 22, 1880.

8. Wild Reports.

9. *Lincoln County Leader* (White Oaks), December 7, 1889. M. G. Fulton characterized Carlyle as "an ex-buffalo hunter and desperado." Whether he was the Bermuda Carlile who figured in the famous fight at Adobe Walls, Texas, on June 27, 1874, has never been confirmed.

10. *Las Vegas Gazette*, December 22, 1880. In Siringo's account of these events, after the posse burned the Greathouse ranch they went to the ranch of a "highly-respected citizen by the name of Spence . . . [who] acknowledged cooking breakfast for [the fugitives]. Now Mr. Spence was dragged to a tree with a rope around his neck to hang him. Many of the posse protested against the hanging of Spence, and his life was spared, but revenge was taken by burning his buildings." James H. Earle, ed., *The Capture of Billy the Kid*, 77–78.

11. Wild Reports.

12. *Las Vegas Gazette*, December 3, 1880.

13. *Las Vegas Gazette*, December 22, 1880; Wallace to Ritch, December 13, 1880, Letters Sent, 1878–81; Governor Wallace, Reward Notice, Executive Record Book No. 2, 1867–82, 472–73, Territorial Archives of New Mexico, NMSRCA.

Chapter 19. Capture

1. Wild Reports. This was effectively Wild's swan song. By December 24 he was home in New Orleans, from which place he reported that "information of the arrest of William Wilson, W. Antrom alias "Billy the Kid" with several members of the gang by deputy United States Marshal Patrick F. Garrett has reached me." In less than a month use of the Kid's nickname had become universal.

2. C. Bowdre to Capt. Lea, December 15, 1878, in Hertzog, *Little Known Facts*, 14; Garrett, *Authentic Life*, 106. The "Frank Clifford" account is from an unpublished manuscript, "Deep Trails in the Old West," by John Francis Wallace, reproduced here courtesy of Michael E. Winter.

On May 29, 1879, the *Barber County Mail* (Kansas) noted that "the man Charley Jones arrested as Lewis Bousman, alias Chas. Smith, proves to be Frank Johnson, a young fellow well known at Kiowa during the Withers stay at that place." In May, 1879, Bousman was arrested at Dodge City and taken to Topeka, but on what charge is unknown, as is the outcome of the case. He "disappeared" for half a century, reappearing in Texas in the 1930s to write the memoir cited below, note 6. He died at Waurika, Oklahoma, January 2, 1942.

3. C. Carson, "Supervisor of Indians," to General, July 14, 1864, Letters Sent, District of New Mexico, Fort Sumner, Microform M619, Roll 286, RG 94, NA; U.S. Census, Cedar Springs, San Miguel County, 1870; U.S. Census, Los Ojitos, San Miguel County, 1880.

4. James H. East to Charlie Siringo, May 1, 1920, cited in Earle, *Capture*, 82.

5. "Life of C. W. Polk Commenced January 25, 1896," unpublished manuscript, Jessie Polk McVicker, Burneyville, Okla., private collection, copy in author's collection, cited in Earle, *Capture*, 26. According to Frank Clifford, there was no warning. "When they got opposite to where Pat's men were hiding," he said, "Pat opened fire on them *without calling to them to surrender*, according to the definite words of these men who told us about it—men who were in the posse: Lon Chambers, Tom Emory, Jim East, the Animal, Cal Polk, and Lee Hall, all men who were from our expedition."

6. Interview with Louis Bousman, Wichita Falls, Texas, 1934, cited in Earle, *Capture*, 52.

7. James H. East to Charlie Siringo, cited in Earle, *Capture*, 83.

8. Garrett, *Authentic Life*, 122.

9. James H. East to Charlie Siringo, cited in Earle, *Capture*, 83–84.

10. Interview with Louis Bousman, Wichita Falls, Texas, 1934, cited in Earle, *Capture*, 53.

11. "Life of C. W. Polk," January 25, 1896, cited in Earle, *Capture*, 28. Once again, Frank Clifford takes issue with this version of Bowdre's death. "Shortly after daybreak, Charley Bowdre, who was the same size and build as the Kid, came out with the Kid's hat on, and started to break up some wood to build a fire. Pat, according to the boys' story, shot Bowdre down without warning the same as he did Tom O'Phalliard the evening before."

12. Garrett, *Authentic Life*, 125.

13. *Las Vegas Gazette*, December 28, 1878.

14. James H. East to Charlie Siringo, and "Life of C. W. Polk," both cited in Earle, *Capture*, 28, 84.

15. Ibid., 31, 84–86; Wallace, "Deep Trails in the Old West"; *Las Vegas Gazette*, December 28, 1880.

16. Leon Louis Branch and Charles Frederick Rudulph, *"Los Bilitos": The Story of "Billy the Kid" and His Gang*, 214; James H. East to Charlie Siringo, cited in Earle, *Capture*, 86.

17. James H. East to Charlie Siringo, cited in Earle, *Capture*, 86; J. Evetts Haley, Interview with William Weir, June 22, 1937, Vandale Collection, Barker History Center, University of Texas, Austin.

18. James H. East to Charlie Siringo, cited in Earle, *Capture*, 88.

19. Garrett, *Authentic Life*, 127.

20. J. Evetts Haley, Interview with James H. East, September 27, 1927, HHC.

21. Albert E. Hyde, "The Old Regime in the Southwest: The Reign of the Revolver in New Mexico," *Century Magazine* 33 (March 1902): 690–701; *Las Vegas Gazette*, December 28, 1880.

22. Benjamin S. Miller, *Ranch Life in Southern Kansas and the Indian Territory, as Told by a Novice*, 132–34; Garrett, *Authentic Life*, 129–30.

23. *Las Vegas Gazette*, December 28, 1880; *Daily New Mexican*, December 29, 1878.

24. Haley, Interview with James H. East, September 27, 1927, HHC.

25. *Las Vegas Gazette*, December 28, 1880.

Chapter 20. Trials

1. *Las Vegas Daily Optic*, December 31, 1880.

2. *Daily New Mexican*, December 30, 1880.

3. With the exception of the one dated March 2, 1881, which is in the Lincoln County Heritage Trust museum at Lincoln, the Kid's letters, seriatim, are in the Wallace Collection, William Henry Smith Memorial Library, Indiana State Historical Society, Indianapolis.

But are they all the Kid's letters? Analysis by Chicago forensic document examiner Maureen Casey Owens in 1991 confirms that the bill of sale given by the Kid to Henry Hoyt and the first "surrender" letter to Wallace were written by the same person, whereas the December 12, 1880, letter from Fort Sumner and the jail letters of January 1 and March 2, 4, and 27, 1881, are in a different hand. This has led to speculation that the latter letters are forgeries, but no evidence has ever been adduced to support the proposition. In addition, the phraseology and construction are persuasively authentic; bearing in mind the fact that the Kid was ambidextrous, it might be as well to keep an open mind on the subject.

4. *Las Vegas Gazette*, January 7, 1881.

5. *Daily New Mexican*, March 1, 1881.

6. *Las Vegas Gazette*, March 12, 1881.

7. Ibid., April 28, 1881.

8. *Daily New Mexican*, April 3, 1881.

9. Robert J. Torrez, "Forgotten Desperadoes," *True West* 43, no. 2 (February 1996): 46–49.

10. Robert N. Mullin, "An Item from Old Mesilla."

11. *The United States* vs. *Henry Antrim alias "Kid."* Opinion of the Court, April term, A.D. 1881, Sidney M. Barnes to Attorney General of the United States, May 30, 1881, Records of U.S. Court, 3rd Judicial District, RG 60, NA.

12. *Newman's Semi-Weekly* (Las Cruces), April 2, 1881. "Mob rule," said Newman, "*must* be avoided. Kid himself has been the most terrible exponent of that law in Southern New Mexico and his punishment should be meted out in due form and with all the solemnity attaching to the dignity of the laws he has outraged. His punishment by a mob would be an evil to be deprecated scarcely less than his

escape into the mountain fastnesses of Lincoln county; and yet any delay in bringing him to justice may possibly result in such a scene."

13. Helen Irwin, "When Billy the Kid was Brought to Trial," *Frontier Times* 6 (March 1929): 214–15.

14. Randy Russell, *Billy the Kid: The Story, the Trial,* 47–64.

15. Ibid., 65–67.

16. *Mesilla News,* April 15, 1881.

17. The letter originally appeared in a 1930 publication, *History of the Mesilla Valley, or, the Gadsden Purchase,* by George Griggs, who established the Billy the Kid Museum in La Mesilla. Caypless, whose practice was based at Cimarron, pursued the Kid's case and won a judgment of fifty dollars in the San Miguel County Court late in July 1881. By that time, of course, the Kid was not around to collect.

18. *Newman's Semi-Weekly,* April 20, 1881. The Mesilla jail, the Kid told Newman, was "the worst place he had ever struck." Simeon Newman gave him some paper and an addressed envelope in which the Kid promised to send him "some things he wanted to make public" about John Chisum which when published "would be some satisfaction to him to know that some men would be punished after he had been hung." He may even have sent the letter, who knows? Newman never produced another issue of the *Semi-Weekly.* He moved to El Paso soon thereafter and the following October started up a new and equally short-lived paper, *The Lone Star.*

19. *Las Vegas Daily Optic,* January 21, 1881. On January 16, at White Oaks, Bell gave an account of his meeting Billy Wilson at Las Vegas. Wilson asked him if he could help him in any way, to which Bell replied, "That is a hard thing to ask of me after you killed Carlyle in cold blood." Wilson hung his head and replied, "I didn't shoot at him and tried to keep the others from doing so." Rudabaugh, overhearing this, put in with, "You are a damned liar. We all three shot at him. You and I fired one shot apiece and Kid twice."

20. Garrett, *Authentic Life,* 134. The day before he escaped, Billy said, "People thought me bad before; but if ever I should get free, I'll let them know what bad means" (*Daily New Mexican,* May 3, 1881).

21. *Daily New Mexican,* May 3, 1881.

Chapter 21. Adios, Boys!

1. Blachly, Interview with Wayne Whitehill, March 23, 1952.

2. *Lincoln County Leader,* March 1, 1890.

3. Meadows, "Billy the Kid as I Knew Him."

4. *Daily New Mexican,* May 3, 1881. A Lincoln correspondent reports that "Bell lay dead in the back yard with one bullet through him and two gashes on his head, apparently cut by a blow from the handcuffs."

5. The story of the pistol in the privy originated with the Baca family and was first cited in Leslie Traylor, "Facts Regarding the Escape of Billy the Kid," *Frontier Times* 13 (July 1936): 509. It seems at least as likely as the version allegedly told to Meadows by the Kid.

6. Otero, *Billy the Kid,* 186; Santa Fe *Daily New Mexican,* May 3, 1881; *Las Vegas Daily Optic,* May 3, 1881; *New Southwest and Grant County Herald* (Silver City), May 14, 1881.

7. *Lincoln County Leader,* March 1, 1890.

8. *Las Vegas Gazette,* May 3, 1881; *Alamogordo News,* June 25, 1936; Otero, *Billy the Kid.*

9. *Las Vegas Daily Optic*, May 9 and 10, June 10 and 13, 1881; *Las Vegas Gazette*, May 12 and June 17, 1881; *Daily Nugget* (Tombstone), June 30, 1881.

10. *Las Vegas Morning Gazette*, June 16, 1881.

11. Haley, Interview with Yginio Salazar, August 17, 1927, HHC; *Lincoln County Leader*, March 1, 1890.

12. Meadows, "Billy the Kid as I Knew Him"; *Las Vegas Morning Gazette*, June 16, 1881.

13. Otero, *Billy the Kid*, 155.

14. Jerry Weddle, "The Kid at Old Fort Sumner," *The Outlaw Gazette* 5, no. 1 (December 1992). The story is confirmed in J. Evetts Haley, Interview with Deluvina Maxwell, June 24, 1927, HHC.

15. Garrett, *Authentic Life*, 143; John W. Poe, *The Death of Billy the Kid*, 12–15.

16. Poe, *Death*, 22–25.

17. Ben Kemp, "Dead Men Who Rode across the Border," Rasch Collection, Lincoln County Historical Society, Lincoln, N.M. Rasch said Collins's real name was Abraham Gordon Graham. But if Poe had never been in Fort Sumner, how did Collins know who he was? And more important, how did the Kid know who Collins was talking about?

18. Poe, *Death*, 27–28. Local tradition has it that Saval Gutiérres disliked Garrett intensely, which was why the Kid hid out in the Gutiérres house: he knew it was unlikely Garrett would go there.

19. Garrett, *Authentic Life*, 144; Poe, *Death*, 28–29.

20. Garrett, *Authentic Life*, 145–47; Poe, *Death*, 31–35. An alternative version of Billy's reaction to Garrett's presence appeared in the *Albuquerque Daily Journal* on July 18, 1881. In their account, "He could distinguish Garrett but indistinctly, in the dark sitting at a table, and as soon as he saw him he drew his revolver and started back saying 'What s—— of a b—— is that?'" It does sound a shade more authentic.

21. Poe, *Death*, 37–38. I have taken the liberty of converting Poe's "literary" version of what was said into something nearer reality.

22. Haley, Interview with Deluvina Maxwell, June 24, 1927, HHC.

23. Rudulph, *"Los Billitos,"* 252; Poe, *Death*, 44.

24. Poe, *Death*, 54–58.

25. Otero, *Billy the Kid*, 154–58; Poe, *Death*, 41–42; Keleher, *Violence*, 346. Ever since the night of July 14, 1881, conspiracy theorists have been running rings around the truth of the events surrounding the Kid's death, their suspicions that all was not as Garrett and Poe told it that night fueled by the fact that not only does there seem to have been an earlier coroner's inquest whose findings were abandoned, but also that both the Garrett and Poe versions are notable for another major omission—the testimony of the third member of the posse, "Kip" McKinney. Although Garrett and Poe were extensively interviewed at the time, and both wrote their own versions of the story at later, greater length, McKinney was never sought out, nor as far as is known did he ever write down his version of events. All we have is the strange tale told by a roving Englishman named Frederick W. Grey.

"There used to be a man named Kipp Kinney at the mines, who really was a genuine gunfighter," Grey wrote. Kinney and Garrett

> found out a Mexican girl whom the Kid used to visit, and lay in wait for
> him there after tying and gagging her. Garrett stayed in the house behind a
> sofa and Kipp was to stay outside to see that the Kid did not get to his horse
> again after the shooting commenced. The Kid rode up when night fell and
> walked into the house; but like all hunted animals, his suspicions were easily

aroused, for he had hardly entered the dark room when he drew his pistol and asked who was there. As he called out, Garrett rose from behind the sofa, and sighting the Kid against the light of the doorway, fired twice, killing him instantly.

Bearing in mind the evidence suggesting that Garrett shot down both Tom O'Folliard and Charlie Bowdre without warning, there is a faint ring of truth to this account. To further muddy the water, however, McKinney's present-day descendants believe his (reported) statement that "Pat Garret mistakenly shot a Mexican boy in Maxwell's bedroom. After some discussion it was agreed that the dead boy would be buried that night as 'Billy the Kid' so Garret could collect the reward and split with Grandfather and another party who had been called in to assist (John Poe)." Frederick W. Grey, *Seeking Fortune in America*, 110–19; Leonard Huffman to Heather, October 22, 1990, courtesy Morgan Nelson.

26. Not surprisingly, widely varying accounts of the Kid's funeral have appeared through the years. One of the best is a report attributed to Jack Potter, who came to Sumner three years after the Kid was killed. In Potter's version, Garrett

> instructed several Mexican ranch hands to remove the dirt roof of an abandoned adobe building and pull out enough ceiling planks to make a coffin, as time was too short to have new lumber shipped from Las Vegas. Late in the afternoon the corpse was loaded into old Vicente's [Vicente Otero's] wood hauling wagon which proceeded to the government cemetery followed by every person in Fort Sumner, even the saloonkeeper who rarely closed. The Sanctified Texan [Hugh Leeper], who believed in predestination, preached the funeral and said that Billy's time had certainly come at last. They told me he made remarks about Billy, "our beloved young citizen," and read from the 14th chapter of Job—"A [M]an that is born of [a] woman is of few days and is full of trouble[. He cometh forth like a flower and is cut down;]—he fleeth [also as] like a shadow and continueth not." In closing he said, "Billy cannot come back to us, but we can go to him and will see him again up yonder. Amen." ["A Grave Matter," *The Outlaw Gazette*, December, 1993, 12.]

Amen, indeed.

Chapter 22. The Men Who Made the Myth

1. Leon Metz, *Pat Garrett: The Story of a Western Lawman*, 127; *Daily New Mexican*, March 31, 1883. It should be pointed out that apart from the extremely dubious sanction of the deputy U.S. marshalship conferred upon Garrett by Azariah Wild—even accepting that it was U.S. Marshal Sherman's intent to make Garrett his deputy, the fact remains that the documents both named John Hurley, and Wild had not the slightest authority to alter one of them—Pat Garrett's legal jurisdiction in San Miguel County was at best uncertain. No modern law enforcement officer would dare act today on such tenuous "authority."

2. Thomas Fulton Kelly, "The Life of M. A. Upson (From Original Letters)," Mullin Collection, HHC. From 1885 to 1887 Upson spent most of his time in Seven Rivers and did not return to Roswell until 1888. He spent the next four years living there on Garrett's ranch, and when Garrett decided to relocate in Uvalde, Ash went along.

It is said that it was Upson's intention to follow up the Garrett book with one of his own, a history of Lincoln county that covered not only its "wars" but also its

Indian troubles. There is a persistent tradition that he kept all his materials for this book—newspaper clippings and other documents—in a small trunk he carried everywhere, and that when he accompanied Garrett from the Pecos Valley down to Uvalde in 1892, he took the trunk with him, intending to finish the book there. He never did, of course, and if the trunk ever existed, it has long since vanished.

At Uvalde, Upson reported that Garrett had built him "a beautiful office with a bedroom attached," but he does not appear to have had much chance to use it. In 1894 he made a trip back East to see his people in Connecticut, and there he caught influenza. He returned to Uvalde, where he died on October 6, 1894, and he is buried in an unmarked grave.

3. James D. Shinkle, *Reminiscences of Roswell Pioneers*, 22.

4. There have been many reprints of *The Authentic Life*, notable among them the first, edited by Maurice Garland Fulton and published in 1927. Fulton rearranged and added to much of the text, appending his own early findings to clarify and correct Upson's sins of error and omission. It was and remains the most historically valuable edition published to date.

In 1946 a fly-by-night New York paperback publisher, Atomic Books, issued a twenty-five-cent paperback of 128 pages entitled *Billy the Kid the Outlaw* on the cover and *Authentic Story of Billy the Kid by Pat F. Garrett, Greatest Sheriff of the Old Southwest* on the title page. Omitting only the chapter heads of the original, this volume reproduced the main text and offered as extras a (pirated) foreword by John Milton Scanland "and Eyewitness Reports edited by J. Brussel," an uncredited "Ballad of Billy the Kid," and a "Life of Pat F. Garrett," which, like the foreword, was lifted verbatim from Scanland's 1908 publication *The Life of Pat F. Garrett and the Taming of the Border Outlaw*. Also included was an uncredited reprint of a 1905 *Outing Magazine* article by Arthur Chapman, "[Billy the Kid—] A Man All Bad," and an analysis of the Kid's handwriting by "psycho-graphologist" Nadya Olyanova of New York City.

In 1953 *The Authentic Life* was reprinted by the Frontier Press of Houston, and the following year it appeared yet again as the third volume in the Western Frontier Library of the University of Oklahoma Press; in the latter edition it featured a long and studied introduction by bibliographer J. C. Dykes. This modest little version of the book, which also reproduced the original illustrations and title page, has probably sold more copies than all the other editions combined.

Another valuable edition appeared in 1963 when Horn & Wallace of Albuquerque persuaded Pat Garrett's son Jarvis to contribute a new and fascinating foreword which covered Garrett's attempts to arrest Oliver Lee and Jim Gilliland for the murder of Albert J. Fountain and his son and which also discussed Garrett's murder.

In 1973 an English paperback publisher, Sphere Books, reissued the book to tie in with the English release of the Sam Peckinpah movie *Pat Garrett and Billy the Kid*. Once again the chapter heads are dispensed with, and the only additional material is two short essays: the first a "Historical Introduction" and the second, "Pat Garrett: A Postscript," both by Frederick H. Christian. I mention it only because that happens to be my pen-name.

5. Walter Noble Burns, who once claimed he had interviewed 54,750 persons during his twenty-five years as a newspaperman, died following an operation at Chicago on April 15, 1932, just a few weeks after the publication of his book *The Robin Hood of El Dorado*. One cannot help but wonder whether it is altogether accidental that the best known of all Chicago newspaper editors, the ruthless

monster created by Ben Hecht and Charles McArthur for their 1928 stage play (and later movie) *The Front Page*, was given the name "Walter Burns."

Bibliography

Unpublished Sources

Ball, Eve. Interview with Amelia Bolton Church, December 3, 1951. Lincoln County Historical Society, Lincoln, N.M.

Barber, Susan E. "Notes of Correction on *The Saga of Billy the Kid*" [1926]. Fulton Papers. Special Collections, University of Arizona Library, Tucson.

Barker, Allen. Correspondence with Frederick Nolan, 1994–1997. Author's collection.

Blachly, Lou. Interview with Mrs. Louis Abraham, Tape No. 2 [1952], MSS 123B, Folder 2.

———. Interview with Agnes Meader Snider, March 29, 1952, MSS 123B, Folder 273.

———. Interview with Wayne Whitehill, March 23, 1952, MSS 123B, Folder 503. All in Special Collections, University of New Mexico General Library, Albuquerque.

Boyle, Joseph. Letter to H. C. Smith, February 18, 1878. Hank Smith Collection, File 41. Panhandle-Plains Historical Museum, Canyon, Texas.

Burns, Walter Noble. Letter to W. A. Carrell, February 16, 1930. Carrell Collection, Lincoln County Heritage Trust, Lincoln, N.M.

Cantillion, Daisy Denton. "Mrs. Amanda Ballard" (Reminiscences of Daisy Denton Cantillion). Wichita–Sedgwick County Historical Museum Collections, Wichita, Kansas.

Chapman, Huston I. Letter to J. P. Tunstall, February 10, 1879. Tunstall Family Papers. Original in the private family collection. Copy in author's collection.

Chisum, Sallie. Notebook (copy). Historical Center for Southeast New Mexico, Roswell.

Coe, Frank. Letter to William Steele Dean, August 3, 1926. Museum of New Mexico History Library, Santa Fe.

Corbet, Samuel. Letter to John Middleton, February 3, 1880. Fulton Papers, Box 11, Folder 8. Special Collections, University of Arizona Library, Tucson.

———. Letters to J. P. Tunstall, September 23 and October 1, 1878, Tunstall Family Papers. Originals in the private family collection. Copies in author's collection.

Cunningham, Eugene. Correspondence with Frederick Nolan, 1953–1957. Author's collection.

Ealy, Lawrence O. Correspondence, diaries, and memoirs of Taylor F. and Mary Ealy, including Taylor F. Ealy to Dear Father, February 25, 1878. Special Collections, University of Arizona Library, Tucson.

———. "The Lincoln County War as I Saw It" (several versions). Special Collections, University of Arizona Library, Tucson.

Ealy, Mary. "The Lincoln County War." Special Collections, University of Arizona Library, Tucson.

Erwin, Allen. Interview with Will Chisum, 1952. Arizona Historical Society, Tucson.

Germen, Bertha. "First Experience on a Prairie Farm" (Reminiscences of Mrs. Bertha Germen). Wichita–Sedgwick County Historical Museum Collections, Wichita, Kansas.

Gildea, A. M., Letter to M. G. Fulton, December 14, 1929. MS 57, Fulton Papers, Box 2, Folder 2. Special Collections, University of Arizona Library, Tucson.

Haley, J. Evetts. Interview with Susan E. Barber, August 26, 1927.

———. Interview with Robert Casey, June 25, 1937.

———. Interview with Florencio Chaves, August 15, 1927.

———. Interviews with George Coe, August 18, 1927; June 12, 1932.

———. Interviews with Frank Coe, March 20 and 27; April 20; August 14, 1927; February 20, 1928.

———. Interview with James H. East, September 27, 1927.

———. Interview with Deluvina Maxwell, June 24, 1927.

———. Interview with W. R. "Jake" Owen, March 2, 1933.

———. Interview with Yginio Salazar, August 17, 1927.
    All in History Center, Nita Stewart Haley Memorial Library, Midland, Texas.

———. Interview with William Weir, June 22, 1937. Vandale Collection, Barker History Center, University of Texas, Austin.

Kelly, Thomas Fulton. "The Life of M. A. Upson (from Original Letters)." Mullin Collection, History Center, Nita Stewart Haley Memorial Library, Midland, Texas.

Kemp, Ben. "Dead Men Who Rode across the Border." Rasch Collection, Lincoln County Historical Society, Lincoln, N.M.

Kimmerle, Pauline. "Date: July 1870. Place: Wichita" (Reminiscences of Mrs. Pauline Kimmerle). Wichita–Sedgwick County Historical Museum Collections, Wichita, Kansas.

Klasner, Lily Casey. "The Kid." Lillian Klasner Collection, Harold B. Lee Library, Brigham Young University, Provo, Utah.

McKinney, Calvin. Notes on "Kip" McKinney, June 1990. Lincoln County Historical Society, Lincoln, N.M.

Mead, James R. "Reminiscences of Frontier Life." Kansas State Historical Society, Topeka.

Meadows, J. P., in collaboration with M. G. Fulton. "Billy the Kid As I Knew Him." Rasch Collection, Lincoln County Heritage Trust, Lincoln, N.M.

Middleton, John. Letter to R. A. Widenmann, August 30, 1878. Tunstall Family Papers. Original in private family collection. Copy in author's collection.

"Public Meeting Held at Mescalero, New Mexico, June 12, 1932, under the auspices of the Alamogordo Chamber of Commerce." Unsigned typescript. Historical Center for Southeast New Mexico, Roswell.

Rasch, Philip J. Personal communication with Frederick Nolan, August 17, 1990.

Truesdell, Chauncey O. Reminiscence, September 29, 1950. Biographical File, Silver City Museum, N.M.

Tunstall, John H. Letters, 1872–1878. Letter to My Much Beloved Trinity, November 16, 1876.

———. Letter to My Dear Parents, November 17, 1877.

———. Letter to My Much Beloved Parents, November 29, 1877.

————. Letter to My Dear Parents, December 6, 1877.

————. Letter to My Much Beloved Parents, January 20, 1878.
  All in Tunstall Family Papers. Originals in private family collection. Copies in author's collection.

Upson, M. A. Letter to Ad Casey, September 9, 1879. Lillian Klasner Collection, Harold B. Lee Library, Brigham Young University, Provo, Utah.

Vail, Edward, "Reminiscences," Manuscript 827, Box 2, Vail Collection, Arizona Historical Society, Tucson.

Vail, Walter L. Letter to Edward Vail, March 24, 1877. Vail Collection, Arizona Historical Society, Tucson.

Wallace, John Francis [Frank Clifford]. "Deep Trails in the Old West." Courtesy Michael E. Winter, Beebe, Ark.

Weeks, Mary. "Date 1870–71. Place: 12 miles northeast of Wichita, section 24" (Reminiscences of Mrs. Mary Weeks). Wichita–Sedgwick County Historical Museum Collections, Wichita, Kans.

Wheaton, Helen. Interview with Harry Whitehill, September 3–4, 1928. Historical Files, Silver City Museum, Silver City, N.M.

Widenmann, Robert A. Letters to J. P. Tunstall. February 28, 1878, and February 15, 1881. Tunstall Family Papers. Originals in private family collection. Copies in author's collection.

Wood, Miles. "Life Notes of M. L. Wood." Arizona Historical Society, Tucson.

Documentary Records

Adjutant General's Office (AGO), Letters Received 1871–80. RG 94, NA.

Consolidated File 1405 AGO 1878, Microfilm M666, Rolls 397–98.

Appointments, Commissions, and Personal (ACP) and Commission Branch (CB) Files.
  Daniel Mitchell Appel, 679 ACP 1880.
  Nathan Augustus Monroe Dudley, 6674 ACP 1876.
  James Hansell French, 7940 ACP 1874.
  Millard Fillmore Goodwin, 3548 ACP 1883.
  Lawrence Gustave Murphy, CB.
  Samuel Speece Pague, 3690 ACP 1876.
  George Augustus Purington, 2330 ACP 1877.
  George Washington Smith, 2838 ACP 1880.

British Foreign Office. "Correspondence Respecting the Murder of Mr. J. H. Tunstall on the 18th February, 1878, in Lincoln County, New Mexico, United States, 1878–86." File FO5 1964. Public Records Office, Kew, England.

District of Arizona.
  Record of Events register, Fort Grant. Returns from RA Cavalry Regiments, 1833–1916: 6th Cavalry, 1875–1880. Microcopy 744 Roll 63. RG 94, NA.
  Record of Events register, Fort Thomas, Co. F, 6th Cavalry, February 1877. Microcopy M617 Roll 1265. RG 94, NA.

District of New Mexico.
  Letters Sent, Fort Sumner. Microform M619, Roll 286. RG 94, NA.
  Returns of the 8th Regt. of Cavalry, January, 1876. RG 94, NA.
  Letters Received, Headquarters, 1879. Microfilm M1088, Roll 38. RG 94, NA.

Letters Received. Letters File 520-M-1876, RG 94, NA.

Doña Ana County, N.M.

Criminal Case #451. NMSRCA.

Records of the U.S. Court, 3rd Judicial District, RG60, NA.

Grant County, N.M.

Deed Book No. 2: 14, Grant County Courthouse, Silver City, N.M.

Judge Advocate General's Office, RG 153, NA.

Records Relating to the Dudley Court of Inquiry. CQ 1284.

Lincoln County, N.M.

Fritz and Scholand vs. *McSween*, Civil Case No. 141; Probate Court Journal, December 1, 1876–March 24, 1881. NMSRCA.

Lincoln County Commission. Records, April 10, 1878. NMSRCA.

A. A. McSween Probate File. Lincoln County Courthouse, Carrizozo, N.M.

Office of the Quartermaster General, RG 92, NA.

Records Relating to Functions: Cemeterial, 1828–1929.

General Correspondence and Reports relating to National and Post Cemeteries, 1865–1890.

Steilacoom to Vicksburg. Box No. 64.

Cemeterial Files: Fort Sumner 1863–1868. 8W2/3/8/B/Box 64.

RG 92, NA.

San Miguel County, N.M.

Territory vs. *The Kid.* Criminal Case No. 1005, District Court Records, NMSRCA.

Santa Fe County, N.M.

Records of the First Presbyterian Church, Libra de Matrimonios [Marriage Book] A, 35–36, NMSRCA.

Sedgwick County, Kansas.

Deed Records Book A, 129 and 478.

Deed Records Book B, 165 and 168.

Both in Wichita–Sedgwick County Historical Museum Collections, Kansas.

Territorial Archives of New Mexico

Letters Sent, 1878–81, Gov. Wallace, Executive Record Book No. 2, 1867–82, 472–73. NMSRCA.

U.S. Bureau of the Census

Arapahoe County, Colo., 1885.

Doña Ana County, N.M., 1870.

Grant County, N.M., 1880.

Lincoln County, N.M., 1870 and 1880.

Pima County, Ariz., 1876.

San Miguel County, N.M., 1870 and 1880.

Sedgwick County, Kans., 1870.

Also the complete state censuses for

Indiana, 1860.

Missouri, 1860 and 1870.

New York, 1860.

U.S. Department of the Interior, Bureau of Pensions.

Pension Records of

William H. H. Antrim.

Daniel M. Appel.

Saturnino Baca.

George B. Barber.

Joseph H. Blazer.

William Brady.

Robert A. Casey

Charles E. Compton.

Byron Dawson.

James J. Dolan.

Gottfried G. Gauss.

William H. Johnson.

John R. Mackie.

John Kinney.

George W. Peppin.

David P. Shield.

George W. Smith.

Harvey H. Whitehill.

All in NA.

U.S. Department of Justice.

General Records, RG 60, NA

Letters/Judiciary Accounts, New Mexico, 4W1/3/1/2, Boxes 476, 477, 478.

"In The Matter of the Cause and Circumstances of the Death of J. H. Tunstall, a British Subject" (cited as Angel Report), 44-4-8-3.

———. Bureau of Land Management, RG 49, NA.

"Application and Proof of Catherine McCarty."

———. Bureau of Indian Affairs.

Letters Received, 1878. RG 75, NA.

Selected Documents Relating to the Mescalero Apache Indian Agency. University of New Mexico General Library, Albuquerque. Microfilm E99 M45 U55x.

U.S. Treasury Department, Secret Service Division.

Reports of Azariah F. Wild, New Orleans District, in Records of U.S. Secret Service Agents, 1875–1936, Microfilm T915, Roll 308. RG 87, NA.

Wallace (Lew) Collection. William Henry Smith Memorial Library, Indiana State Historical Society, Indianapolis.

Published Sources

Ball, Eve. "Charles Ballard, 'Lawman' of the Pecos." *English Westerners Brand Book* 7, no. 4 (July 1965): 1–6.

———. *Ma'am Jones of the Pecos*. Tucson: University of Arizona Press, 1969.

Bartholomew, Ed. *Jesse Evans, A Texas Hide-burner*. Houston: Frontier Press of Texas, 1955.

Bender, Norman J. *Missionaries, Outlaws and Indians: Taylor F. Ealy at Lincoln and Zuni, 1878–1881*. Albuquerque: University of New Mexico Press, 1984.

Berry, Susan, and Sharman Apt Russell. *Built To Last: An Architectural History of Silver City*. Santa Fe: New Mexico Historic Preservation Division, 1986.

Biographical and Historical Catalogue of Washington and Jefferson College 1802–1902. Philadelphia: George H. Buchanan & Co., 1902.

Boyle, Andrew J. "Report to Thomas B. Catron," *Mesilla Valley Independent*, June 23, 1877.

Branch, Leon Louis, and Rudulph, Charles Frederick. *"Los Bilitos": The Story of "Billy the Kid" and His Gang.* New York: Carlton Press, 1980.

Bryan, Howard. *Wildest of the Wild West.* Santa Fe: Clear Light Publishers, 1988.

Burns, Walter Noble. *The Saga of Billy the Kid.* Garden City: Doubleday Page & Co., 1926.

Burroughs, Jean. *On The Trail: The Life and Tales of "Lead Steer" Potter.* Santa Fe: Museum of New Mexico Press, 1980.

Church, Amelia Bolton. "Notes for [an] Informal Talk on Her Recollections of Life, February 16, 1950." Lincoln County Historical Society, Lincoln, New Mexico.

Clarke, Mary Whatley. *John Chisum: Jinglebob King of the Pecos.* Austin, Tex.: Eakins Press, 1984.

Cline, Donald. *Alias Billy the Kid: The Man Behind the Legend.* Santa Fe: Sunstone Press, 1986.

Coe, Frank. "A Friend Comes to the Defense of Notorious Billy the Kid," *El Paso Times,* September 16, 1923.

Coe, George. *Frontier Fighter.* Ed. Doyce B. Nunis, Jr. Chicago: Lakeside Press, R. R. Donnelley & Sons, 1984.

Conner, Anthony. Letter to Silver City *Independent,* March 22, 1932.

Cullum, Bvt. Maj-Gen. George W. *Biographical Register of the Officers and Graduates of the U.S. Military Academy at West Point, N.Y., from Its Establishment in 1802 to 1890.* Boston: Houghton, Mifflin & Co., 1891.

Curry, George. *George Curry, 1861–1947: An Autobiography.* Ed. H. B. Hening. Albuquerque: University of New Mexico Press, 1958.

Denton, J. Fred. "Billy the Kid's Friend Tells for the First Time of Thrilling Incidents." *Arizona Daily Citizen* [Tucson], March 28, 1931.

Dillon, Richard. "Adventures of an Army Post Photographer." *Old West,* Fall, 1977.

Earle, James H., ed. *The Capture of Billy the Kid.* College Station, Texas: Creative Publishing, 1988.

Edwards, Harold L. "Barney Mason: In the Shadow of Pat Garrett and Billy the Kid." *Old West* 26, no. 4 (Summer 1990): 14 –19.

———. "Capt. Saturnino Baca in the Shadow of the Lincoln County War." *Los Amigos* 2, no. 2 (April 1993): 9–14; 2, no. 3 (July 1993): 9–12; 2, no. 4 (October 1993): 10–11.

———. *Goodbye Billy the Kid.* College Station, Texas: Creative Publishing, 1996.

Fleming, Elvis E. "Deputy J. B. "Billy" Mathews: The Lincoln County War and Other Lives." *New Mexico Historical Review* 72, no. 3 (July, 1997): 239–56.

———, and Minor S. Huffman, eds. *Roundup on the Pecos.* Roswell, N.M.: Chaves County Historical Society, 1978.

Gard, Wayne. *The Chisholm Trail.* Norman: University of Oklahoma Press, 1954.

Garrett, Pat F. *The Authentic Life of Billy the Kid.* With intro. by J. C. Dykes. Norman: University of Oklahoma Press, 1954.

Grey, Frederick W. *Seeking Fortune in America.* London: Smith, Elder, 1912.

Griggs, George. *History of the Mesilla Valley, or, The Gadsden Purchase.* Las Cruces, N.M.: Bronson Printing Co., 1930.

Hertzog, Peter. *Little Known Facts about Billy the Kid.* Santa Fe: The Press of the Territorian, 1964.

Hinton, Harwood P., Jr. "John Simpson Chisum." *New Mexico Historical Review* 31, no. 3: 177–205, and 31, no. 4: 310–37 (July and October 1956); 32, no. 1:53–65 (January 1957).

Hough, Emerson. *The Story of the Outlaw.* New York: Outing Publishing, 1907.

Hoyt, Henry. *A Frontier Doctor.* Ed. Doyce B. Nunis. Chicago: Lakeside Classics, R.

R. Donnelley & Sons, 1979.

Hunter, J. Marvin, comp. and ed. *The Trail Drivers of Texas.* Austin: University of Texas Press, 1985.

Hyde, Albert E. "The Old Regime in the Southwest: The Reign of the Revolver in New Mexico." *Century Magazine* 33 (March 1902): 690–701.

Irwin, Helen. "When Billy the Kid Was Brought to Trial." *Frontier Times* 6 (March 1929): 214–15.

Jaramillo, Pauline. *Genealogical and Historical Data of the Jaramillo Family 1598–1989.* N.p., 1989.

Jones, Walter N. *Tree Branches.* Greenbank, Wash.: N.p., 1994.

Kadlec, Robert F. *They "Knew" Billy the Kid.* Santa Fe: Ancient City Press, 1987.

Keleher, William A. *The Fabulous Frontier.* Albuquerque: University of New Mexico Press, 1968.

——. *Violence in Lincoln County, 1869–1881.* Albuquerque: University of New Mexico Press. 1957.

King, David. "The Pecos War." *True West* 43, no. 12 (December 1996): 19–22; 44, no. 1 (January 1997): 12–16.

Klasner, Lily. *My Girlhood among Outlaws.* Ed. Eve Ball. Tucson: University of Arizona Press, 1972.

Koop, Waldo. *Billy the Kid: The Trail of a Kansas Legend.* Wichita: Kansas City Posse of The Westerners, 1965.

Lavash, Donald R. *William Brady, Tragic Hero of the Lincoln County War.* Santa Fe: Sunstone Press, 1986.

——. "Thomas G. Yerby and Nasaria." *The Outlaw Gazette* 5, no. 1 (December 1992): 10–11.

McCarty, John L. *Maverick Town: The Story of Old Tascosa.* Norman: University of Oklahoma Press, 1946.

McGaw, Bill. "Out of the West: Billy the Kid's Teacher Saw Him as Sensitive, Effeminate, Fearful Youth." *El Paso Times,* December 17, 1960.

McLean, William Hunter. *From Ayr to Thurber: Three Hunter Brothers and the Winning of the West.* Fort Worth: New Printing Co., 1978.

Maynooth Students and Ordinations Index, 1795–1895. St. Patrick's College, Maynooth, Ireland.

Mazzanovich, Anton. "Tony Tells about the Kid," *Tombstone Epitaph,* March 9, 1933.

Metz, Leon. *Pat Garrett: The Story of a Western Lawman.* Norman: University of Oklahoma Press, 1974.

Miller, Benjamin S. *Ranch Life in Southern Kansas and the Indian Territory, as Told by a Novice.* New York: Fless and Ridge Printing Co. 1896.

Miller, Darlis A. "William Logan Rynerson in New Mexico, 1862–93." *New Mexico Historical Review* 48, no. 2 (April 1973): 101–32.

Miller, Nyle H., and Joseph W. Snell. *Great Gunfighters of the Kansas Cowtowns, 1867–1886.* Lincoln: University of Nebraska Press, 1963.

Miner, H. Craig. *Wichita: The Early Years, 1865–80.* Lincoln: University of Nebraska Press, 1982.

Mullin, Robert N. *The Boyhood of Billy the Kid.* Southwestern Studies 5, no. 1. El Paso: University of Texas at El Paso, 1967.

——. "An Item from Old Mesilla." N.p., n.d., privately published.

Nolan, Frederick. *The Life and Death of John Henry Tunstall.* Albuquerque: University of New Mexico Press, 1965.

——. *The Lincoln County War: A Documentary History.* Norman: University of Oklahoma Press, 1992.

———. "The Search for Alexander McSween." *New Mexico Historical Review* 62, no. 2 (July 1987): 287–301.

———. "Dick Brewer, The Unlikely Gunfighter." *NOLA Quarterly* 15, no. 3 (July–September 1991).

———. "The Horse Thief War." *Old West* 30, no. 4 (Summer 1994): 16–23.

———. "A Note on Jose Chavez y Chavez." *Lincoln County Historical Society Newsletter,* August 1994.

———. "Boss Rustler: The Life and Crimes of John Kinney." *True West* 43, no. 9 (September 1996): 14–21, and 43, no. 10 (October 1996): 12–19.

———. "Lesser Lights: A Note on Some of 'The Boys.'" *Los Amigos* (July and October 1995; January, April, and July 1997).

Otero, Miguel Antonio. *The Real Billy the Kid.* New York: Rufus Rockwell Wilson, 1936.

Pearson, Jim Berry. *The Maxwell Land Grant.* Norman: University of Oklahoma Press, 1961.

Poe, John W. *The Death of Billy the Kid.* Boston: Houghton Mifflin Co. 1933.

Poe, Sophie. *Buckboard Days.* Ed. Eugene Cunningham. Caldwell,   Idaho: Caxton Printers, 1936.

Potter, Jack. "The Death and Burial of Billy the Kid." Undated clipping, Clayton, N.M., *Union County Leader.* In Potter Files, Museum of New Mexico Library, Santa Fe.

Rasch, Philip J. *Trailing Billy the Kid.* Stillwater, Okla.: Barbed Wire Press, 1995.

———. *Gunsmoke in Lincoln County.* Stillwater, Okla.: Barbed Wire Press, 1997.

———. "A Man Named Antrim." *Los Angeles Westerners Brand Book* 6 (1956): 49–54.

———. "They Fought for the House." In *Portraits in Gunsmoke,* 34–64. Ed. Jeff Burton. London: English Westerners Society, 1971.

———. "These Were the Regulators." In *Ho! For the Great West,* 50–69. Ed. Barry C. Johnson. English Westerners Society, 1980.

———, and Robert N. Mullin. "New Light on the Legend of Billy the Kid," *New Mexico Folklore Record* 7 (1952–53): 1–5.

———, and Lee Myers. "The Tragedy of the Beckwiths." *English Westerners Brand Book* 5, no. 4 (July 1963): 1–6.

———, and Allan Radbourne. "The Story of 'Windy' Cahill." *Real West* 28 (August 1985): 22–27.

Rickards, Colin W. "Better for the World That He Is Gone." *English Westerners Brand Book* 2, no. 3 (April 1960): 2–8.

———, "More on Henry Newton Brown." *English Westerners Brand Book* 3, no. 1 (October 1960): 8–10.

Rucker, Alvin. "The True Trail of Billy the Kid." *Daily Oklahoman* [Oklahoma City], July 7, 1929.

Russell, Randy. *Billy the Kid: The Story, the Trial.* Lincoln, N.M.: Crystal Press, 1994.

Shinkle, James D. *Reminiscences of Roswell Pioneers.* Roswell, N.M.: Hall-Poorbaugh Press, 1966.

Smith, Colonel C. C. "Concerning the Capture of Billy the Kid." *Tombstone Epitaph,* March 30, 1933.

Thrapp, Dan L. *Encyclopedia of Frontier Biography.* 3 vols. Rev. ed. Spokane: Arthur H. Clarke Co. 1990.

———. *Encyclopedia of Frontier Biography: Supplement (Vol. 4).* Spokane: Arthur H. Clarke Co., 1994.

Torrez, Robert J. "Forgotten Desperadoes." *True West* 43, no. 2 (February 1996): 46–49.

Traylor, Leslie. "Facts Regarding the Escape of Billy the Kid." *Frontier Times* 13 (July 1936): 509.

Wallace, Lew. *An Autobiography.* 2 vols. New York: Harper & Bros., 1906.

Weddle, Jerry. "The Kid at Old Fort Sumner." *The Outlaw Gazette* 5, no. 1 (December 1992): 8–9.

———. *Antrim Is My Stepfather's Name.* Tucson: Arizona Historical Society, 1993.

Whitehill, H. H. "Billy the Kid: The Subject of an Interview with H. H. Whitehill of This City." *Silver City Enterprise,* January 3, 1902.

Younger, Cole. *The Story of Cole Younger, by Himself: Being an Autobiography of the Missouri Guerilla Captain and Outlaw, His Capture and Prison Life, and the Only Authentic Account of the Northfield Raid Ever Published.* Chicago: Press of Henneberry Co., 1903.

Newspapers and Periodicals

Alamogordo News
Albuquerque Daily Journal
Albuquerque Review
Amarillo Sunday News and Globe
Arizona Citizen (Tucson)
Arizona Daily Citizen (Tucson)
Arizona Weekly Star (Tucson)
Barber County Mail (Kansas)
Carlsbad Current
Cimarron News & Press
Daily Oklahoman (Oklahoma City)
Daily New Mexican (Santa Fe)
Denison Daily News
Denver Post
El Paso Times
Fort Worth Star Telegram
Grant County Herald (Silver City)
Indianapolis World
Las Cruces Thirty Four
Las Vegas Daily Optic (New Mexico)
Las Vegas Gazette (New Mexico)
Las Vegas Morning Gazette (New Mexico)
Las Vegas Optic (New Mexico)
Lincoln County Leader (White Oaks)
Mesilla News
Mesilla Valley Independent
New Mexico State Tribune (Albuquerque)
New Southwest and Grant County Herald (Silver City)
Newman's Semi-Weekly (Las Cruces)
Newton Kansan
Santa Fe New Mexican
Silver City Enterprise
Silver City Independent
Silver City Mining Life
Tombstone Daily Nugget
Tombstone Epitaph
Union County Leader (Clayton)
Weekly New Mexican (Santa Fe)
Wichita Eagle
Wichita Tribune
Wichita Vidette
Wichita Weekly Eagle

Index

References to illustrations are printed in boldface type.

CPSIA information can be obtained
at www.ICGtesting.com
Printed in the USA
BVHW06s1318130718
521327BV00001B/1/P